Before the Oath

Before the Oath

How George W. Bush and Barack Obama
Managed a Transfer of Power

MARTHA JOYNT KUMAR

Johns Hopkins University Press
Baltimore

© 2015 Johns Hopkins University Press
All rights reserved. Published 2015
Printed in the United States of America on acid-free paper
2 4 6 8 9 7 5 3 1

Johns Hopkins University Press
2715 North Charles Street
Baltimore, Maryland 21218-4363
www.press.jhu.edu

Library of Congress Cataloging-in-Publication Data

Kumar, Martha Joynt.
Before the oath : how George W. Bush and Barack Obama managed a transfer
of power / Martha Joynt Kumar.
pages cm
Includes bibliographical references and index.
ISBN 978-1-4214-1659-5 (paperback) — ISBN 978-1-4214-1660-1 (electronic) —
ISBN 1-4214-1659-X (paperback) — ISBN 1-4214-1660-3 (electronic)
1. Presidents—United States—Transition periods. 2. Presidents—United
States—Transition periods—Planning. 3. Administrative procedure—United
States. 4. Executive departments—United States—Management.
5. Presidents—United States—Election—2008. 6. Bush, George W. (George
Walker), 1946– 7. Obama, Barack. 8. United States—Politics and
government—2001–2009. I. Title.
JK516.K85 2015
973.931—dc23
2014029355

A catalog record for this book is available from the British Library.

*Special discounts are available for bulk purchases of this book. For more information,
please contact Special Sales at 410-516-6936 or specialsales@press.jhu.edu.*

Johns Hopkins University Press uses environmentally friendly book materials,
including recycled text paper that is composed of at least 30 percent
post-consumer waste, whenever possible.

To
the women on whose shoulders I stand:
May Lepley Joynt (1907–1995)
Jean Cunnian Lepley (1887–1948)
Minnie Lee Spencer Ward (1875–1957)

the men whose love and support inspires me every day:
Vijayendra Kumar
Zal Alexander Kumar
V. Cameron Kumar
Kiran Zal Kumar

CONTENTS

ACKNOWLEDGMENTS

The preparations for the coming change of power from George W. Bush to Barack Obama were undertaken on both sides with a sense of the gravity of what it meant to prepare for the incoming administration; partisanship played only a minor role. General James Jones, President Obama's national security advisor, spoke for many when he discussed the transition work he did with the outgoing secretary of state, Condoleezza Rice, and the outgoing national security advisor, Steve Hadley. "These are two extraordinarily decent, thoughtful people who went out of their way, especially Steve, because he was the national security advisor, to prepare a glide path where I think the transition was . . . pretty darn close to being ideal," he said. Jones said that Hadley "certainly set up an orderly process of briefings and turnover of key documents and papers and issues that were being worked that made it very comfortable." The same could be said for other exchanges of information between outgoing and incoming transition team members.

The people who participated in transition preparations established the cooperative tone and set its direction, including President Bush and Senators Barack Obama and John McCain. Understanding the 2008 transition means viewing it from the perspectives of those who participated in it. The voices on which the book is based are those of the participants who shaped the transition through their work in the White House, the campaigns of both candidates, government agencies, those working from outside of government, and the official candidate transition operations. Among the people interviewed for this book are members of the George W. Bush White House team, including Chief of Staff Joshua Bolten; Deputy Press Secretary Tony Fratto; Counselor to the President Ed Gillespie; Director of Presidential Personnel Joie Gregor; National Security Advisor Stephen Hadley; Deputy Director Office of Management and Budget Clay Johnson; Deputy Chief of Staff Joel Kaplan; Chief of Staff to the First Lady Anita McBride; Press

Secretary Dana Perino; Director of Communications Kevin Sullivan; and Chief Usher Gary Walters.

The officials interviewed who were involved in the Obama transition include the following people: Staff Secretary Lisa Brown, who was also co-chair of the agency review teams; Deputy Press Secretary Bill Burton; Dan Chenok, who served on the technology and Office of Management and Budget transition agency review teams; Communications Director Anita Dunn; Deputy Press Secretary Joshua Earnest; Press Secretary Robert Gibbs; Personnel Director Donald Gips; National Security Advisor James Jones; Deputy Secretary of Labor Christopher Lu; Communications Director Ellen Moran; Communications Director Dan Pfeiffer; and Obama Transition co-chair John Podesta. Additionally, I interviewed three senior White House officials who asked to be cited on background. An interviewee outside of the administration but who worked with transition officials is Washington lawyer Harrison Wellford, who has served as the keeper of transition records for several Democratic transition efforts. For the McCain transition, former Navy secretary Will Ball was tasked with gathering information on past transitions, and Russell Gerson, who heads his own personnel recruiting firm, prepared the personnel piece. People on Capitol Hill were also helpful in their interviews, including former Senator Ted Kaufman (D-Del.); Representative Dutch Ruppersberger (D-Md.); and James Manley, former senior aide to Senate Majority Leader Harry Reid. Other government officials—past and present—I interviewed are Jonathan Breul, who served through several administrations in the Office of Management and Budget working on management reform issues; Dan Chenok, who heads the IBM Business of Government organization; John Kamensky, who is also at the IBM office, worked at the Government Accountability Office and on the staff of Vice President Gore's National Performance Review initiative; Gail Lovelace, who directed GSA transition operations in 2008; and Robert Shea, chief of staff for Clay Johnson in the Office of Management and Budget. Max Stier, president and CEO of the Partnership for Public Service, was helpful as well.

Many people who work on transition issues and White House operations have been helpful by reading all or part of the book. Among those to whom I owe special thanks for their comments are Dan Blair, president of the National Academy of Public Administration; Jonathan Breul; John Burke, transition author and expert at the University of Vermont; Lisa Brown; Dan Chenok; George Edwards, who specializes in presidential leadership issues in the political science department at Texas A&M University; Steve Hadley; Christopher Lu; James Pfiffner, transition expert and political science professor at George Mason University; and Alexis Simendinger, White House correspondent for RealClearPolitics. Their comments were helpful in identifying areas that required further discussion; they also brought up items I might have missed.

The book benefited from the articles I published that prepared the way for a more well-rounded work. Earlier versions of book sections and chapters were published in *Presidential Studies Quarterly* and *Public Administration Review*. The two *Presidential Studies Quarterly* pieces are, "The 2008 National Security Council Transition: Providing Continuity in a Bipartisan Environment" (September 2013) and "The 2008–2009 Presidential Transition through the Voices of Its Participants" (December 2009). The *Public Administration Review* piece is "Getting Ready for Day One: Taking Advantage of the Opportunities and Minimizing the Hazards of a Presidential Transition" (July/August 2008). Readers' responses to these pieces helped me further develop points for the book.

Professor Toni Marzotto, chair of the Department of Political Science at Towson University, and Terry Cooney, dean of the College of Liberal Arts at Towson, both found ways to help me find the time to research and write this book. The Johns Hopkins University Press has been supportive of my work since the mid-1970s, when I first began working with my editor and friend, the late Henry Tom. He first encouraged me to write this book, and Suzanne Flinchbaugh then picked up where he left off after he retired in 2010. I am thankful to both of them for their suggestions and support in the development of this book. Many thanks as well to the Johns Hopkins University Press team that worked on my book, including managing editor Juliana McCarthy; marketing team members Kathy Alexander and Brendan Coyne; the editorial staff members I worked with, Kelley Squazzo, Hilary Jacqmin, and Catherine Goldstead; as well as my copy editor, Martin Schneider. Special thanks go to David Hume Kennerly for the front and back cover photographs that capture both presidents as well as the Oval Office at a pivotal point in the transition.

My family gave me love and support while I worked on the manuscript and encouraged me at each point when I flagged. My husband, Vijay Kumar, and our sons Zal and Cameron read and commented on the book, with Zal paying particular attention to what areas required further clarification and development.

Before the Oath

The Presidential Transition of 2008–2009

Inauguration Day is a mix of traditional, personal, institutional, and unanticipated elements, and January 20, 2009, was no exception. President George W. Bush visited the still-furnished Oval Office before going back to the White House itself. He described the atmosphere in the West Wing on his final visit there. It was not "bustling with aides," as on a normal day. "It was eerily quiet. There were no ringing phones, no television sets tuned to the news, no meetings in the hallways. The only sound I heard was the occasional buzz of a workman's drill, refitting the offices for a new team."[1] After that final office visit, he went to the East Room to join his family for a ceremony that mixed the personal with White House tradition. Before the formal ceremony of the day took place, the president joined former president George H. W. Bush, Barbara Bush, and the Bushes' daughters, Barbara and Jenna, as well as Laura Bush's mother in the East Room with the nearly one hundred members of the White House residence staff.

President George W. Bush described the scene: "Nearly every member of the residence staff was there: the florists who put fresh bouquets in the Oval Office every morning, the butlers and valets who made our life so comfortable, the carpenters and engineers who keep the White House in working condition, the chefs who cooked us such fabulous meals, and, of course, the pastry chef who fed my sweet tooth."[2] President George W. Bush and Laura Bush then shook hands with the staff. Anita McBride, Mrs. Bush's chief of staff, commented, "They went and greeted every single one and hugged every single one. . . . Barbara Bush and George H. W. Bush were standing there as well and greeting some of them. But [they] really let George and Laura do it."[3]

In a traditional White House ritual, Chief Usher Stephen Rochon presented the Bushes with two flags, the one that flew over the White House the day President Bush came into office and the one from that morning, his last day. The ritual first began in 1989 when Chief Usher Gary Walters presented outgoing President Reagan with a flag from his last day in office.[4] The flags for President Bush were placed in a wood box made in the White House carpenter's shop with a plaque noting the president and his terms of service. The wood was original to the White House rebuilt in 1815–16 after the War of 1812 when the White House interior was burned to the ground. The flags are in the Bushes' home in Dallas.[5] President Bush spoke to the assembled household staff with Laura Bush and his daughters near him: "You've been like family to us. . . . There are some things I am not going to miss about Washington, but I am going to miss you a lot. Thank you from the bottom of our hearts."

Then it was to the North Portico to greet Barack and Michelle Obama, who arrived at the White House in the new, heavily armored presidential limousine called "The Beast." At approximately 15,000 pounds, 18 feet long, and with 8-inch-thick doors, the imposing vehicle rolled up to the White House shortly after 10:00 am.[6] The four of them then entered the building. President and Mrs. George W. Bush were hosting the traditional preinauguration coffee in the Blue Room for President-elect and Mrs. Obama as well as the Cheneys and the Bidens and the Joint Congressional Committee on Inaugural Ceremonies.

A critical and unanticipated situation arose that morning requiring the attention of the senior representatives of the outgoing and incoming administrations. The chiefs of staff for the outgoing and incoming chief executives, Joshua Bolten and Rahm Emanuel, went over to the Situation Room in the West Wing, where they joined the national security teams for both administrations. A three-hour meeting focusing on issues of immediate and crucial importance to the incoming and outgoing national security teams was under way. "I was there," said Steve Hadley, national security advisor to President Bush. "Condi [Rice] was there, Bob Gates was there, Admiral [Michael] Mullen was there, Mike Hayden, and Mike Chertoff. We had the attorney general, and Bob Mueller [FBI] came for part of it."[7] Except for General James L. Jones, the counterparts for the incoming team were present as well.[8] As the terrorism advisor for President-elect Obama, John Brennan was at the table rather than the national security advisor. All in the room were alert to new developments in an unfolding security threat pegged to the inauguration, which would, if it occurred, be witnessed on television by millions throughout the world.

By this point at the end of the transition, the principals in both national security teams knew their counterparts from their January group crisis training sessions and through one-on-one meetings that began after the election. Each time President-elect Obama designated an official for his administration, that person met with the corresponding officeholder in the Bush administration. During the summer, designated transition officials in both the Obama and McCain campaign operations met with White House and Justice Department officials to work on transition issues that needed a long lead time, such as security clearances.

During the months following their first contacts in June with White House officials, a small number of staff members in both campaigns met with Bush administration officials to discuss aspects of the transition ahead. President Bush and Chief of Staff Joshua Bolten were committed to establishing an environment where no matter which side won the election, that candidate and his team would be well informed when they came into the White House on January 20. Now, just hours before they were to come in as the staff of President Obama, they were sitting with their counterparts, whom they knew fairly well. Following the election, the number of White House and Obama officials dealing with one another grew, as did the quality of the communication. Thus, by the time they came to the White House on January 20 on the cusp of the inauguration, officials knew one another well and were consumers of reports, memoranda, and regularly held conversations with the outgoing team. The level of comfort they had was important for the dilemma that confronted them in the hours before the new team took office.

The Bush administration had prepared information for the officials from the Obama team. "We talked about a threat to the inauguration, which had just surfaced in the previous twenty-four hours. And the FBI briefed the threat—the intelligence community briefed the threat, what we were doing about it, how credible we thought it was. . . . It involved an attack on the Mall," said National Security Advisor Steve Hadley, who was in the room and was involved in the response.[9] The night before the inauguration, an FBI/Homeland Security bulletin issued to state and local law enforcement identified a possible threat on the event from a Somalia-based Islamist organization, al-Shabaab, a group with links to al-Qaeda.[10] President Bush's NSC deputy dealing with terrorism strategy, Juan Carlos Zarate, described the atmosphere: "All the data points suggested there was a real threat evolving quickly that had an overseas component."[11]

With all of the events and ceremonies taking place that morning, well-laid plans—and contingency ones too—were going to be essential to the successful handoff of the presidency as George W. Bush and Barack Obama changed places. It was a morning with a mix of the traditional and the sentimental, with the added pressure of a critical situation requiring precise information for the assessments the participants were making. The safety of the two presidents and the inauguration depended on both men and their staffs and nominees for executive branch positions all being well prepared for the events of the day ahead of them.

* * *

One of the enduring characteristics of the American political system is its ability to manage, peacefully and decisively, the changeover of presidential power, regardless of whether the election results are close or dictate a change in the party in power. Our presidential elections have almost always been swift to declare a winner. With the exceptions of the elections of 1800, 1824, 1876, and 2000, the public has known relatively quickly who was elected president. Our election process has worked; we have held elections on the timetable outlined in the Constitution, and the system provided winners. Once we have a winner, we then go into a somewhat lengthy process between the election and the inauguration. During that time period, the incumbent chief executive and the incoming president chart the course for how information will be transferred between the two and how the new staff will learn the current state of policy, programs, and government operations prior to the inauguration.

Nothing was prescribed in law or the Constitution for what should take place during the seventy-seven days between the presidential election and the inauguration. There is a body of law relating to the resources a president-elect can draw on to prepare for the presidency, but there are no prescriptions for what candidates or presidents-elect are legally required to do or actions they must take during this time period as they move from the election to the presidency. For the incumbent president, there are few rules for what he must provide to the incoming administration. As crucial as information is for a new president on subjects such as the organization of White House operations, ongoing activities in the departments and agencies and in the national security areas, the incumbent president has no prescribed responsibility to smooth the path into office for his successor. That has led to many different patterns for what candidates have done to prepare for office and what sitting administrations have felt responsible for providing to their successors. Transitions have been driven by tacit understandings as well as what presidents have chosen to do.

As the presidency grew in importance in the twentieth century, midcentury presidents began to provide information on the positions and programs of their administrations. President Truman was the first to have a government agency—the Bureau of the Budget—collect and give administrative information to his successor. From Dwight Eisenhower through Barack Obama, eleven people have become chief executive. Of those eleven, Presidents Johnson and Ford came in without a presidential transition because of President Kennedy's death and President Nixon's resignation from office. That leaves nine presidents, eight of whom came in under circumstances of a change in party power. These were Presidents Eisenhower, Kennedy, Nixon, Carter, Reagan, Clinton, Bush, and Obama; President George H. W. Bush is the only post-Truman president to be elected to follow a president of the same party. Same-party transitions, especially when the incoming chief executive is vice president, do not involve the same kind of transfer of information as when there is a change of party where people inside an administration may or may not be reluctant to provide material about operations and people.

A look at the eight transitions that involved a change in the party in power reveals the gradual development of a more formal handover of power from one president to another.

Gradually, outgoing incumbent presidents felt a responsibility to gather information for their successors. A persistent problem, though, has been that the information went unused and the advice unheeded. Former chief of staff to President Ford, Richard Cheney, who presided over the transition to the Carter administration, noted in 1999 that in a change of party transition it is often difficult to get the new team to listen, especially when the incoming president defeated the outgoing one. "You really want to help the new crowd. There is an institutional sense of responsibility; you want things to go well. In our case, certainly President Ford, even though he had a fairly bitter battle with Jimmy Carter, felt strongly about having the transition work, and that was his charge to us. So you get organized for it, to help the new crowd coming in, and basically they're not interested. The basic attitude is, 'If you're so smart, how come we beat you? Why do we need to take your advice? You guys lost.' There's just a disconnect there in terms of the desire on the part of the incoming party and the outgoing party in terms of how much they want to work together."[12]

In 2008 there was a concerted effort by officials in the George W. Bush administration to gather information, and the transition team working for President-elect Obama used some of it as the basis for their preparatory work. Because he was completing a second term and could not run again, President Bush had his staff begin preparations in late 2007 for the 2009 handoff of power. For his part, Senator Obama talked to staff about transition issues and then assembled a team well before the election to work on issues related to governing. With both sides productively working together, there may have been a precedent set for future transitions. What was it that made the 2008 transition such an effective one and a worthy one for a model to be followed by future incoming and outgoing administrations? This book focuses on the preparations made by President Bush's transition team as well as the preparations for office Senators Obama and McCain made as they thought through a possible presidency. In addition to the efforts of President Bush and his White House staff, congressional legislation paving the way for the distinctive conditions of the 2008–2009 transition, the early and continuing actions by the General Services Administration to plan and to set up transition offices, the work on financial disclosure issues handled by the Office of Government Ethics, and the preparations by the Office of Management and Budget are all important ingredients in the early efforts made by governmental institutions and officials to bring about a smooth passing of power.

The Elements of the 2008–2009 Presidential Transition

The 2008–2009 transition took place in a permanently altered environment. White House officials who came into office in 2001 saw their transition as a successful one, but after the events of September 11 they acknowledged that they needed to prepare for a different type of transition when they left office. Joshua Bolten, who came into the George W. Bush administration as deputy chief of staff for policy and left as White House chief of staff, commented on the transition and the impact of the 2001 attacks. "Relatively speaking, we were prepared, but 9/11 gave us all a pretty pungent taste that even though we were relatively more prepared than some other incoming White House staff have been, we were not well prepared to deal with a crisis," he said. "9/11 gave us all the sense that a crisis was not only possible but also likely. So the mentality changed after 9/11, and I think everybody had thoughts about 'what about the next guys.'" As Bush administration officials prepared for the transition, they viewed it differently than any experienced by earlier presidents. Bolten said, "As we worked to get ourselves prepared, what about making sure that the next guys were not as, candidly, ill prepared as we and all of our predecessors had been?"[13]

The same sentiment ran through government agencies, members of Congress and the committees preparing for the next transition, executive branch agencies, officials and former officials of both political parties, and groups focused on effective government operations. Together, the preparations for the 2008 transition were more extensive and polished than any preceding one. That makes the 2008–2009 transition important to document for what happened during this time, who was involved, what they did, and why they made the choices they did. The preparations are important as well as a guide for future transitions. The collective groundwork undertaken by government officials and others improved the quality and efficiency of the work undertaken during the period before and after President Obama took office.

This book focuses on the prominent elements in the Obama transition into the White House and the transition out of the White House by President Bush and his team. Both aspects of a transition—the transition into the White House and the one taking place simultaneously to organize the way out of government—are important for an understanding of how the operation was organized and played out. The White House was at the center of the transition for both the outgoing and incoming teams. How the handoff of power worked at that central place is key to understanding how one president left and a new one came into the office. They include the place of transitions in governing, decisions by Congress and executive branch agencies shaping transition preparations, the quality of the transition out of office developed by the incumbent administration, the sequencing and coordination of decisions during the transition, and an exploration of what happens when a new team enters the White House. Two studies in the book demonstrate important aspects of the transition: the handling of presidential appointments and the central place of national security issues in a solid start to an administration. Together these subjects develop a portrait of how the change took place between Presidents Bush and Obama in early 2009.

All of these elements helped to create an environment in which President Obama took the oath of office and entered the White House on January 20 with a decision-making system of his choice in place, policy initiatives ready to present to the public and to Congress, a sense of his priorities, and a functioning personnel process. That is what a well-prepared transition can provide an incoming president. It does not happen by chance; it requires solid preparation from the outgoing as well as the incoming administration to achieve a smooth handover of power, especially when there is a change of parties involved.

CHAPTER ONE

A Time of Opportunity and Hazard

The approximately seventy-five days between a presidential election and the in-auguration of the new chief executive are a time of opportunity and hazard for an incoming administration—and for an outgoing one as well. For the president-elect, the ability to begin his administration with a productive start is on the line. There are no constitutional requirements or guidelines for the shape of the tran-sition nor the actions that the incoming and outgoing administrations should take during this period. There is legislation dating back to 1963 with several amend-ments through the years that provide resources—monies and agency help—but it does not address what needs to be done between the presidential election and the inauguration. The legislation originally provided for a transition appropriation of $900,000 to cover both the incoming and outgoing presidents but without any explicit instruction on how the money was to be divided. In 2012 the funds for an incoming president (had there been a transition) stood at $5.6 million, with the outgoing president getting $2.35 million. Even adjusting for inflation, the fund-ing has increased as a result of an understanding of how important this period is for the quality of the beginning of a president's tenure in office.

Instead, what happens during this period depends on what the winning pres-idential candidate does to prepare for office and what the incumbent president chooses to do as he leaves office. There isn't a template for the plans a candidate should make, and the same is true for what a retiring chief executive should provide to his successor and his team. It is up to those departing and entering the White House to determine how they want to prepare to leave or come into office. Yet as amorphous as the legal requirements of a transition are, the 2008–2009 transition demonstrated productive ways for those leaving the White House and those coming in to gather and process information for the newcomers as they prepare to staff up and organize their administration, develop their policy proposals, and establish their priorities. Although there is flexibility in how the transition takes shape, some ways of handling transitions are more effective than others. Political scientists and others studying transitions have focused on management, personnel, policy, coordination, and timing issues that make a difference in the ways in which a president prepares for office.[1]

The 2008–2009 transition provides future presidents and their staffs with an institutional memory of a transition that worked, a timetable for what actions need to be taken and when, and a prescription of how to bring together people who have amassed considerable experience on executive branch programs, operations, and institutions and those coming into office when the new administration takes office. Also included in the 2008 transition was a commitment from Congress to support transition planning with resources and early, though not sustained, attention to the appointments and priorities of the new administration. The transition left behind a well-informed group of people in both parties and in the incoming and outgoing administrations who know transitions well.

One of the distinguishing features of the transition was the series of templates used by President George W. Bush's staff and administration officials as well as by members of the transition team working for President-elect Barack Obama. On both sides and independent of one another, staff created a series of templates for acquiring what information they would need and when they should begin gathering it. The templates covered such diverse functions and institutions as national security memoranda, contingency plans gathered by the National Security Council, and information gathered by the President's Management Council on department and agency programs and operations. The templates also addressed the requirements and demands for the approximately twelve hundred executive branch positions a chief executive has to fill and the process of gathering information by the Obama transition agency review teams. President Bush and his White House team left behind a solid outline for the steps future administrations can take to provide a productive start for their successors.

Additionally, the Bush and Obama teams made certain that those leaving the administration and those taking over the same positions supplemented the printed material they left behind with one-on-one meetings in which the sitting official held frank discussions about the nature of the position the newcomer was about to assume. Both the printed record and the personal discussions were key to the successful preparation for office of the White House staff members brought in by President Obama. Initially through memoranda and later in sessions with those holding the posts, incoming and outgoing officials discussed what worked in their jobs and what did not.

The work the Obama team did to prepare for office and the Bush staff did to make sure the incoming president had the information he needed made a difference in how ready President Obama and his team were that first day. It was important because the incoming president faced at least one important decision within hours of his taking office. The familiarity of President Obama's leadership team with the cabinet and White House team members involved in the transition made a difference in how smooth and effective the meeting described below was. So too did the familiarity of the new team with the issues, programs, and people they would be dealing with.

Terror Alert on Inauguration Day 2009

The day before the inauguration, President-elect Obama first received news about the threat from his national security team. The threat had an impact on his plans. David Axelrod noted that Obama canceled the session he had scheduled with aides to practice his inaugural address. Axelrod told Peter Baker of the *New York Times* that Obama "seemed more subdued than he had been. . . . It's not as if you don't know what you're getting into," Axelrod said. "But when the reality comes and the baton is being passed and you're now dealing with real terrorism threats, it's a very sobering moment."[2] The following day, national security advisors for President Bush and President-elect Obama discussed the unfolding threat at a meeting in the Situation Room.

The threat did not provide national security teams on either side much time to process and plan for the situation. It surfaced "about 96 hours before," said Hadley. "For the first 48 hours, it didn't seem serious, and then maybe 36 hours before, we got something suggesting it was more serious. At that point, we ramped up quite a bit."[3] Part of that ramping up was to prepare cabinet officials coming into the administration. The preparation was done at the White House that morning.

Cabinet members and designees felt sufficiently comfortable with one another to discuss responses the incoming president could have. "Senator [Hillary] Clinton really showed . . . the sense of both a politician and also [was] able to see things from the president's perspective," said Hadley.[4] "And she asked the best question of the meeting, which was 'So what should Barack Obama do if he's in the middle of his inaugural address, and a bomb goes off way in the back of the crowd somewhere on the Mall? What does he do? Is the Secret Service going to whisk him off the program—or the podium, so the American people see their incoming president disappear in the middle of the inaugural address? I don't think so.'" While there was no certainty what shape the attack would take, "people were pretty confident that it would be pretty far back," said Hadley. With the amount of security on the Mall that day, Hadley added that "it clearly wasn't going to be a vehicle so it would have been something somebody would have had on themselves. It would have killed people."[5]

The Obama officials present "then went back and talked with President-elect Obama and walked him through what they thought he should do, so he could think about what he decided he would do in that situation."[6] Mercifully, Hadley said, the threat "melted away" in those minutes before the new president took office. With the inauguration ceremony soon to begin, the situation was a dramatic one, and everyone needed to be at top performance. The only way for the new team to be in a position to handle such a situation was for incoming officials to be well briefed on the offices they were to hold in the coming days as well as on the programs and people associated with their positions. Fortunately, President-elect Obama assembled his team early enough for them to learn about the operations of their offices, and the outgoing Bush team brought together information that would get them quickly up to speed. Then the Obama team went to the president-elect and discussed the issue with him. "There wasn't a recommended response," said Hadley. "I mean, the outgoing administration was not in a position to make a recommendation to the new President, but it was discussed among the representatives of the old team and the new team, and I think the view was you couldn't have him duck and cover, you couldn't have him pulled off the stage; he needed to stay and finish his speech, as long as it was not an immediate threat to him. That was just not the right visual of a new presidency. But the bottom line was . . . this will be a decision for the president-elect to make."[7] The situation did not require a final decision because the threat evaporated as quickly as it arose.

The threat discussion with all of the principal officials in the outgoing and incoming administrations allowed everyone to work through a potential crisis event on the first day for Barack Obama as president and the last one for George Bush. It also demonstrated how well people were able to work together. Joshua Bolten commented about the handling of the situation: "Rahm was well informed, and he had informed Obama about what was going on. So at that moment I was proud of the way that we had managed to integrate the incoming folks into the management of a potential crisis."[8] That important and effective discussion could not have taken place if both sides had not dedicated a significant amount of staff time and resources preparing for President Obama's entry into office. At the same time, it remained unclear just what would have happened if the assault had occurred during the point of transition. "They were jointly making judgments about that and I guess technically the authority was still with the Bush administration.

But it's an interesting question about how you would handle an event that happened literally at the moment of transition," said Bolten.[9]

President Bush has described the contrast between the coffee he and Laura Bush had with President-elect Obama and Michelle Obama in the Blue Room and what was then going on in the Situation Room. "The Obamas were in good spirits and excited about the journey ahead. Meanwhile, in the Situation Room, homeland security aides from both our teams monitored intelligence on a terrorist threat to the Inauguration," he wrote in his memoir *Decision Points*.[10] "It was a stark reminder that evil men still want to harm our country, no matter who is serving as president."

How serious was the threat on the inauguration of President Obama from the Somalia-based group, al-Shabaab? On February 25, 2012, when a new president, Mansour Hadi, was sworn into office in Sanaa, Yemen, a car bomb exploded outside a presidential complex, killing 25 people. Authorities blamed al-Qaeda in the Arabian Peninsula, an organization with a close relationship with al-Shabaab. Hours before the attack, President Hadi vowed in his inaugural address to "fight al-Qaeda" and "restore stability" to his nation with its violent recent history.[11] Terrorist groups wanted to challenge that stability before the new president could come into office and have subsequently continued its bombing campaign against the president.

President Truman and Modern Presidential Transitions

In the period since the first formal presidential transition from the Truman to Eisenhower administrations in which the incumbent and the president-elect worked to prepare information for the incoming chief executive, transitions have varied greatly in the types of preparation presidents and their staffs have made and the success they have had in setting the direction of their tenure in office in the days after the election through their first three months in office. Since President Truman first reached out to his successor to provide him with information on administration programs and activities, presidential transitions have become more formal and complex, as have the office of the presidency and the scope of what the chief executive is responsible for handling. Beginning in 1963, there is a formal government structure to provide assistance to the president-elect that comes with funds to support such an operation. Yet there is a great deal of flexibility on the part of the incumbent president and the incoming one as to how and when they structure their part of the transition of power from one chief executive to the next. Incumbent presidents can choose how much information they want to provide the president-elect, and the incoming chief executive can decide how interested he or she is in what the sitting president has to offer.

Whatever they do, early planning is a must for both candidates, even at the risk of charges of hubris leveled by the other side or by reporters covering the election. No matter their level of preparation, at one time presidents and their staffs were reluctant to admit advance planning even while they were doing it. They feared a public perception of arrogance on their part. By 2000, the perception of the wisdom of early planning began to take hold. In June 2000, *Washington Post* columnist and reporter David Broder discussed the good judgment of early planning and quoted officials from all recent administrations in calling for preparation for governing. "In fact, such advance planning has been done in many past campaigns but covertly, to avoid conveying a sense of smug overconfidence to the voters. . . . The reality is that when a new president moves in, his top aides find bare desks, empty filing cabinets and disconnected computers. They need help."[12]

Yet when Senator Obama let it be known in late July 2008 that he was assigning former Clinton chief of staff John Podesta to head his transition planning operation, he faced criticism in some quarters for his early planning. MSNBC anchor David Shuster criticized Senator Obama for the move. "That does seem a little bit premature, right?" Shuster said to veteran White House correspondent Ken Walsh of *U.S. News and World Report*. Walsh replied: "But this is very early, and it plays into this notion that the Republicans are talking about, about Obama being too arrogant, that . . . a sense of inevitability has set in there. And Americans don't like the idea that . . . a candidate thinks that he's got the thing won without really pushing at it and trying really hard, and so I think that that's a danger. Putting out this transition statement, I think, was not a smart thing to do."[13]

Criticism did not impact John Podesta's operation, as he felt little pressure. When asked if the criticism of their early planning had an impact on what he was doing or how he did it, Podesta answered "No."[14] He knew that the public understood the need to prepare for a presidential change in power. He also credited President Bush for making it clear that transition planning was important. "I welcome their willingness to stand up in public and say both sides should be planning for a transition. . . . Hopefully that lesson will be followed by future presidents," Podesta commented. Indeed it was. In 2012, when former George W. Bush cabinet secretary and Utah Governor Michael Leavitt was announced as Republican candidate Mitt Romney's transition team leader for what was dubbed the "Readiness Project," there was no criticism from the press or his opponents. With the example of the success of early planning in 2008 and the passage of the

Pre-Election Presidential Transition Act of 2010, early planning is now an accepted part of the passage of power between administrations. Then too in 2008, President Bush was the first chief executive since President Truman was in office whose vice president did not become his party's candidate to succeed him in the presidency. That meant that President Bush was in the unusual position of having no official ties to his party's candidate and could therefore step back from the presidential race in a way that his predecessors could not.

With the exceptions of President Kennedy's assassination and President Nixon's resignation, there have been nine planned transitions between elected presidents since the transition period was shortened in 1933 from the original approximately 120 days between the November election and March 4 to the roughly 75 days currently scheduled from the election in the first week in November to January 20. With the original long stretch between the election and the inauguration, presidents were not pressed for time to prepare for office in the same way they are today. The first transition scheduled to come under the umbrella of the January inauguration date was the 1953 one between Presidents Harry S Truman and Dwight D. Eisenhower. In that first shortened transition period, President Truman reflected a new concern for planning out the information-gathering and -dissemination processes. In an effort to accommodate the abbreviated schedule as well as the rapidly accumulating national security, budget, and policy information that should be exchanged between the incumbent administration and the presidential candidates, President Truman wanted to lengthen the information exchange period beyond the restricted 75-day schedule to well before the election.

President Truman began his preparations for the change of power during the spring of 1952, many months before the presidential election in November. Truman's plans included providing domestic, foreign policy, and national security policy information to the presidential candidates in the summer of 1952. That early dissemination of information to both major-party candidates following their nomination did not take place in the manner he planned, however. Nor did his successors work with the major-party candidates before the presidential election. It took until 2008 for an incumbent president to work successfully with both party candidates prior to the election. Through his work and that of people in his administration, President George W. Bush completed the transition preparation model first outlined by President Truman. Indeed, early planning had important payoffs for President Obama, payoffs that would have served Senator McCain equally as well if he had been elected.

In part, President Truman was moved to early transition planning by the circumstances of his own ascendancy to power. He entered the office in 1945 as a result of President Franklin D. Roosevelt's death with little knowledge of what was going on in government, including the planning for the atomic bomb. Ken Hechler, White House assistant to President Truman, commented that the president brought his staff together the day after his speech to Democratic party members at the annual Jefferson-Jackson dinner on March 29, 1952. At that dinner, Truman had announced that he would not be running for reelection in the coming year. He promptly began his planning in earnest for his transition out of power, which relied heavily on preparing the next president. "He called us all together and said, 'Now, whoever's elected this fall, whether he be a Republican or a Democrat, I don't want him to face the kind of thing that I faced when I came into office in 1945, completely unbriefed and unprepared."[15] Truman continued: "I want this to be a smooth transition. . . . I want everybody to work hard on it between now and next January."[16]

President Truman's preparations covered the areas of central planning currently required of a president to effectively assume power: budget, foreign and intelligence policy, and domestic programs. The president turned to the Bureau of the Budget as his first line of preparations because of the broad reach of the agency as an information-gathering unit and the experience he had using the Bureau to prepare for a possible 1948 transition. Roger Jones, who worked at the Bureau of the Budget during Truman's term, described the president's efforts: "In the last year or so of Mr. Truman's administration, he looked to the Bureau to provide most of the tissue for transition to the next administration since he knew there was going to be a new president."[17] Truman also relied on the Bureau because he had done so in 1948 when he was running for election, though that effort was a very low-key one. Roger Jones observed that the president "said it was essential for the Budget Bureau as the chief on-going piece of presidential machinery be prepared for a new president in case a new president was elected. . . . But he did ask that we very carefully analyze the party platforms, that we watch the statements made by the party candidates and that we be prepared to give briefings on where the government stood on these issues."[18] The same kinds of preparations were taken in 2008, with Clay Johnson, deputy director of the Office of Management and Budget, organizing administrative agencies in the information-gathering process. They too followed the party platforms and the statements by candidates on their policy intentions.

Both Truman's experience and the new inauguration date for an incoming president led Truman to plan in a way his predecessors had not. While the gathering of information on programs and positions was important as a precedent to be followed by all of his successors, one aspect of his transition planning was not adopted by his successor: preelection transfer of information to both of the major-party candidates. Adlai Stevenson accepted Truman's information offer, but Dwight Eisenhower did not. President Truman's idea of preelection planning was not adopted in 1952 but became an important consideration for those planning the 2008 transition.

The transition of 2008 was notable for closing a circle on transition planning that began with President Truman's early efforts in the modern transition period to bring about pre- as well as postelection preparation of candidates for the presidency. While Truman and those chief executives who followed him all provided some information to the president-elect and his team, the same was not true in the days before the November election, except in the area of intelligence information. Even after the election, there is no previous transition where there was a more systematic effort by the outgoing president and his White House staff to gather information administration-wide for the new team coming in.

Truman wanted to have the two major-party presidential candidates knowledgeable on government operations before the election, including White House and departmental operations. He wanted the candidates to be able to interact with the White House on issues other than national security policy. In 2008, representatives of the major-party candidates did work with White House staff on a variety of issues that went beyond candidate intelligence briefings, such as personnel and transition process issues. While not exactly what Truman was seeking, the 2008 transition caught the spirit of what Truman wanted to do. Through Chief of Staff Joshua Bolten and his staff, President Bush kept the major-party candidates well informed before the election about White House operations and any transition plans that were under way and the clearance process for nominees and also provided them with lists of positions a president can fill. Bolten brought together the candidates' representatives and let them know what information the president-elect and his team would get following the election and brought the two sides together to plan for the appointments process.

In 2008, the president and the White House staff involved in transition operations were able to get beyond the partisan suspicions that had crippled President Truman's 1952 efforts. During the summer after the two party nominating conventions, President Truman offered the party candidates, Adlai Stevenson and Dwight Eisenhower, meetings with members of his cabinet. Truman wanted the candidates to get briefings from the secretaries on the departmental issues they had been dealing with. Truman offered the candidates other briefings as well. In a letter to Eisenhower dated August 13, 1952, the president wrote to the candidate: "I'll have General [Walter Bedell] Smith and the Central Intelligence Agency give you a complete briefing on the foreign situation."[19] Following the briefing with the director and other members of the Central Intelligence Agency, Eisenhower and Truman would have lunch with the cabinet. President Truman also indicated to Eisenhower that the CIA would provide him with information on the "world situation" on a weekly basis. After his initial CIA briefing, "we will have luncheon with the Cabinet and after that if you like I'll have my entire staff report to you on the situation in the White House and in that way you will be entirely briefed on what takes place."[20]

Dwight Eisenhower was reluctant to take advantage of President Truman's offers. He viewed the offer with a high level of suspicion. In his response to President Truman, Eisenhower wrote: "In my current position as standard bearer of the Republican Party and of other Americans who want to bring about a change in the National Government, it is my duty to remain free to analyze publicly the policies and acts of the present administration whenever it appears to me to be proper and in the country's interests. . . . I believe our communications should be only those which are known to all the American people. Consequently I think it would be unwise and result in confusion in the public mind if I were to attend the meeting in the White House to which you have invited me."[21] Feeling slighted by Eisenhower's brusque turndown, President Truman wrote a heated handwritten response to him. "I am extremely sorry that you have allowed a bunch of screwballs to come between us. You have made a bad mistake and I'm hoping it won't injure this great Republic."[22]

The exchanges between the two men colored the remainder of their transition; although President Truman offered his plane to Eisenhower for the president-elect's trip to Korea, Eisenhower made his own arrangements, which included travel by military transport and by ship over a 15-day period. During his campaign, Eisenhower said that he would go to Korea to see the conditions for himself and work at finding a solution for the conflict. Truman offered to facilitate his journey, but Eisenhower demurred. The suspicion between opposing party presidents and their teams remains an issue, but today the need to cooperate in preparing for office is deemed more important by both sides than are the points that divide them. Deputy Chief of Staff Joel Kaplan, who worked on domestic policy issues in the final year of the George W. Bush administration, spoke about the need to cooperate that brought the Bush and Obama teams together. "What I think is great about it was there was just a recognition on both sides that there was just a lot at stake and we had to get it right," he said.[23] "We took it from the president and Josh [Bolten] and Blake [Gottesman, deputy chief of staff for operations] and Steve [Hadley] really took it incredibly seriously, and to their credit so did the incoming team." The party divisions that stopped earlier administrations from cooperating with one another did not prevent the two sides from working together. "Even though we are from different parties and obviously they spent the year beating us up and all of that, everyone put that aside, and I thought it was really terrific." Transitions have so many benefits for governing that presidential candidates and their teams now view planning as a central part of the passage from the campaign to the presidency, no matter which party is in office or coming in.

Ten Ways an Effective Transition Benefits a President

The preparations of the Bush and Obama national security teams set the stage for them to consider in an informed manner a very important issue arising as the new president prepared to take office. This benefit alone justifies the kind of work both sides did in holding principal-to-principal meetings and preparing templates to gather the information each side regarded as important to understanding the issues the incoming president would soon have to deal with. In a broader sense, an effective transition buys a new administration the chance to take advantage of the opportunities that exist at the beginning of an administration and to reduce the hazards that inevitably lie in wait. The benefits range from the direction of government to the reputation a president establishes in his early days.

1. Continuity in Government

Personnel, knowledge, and programs are in a volatile state when experienced people are leaving an administration and new ones are coming in. Continuity in government programs and decisions as well as crisis contingency plans are important in such a vulnerable time. The threat on the 2009 inauguration is a good example of the difference a transition can make to a president's effective handling of a potential crisis early in his presidency. "At a time of war, you don't want there to be any gaps, but particularly any extended gaps in having knowledgeable people [in office]," said Joe Hagin, deputy chief of staff in the George W. Bush administration.[24] Hagin was the White House staff member responsible for overseeing emergency preparations. Chief of Staff Joshua Bolten explained the importance of what Hagin was doing in terms of continuity of government. "Joe spent a lot of time trying to make sure that, before we left, we had in place the best possible emergency procedures and that we had mechanisms to make sure that people were trained and that there would be continuity between the administrations," Bolten said. "He worked a lot with the military office as well as on the infrastructure, the physical and technological infrastructure that goes with responding to an emergency."[25]

Recent examples of attacks on democratic governments provide a sense of the vulnerabilities that exist at election and transition times. On June 30, 2007, three days after Prime Minister Gordon Brown took office in the United Kingdom, there was a terrorist attack at Glasgow International Airport. A day and a half earlier two bombs had failed to go off in London. The March 2004 Madrid train bombings that killed 191 people came three days before that country's general election. With war in Afghanistan and Iraq under way in 2008, continuity in governing was essential to make sure the nation was protected during a vulnerable time.

Continuity in government is important in more than a national security sense. With few guidelines for how personnel and programs are to make a transition from one chief executive to another as well as from one department secretary to another, presidents need to take action when they leave government that assure continuity in programs and in the personnel assigned to carry on staff functions. The number of positions an incoming president will fill during his tenure is too large to fill in the first month in office or even the first year. Bradley Patterson, who once served in the White House and today studies its organization, estimated in 2008 that the president and his White House staff have an estimated 7,854 positions they can fill.[26] These include approximately 1,200 presidential appointees requiring Senate confirmation; about 1,500 part-time appointees for boards and commissions; 154 commissioned White House staff members; 2,300 non-career Senior Executive Service and Schedule C positions; and another 900 people who fill the White House staff offices as well as executive residence staff.[27] With so many positions to fill, a president and his staff need to set priorities.

In order to assure continuity in government programs, a president sets up a transition team focused on the budget as a priority. The president is called upon by law to present a budget to the Congress in February, less than a month after he comes into office. He must consider as well how the executive branch departments and agencies are going to implement the programs in operation and ones that may be coming online. With a budget of $3.8 trillion in spending for FY 2013 and 2.1 million civilian employees in the federal government, it is not easy to establish direction of government.[28]

2. Direction of Government

The presidential transition is an important element in establishing the direction of government. With a clear campaign agenda, an incoming president can quickly signal his governing priorities. President Reagan signaled his intention to carry through on his budget and tax cut priorities in his first days in office. Less than an hour after he had been sworn into office on January 20, 1981, President Reagan signed a memorandum that was followed the next day by an executive order freezing the hiring of civilian federal workers. "I pledged last July that this would be a first step toward controlling the growth and the size of Government and reducing the drain on the economy for the public sector," the newly inaugurated president said. "And beyond the symbolic value of this, which is my first official act, the freeze will eventually lead to a significant reduction in the size of the Federal work force. Only rare exemptions will be permitted in order to maintain vital services."[29] The following day he signed a memorandum cutting by 5% "obligations for consulting, management and professional services, and special contract studies and analyses. . . . Cut obligations for travel by 15 percent" and halting the "procurement of furniture, office machines and other equipment, except military equipment and equipment needed to protect human life and property." As a last measure, Reagan provided: "I am directing that Members of the Cabinet and other appointees set an example by avoiding unnecessary expenditures in setting up their personal offices. Appointees are not to redecorate their offices."[30] In an area where the president had discretion, Reagan moved quickly to set the tone. Just as quickly, the Senate confirmed all but two of his cabinet nominees that first day.

For other presidents as well, transition planning meant an early start on their policy initiatives. "We weren't stumbling around the first couple of months of the administration," commented Deputy Chief of Staff Joe Hagin about the transition of George W. Bush in 2000–2001. "We were able to get right down to business."[31] Because those handling the White House transition—Andy Card, Joshua Bolten, and Hagin—had served in previous administrations, they knew where the traps lay. "We knew all the basics that allowed us to at least walk from the first day rather than crawl," he said. "That is important." From that beginning, the president and his administration focused on their priority issues at a tempo of their choosing without being sidetracked by the agendas of others. In their first year, though, they found that they had to change course. First, on June 6, 2001, the Republicans effectively lost control of the Senate with the change of party affiliation of Senator James Jeffords of Vermont from Republican to Independent and his indication he would caucus with the Democrats. That switch meant, at a minimum, alterations to some of President Bush's agenda items, such as his tax cuts. September 11 meant further changes in policy priorities as well as significant challenges to the economy.

In the case of President Obama and his team, the first weeks were productive ones with executive orders, memoranda, proclamations, and legislation important to the administration and the Democratic majority in Congress. With a financial collapse a distinct possibility, the president wanted to establish early that his administration was under way and taking hold of the crisis. In his first ten days in office, President Obama took executive action through a series of ten memoranda directing the bureaucracy to take action on certain subjects. He also signed nine executive orders dealing with a range of domestic and national security issues, including a review of our policies dealing with detainees in Guantanamo Bay, abortion, and ethics requirements for members of the administration. All of these actions required a great deal of preparatory work during the transition period.

3. Seizing Political Momentum

Getting off to a fast start has the benefit of leaving little blank space for your critics to fill and represents an opportunity to discuss what you want to talk about. Max Stier, president of the Partnership for Public Service, a group that facilitated transition discussions in the late spring of 2008 and 2012 with teams representing those running for the presidency, commented on the importance of the transition in dominating discussion as a president comes into office. "I think especially in today's political climate to actually have an affirmative agenda, your honeymoon period gets shorter and shorter and shorter. Your opportunity for change is much, much greater at the very front end of your term. And so the faster you do your transition, the faster you actually have the ability to have people in place to execute on your positive agenda, and you spend a lot of time reacting to things as the term lays out," he said. "The idea of a quick transition also means you improve your likelihood of actually making it happen by making it fast, because there are fewer things—the political momentum is with you in a way that just dissipates really quickly, and there are going to be fewer people that are going to stand in your way to get your stuff done at the front end. That's the up side."[32]

President George W. Bush had an agenda ready to go that rolled out their chief initiatives in a weekly order. That way, the amount of time spent on the outcome of the election was held to a minimum. He had an order of initiatives that went from his first week in office until his sixth. Each week had a policy theme to it. The issues went from education in the first week to establishing the Office of Faith-Based Community Initiatives in his second. That week President Bush also signed an executive order designed to clear away bureaucratic hurdles for non-profit agencies dealing with five executive branch departments that often interact with community organizations: Justice, Housing and Urban Development, Health and Human Services, Labor, and Education.

Each week the president spoke on the issue of the week, and so too did members of his cabinet. He followed those first three weeks of education and faith-based issues with ones devoted to increasing military spending and tax reform. With each of the issues, President Bush spoke on the issue, often brought in congressional leaders to discuss the subject, and traveled outside of Washington to speak to relevant groups. The discussion of military spending, for example, included speeches to troops at Fort Stewart, Florida, and at the Norfolk Naval Station in Virginia as well as to National Guard members in Charleston, West Virginia.

While he spoke on issues of his choice, he also worked on issues that surfaced requiring presidential attention, including the early April downing of a military intelligence plane over China. He emphasized his role as chief executive through his swearing-in ceremonies with each of the cabinet members and a talk about the subjects that they handled in their individual departments. Taken together, there was little room for his critics to surface and get attention for their positions. News organizations were interested in following the new faces in the executive branch, most especially the president. President Bush gave them a great deal to write about. So much so, in fact, Democrats and reporters spent little time on President Bush's status as the last president since Benjamin Harrison in 1881 to enter the presidency with fewer popular votes than his opponent. Their early transition planning enabled Bush to enter office as a reasonably strong president, not one weakened irreparably by a cloudy election.

4. Quality of Information

Gathering information well before a president comes into office is important because the previous administration removes its papers and digital records from the White House before the new occupant comes in. The more a president and his team know when they come into the White House, the more quickly they can get started. Chief executives come into the White House with no institutional memory awaiting them as an informational support system; only the Counsel's Office and the National Security Council retain files from the previous administration that the new presidential team can use. The Presidential Records Act of 1978 requires that presidential records leave a White House with the outgoing president. How much information is available to the incoming team about the operations of the White House and the fifteen cabinet departments depends on the preparations provided for by the incumbent White House and the cooperation of the department secretaries and their deputies. The trucks begin pulling up to the White House in December to load in the boxes of White House Central Files that are still in the building. The end result is that when a new administration comes into office, the desks and file cabinets are empty. Having so many records leave the building is a big hurdle for the new team, which wants to get up to speed quickly.

The outgoing administration helps the new team assemble information important to a fast start. The agency review teams assembled by the transition team for President-elect Obama during the transition period made a difference in the kinds of information the policy teams worked with as they developed initiatives for the early days of the administration. They had 517 people on the agency review teams fanned out through government to find the status of programs in the departments and agencies and what was working and what was not. They had information assembled by the General Services Administration on the functions and responsibilities of each of the units. The President's Management Council, composed of the chief operating officers in the government, typically the deputy secretary of the departments and the largest agencies, produced information for the transition team about the hot issues and upcoming schedules important for each unit. Once the new team came into office, they had current information on the department or agency from both their own review teams and from those in office in 2008.

In coming into the White House, an early start is important because incoming staff need time to figure out the functioning of the offices they are going to occupy. There are many ways in which White House functions and operations will continue whether a Democrat or Republican holds the presidency, but there are fewer people serving across administrations in those offices at the career level as in the past. Anita McBride, who came into the White House at the beginning of the Reagan administration and returned for each Republican administration thereafter, noted the gradual loss of institutional memory from the time she first served in the White House in 1981. "People who had been there twenty and thirty years that were training all the new administrations weren't there, and that was very striking to me coming back in 2001 and coming in as acting director of White House personnel and not having the go-to people that I was used to in the past just to help you get started," said McBride.[33] With fewer people to train those coming in, an early start is important to develop the necessary information from other sources than career people.

5. Reducing Mistakes

The transition is a vulnerable decision-making period. There are important choices to be made, and mistakes are costly, especially in the appointments area. If a president-elect makes a mistake, it can drag on well into the new administration. The area of presidential appointments has tripped up several recent administrations as they started out of the gate. It took President Clinton until the middle of March to get his candidate for attorney general confirmed. It turned out that his first nominee, Zoë Baird, had not paid the required Social Security taxes for two household staff members. *Time* magazine carried a headline: "Clinton's First Blunder: How a Popular Outcry Caught the Washington Elite by Surprise."[34] *Newsweek* early on painted a portrait of an administration coming into the White House without a grasp on governing. "The transfer of power may have looked seamless on TV, but behind-the-scenes chaos reigned during the first days in the Clinton White House," the authors wrote. "The switchboard was overwhelmed, in part by callers complaining about Zoë Baird's nomination as attorney general. Many top aides were unreachable because offices—and direct phone lines—were still being assigned. Even the computer system wasn't working."[35]

In such an environment, it was difficult for the president and his staff to handle the problems associated with the attorney general position. President Clinton went through another nominee, federal judge Kimba Wood, before finally settling on the Florida state attorney in Miami, Florida, Janet Reno. It was February 11 when he nominated her and a month later before she was confirmed by the Senate. The problems from that one nomination caused trouble for him in other areas.

In contrast, President George W. Bush wasted little time at the start of his administration over inappropriate cabinet nominees. He had one nomination that caused trouble, but the situation was resolved fairly quickly. When Linda Chavez was named secretary of labor, information surfaced that she may have previously had undocumented workers as household help. When confronted with information that she had helped support an illegal worker, she stepped down. While the Clinton attorney general process took over three months from the naming of the first nominee to Reno's confirmation by the Senate, the Bush labor secretary flap traveled the same distance in three weeks.

Max Stier discussed the protection an administration has if it starts planning early. "There's also a protection against a down side, which is there are lots of risks out there. The world is an ugly, scary place, and not having a quick transition means you are more likely to be subject to a risk that you don't have your team in place to deal with," he said.[36] In his view, there is an opportunity a president squanders if he does not begin planning early. "I think there's both upside loss and downside risk that you can avoid by effective, quick transition, and I do think that the metric of doing better than the last person is insufficient not only because no one's done it well but also because the world is changing so quickly that the requirements for doing it faster are all the more important."

6. Effective Working Relationships

When presidents establish early relationships with congressional leaders, what difference does it make for them? While the relationships may come apart, they sometimes exist long enough for a president's policy priorities to get enacted. President George W. Bush provides a good example with the early relationship he built with Senator Edward Kennedy. Jim Manley, a Kennedy aide who was present at the time, recalled an exchange between President Bush and Senator Kennedy that helped them work together to further the president's No Child Left Behind legislation.[37] President-elect Bush's initial foray into education was to bring together key congressional players in the area of education as he planned an initiative his first week in office. In late December, he brought together at his Texas ranch those he and his staff considered the key players. Senator Kennedy was not invited to the gathering.[38]

In his first week in office, President Bush had another meeting of Senate and House members involved in education issues. This time the meeting was at the White House and included the key players on education, Democrats as well as Republicans. This time the president saw an opportunity to work with Senator Kennedy. "At the end of the meeting, the President looked around the room and said to Senator Kennedy, 'The press is waiting for you out there, and they're going to try and drive a wedge between you and I right away over the issue of'—I think it was probably testing and standards—'and I hope you won't do anything to fall into that trap.'"[39] Manley said "Kennedy agreed, and sure enough we walked out the door. I don't think we ended up going to the microphones. We started walking right to his van, which was parked on the drive, . . . There was a large pack of . . . reporters, and they're just shouting questions at Kennedy. 'What's your view on this? What's your view on that?' And Kennedy just kept right on going and got in the van and said a few innocuous words." Manley viewed the senator's response as important to the two men's working relationship: "That sent an important signal to the administration, to the President that he was someone that could be trusted." In Manley's view, the discussion and understanding between Bush and Kennedy was "probably a key, defining moment in the relationship, because the

White House was astute enough to realize that the potential for a stakeout had disaster written all over it, and Senator Kennedy was smart enough not to fall into the trap." It was, he said, "a pretty subtle, but pretty important telling point. "After the initial mix-up, they identified Senator Kennedy as someone that they could do business with. And under great opposition, if you will, from many within the party and within the leadership, Senator Kennedy worked to pass No Child Left Behind," he added.[40]

Beyond the White House, a good presidential transition can make a difference to the quality of the relationship between the political team coming in and the career staff in the departments and agencies. An effective transition "enables you to get the trust very quickly of the career staff," said Dan Chenok, who worked in the Office of Management and Budget as a career staff member during both Democratic and Republican administrations before leaving to the private sector. As a member of two agency review teams for the Obama transition, Chenok saw the importance of the president-elect's transition operation to acquiring the trust of career staff: "It is really important for there to be a good trust relationship as quickly as possible between the incoming team and the career staff. The trust relationship often gets built up in the transition."[41] In addition to the relationships, in those early days it is also necessary to build the "working parameters" of the relationship, said Chenok. One of the ways the Obama transition operation built links with career staff was to bring onto their transition teams former members of the agencies who had both knowledge of agency operations and who had preexisting relationships with career staff.

7. Taking Advantage of Goodwill

For a short while, the president has the goodwill and attention of the public and the Washington community. Even in politics, people do not want to attack the newcomer until there is substantial reason to do so. In the early days, if he has strong poll numbers, there is little advantage for a president's opponents to go on the attack against the administration's people and positions. Instead, they wait.

The early months are ones where the president ordinarily can count on the public backing the job he is doing. But it doesn't last. Presidents need to make use of that time to introduce their people and programs. President Obama won election with 53 percent of the popular vote. Yet by the time he was sworn into office, he had 68 percent job approval. He maintained that level through his first hundred days even though his job disapproval ratings went from 12 percent in his first days in office to 29 percent at the hundred-day mark. A year into his presidency, President Obama had a 49 percent job approval rating and 44 percent in-

TABLE 1.1
Gallup Presidential Job Approval Ratings and Percentage of Popular Vote

	Percentage of popular vote[1]	Gallup job approval in first days in office[2]	Gallup job approval at 100-day mark[3]	Gallup job disapproval at 100-day mark[3]
Dwight Eisenhower	54.9	68	73	10
John F. Kennedy	49.7	72	83	5
Richard Nixon	43.4	59	62	15
Jimmy Carter	50.1	66	63	18
Ronald Reagan	50.7	51	68	21
George H. W. Bush	53.4	51	56	22
Bill Clinton	43.0	58	55	37
George W. Bush	47.9	57	62	29
Barack Obama	52.9	68	65	29

[1]American Presidency Project, "Presidential Elections Data."
[2]"Two-Thirds Approve of Obama's Job."
[3]American Presidency Project, "Presidential Job Approval Ratings Following the First 100 Days, Eisenhower–Obama."

dicating disapproval. A president needs to move during those early months, because support is not going to last once the chief executive submits his legislative proposals and his critics surface.[42]

Nor was President Obama alone in having a relatively high presidential job approval rating early in his presidency when compared with the percentage of the popular vote he received in the November election. Except for President George H. W. Bush, all recent presidents have had a substantially higher early approval rating than their percentage of the popular vote in their election to office. Of the nine presidents elected to the presidency from Dwight Eisenhower through Barack Obama—not counting Lyndon Johnson and Gerald Ford, who ascended to the presidency through the death or resignation of their predecessors—five of the nine presidents experienced at least a fifteen-point increase from the popular vote percentage to the early presidential approval rating. President Eisenhower was close, with a thirteen percent increase from his percentage of the popular vote to his early Gallup approval rating, while President George W. Bush had an increase of nine percent. Only two presidents—Ronald Reagan and George H. W. Bush—saw little movement between their election and early approval numbers.

The willingness of the public to give the new president a chance and look at him in a positive way is an important resource for a chief executive. That goodwill helps spur the Senate into confirming a president's cabinet-level nominees. He may have trouble down the line with deputies to the deputy secretaries, but at the top level, the Senate is willing to move quickly. In change of party transitions from Presidents Carter through Obama, unless a president withdrew a nominee, the Senate confirmed them within days. All but two of them were confirmed less than a month after the inauguration, which was when their names were formally sent to the Senate. Goodwill translates into positive steps for a new administration as it assembles its team. For President Obama it led to a string of early legislative victories, such as the American Recovery Act and, several months later, the Affordable Care Act.

8. Capturing Public Attention

In addition to being willing to give the new president support for how he is handling his job as he begins his term in office, the public pays more attention to what the president says and does in the first months of his administration. That willingness to listen does not last through the chief executive's term. The inaugural address is important not only because it is a statement of the president's priorities but also because it draws strong public attention. Even though the ceremony is usually held on a weekday, a significant segment of the public watches the presidential address.

Individual speeches early in a president's term receive the attention of the public. President Reagan kept up the theme of getting the budget under control through a televised address less than a month after he came into office. In reviewing all of the televised addresses to the nation from his eight years in office, his February 18, 1981, budget speech had the largest audience. In a poll conducted by Richard Wirthlin of the audiences for twenty-two of President Reagan's major speeches, the average number of people who heard "all" of a Reagan speech was 21%, "part" of a speech was 24%, "read about later" was 16%, and "heard/read nothing" was 39%.[43] For his budget speech, however, 39% heard all of it, 25% part of it, 18% read about it later, and only 18% heard or read nothing about it. Reagan knew that this early period of his presidency would be important for getting the attention of the public, and he took advantage of it.

In part it was the subject, but the timing of Reagan's budget speech was important too. President Clinton delivered an economic speech on February 17, 1993, one day earlier in his presidency than Reagan delivered his. Clinton's result was similar to Reagan's experience in terms of the size of his television audience. To the question if a person watched all, some, a little, or none of the Clinton speech, 70% saw some part of the speech, while only 30% said they saw none.[44]

At the same time the public is watching, the press's treatment of presidents in the early days is fairly positive as well. The Center for Media and Public Affairs found in its charting of news coverage by ABC, CBS, and NBC that in the first fifty days of the George H. W. Bush, Bill Clinton, and George W. Bush adminis-

trations, presidents got positive coverage for particular aspects of their administrations. The center's evaluation of press coverage of President George H. W. Bush
was 61% positive, while those numbers in the three major networks fell in the
Clinton first fifty days to 44%, and rose in a similar period of George W. Bush's
tenure to 48%.[45] Even if their overall coverage was under 50% in its favorability,
the coverage of individual policy areas came out well in the George W. Bush administration: faith-based initiatives 60%; defense 50%; taxes 49%; domestic policy 48%; other economic 54%.[46] While President Clinton did not receive as many
favorable as unfavorable stories in his first fifty days, he did come in with favorable television pieces about himself and by members of his administration, which
is the medium toward which recent administrations have aimed their publicity
efforts. In the period between his election and inauguration, President Clinton
had 64% favorable television pieces, and the coverage of his new team was even
more favorable, except for controversial cabinet nominees Zoë Baird for attorney
general and Ron Brown for commerce secretary.[47]

While poor transitions may not hobble a presidency, they prevent a new president from taking advantage of all of the opportunities that come to him when he
enters the White House. In a wartime situation, an ineffective start means there
will be a break in the continuity that is so important to carrying on the tasks and
programs already in place.

9. Presidential Reputation

It is said that you only get one chance to make a first impression, and presidents
are mindful of their need to use the early days to establish themselves with the
public. One of the first and most important transitions a president needs to make
is the one from candidate to chief executive. A president is responsible to all of
the people, not just those of his party or those who voted for him. He needs to
make the switch from candidate to president of all of the people.

If he is to be successful as chief executive, the president-elect needs to make
that move during the transition rather than at the beginning of his presidency.
One of the ways presidents-elect make that switch is by staying out of view for a
time after the initial announcements related to the senior White House staff and
domestic and foreign policy and national security teams. Once this group of aides
is chosen, the president-elect can then head out of public view. It is a natural
move to make because the stresses and strain of campaigning leave candidates
exhausted. President Ford was so hoarse when he ended his campaign that Betty
Ford read his concession telegram with him standing behind her.

The natural move for a president-elect, once he has rested, is to come to Washington. The length of that hiatus depends on circumstances. President Reagan went to his ranch and then in mid-November came to Washington for a brief visit and did so as president-elect, not as the Republican candidate. His schedule emphasized a bipartisan tone. He gave one dinner for the Washington community and was hosted by columnist George Will for another. The dinner the Reagans hosted included as guests the leaders and minority leaders of Congress as well as committee chairs, lobbyists, party officials, reporters and columnists. He included Democrats and Republicans and all of those whose support he needed to achieve his goals. It was a formal affair given by the president-elect and his wife Nancy at the F Street Club. The Washingtonians attending the event appreciated the manner in which Reagan was seeking to build connections with them.

"After four long years as wallflowers, members of the Washington establishment will finally have a suitor in the White House. Never was a neglected belle more eager to be wooed," noted Lynn Rosellini in the *New York Times*.[48] Edward Bennett Williams, a Democrat and member of the Washington establishment, commented: "Obviously, he is reaching out. . . . That is something the current President [Carter] never did." Clark Clifford, who advised Carter on foreign affairs, expanded on that theme for Rosellini: "The [Carter] White House missed an opportunity to ease their problems by remaining apart from the social activity of this city." The day after his meeting with President Carter, Governor Reagan went up to Capitol Hill and called on Democratic and Republican leaders in the House and Senate. Those he went to see included Democratic Senator Edward Kennedy. Additionally, he stopped by the Supreme Court to see Chief Justice Warren Burger and then the other members of the Court. His message was clear: He wanted their support, and he was willing to come to them to get it.

Once he got into office, he got off to a quick start with a slew of executive orders and administrative memoranda. That led to favorable publicity about his leadership style, which portrayed a man who knew what he was doing. Veteran White House reporter Helen Thomas wrote about his focus on the economy one month into his presidency: "President Reagan is living up to his campaign promise to make the economy his No. 1 priority. As his one-month anniversary in office nears and he prepares to unveil his economic package Wednesday, he has kept the nation's eyes riveted on that issue alone."[49]

At the hundred-day mark of his presidency, President Reagan received continued praise for his leadership on the economy and for his overall good start. "With a gift for political theater, Mr. Reagan has established his goals faster, communicated a greater sense of economic urgency and come forward with more comprehensive proposals than any new President since the first 100 days of Franklin D.

Roosevelt, the hero of his youth and the man whose record of achieving social change Mr. Reagan seeks to emulate—albeit at the opposite end of the political spectrum," wrote Steven Weisman in the *New York Times Magazine*.[50] "In Rooseveltian fashion, Mr. Reagan has commanded the attention of the public, the Congress and America's allies and adversaries. He has skillfully courted new and old friends, kept Democrats and liberals on the defensive and maintained a friendly posture even to those who, like labor leaders and blacks, regard his program as anathema." Weisman noted as well Reagan's knack for avoiding the early mistakes of earlier administrations: "And, perhaps by luck, he has managed to avoid the serious blunders of many predecessors. Before the end of their first 100 days, after all, John F. Kennedy had the Bay of Pigs, and Jimmy Carter had already alienated his congressional allies and had been dramatically rebuffed by the Russians on his early arms-control initiative, setting negotiations back as much as a year for the ill-fated nuclear arms treaty."

With his budget cuts and tax cuts legislation passed that year, President Reagan established a pattern of leadership that shot up his Gallup poll numbers at the hundred-day mark. Table 1.1 shows the figures. Seven of the nine elected chief executives from Presidents Dwight Eisenhower to Barack Obama had job approval ratings of at least 62%, with only two in the fifties (Presidents George H. W. Bush and Clinton had 56% and 55%, respectively). Two of the presidents, John Kennedy and Dwight Eisenhower, had ratings of 83% and 73%. Since 1960, though, presidents have had to settle for significantly lower but still strong numbers. Yet Presidents Obama and George W. Bush had 65% and 62%, respectively. The relatively robust public approval numbers for almost all of these chief executives made a difference in their approach to their jobs and their relationships with the public and the Washington community. Reputations are formed early in Washington, and when important players view presidents as knowing what they are doing, they are more willing to give them more support for their programs.

10. A Good Transition Benefits the Outgoing President

How a president leaves office can be a significant factor in his legacy. Certainly it influences the stories written about him as he leaves office. For President Clinton, the end of his presidency brought criticism from Democrats as well as Republicans. News articles and broadcasts at the end of his presidency reflected the questions about the 176 pardons he granted, particularly the one to exiled financier Marc Rich, as well as the plea deal he struck on that final day to avoid further investigation of his lying in the deposition he gave in the Paula Jones case. The Rich pardon was particularly damaging. A 2013 Associated Press obituary on Rich described the conditions under which Rich left the United States for Switzerland in 1983. He left "after he was indicted by a U.S. federal grand jury on more than 50 counts of fraud, racketeering, trading with Iran during the U.S. Embassy hostage crisis and evading more than $48 million in income taxes—crimes that could have earned him more than 300 years in prison."[51] Rich was on the FBI Most Wanted List when Clinton pardoned him.

Later newspaper articles mentioned vandalism by junior White House staff that was purported to have occurred as he left office. The vandalism reports spread so far and wide that Congressman Bob Barr (R-Ga.) requested the General Accounting Office to investigate the claims. The agency's June 2002 report concluded: "Damage, theft, vandalism, and pranks occurred in the White House complex during the 2001 presidential transition. Incidents such as the removal of keys from computer keyboards; the theft of various items; the leaving of certain voice mail messages, signs, and written messages; and the placing of glue on desk drawers clearly were intentional acts."[52] But the GAO concluded: "It was unknown whether other observations, such as broken furniture, were the result of intentional acts, when and how they occurred, or who may have been responsible for them." The GAO estimated the costs associated with the repair and replacements of items at the beginning of the new administration at $9,324.[53] Questions arose too about items of American porcelain and decorative arts acquired by the Clintons said to total $190,027.[54] The initial piece over the Clintons' gifts raised questions posed by the chief usher about the uncertainty of whether the items belonged to the White House or the Clintons.[55] By early February, the Clintons paid for or returned the items where ownership was an issue.[56] All of the Clinton controversies led to articles such as one by Godfrey Sperling appearing in the *Christian Science Monitor*: "Bush's Promising Start and Clinton's Sorry Exit," was the headline of his article.[57]

A month after President Clinton left office, the controversies surrounding his exit had still not quieted down. The *Washington Post* reported that the hullabaloo created by his exit had elevated President Bush's early poll numbers and were responsible for the precipitous fall of Clinton's figures. "There is widespread agreement that Republican gains have been the result," John Harris and Dana Milbank reported in their *Post* article. "The questions around Clinton have helped reinforce Bush's pledge to 'restore dignity' to the White House. A poll last week by Zogby International showed that 64 percent of respondents said they had an 'overall favorable' impression of Bush, up 10 points from a month before. Clinton scored 48 percent favorability, down eight points in a month."[58] President Clinton worked his way back up to his earlier highs, but his exit cost him in popularity.

TABLE 1.2
Gallup Presidential Job Approval Ratings

	Gallup average job approval while in office (%)	Gallup final job approval rating while in office (%)	2010 Gallup retrospective approval (%)
John F. Kennedy	70	58	85
Lyndon Johnson	55	49	49
Richard Nixon	49	24	29
Gerald Ford	47	53	61
Jimmy Carter	45	34	52
Ronald Reagan	53	63	74
George H. W. Bush	61	56	64
Bill Clinton	55	66	69
George W. Bush	49	34	47

Source: Saad, "Kennedy Still Highest-Rated Modern President, Nixon Lowest."

His last Gallup poll while in office had him at 66%, with the Zogby poll showing him a month later at 48%. A poor exit had a sharp, if transitory, impact on his public approval ratings.

All around, President Clinton's exit was viewed as one of the messiest in memory and one future presidents would want to avoid. In fact, one of the issues discussed in a White House meeting at the end of President Bush's time in office was how to avoid a situation of petty vandalism similar to what happened in the end of Clinton's presidency when some junior staffers took the letter W (a common nickname for George W. Bush) off of some White House computer keyboards.[59] While the actual instances of defacement were few, articles abounded about the destruction.

What happens in his transition out of office is significant for how people view the president. While President George W. Bush left office with a low public approval rating, his transition out of office continues to receive considerable praise as the most successful one a president has had. It is one element in the rise of President Bush's ratings in the years following his presidency.

Transition Challenges

In order to take advantage of the opportunities a transition offers as well as to avoid its hazards, the presumptive party candidates need to prepare for the presidency before they come into office—ideally, well before the party conventions. By taking advantage of the opportunities a presidential candidate has to begin early information-gathering on personnel, programs, and presidential actions, a president-elect has a better chance than he otherwise would have of successfully establishing the direction of the new administration. In addition to setting the course of presidential policy, an effective transition will help the incoming president staff up the White House and the administration.

While an effective transition provides a good start for an administration, the duration of its beneficial effects will last only as long as the president and White House as well as administration officials are responsive to their new environment. Their operation must be flexible and able to detect changes in conditions and sense new issues rising. Without that capacity, the benefits of a good transition will prove transient.

CHAPTER TWO

Transition Foundations

The importance of governmental institutions to the president-elect is symbolized by the role of the administrator of the General Services Administration in declaring the election winner. On election night 2008, it was Acting Administrator Jim Williams who signed the documents declaring Barack Obama winner of the presidential election, documents that signaled the beginning of the formal transition process.[1] In a GSA-produced video, officials explained: "Jim Williams' signature released about six million of the more than eight million dollars designated for the transition. It also gave the GSA staff the okay to hand over the keys to the offices of the incoming president." All of these actions were taken less than twenty-four hours after the polls around the country had closed and an apparent winner was declared by election specialists and news organizations. The GSA administrator's role in declaring a winner is provided for in Section 3 of the Presidential Transition Act of 1963. Behind our presidential transitions is a welter of legislation, presidential action, administrative decisions taken by government agencies, and a strong record of congressional legislation. Additionally, there are those in the Washington community who live outside of government but are important to the information and resources that presidential candidates and then presidents-elect can call upon for support.

The development of government-wide presidential transition planning in the United States has a relatively short history. Until 1937, presidential inaugurations occurred on March 4, not January 20 as became the practice in that year. Before, transitions had been approximately 120 days. Gradually, over the years since 1952 when transitions moved to an approximately seventy-five-day calendar and presidents were limited to two terms, people inside and outside of government have adopted practices encouraging transition planning by providing resources to the president-elect. The foundation for presidential transitions is made up of legislation, government agency practices, and an institutional memory developed by supportive groups. Additionally, people outside of the government have combined with incumbent presidents to develop a solid path to the presidency shaped by transition planning. While most legislation and government agency action is aimed at facilitating a smooth running transition, laws, congressional actions, and agency requirements have added hurdles to the transition process, particularly in the nomination process to fill executive branch positions.

When President Truman prepared for his transition out of office in 1952, he focused his attention on gathering the information the Central Intelligence Agency and the Bureau of the Budget could provide. He wanted to make certain that the incoming president would be knowledgeable on issues of war and peace as well as the budget and the status of government programs. Congress did not weigh in on the transition, nor would President Truman have been interested in listening if the legislative branch had sought a role. There was no office space in Washington or New York for the incoming team. Candidates and even the president-elect fended for themselves without government support and no obligations of others to provide for aid to the new president. Furthermore, outgoing presidents received no resources as they made the adjustment to civilian life.

Today the situation of a president-elect is much different than was the case in the Truman era. Through a consideration of congressional action, executive agency initiatives, the work by those who form an institutional memory of previous transitions, and public service groups, we can see how far we have come in government institutions accepting an obligation to prepare for a president's entry into office with support coming from outside institutions and individuals as well. Beginning with the Presidential Transition Act of 1963, government officials have gradually taken on the responsibility of facilitating a good transition by providing funds and resources to the president-elect for his postelection transition.

Those outside of government feel no similar need to provide help to the president leaving office. After all, he has all of the resources of the government at his disposal. What that means is each president leaving office makes up plans anew for how to exit the presidency. How they leave depends on two points: whether the transition is one where there is a change in party control of the presidency and whether the president was running for reelection. Presidents who leave after two terms often have both the time and the inclination to prepare for the transition out of office. Those who are running for reelection do not have the incentive to do much more than basic preparations for a new team because they do not focus on the transition until after they lose the election. Thus, they have little time to make preparations for a new team.

Transition Foundations Established by Law

By the 1960s, Congress as well as presidents had recognized the need to prepare for an orderly transfer of power by establishing information practices as well as financial and office support. Incumbent presidents were active behind the scenes in providing intelligence information, and the president-elect's political party provided whatever support their winning candidate needed. By 1963, members of Congress realized that providing support for a president-elect was a role for government. That recognition is established in the Presidential Transition Act of 1963. Along with the many amendments over the years adding funds and more government support, the act is the basic law governing presidential transitions. The thrust of the law and its amendments is often to establish in law presidential transition practices that were already being followed during the one or two transitions preceding the congressional provisions. Congress recognized the importance of what candidates were doing and brought their practices under the umbrella of the law. They did so because they wanted to make certain that funds and government resources were available, but they also did it because they wanted to establish guidelines and restrictions of what private monies and resources presidents-elect raised and spent. From 1988 onward, transition law requires reporting on the sources, amounts, and nature of the support presidents-elect receive from the private sector.

Over the almost fifty-year history of transition legislation, Congress has supported presidential transitions with funds and government resources, especially the services and support of the General Services Administration. Congressional legislation mirrors growing transition needs and practices. From the 1960s forward, transition planning expanded with the growth in the number of government programs, agencies, and presidential appointed positions. It did not take long for presidents-elect to feel a need for a greater amount of financial and staff support than the government was guaranteeing and to want that support before the election, not just after it. Those needs led President-elect Reagan in 1980 to create a private corporation, Presidential Transition Foundation, Inc., to raise whatever he funds he needed. The foundation did not publish its expenditures or monies raised. That led Congress to establish ground rules for transition fundraising and spending along with strict reporting requirements. Gradually congressional action moved from providing funds and basic services to placing conditions on private fundraising as a condition of presidents-elect taking transition funding under the 1963 act.

Laying the Groundwork for Presidential Transitions: 1963–1988

The Presidential Transition Act of 1963 came about in recognition of the vulnerability of the United States during the change in power from one president to his successor. The section of the act detailing its purpose states:

> The Congress declares it to be the purpose of the Act to promote the orderly transfer
> of the executive power in connection with the expiration of the term of office of a
> President and the inauguration of a new President. The national interest requires that
> such transitions in the office of President be accomplished so as to assure continuity
> in the faithful execution of the laws and in the conduct of the affairs of the Federal
> Government, both domestic and foreign. Any disruption occasioned by the transfer
> of the executive power could produce results detrimental to the safety and well-being
> of the United States and its people. Accordingly, it is the intent of the Congress that
> appropriate actions be authorized and taken to avoid or minimize any disruption.[2]

In order to facilitate the transition, the act provided for funding and government office space for the new administration and for the outgoing team as well. The act is clear on the limited nature of the funds to be dispersed: "The Administrator shall expend no funds for the provision of services and facilities under this Act in connection with any obligations incurred by the President-elect or Vice-President-elect before the day following the date of the general elections held to determine the electors of the President and Vice President."[3] The act provides for government office space provided under the direction of the General Services Administration, staff salaries, and expenses including travel and experts. Transition expenditures were capped at $900,000, but the act did not specify how the $900,000 should be divided between the incoming and outgoing teams.[4] For the 1968–1969 presidential transition, President-elect Nixon was allotted $450,000 but raised an additional one million dollars privately.[5] In 1976 the sums were increased to three million dollars, with two-thirds of the funds designated for the incoming president and vice president and the remainder to the outgoing team.

Much of our transition legislation has been developed in response to practices and issues occurring during presidential transitions. Amendments to the 1963 legislation raised the amounts allotted to candidates, but Congress later became interested in placing some limits on the ever-increasing amounts of private funding coming into play in transition before and after the election. Political parties no longer funded transition efforts, as the candidates preferred to raise their own funds.

Changes in Transition Needs and Rules: 1988–2000

Gradually presidents-elect had more they wanted to do to prepare for office and created privately funded foundations to accomplish their goals. With government transparency demands increasing, the two trends came together in the Presidential Transition Effectiveness Act of 1988. The act acknowledged the need for private funding and placed reporting restrictions and contribution limits on these private organizations.

By 2000, Congress had a laundry list of complaints about the shortcomings of government efforts to facilitate smooth transitions and also began to recognize the growing need for agencies to deal with representatives of the major-party candidates prior to the election. Congress sought solutions to alleviate what presidents-elect and their nominees for executive branch positions were coming to regard as onerous financial disclosure regulations. Congress recognized that an incoming administration needed to have information on the functions of executive branch departments and agencies. The Presidential Transition Act of 2000 called on the National Archives and Records Administration and the General Services Administration to provide a directory with the functions and statutory description for each department and agency. The General Services Administration has carried out this function as well as the gathering of information on transition practices. Gail Lovelace, who handled presidential transitions on behalf of the General Services Administration, discussed with representatives of the two candidates the work her agency team did to prepare to meet these transition tasks.[6] The 2000 law directed the General Services Administration to meet with the major-party presidential candidates to develop their communications and software. The White House, also involved in the question of software development, brought the candidates in to discuss the issue. That work as well as everything the outgoing George W. Bush administration did on the presidential appointments process is the subject of chapter 3.

While most of the provisions have served the presidents-elect well, not all of the provisions have been clear to those they are designed to help. The 2000 legislation, for example, calls for a million dollars for training programs for the new presidential appointees to executive branch positions, but the law did not flesh out for what the money was to be used. Clay Johnson talked about their use of the funds: "The language in there that deals with orientation and training of new Cabinet members or senior Cabinet members, it's very vague. When you say 'train' it doesn't say training to do what? . . . So we used it strictly for orientation, not training. . . . Our goal was not to teach people about ethics or teach people

TABLE 2.1
Government-Allocated Funding of Presidential Transitions

Election year / Transition laws governing funding and resources	Allocated government funds	Incoming president and vice president funds spent	Outgoing president and vice president funds spent	Private funds raised for incoming presidential transition / other provisions of law
1964: Presidential Transition Act of 1963 [PTA] Public Law [PL] 88-277 signed by President Johnson on March 7, 1964	$900,000; President Johnson decided the division between incoming and outgoing presidents. Legislative history of PTA said funds to be equally divided.	$900,000 total	$900,000 total	
1968: PTA PL 88-277 [President Johnson established money would be equally divided][1]	$900,000	$442,276 spent out of $450,000 allocated. President Johnson spent $370,276; Vice President Humphrey spent $72,000.[1]	$370,276 spent out of $375,000 allocated	President-elect Nixon raised $1 million
1974: PTA does not come into play as there was no president-elect.				Supplemental Appropriations Act of 1975 appropriated $100,000 to former president Nixon under PTA for 6 months ending February 9, 1975
1976: Amendments to PTA: PL 94-499 raised transition spending and provided support provisions for Nixon as former president and Ford on his entry. Signed by President Ford on October 14, 1976.	$3 million [1976 bill establishes how much incoming and outgoing presidents receive]	$1.7 million spent of $2.0 million allocated	$686,292 spent out of $1 million allocated. President Ford spent $635,000; Vice President Rockefeller spent $51,292.	No private funds spent though Carter had requested permission from the FEC to do so. Request denied based on FEC decision that campaign funds cannot be used for transition planning.[2]

Year/Law				
1980: PTA PL 94-499	$3.0 million	$1.75 million spent out of $2.0 million allocated. Vice President Bush spent $63,378 of those funds.	$861,526 spent out of $1 million allocated. President Carter spent 672,659; Vice President Mondale spent $188,867.	The Reagan Transition Foundation raised and spent 1.25 million. No public reporting of funds raised or spent. Federal Election Commission allowed creation of separate campaign and transition accounts.[2]
1988: Presidential Transitions Effectiveness Act of 1988 as amended PL 100-398 signed by President Reagan on August 17, 1988	$4.75 million	$2.3 million spent out of $3.5 million allocated ($1 million transferred to Washington, D.C., government for inaugural expenses)	$697,034 spent out of $1.25 million allocated ($250,000 authorized to Vice President Bush for his VP transition out if he was not elected president and none if he was elected. Unspent funds were transferred to FEC)	No private funds spent. PTEA requires reporting for private contributions, including in-kind contributions, and staff information; maximum contribution limit set at $5,000 for any person or organization.
1992: PTEA of 1988 PL 100-398	$5.0 million	$3,485,000 spent out of $3.5 million allocated (funds used jointly)	$1,152,131 spent out of $1.5 million allocated. President Bush spent $907,939; Vice President Quayle spent $244,192	About $5.3 million in private funds raised[3]

(continued)

TABLE 2.1
Continued

Election year / Transition laws governing funding and resources	Allocated government funds	Incoming president and vice president funds spent	Outgoing president and vice president funds spent	Private funds raised for incoming presidential transition / other provisions of law
2000: Presidential Transition Act of 2000 PL 106-293 signed by President Clinton on October 13, 2000	$7.1 million	$4,000,836 spent out of $4.27 million allocated	$1,788,623 spent out of $1.83 million allocated. President Clinton spent $1,505,688 Vice President Gore spent $282,935.	Nov. 27: The General Services Administration refused to release any funds until there was a candidate declared as the winner, which occurred December 13. Governor Bush team rented space in McLean, Virginia, and worked from there until he was declared the winner. About $5.0 million in private funds raised. Governor Bush establishes a $5,000 contribution limit with no funds from lobbyists: • $1 million provided for orientation of cabinet, senior executive branch personnel: $983,507 spent for briefings • NARA and GSA required to create directory of information on federal departments and agencies • GSA required to talk to candidates about communications and computer systems • OGE to give report on improvements for financial disclosure process[4]
2008: Presidential Transition Act of 2000 PL 106-293	$8.52 million with $1 million dedicated to briefings and other personnel activities designed for those chosen to serve in the new administration	$5.3 million allocated	$2.2 million allocated	Sought private funds of approximately $6.8 million for the transition.[5]

| 2012: Pre-Election Presidential Transition Act of 2010 [PEPTA] PL 111-283 signed by President Obama on October 15, 2010 | Beginning following the Republican convention when he was declared the Republican nominee, Governor Romney was provided office space, furniture, supplies, travel support and administrative support. Communications and information security. | $5.6 million allocated for a president-elect if there was a change in administrations. $2,347,000 allocated in 2013 budget for the former president and vice president if there was a change in administrations.[7] | Calls for non–government funded preelection planning following presidential conventions. Through his organization R2P, Inc., led by Michael Leavitt, Republican candidate Governor Romney spent $8.9 million in public funds August 30–November 9.[6] Acceptance of funds calls for restrictions on private funding with no more than $5,000 from any person or organization. (Memorandum of Understanding called for personnel and operations to be completed three days following election if candidate loses election.)
• President may create transition coordinating council; create an agency transition directors council composed of career service designees; guidance to executive agencies; development of information from past transition for eligible candidates.
• GSA makes sure computers secure; give report on modern presidential transition activities; computer software transition activities; GSA reported to Senate and House on administration preparations. |

Source: The information in this table is drawn from Stephanie Smith, "CRS Report for Congress, Presidential Transitions."

[1] Smith, "CRS Report for Congress, Presidential Transitions."

[2] Burke, *Presidential Transitions,* 46n, 132, 134–35.

[3] Broder, "Raising Millions More for Separate Transitions."

[4] Johnson, "2000–2001 Presidential Transition," 314.

[5] Cooper and Zeleny. "Obama's Transition Team Restricts Lobbyists' Role" (quoting John Podesta).

[6] GSA. Memorandum of Understanding Between The General Services Administration and R2P, Inc. On Behalf of Governor Mitt Romney," signed September 17, 2012 by Michael Leavitt representing R2P, Inc. and on September 19 by Darren Blue, representing the General Services Administration, http://timeswampland.files.wordpress.com/2012/12/memorandum-of-understanding1.pdf.

[7] General Service Administration Report (redacted), June 2012.

about how to deal with the Senate, or deal with Congress, or deal with the press, or learn about the ethics laws. We figured that's what your legal affairs, your ethics officer, are for."[7] Without clear guidance on what training meant or how the funds were to be spent, the incoming Bush team later used the funds to develop a website at results.gov. Their purpose of creating the website, Johnson said, was to "create a sense of community amongst the sub-Cabinets so they knew what the President's expectations were, and some idea of who else was on the team, and they had some perspective on what the working federal government was like." They had the idea of bringing "George Shultz and a couple of people to come in. It was a nice thing to have, but by that time we were a year into the administration and we figured that people had either gotten it by then or they hadn't gotten it. . . . I do think there's some community building or some team building kinds of activities that make sense."[8] There is little evidence that there was a strong training program in the 2008–2009 transition. It may be difficult both to select people and to provide a good training program for them early in any administration because those who would need to direct such a program are themselves new to governing.

For 2008, the incoming president was allotted $5.3 million out of the $8.52 million provided for in the congressional budget resolution of that year. The provisions of the 2000 law called for the General Services Administration to gather information on government programs and agencies as well as their statutory requirements. The major-party candidates were called on to receive information following their selection at the national party nominating conventions. As we shall see, with the White House facilitating early preparations for the next president, GSA and other agencies as well began working with the two presumptive major-party candidates prior to their formal nomination at the conventions in late August and early September.

The Pre-Election Presidential Transition Act of 2010

The 2008 transition was deemed such a success by those in Congress and outside of government that Congress chose to legitimize the notion of transition planning prior to the major-party nominating conventions. The report of the Senate Homeland Security and Government Affairs Committee explained the need for the legislation.[9] They based it on the increased national security need to begin early planning as well as the fear candidates have of appearing presumptuous if they are to plan early for a transition to power. "The post-September 11 security environment has made the old transition model obsolete," the report stated. "Numerous challenges now necessitate earlier planning and closer cooperation between incoming and outgoing administrations; the period between Election Day and the inauguration of a new president simply provides too short a timeframe for an incoming administration to do everything it needs to prepare for taking office. The selection process for incoming senior administration officials, many of whom require extensive security clearance background checks, for example, can be long and cumbersome."[10]

The act is designed to diminish the national security vulnerabilities inherent in a transition and also to create an environment within and outside of government where preelection planning is viewed as a legitimate and necessary activity:

> The Pre-Election Presidential Transition Act seeks to mitigate the risks inherent in the transfer of power and encourage early transition planning by providing resources and educating the campaigns, the press, and the public on the importance of early transition activities . . . candidates tread into such early transition planning carefully, fearing the portrayal of such planning as a presumptuous "measuring of the drapes," an accusation they worry could damage them politically. By codifying Congress's view that candidates should start transition planning before the election, this legislation seeks to remove the stigma related to it and make pre-election transition planning an accepted part of a successful transition process.[11]

The Senate sponsor of the legislation was Senator Ted Kaufman (D-Del.). As chief of staff to Senator Joseph Biden during the election period, Kaufman served also as co-chair of the senator's transition team. Before the inauguration, he was named by Governor Ruth Ann Minner to fill Biden's Senate seat now that he was moving into the vice presidency. While his time as a transition coordinator for Biden was short, he was there long enough to know that there were timing and resource issues that needed to be faced. Once Kaufman got to the Senate, he addressed those issues with what became the 2010 transition bill: "I just realized the sheer idiocy of the way we do it in terms of it's all sub rosa even though it was very well organized by Podesta. Still, sub rosa, and everybody is afraid they're going to get the story that says, 'Barack Obama or John McCain or someone else is measuring the drapes in the White House.'"[12] Kaufman wanted to up the planning calendar from after the election to following the national party nominating conventions. "Instead of setting up one GSA-type operation, you set up two," he said. "And if there is a third party that did well, three, so that right after [the election] . . . it's all above board, everybody knows what's going on . . . and not having to hide what they're doing, not trying to keep it secret."

The specifics of the two sections of the Pre-Election Presidential Transition Act of 2010 are as follows. First, after the national conventions, it makes available to the major-party candidates and "certain third party candidates certain GSA services and access to facilities previously provided only to the President-elect and Vice President-elect for the purposes of preparing to transition into office. The services offered would include office space and suitable furnishings; communications services; payment for printing and binding; funds for briefings, workshops, and other orientation activities for incoming staff; and a transition directory with information on the officers, organization, authorities, and responsibilities of each department and agency."[13] The funding the candidates will receive will not include "salaries, travel expenses, contractor or consultant fees, and postal reimbursements."[14] However, candidates may create a fund "to pay for transition services and facilities. An eligible candidate may transfer into this fund contributions received for his or her general election campaign and may also solicit and accept donations directly into it." Candidates creating such transition funds at this early stage are required to report their contributions according to the provisions in the Presidential Transition Act of 1963. The limit for such contributions is under $5,000, as provided in the original act. The candidates eligible for the early support provided for in the act can also ask the administrator of the General Services Administration for coordination on technology, "including the development of a systems architecture plan for computer and communications systems of an eligible candidate to transition to federal systems should the candidate be elected."[15]

The second substantive section calls for major-party candidates to have access to some of the preparations President Bush chose to undertake in 2008. Without using the names of the bodies, the section calls for a president to have an option to create a Transition Coordinating Council and to use the President's Management Council as a tool to coordinate government-wide transition efforts. The law obligates the president to take actions to "facilitate an efficient transfer of power, including the establishment of a transition coordinating council comprised of high-level executive branch officials; the formation of an agency transition directors council that includes career employees designated to lead transition efforts within their agencies; the development of guidance to departments and agencies regarding briefing materials for an incoming administration and the development of such materials; and the development of computer software, contingency plans, memoranda, training and exercises, and other items for improving the effectiveness and efficiency of a President transition."[16] All of the items listed here the Bush administration provided in 2008.

Additionally, the legislation calls for the incumbent administration to report to the Senate Homeland Security and Government Affairs Committee and the House Committee on Oversight and Government Reform. The reports are to "describe activities undertaken by the incumbent administration to prepare for a transfer of power." The reports are to be provided six months and three months before the general election. The first two-page letter from GSA and the five-page report were sent to Senator Joseph Lieberman in June, and then GSA sent a two-page follow-up letter on September 28, 2012.[17] That one had no separate report but did provide a summary of activities. Committee staff provided both reports to me following my requests for the information and a subsequent review by the committee to determine if they could be released. Two White House officials indicated in separate conversations with me that they had seen the reports before they were sent to the House and Senate committees, but the reports were the responsibility of GSA as the lead for the administration on transition preparations.[18]

The legislation achieved its goals in 2012. On June 3, 2012, *Politico* ran a story that Mike Leavitt, former governor of Utah, health and human services secretary, and friend of Mitt Romney, was heading a project then dubbed the "Ready Project" (later to be called by the Romney team the "Readiness Project") to plan a transition into office for the presidential candidate.[19] Instead of the usual criticism most news organizations and others in the political system directed toward the candidate, the Romney move was viewed as sensible planning. When reporters asked Andrea Saul, press spokesperson for Mitt Romney, about the planning project, she cited the 2010 legislation. "This is exactly what the bipartisan legislation signed into law by President Obama in 2010 encouraged candidates to do," Saul said.[20]

Additional Legislation on Presidential Transitions

While legislative developments over the last fifty years have a common theme of facilitating an effective presidential transition, there is non-transition-related legislation that has complicated the changeover from one administration to the next. Since the 1963 Presidential Transition Act became law in March 1964, six departments (housing and urban development, transportation, energy, education, veterans affairs, and homeland security) have been added to the federal government bureaucracy. That is a growth of 40 percent in the number of departments alone. The number of federal government employees has increased, while the percentage of employees who are covered by merit appointment has decreased. In 1964, there were 2,500,503 federal civilian employees and 86 percent were under merit civil service. By 2008, the number of civilian employees had grown to 2,758,468, but only 48.6 percent were under the merit system.[21] When President Kennedy was in office, there were 850 positions appointed by the president and confirmed by the Senate.[22] That number grew to 1,143 by the time President George W. Bush came into office and to 1,215 as President Obama became chief executive. Even the White House staff has doubled the number of commissioned positions at the assistant to the president and deputy and special assistant levels. The result is a complicated government structure that requires a great deal of preparation for those assuming office as president, staff, or officials serving in departments and agencies. There are more positions to fill in more agencies and, as we will see, more restrictions surrounding their service.

Legislation from the past fifty years that shapes government processes has an important secondary impact on transition planning and preparations. The 1978 Ethics in Government Act, for example, establishes conflict of interest rules and empowers the agency to work with nominees to executive branch positions in order to avoid conflicts. The result is a protracted process that makes the appointments process more arduous than it was in 1963, when the first transition legislation was enacted. The Presidential Records Act of 1978 is another piece of legislation with an impact on the transition process because it dictates how records are to be kept and maintained. The record-keeping demands require early preparation for office. In the 2000 and 2010 transition legislation, Congress recognized the weight of the demands of the varied bills and sought to provide early help to presidential candidates following their nomination.

Security Clearances for Presidential Appointees

Other than the Presidential Transition Act of 1963 and its amendments, the most important piece of legislation for the 2008 transition was the Intelligence Reform and Terrorism Prevention Act of 2004. While the act was designed to deal with intelligence issues in the wake of the attacks on the United States on September 11, 2001, the bill is important for dealing with the issues stemming from the large number of appointments an incoming president has to make in a short time.

Concerns about national security contributed to making the 2008–2009 transition so well thought out. The Congress and the president viewed a smooth transition a national security necessity, and both branches took action on issues related to getting a new administration up and running as soon as possible. The impetus for much of their preparatory work was the events of September 11, 2001. In two particular subject areas discussed here, security clearances for administration nominees and contingency crisis plans, the National Commission on Terrorist Attacks Upon the United States (also known as the 9/11 Commission) made recommendations that Congress and the president turned into policy. There are other transition security issues as well, such as those concerned with ensuring a smooth first transition for the Department of Homeland Security, but our discussion is focused on the examples of security clearances and contingency plans.

The government adopted the Commission's recommendations to improve the national security clearance process and to gather and provide information on security threats. In recent transitions, security clearances have consistently been an issue because they represent a major pinch point in getting presidential appointees from announcement to confirmation, which already is a slow process.

The 9/11 commissioners criticized the lack of a full complement of presidential appointees in national security positions at the time of the September terrorist attacks. One of their recommendations to Congress and the president was to see future national security teams in place sooner than was the case in 2001:

> Since a catastrophic attack could occur with little or no notice, we should minimize as much as possible the disruption of national security policymaking during the change of administrations by accelerating the process for national security appointments. We think the process could be improved significantly so transitions can work more effectively and allow new officials to assume their new responsibilities as quickly as possible.[23]

In the Intelligence Reform and Terrorism Prevention Act of 2004, Congress and the president responded to the commission's recommendations for a smooth transition by providing for changes in the security clearance process for nominees to executive branch positions. In the section on presidential transitions, the act calls for the president-elect to submit names for clearance as soon as possible after the election results are affirmed:

> The President-elect should submit to the Federal Bureau of Investigation or other appropriate agency and then, upon taking effect and designation, to the agency designated by the President under section 115(b) of the National Intelligence Reform Act of 2004, the names of candidates for high level national security positions through the level of undersecretary of cabinet departments as soon as possible after the date of the general elections held to determine the electors of President and Vice President under section 1 or 2 of title 3, United States Code.[24]

At the same time, the act provides that the two major-party candidates can begin setting up their organizations for the transition by submitting names for national security clearance prior to Election Day: "Each major party candidate for President may submit, before the date of the general election, requests for security clearances for prospective transition team members who will have a need for access to classified information to carry out their responsibilities as members of the President elect's transition team."[25] This section of the act is a potentially useful tool for the presidential candidates. They can submit names to the FBI for security clearances so that the eventual victor will be prepared for national security events on Election Day and following the election.

The Bush White House was particularly interested in having the transition teams for the presidential candidates make effective use of the new legal provision allowing the candidates to clear their names early. Joshua Bolten talked about his discussions with representatives of the candidates: "I thought the most important thing for them to focus on was the personnel side and that they really needed to get that going early; that we were there, ready to use the authorities from the legislation to get them clearances and that we wanted to put in place a mechanism that would permit them, without fear of compromise either on the general issue of being presumptive and sort of arrogantly starting to name people, or on just the specific side of names getting out."[26] The question for Bolten was how to create a way for the transition teams to submit names without leaks to reporters and others. "We were keen to put in place a mechanism and a commitment that they would face no risk from us, the White House, in pushing that process forward. Both sides were, I thought, naturally reticent about taking a political ding for naming people too early and I think the Obama people might have been nervous that if they gave us names that we would leak the names. But we were able to assure them that we were not going to make the situation any worse for them."

The Obama transition team began submitting names in the summer of 2008 after they met with Justice Department officials in a joint discussion with Republican presidential nominee Senator John McCain's representative to discuss transition resources. Chris Lu, executive director of the Obama transition, described the Bush administration's effort to implement the clear-early provision in the 2004 act. "They said first, 'Shoot for maybe submitting a hundred people's names for clearances, for interim clearances.' . . . We probably submitted about 150, 200 [names]. We submitted well more than a hundred."[27]

The Obama transition operation made early use of the law's new allowance section and submitted the names of people they wanted in their administration. There was no requirement in the law or by the agencies performing the clearances that those submitting the names stipulate the positions to be held along with the identity of the people the presidential candidate wanted to serve in his administration. In early December, David Shedd, deputy director of national intelligence for policy, reported to attendees at a meeting of President Bush's Transition Coordinating Council that President-elect Obama had received the President's Daily Brief from the Bush intelligence community, as had Rahm Emanuel, his designated White House chief of staff. "Not a single daily briefing has been missed," Shedd reported.[28] Emanuel could only have participated with an FBI security clearance.

Should Senator McCain have been elected in November 2008, the situation would have been different because of a decision he made. The McCain transition team would have had no one cleared to work on information requiring a national security clearance unless they had come to work for McCain with a current, pre-existing clearance. Will Ball, Senator McCain's representative who met with Bush administration officials and served on the transition board, said that they did not submit any names to the FBI for review during the transition period: "We met with the Justice Department, FBI, and IRS representatives about the process, but we did not turn names in to initiate the process. We had lists of names compiled internally for Senator McCain, but he did not wish at that point to turn names in to begin the clearance process on any individual."[29]

Russell Gerson, who handled the personnel piece of the transition planning for McCain, explained why the senator chose not to submit names early. First, McCain was concerned that the names would be publicly released: "We didn't trust that the names wouldn't be leaked, and McCain was just completely focused on no leaks. He didn't want anything to distract from the campaign. He didn't want anything getting out, and he felt that if we started giving names to the Justice Department to get cleared or pre-cleared, the names would get out. That was number one."[30]

At the same time, McCain believed that the clearance process would not be a substantial hurdle for those he wanted to appoint. "He didn't feel he was being irresponsible because he felt many of the people that would be in sensitive positions either already had clearance or could get clearance immediately," Gerson said. They envisioned keeping on some of the people who already were in executive branch positions because it would be a second successive Republican administration. "Even if it was for a short term, we knew that we could get people cleared immediately because many of the guys were already cleared related to the more sensitive positions in the State Department, in the Defense Department. We felt . . . we could get people cleared immediately because some of these people already had clearance."[31] Many people who worked in the Senate who he might bring into an administration had security clearances.

Executive Branch Agencies

There are four executive branch agencies that are particularly involved in transition preparations: the General Services Administration, the Office of Government Ethics, the Government Accountability Office, and the National Archives and

Records Administration. Other agencies, such as the Secret Service, work with GSA on transition preparations; the Federal Bureau of Investigation and the Office of Personnel Management combine with GSA on clearances and job lists. Within the Executive Office of the President, the White House Office and the Office of Management and Budget are keys to transition planning. These two institutions are discussed in chapter 5.

The General Services Administration is particularly important because it is called on to find and provide office space and then set up the transition office for presidents-elect. GSA is also called on to provide space for the outgoing president. In addition, in recent years, Congress has passed legislation that relates to specific transition areas, especially the presidential appointments process. Presidents-elect need to be prepared to meet the requirements for handling presidential records outlined in the act, and outgoing administrations must ready their papers by the time they leave. The legislation provides that beginning with the Ronald Reagan administration, presidential papers are public property, not the property of the president who then deeds them to the federal government.

The General Services Administration

This is the place where transition planning never sleeps. It is the physical step toward a transition and must be in place on a continual basis in order to make the decisions about physical space and the resources required for a possible transition. Gail Lovelace, the person at GSA who worked on transition operations for the agency since 1996, spoke of transition preparations. "We never stopped," she commented in June 2009.[32] "We are already today at work [on preparations for a possible 2012 transition]. Because we don't know what the outcome of the election is going to be, so we have to prepare for whatever the outcome will be in four years." The GSA piece of the puzzle involves resource development and coordination. A key part of a transition is getting the physical location in place for the transition. Doing so requires acquiring office space as well as furnishings for the space, working with communications technology that can insure safe phone communications, and meeting the specific needs of the potential president-elect.

The first step for the General Services Administration is identifying properties to house transition staff. Lovelace talked about the importance of finding appropriate transition opportunities. "The biggest issue . . . , and the thing we focus on early, is the space issue because we're in downtown D.C. There's not a lot of vacant space available." They want to "keep it within a government facility, not some kind of a leased facility. So what we do, and what we did this past time, is we try to find space where there is some part of the government—and this past time it just happened to be Department of Justice—where there is some department who is getting ready to outfit a space for their agency, and then we try to latch onto that and work with that agency to say 'Hey, can we utilize this space for this short period of time?'"[33] Then GSA will restore the space to the government agency that has claim to it. Lovelace said in June 2009, "We're already working on looking at what are those renovations that are in process now that we might be able to tap an agency or two on the shoulders and say, hey, can we interrupt your moving into this space temporarily. We're already working on that." By June 2011, GSA officials identified a space that met all of their needs and that the Secret Service found fit the security requirements for the transition headquarters and for the inaugural committee as well.

The reason GSA has to identify the space early is because of the work required to bring it up to the required standard. Dealing with the Secret Service is one of the first steps: "We work lockstep with the Secret Service on creating the space because you have to imagine you're creating this space assuming the president-elect will be in that space. And so the Secret Service jumps into that. So we have to work hand in glove to make sure that the space is outfitted and meets their requirements. So they literally were on site with us in that space," commented Gail Lovelace.[34] In preparing for the transition, the Executive Steering Committee—a body Lovelace originated—had representatives from each required GSA area to find resources and then implement them within the appropriate laws. But there is only so much that GSA can do until there are two presumptive party candidates. GSA does not wait until the convention to make contact with the candidates' operations, but they do not move until there is a clear Democratic and Republican frontrunner.

GSA is responsible for developing space for both operations and for making certain that the two are within the same building but at the same time separate from one another. The security needs are different for the transition and inaugural groups because the transition operation has a much higher security threshold to meet. In order to choose an appropriate space, GSA consults with the Secret Service and the Federal Protective Service. In 2011, Lovelace said that both were involved in the choice of space for 2012. "We've already walked the Secret Service and Federal Protective Service through the space," she said. "We actually showed them several spaces, and they liked this one, and we do as well, because there's ways that they can move around in the space without too many issues."[35]

In 2008 prior to the election, preparing space for the president-elect was more difficult than it sometimes is because of the increased post-9/11 security requirements. Another element was preparing for a second transition office in Chicago as Senator Obama indicated that he wanted to work there until he went to Washington close to the inauguration. Chris Lu discussed their plans with GSA: "GSA really dealt with us in a very even-handed way, and they made modifications of this space based on our requirements and our preferences. And we had basically said, look, if we win, we're going to want to have a transition base in Chicago as well. And they started mapping that entire thing out before Election Day. Whatever we asked them to do, they were very amenable to doing."[36] The Chicago office closed down when the Obamas came to Washington on January 13.[37]

Before GSA can get the offices up and running, the person in charge of the transition for the office must sign off on letters to the two candidates with a designation of who won the general election. After determining who the winner was, the GSA administrator turns to the issue of funding the transition operation. "We then signed another letter that gave our chief financial officer authority to expend funds," Lovelace said.[38]

GSA additionally creates a memorandum of understanding (MOU) covering what the agency will provide for the president-elect during the transition. The agency works it out beforehand with both campaigns so that it can move quickly once there is a president-elect. "We have our own memorandum that we create a document with both campaigns in terms of what . . . kinds of services that we provide to them," said Lovelace. They need a formal system because they need to "identify who can authorize the use of their money that we spend on their behalf. They would tell us who that is. We would tell them who our top people are . . . it's just some clarity around our roles and responsibilities." The MOU also "outlines the space and the IT . . . [and] all of the services we provide." In 2008, all of those services began the day after the election. The MOU is "a boilerplate kind of a document that's updated based on the circumstances. But it's longer than a page."[39]

In assessing what GSA did for the 2008 transition, Lovelace in 2010 told members of the Senate Committee on Homeland Security and Government Affairs that GSA preparations included the space they provided and the people they accommodated during the entry of President-elect Obama into office: "We started early in our preparation, had great teams in place, and were well-positioned to provide space, furniture, parking, office equipment, supplies, telecommunications, mail management, travel, financial management, vehicles, information technology, human resources management, contracting and other logistical support as necessary and appropriate."[40] The total number of people served and items provided was impressive: "Specifically, GSA leased and furnished approximately 120,000 square feet of office space in Washington, D.C., in close proximity to both the White House and the Capitol. GSA also provided 600 laptops, Blackberries, and desk phones to support transition staff in both Washington, D.C., and Chicago. GSA's secure IT infrastructure supported 1,300 users, many working remotely throughout the world. To prepare for this high volume of support, GSA proactively met with representatives from the Obama and McCain campaigns prior to the election. In doing so, we ensured the efficiency of the transition while demonstrating the non-partisan spirit of our work."[41]

The GSA group began providing items to members of the Obama team the morning following the election. Lovelace said, "Every day during the transition period, our employees met new members of the Obama-Biden team as they walked in the door, showed them to their offices, explained how to use their computers and blackberries and gave them an overview of the facility, allowing them to get to work right away. Our motto was 'from the street to your seat in 15 minutes.'"[42]

An important part of the work that Lovelace did during 2008 was working with agencies through the President's Management Council, which she and Clay Johnson, deputy for management at OMB, coordinated. "All of the big agencies. All of the cabinet level agencies. And I had made a promise at an earlier meeting that spring about including the Small Agency Council. So I included as many of them as I could get in the room, too. . . . Social Security, EPA, GSA, OPM, all of them and then a whole series of small agencies," she said. The agencies were not equally concerned with getting ready for the first day of a new administration, as small agencies do not immediately get the attention of the president-elect and his team. "Some small agencies weren't quite as concerned about it because of the way in which their political appointees come in. And some don't leave when there's a change of administration, so they were all in a lot of different positions."[43] Even if the agencies were not in the meetings, they were included in the distribution of information.

And there are some agencies where she spent a lot of time. The Office of Personnel Management was important: "I did a lot of work through the Chief Human Capital Offices Council, too, and that was another venue for me to be able to talk to people about transition. Linda Springer was the director [of the Office of Personnel Management] at the time, and she allowed me at every meeting to talk about transition and to have a dialogue, which was really helpful."[44] Much of what she did with the small agencies was to go to groups and attend agency meetings. "I just tried to get out to as many places as we could just talking to people. We talked to the CIO [Chief Information Officers] Council. We went to a lot of the good government groups. We were all over the place just helping people think about it. And we don't have all the magical answers here. . . . I'll tell you, I learned as much from people we talked to as hopefully we were able to share with them as we went around talking."[45]

Other Executive Branch Agencies

The Office of Government Ethics, the Government Accountability Office, and the National Archives and Records Administration all have primary roles in transition preparations.

The Office of Government Ethics (OGE) is responsible for identifying and resolving conflicts of interest of appointees to federal government positions. Under the Ethics in Government Act of 1978, which created OGE, the director of the office works with the White House counsel and identifies the person who will handle conflict issues. Robert I. Cusick, director of OGE, described his duties: "As the Director of OGE, it is my responsibility under the law to certify that a nominee's financial interests do not conflict with his or her prospective Government duties or to certify that, upon taking certain steps after confirmation (for example, the sale of conflicting assets), the individual will have no financial conflicts of interests."[46] There are a substantial number of people whose financial arrangements are considered by the Office of Government Ethics. In 2001, for example, Cusick said that by the end of August, OGE "completed review and conflicts of interest analysis for just over 400 potential appointees."[47]

A great deal of what OGE does involves training the ethics officers who will deal with disclosure issues. It is not a small group. OGE has a pool of reviewers that increases in the transition period so that there is adequate personnel to review the forms that come in from presidential appointees who require Senate confirmation (or PAS nominees, as they are called) before the inauguration and in the early months when people come into office. In preparation for the transition, OGE held a fall training session in Washington. Cusick explained that the event included "over 250 experienced ethics officials from more than 70 departments and agencies on financial disclosure issues related to PAS nominees, in order to prepare them for the increased volume and complexity of financial disclosure reports that are expected during the transition."[48]

Congress has sought a more streamlined process for financial disclosure. In the 2000 transition legislation, OGE was called on to report on the possibilities of creating online forms. Since that time, however, financial conditions and concerns have not made the disclosure process any easier for nominees. In 2008, for example, OGE developed written guidelines for those entering and leaving office on the following subjects: "financial instruments, hedge funds, seeking employment, regulations governing book deals, ethics agreements, and post-employment restrictions."[49]

The National Archives and Records Administration worked together with the General Services Administration to carry out the requirement in the 2000 presidential transition legislation that called on the two agencies to create a directory of information on federal departments and agencies. The 2000 act states: "The transition directory shall be a compilation of Federal publications and materials with supplementary materials developed by the Administrator that provides information on the officers, organization, and statutory and administrative authorities, functions, duties, responsibilities, and mission of each department and agency."[50] NARA and the archivist of the United States are responsible under the Presidential Records Act of 1978 for separating records. The 2000 amendments to the Presidential Transition Act call for training that "may include training or orientation in records management . . . on the separation of Presidential records and personal records."[51]

The Government Accountability Office (GAO) has a varied role in presidential transitions even though it is an agency associated with Congress. As an arm of Congress, the acting comptroller general Gene L. Dodaro testified before the House Subcommittee on Government Management, Organization, and Procurement of the Committee on Oversight and Government Reform that the GAO would do the following transition work: "We will be monitoring the transition and reaching out to the new administration, Congress, and outside experts to identify lessons learned and any needed improvements in the Act's provisions for future transitions."[52] In addition to its general role of aiding a new administration as it comes into office, GAO has some specific duties relating to the transition out of power.

Congress tasked the GAO with keeping an eye out for the conversion of noncareer positions in the federal government service into career jobs. That is a situation that is known to happen, particularly at the end of an administration, when people with a political appointment want to stay on the job when a new administration comes in. A new administration wants to appoint its own people and not have jobs closed off with appointees from an earlier time lingering on in positions that were converted by the last administration from political to career service jobs. To ward against the "burrowing in" phenomenon, the GAO is responsible for making sure that the individual conversions have met all of the process requirements.

The Office of Personnel Management (OPM) reviews conversions from noncareer, noncompetitive posts—Schedule C and Noncareer Senior Executive Service (SES)—into career ones.[53] GAO regularly reports to Congress on these conversions and did so in 2008 during the leadup to the presidential election. Dodaro reported in a House subcommittee hearing on the latest review of agency conversions taking place between 2001 and 2006. The GAO findings were as follows: "23 of 41 agencies reviewed reported converting 144 individuals from noncareer to career positions, 130 individuals at the GS-12 level or higher." There were no conversions reported by the remaining agencies. "We found that agencies used appropriate authorities and followed procedures in making the majority (93) of the 130 conversions reported at the GS-12 level or higher. It appeared that agencies did not follow proper procedures for 18 conversions, including by creating career positions specifically for particular individuals, posting SES vacancy announcements for less than the minimum time requirement, and failing to apply veteran's preference; we referred those 18 conversions to the Office of Personnel Management and recommended that the Director determine whether additional actions were needed. For the other 19, agencies did not provide enough information for us to make an assessment."[54] As we will see in chapter 3, the Obama transition team was sensitive to conversions and wary about their taking place.

An Institutional Memory

The institutional memory available to presidential candidates and their staffs has grown broader and deeper. There are now four main sources of information for them to tap in shaping how they will handle their transitions to govern should they win the presidential election. First, there is a great deal of information available through published government sources and online. In the 2000–2001 transition, departments and agencies did not use websites as informational tools in the way they did eight years later. In the 2008–2009 transition, staff for the two presidential candidates did not need to wait for the White House to provide them with significant information about what government agencies are doing and get some assessments of their performance. There is valuable public information they can access online. In addition, there is a growing body of scholarly literature on presidential transitions that transition teams can tap for what works and what does not.[55] New White House staff and administration officials repeatedly cite transition postmortems as helpful to their understandings of their jobs, offices, and preparations to govern.

The second source of institutional memory is the written record that former transition teams and current White Houses officials pass on to aides to the president-elect. Those include the files from previous transitions, the writings of the personnel involved in transitions, and the information gathered by a sitting administration describing its operations.

The third source of memory is the first-person record a president-elect and his staff can draw on. Individuals form one of the most important troves of information because those taking part in earlier transitions and, in many cases, those who held key offices remember a great deal about how they came into office and what happened at the end of their administration.

Outside groups form a fourth type of institutional memory. There are several public service organizations and others interested in management that have gathered information across administrations and provided information at a point when it will make a difference to a new team as they seek transition information. The Partnership for Public Service is a good example of a group that has assembled people familiar with presidential transitions and brought them together with representatives of presidential candidates who are focusing on transition issues.

Available Public Information

As part of their preparation for office, transition staff in 2008 and 2009 had available in public sources a great deal of information about the operation of the agencies, including budget and performance information. "We've made it a requirement that every agency's home page have a section, and I think everybody but Defense and Homeland Security, which are two big departments, have done this, where there's a link on the home page that says something to the effect of 'Department of Agriculture performance and budget. . . . Here's how all the programs work. Here's where all the IG [inspector general] reports are and so forth,'" said Clay Johnson, deputy director for management of the Office of Management and Budget.[56]

Additionally, transition team members can now visit watchdog websites that track the performance of government agencies as well as congressional websites that include hearings, legislation, and reports. The Congressional Research Service and the Government Accountability Office both publish individual assessments of government performance and information about presidential transitions that are important sources of information as candidates task staff to gather information about the presidential transition ahead of them. Academic and other online sites provide easy online access to presidential speeches, statements and announcements, official actions, such as those found on the website for the American Presidency Project. There are other groups that monitor government actions and agencies, such as OMB Watch.

Academics have written books and articles about presidential transitions that were used by transition teams in 2000 and 2008. Beginning with Laurin Henry's 1960 *Presidential Transitions*, political scientists and historians have chronicled the organization and operation of transitions. The body of transition books stretches over several decades but in recent years has grown with the increasingly sophisticated planning operations that have developed to handle the multiple problems a president now faces when he comes into office. There are around a dozen books that are particularly useful for transition teams searching for information on what worked and what did not work during earlier transitions. The key works are Carl Brauer, *Presidential Transitions*; John Burke, *Becoming President: The Bush Transition 2000–2003*; John Burke, *Presidential Transitions: From Politics to Practice*; Kurt Campbell and James Steinberg, *Difficult Transitions*; Alvin Felzenberg, *The Keys to a Successful Presidency*; Laurin Henry, *Presidential Transitions*; Charles O. Jones, *Passages to the Presidency*; Charles O. Jones, ed., *Preparing to Be President: The Memos of Richard E. Neustadt*; Martha Kumar and Terry Sullivan, *White House World*; and Jim Pfiffner, *Strategic Presidency*. The White House Transition Project provided these books and additional scholarly works on White House operations to the representatives of both major candidates in 2008 and to Governor Bush in 2000.

Information about past transitions persuaded the Obama team to put a White House staff together before the cabinet. Starting around May 2008, Chris Lu, Senator Obama's legislative director in his Senate office and early point man for the transition, gathered information as his first step in preparing for a transition into the presidency. "One of the things I did early on was basically read everything I could possibly find about transitions," he said.[57] His reading of the transition literature led him to the conclusion that the sequencing of personnel decisions is very important. "The one thing you learn is that the Clinton folks probably made a mistake in choosing their cabinet first and then the White House staff. If you go back to those articles, some of their White House staff didn't get chosen until right before Inauguration Day. . . . We were very conscious of that. . . . we had our senior White House staff pretty much filled out by Christmas."[58]

Former Secretary of the Navy William Ball is the person who was responsible for gathering information for Senator McCain's transition operation. He explained his approach: "I tried to spend some time studying each transition. . . . By the time we got started, it was a given that you had to start these things early . . . that the organizational effort had to start earlier than before, because of not only the national security situation, but as we learned in October, the economic situation."[59] As a result of what they learned from past transitions, the McCain operation worked on setting up planning the transition and assembling information on administration positions and what types of people each one called for. Then they gathered names that served as a base for recruiting people for administration posts if they were to win.

Predecessors as an Information Source

Predecessors are an important source of information, and most incoming and outgoing officials spend at least some time talking with one another. The Bush national security team met with principals as the inauguration loomed. Steve Hadley recounted: "We agreed we would try to have the new team have some face to face conversations to talk about the key issues that were transitioning, and that came about. Condi had a dinner at the State Department ten days, maybe two weeks before the inauguration, where Jim Jones [Obama's choice for NSC advisor] and Hillary Clinton [Obama's nominee for secretary of state], and Tom Donilon [Obama's incoming Deputy Director of the NSC] were on one side, and Condi, and I, and she had someone from State on the other. . . . And we went over in detail North Korea, and Middle East peace."[60] Hadley thought the dinner session with the national security team was helpful to the incoming administration team members. "And it was very useful because it actually was the night before, or two nights before Senator Clinton [Obama's nominee to be secretary of state] . . . had her confirmation hearing, and . . . she really clearly drew on that with respect to North Korea, maybe the Middle East as well. . . . It gave them, again, a starting point on where we were."[61]

Some Bush White House officials believed that their successors needed only a limited amount of information from them because these officials thought the work the Obama staff had been doing on the campaign and transition was similar to what they would be doing when the senator came into office. President Bush's press secretary, Dana Perino, talked to her successor, Robert Gibbs, about press operations before January 20. "He didn't really need a lot of advice from me. I think that they've seen how the media has operated. . . . The same outlets covering us have been covering them in the campaign."[62] Perino gave Gibbs a sense of the resonance of the presidential spokesperson's words. "I did tell him about how the worldwide audience is listening. . . . And sometimes it's hard to remember that your audience is bigger than the forty-odd people [who] sit in the briefing room. You're taking their questions, but what you say matters to the whole world."

Those who have run for the presidency and their staff form a nucleus of people who understand the transition process and have materials they prepared for their own transitions. Those materials are now part of an institutional memory that passes from presidential candidate to candidate as the two parties prepare for the period following the election. The institutional memory has three parts to it. First is the set of materials—transition budgets, diagrams of how to set up a transition office, organizational breakdowns of recent White Houses, hundred-day plans—that passes from one group within the party to another. Part of that institutional memory is now formed by information institutions, including government sources, now make available on their websites.

The Democrats have gradually built an institutional memory that proved helpful to the Obama transition. Chris Lu, executive director of the Obama transition, explained the importance of the work done by earlier candidates and their transition personnel. Jim Johnson, who handled the projected transition for Senator John Kerry, provided Chris Lu with the information the Kerry people gathered in 2004. One of the areas where Johnson's documents were useful was the information they had on transition finances. Alexis Herman, who served as a co-chair of the John Kerry transition effort in 2004 and worked on transition planning for Albert Gore in 2000, included a breakdown of how they would spend the government transition funds and how much money they needed to raise to augment the public money. "You get about $5 million in federal funding and we ended up raising probably another 4 or 5 million [dollars] on top of that. . . . You have no idea how many people you need to hire, how expensive it is. . . . But they [the Kerry transition team] had done such a detailed budget in 2004 down to . . . you need this many people to staff the call center, this many people to do document retention. . . . We basically took their budget, updated the numbers, tweaked it a little bit, and that was our draft budget. . . . On things like that, there's no sense in reinventing the wheel."[63]

Chris Lu found the written transition record he inherited from Jim Johnson and the Kerry team to be helpful to the Obama transition operations as well as governing. Lu also found discussions with his predecessors about their office practices to be important for how he subsequently ran his White House Cabinet Affairs Office. Having canvassed several people who once held his position as White House cabinet secretary, Lu and the Obama team "took from the best practices of the Clinton administration and blended some of the best practices of the Bush administration. . . . The Bush administration gave us a lot of . . . helpful suggestions that we incorporated."[64] From the Clinton administration, they learned the importance of the status of the White House cabinet secretary. In the Clinton years, the position was classified as an assistant to the president, the highest White House rank, but it was downgraded in the Bush years.

Harrison Wellford was one of the people associated with the Obama transition effort who had worked on several Democratic presidential transitions. He worked on the Carter transitions in and out of the White House and prepared transition information for presidential candidates Bill Clinton and John Kerry. Lu said of Wellford: "Harrison is one of these people with such incredible institutional memory about transition, so he was an invaluable asset." Wellford was involved in early discussions with the General Services Administration. "Harrison did a lot of outside consulting with John Podesta on a variety of issues," said Lu.[65]

Will Ball gathered information for the McCain transition about past transitions from published sources and from speaking with people knowledgeable about transition patterns. An institutional memory was important for Senator McCain's operation, but it did not focus solely on the written record or the information developed by the Bush White House.

The McCain team relied heavily on the experiences of one primary person with decades of experience: William Timmons. Timmons was a White House veteran who had worked in the Nixon and Ford administrations in congressional relations and worked on the transitions of those two chief executives and Presidents Ronald Reagan, George H. W. Bush, and George W. Bush. Timmons was one of six people who made up "the board" of the McCain transition operation. Fellow board member Will Ball recalled: "Bill Timmons had been through all these transitions, and he brought a very fine-tooth, detailed comb, sort of detailed focus on budget—transition budgets, and transition people, and transition procedures."[66] Ball heard anecdotes about Timmons's long track record with Republican administrations: "At Senator Warner's retirement party, John Warner said, 'You know, in 1968, I was involved in the Nixon transition, and my boss was Bill Timmons,'" related Ball.[67] As a person who worked in some way in all of the Republican transitions in the modern period, Timmons knows transition logistics and budgets. Russ Gerson, who handled the appointments portion of the John McCain transition team, talked about the role Timmons had in their overall planning group. "He was the guy who was figuring out telephones, parking, and all the logistical administrative stuff. He wasn't involved in any of the policy issues."[68] He handled the budget planning based on previous patterns, "who was going to go in what office and how much we were going to spend here and how much we were going to spend on private aircraft during the transition."

Outside Groups as Information Sources

Public service groups also have a supporting role to play in a transition. GAO was tasked in the 2000 presidential transition legislation with gathering information on past transitions and on groups doing transition work. Gail Lovelace headed the effort to provide information to the two transitions in 2008.

Lovelace said that in her transition work with outside groups, there are those "we call the 'good government groups,' the Partnership for Public Service, the National Academy of Public Administration. . . . We meet with them, and they actually sometimes are very helpful in facilitating meetings for us or pulling groups of people together where we could talk to different groups of people about transition and what it means."[69] Lovelace spoke to the groups to learn from them and also to provide them with information. "They're like an extension of the government. They represent a group of people that care about public service. They care about the administration. They care about what's going on in government, and they're trying to do their part in helping government be better. . . . They're just a natural part of transition."

The Partnership for Public Service gives us a good view of the role that outside groups can play as facilitators for candidate transition operations. With a grant from the Rockefeller Brothers Fund, the Partnership held a conference in mid-spring of 2008. The group brought together government officials and experts and others with transition experience, including members of the teams working on issues for Senators McCain and Obama. The purpose of the two-day gathering, held at the Rockefeller family estate on May 5–6, 2008, at Pocantico Hills, New York, was to discuss the issues the presidential candidates would need to understand in making their transition preparations. All sides understood that a major transition was coming and that the staffs working for President Bush, Senator McCain, and Senator Obama needed guidance on what they needed to know. That was the goal of the conference: to familiarize people with the issues, actions, deadlines, and past practices of presidential transitions.

As a nonpartisan public service group specializing in management, the Partnership leadership aimed at making sure people working on transition issues met with people in the government tasked with handling transition issues. Getting people together over two days allowed the transition newcomers to meet people they would later call on for information. The sessions were important as well because they acquainted people with the variety of issues they would deal with, including presidential appointments, security clearances, budget decisions, and transition timing. Two days of meals and full group and breakout sessions gave participants a chance to ask questions and to mingle with the people with whom they would be dealing in a few short months. The interactions were important for the government officials as well since they would need to deal with one another. The timing of the conference was important too. Interestingly, the conference was held when it was clear that Senator McCain would be the Republican nominee and that Barack Obama would probably win the Democratic nomination, but the race was not yet settled. Both major-party conventions were months off. But the decision was made that those beginning to work on transition issues already needed to know what faced them.

The group of twenty people assembled for those two days were from the George W. Bush and Bill Clinton administrations, agencies responsible for transition planning, and private sector and management firms; it also included outside experts, those who were involved in planning for coming transition, and people who later came into the Obama administration. It included the following people: William Ball, former secretary of the Navy and a member of the senior transition team for Senator John McCain; Tom Bernstein, president of Chelsea Piers Management; Sheila Burke of the John F. Kennedy School of Government at Harvard University; Andrew Card, former chief of staff to President George W. Bush; Ed DeSeve, professor at the University of Maryland and later senior advisor to President Obama for recovery and reinvestment; Thomas Dohrmann, partner at McKinsey and Company; Jenna Dorn, president of the National Academy of Public Administration; Maria Echaveste, deputy chief of staff to President Bill Clinton; Scott Gould, vice president for public sector strategy and change at IBM Global Business Consulting Services and later deputy secretary of veterans affairs in the Obama administration; Clay Johnson, deputy director for management for the Office of Management and Budget and head of the President's Management Council; Gail Lovelace, chief human capital officer, General Services Administration; Chris Mihm, managing director for strategic issues for the Government Accountability Office; Sean O'Keefe, former NASA administrator and former deputy director of the Office of Management and Budget; Norman Ornstein, resident scholar at the American Enterprise Institute and co-director of the continuity in government project; David Osborne, former senior advisor to Vice President Al Gore for the National Performance Review; Ron Sanders, chief human capital officer, Office of the Director of National Intelligence; Robert Shea, associate director for administration and government performance, Office of Management and Budget; Linda Springer, director, Office of Personnel Management; Christine Varney, former cabinet secretary for President Clinton, commissioner on the Federal Trade Commission and in the Obama administration, assistant attorney general for the antitrust division, Department of Justice; David Walker, former comptroller general of the United States for the Government Accountability Office. This assemblage of people allowed those who later would come into the administration—Christine Varney, Scott Gould, Ed DeSeve—to talk to people in the sitting administration with important roles in planning the transition, in particular Clay Johnson and Robert Shea at the Office of Management and Budget,

Gail Lovelace at GSA, Linda Springer at the Office of Personnel Management, Chris Mihm at the Government Accountability Office; and myself.

Establishing relationships between those who needed transition information and those who had it was a key point of the conference. Max Stier, president and CEO of the Partnership for Public Service, explained what he hoped the conference would produce. "There were several things that happened from the conference," he said. "There were several relationships that we had talked about so people knew who to go to for additional information. . . . There was a knowledge transfer to people who needed to know certain things, but there's a limited period of time. . . . You create a relationship, [and then] they can keep going back to the well again and again and again, and that is much more important than anything else." Stier was correct: The people who met over meals and the sessions did later come back to talk with one another. "I think what you can do is set a framework or at least create an environment in which people can see the opportunity for learning and the need for it."[70]

Four years later, on May 17–18, with the experience of this 2008 conference firmly in mind, Stier brought together people to talk about a 2012 transition. Whether it would be a second term for President Obama or a first one for Governor Romney, there would be management changes in the coming administration. "While the focus will differ depending on the outcome of the election, in either case a well-executed transition is essential for a fast start in 2013," Stier wrote the participants.[71] "At this event, our primary goal is to answer these questions: (1) How should the current administration and challenger begin to prepare for the transition? (2) How can we best prepare political appointees for federal government leadership?" Stier organized his conference around participants who would be involved in a Romney transition or an Obama second term, people in management positions in the Obama administration, officials who worked on the transition out of power of the George W. Bush administration, former members of Congress with experience in transition issues, and people working on management issues in posts outside of government.[72]

Government and Outside Groups

Planning for a presidential transition today is very different than the process was twenty years ago. Congress has enacted legislation supporting the efforts taken by most presidential candidates to start their planning well before the major-party nominating conventions. Congress acknowledged in its legislation the planning needs candidates have if they are to have a successful transition. Gradually, the basic transition legislation has been broadened to cover the workings of the private fundraising efforts and to move the clock for government-covered transition support to the days following the major-party conventions rather than the traditional postelection timing called for in legislation from 1963 to 2010.

The transition work of executive branch agencies has increased because there are now more agencies with congressional mandates than was the case fifty years ago. Now the Office of Government Ethics and the National Archives and Records Administration have specific transition assignments that did not exist before the late 1970s, such as managing a financial disclosure process as well as a presidential records one. These changes have increased the hurdles presidential candidates face in setting up their transition operations and in persuading people to come into their administrations.

While candidate transition organizations have an increasingly complicated set of issues to deal with as they prepare for office, at the same time there is more information for them to rely on as they get ready. In the post-September 11 world, incumbent administrations cannot afford to let their successors come into power without having information and a relatively smooth road to power. With the demands on government to make available information about its personnel, programs, and goals, it is now easier than it was before the advent of a robust internet to gather the facts related to departments, agencies, and their initiatives. Records are routinely passed on from one group of party people to the current ones planning for their possible entry into the White House. Perhaps the most important transfer of information takes place when those who have served in previous transitions talk with those who are only beginning the task.

CHAPTER THREE

The Transition Out of Office

All outgoing presidents say they want to have a good transition; indeed, most assert that they want to have the best transition out of office there has ever been. Yet presidential transitions out of office actually show wide divergence in terms of effectiveness and style. There is no law saying what a president must leave behind for an incoming administration, nor what he must do for the incoming team. The Presidential Transition Act of 1963 and its amendments state what selected agencies must do, but there is no requirement as to what a sitting president is called on to do. The Senate Committee on Homeland Security and Government Affairs stated in its report on the Pre-Election Presidential Transition Act of 2010 that the sitting administration has few required tasks in preparing for its successor: "Currently, incumbent administrations have little formal responsibility to undertake transition activities. The outgoing administration is required to prepare appropriate files and documents for archiving by the National Archives and Records Administration, and outgoing officials are required to brief their incoming counterparts on important national security matters, including ongoing or planned covert and military operations. Apart from these relatively few mandatory transition activities, further transition efforts on the part of the incumbent administration are discretionary."[1]

What this means is that each president leaving office makes up plans anew for how to exit the presidency. A basic reality of presidential transitions is that transition planning of the outgoing administration reflects the imprint the president himself chooses to adopt as he prepares to leave office.

How involved a president is in planning for his successor traditionally depends on two considerations. The transition depends on whether the president was running for reelection and on whether the transition is an inter-party or intraparty one. Those presidents who lose after running for reelection have little time to prepare for their exit. During the election campaign period, they do not have an incentive to prepare for an incoming team and generally settle on just providing intelligence information. Often they believe they are going to win and thus see no payoff in preparing for an opponent to take over the presidency. It is only at the point when a president loses that he focuses on the transition. The seventy-five days until the next inauguration gives those in the White House little time to make preparations for a new team. Second, when the transition is between presidents of the same party, the transition is a more fluid one, with many people staying in their politically appointed jobs. Presidents who complete two terms often have the time and inclination to prepare for the transition out of office. This was the case with President George W. Bush in 2008.

In a November 6 speech on the South Lawn with his cabinet members and White House staff present, President Bush publicly advised his White House staff to help prepare the new team. He spoke of his commitment to the transition as a priority and gave his reasons for doing so: "This peaceful transfer of power is one of the hallmarks of a true democracy, and ensuring that this transition is as smooth as possible is a priority for the rest of my Presidency."[2] In his call to prepare for transition, he explained his reason for making the transition a high priority, especially the vulnerability of the country to attacks by extremists. "We face economic challenges that will not pause to let a new President settle in. This will also be America's first wartime Presidential transition in four decades. We're in a struggle against violent extremists determined to attack us, and they would like nothing more than to exploit this period of change to harm the American people. So over the next 75 days, all of us must ensure that the next President and his team can hit the ground running."

President Bush then explained in broad terms what his administration had done over the preceding year to prepare for the transition. "For more than a year now, departments and agencies throughout the Federal Government have been preparing for a smooth transition." Many government departments and agencies prepared for the transition. "We've provided intelligence briefings to the President-elect, and the Department of Justice has approved security clearances for members of his transition team. In the coming weeks, we will ask administration officials to brief the Obama team on ongoing policy issues, ranging from the financial markets to the war in Iraq. . . . Offices within the White House are at work preparing extensive transition materials. We're preparing career employees throughout the administration to take on added responsibilities to help prevent any disruption to the essential functions of the Federal Government."[3] All of these preparations began early, in some cases starting in the winter of 2008.

President Bush closed his remarks to staff by talking about the unprecedented nature of what they were doing. "Taken together, these measures represent an unprecedented effort to ensure that the executive branch is prepared to fulfill its responsibilities at all times," Bush said. By the time the election was over on November 4, the preparations he listed were either completed or close to completion. What he realized was that presidents all say the right things when they meet the incoming president, but the reality is by the time the two of them meet, the shape of their transition out of office has already been set. What happens before the two meet is what the transition is all about. He prepared early for a solid handoff of power between the outgoing and incoming teams. His preparations were unique in their nonpartisan flavor and their early involvement of transition representatives for Senators John McCain and Barack Obama. Having candidate representatives come together with White House officials was a long time coming. Before President Bush involved the Obama and McCain camps, only President Truman had called for the early preelection participation of both candidates and then he envisioned separate meetings.

Early Transition Planning by President Bush and His Administration

There were several notable aspects to the rhythms of the transition. First, President Bush got the administration planning under way through his timely decision in late 2007. Second, Chief of Staff Joshua Bolten directed the planning work of White House staff and organized the working sessions with the representatives of Senators John McCain and Barack Obama. Third, Deputy Director for Management of the Office of Management and Budget Clay Johnson organized the information-gathering process in the departments and agencies. Fourth, Bush's team responded well to unanticipated events and the necessity of facilitating whatever responses are appropriate, including working with the president-elect and his team. The financial crisis loomed large for President Bush and for the two senators. There were many exchanges with the administration, especially late in the campaign and in the postelection period.

Once President Bush assigned Bolten to organize and handle transition planning, there were several points within the administration that served as centers for transition planning. President Bush was the ultimate authority. As we will see in chapter 6, he especially focused his attention on national security preparations and occasionally got into specific issues related to the transition. In addition to extensive planning in the area of national security, the early part of the planning operations in the spring of 2008 were initiatives involving administrative operations and domestic policy.

While most incumbent presidents turn to transition preparations in the final months of their administrations, President Bush began over a year ahead of time. That early start gave the administration the opportunity to communicate with representatives of the presidential campaigns after the primary season ended, well before the election. Beginning in the spring of 2008, the Bush team directed preparations of executive branch agencies and streamlined the process of issuing "midnight" regulations. The deputy director of the Office of Management and Budget and the chair of the President's Management Council led twenty-six major departments and agencies to develop criteria for the information-gathering phase of the handover of executive branch information for the new team of the winning candidate.

Within the White House, Chief of Staff Joshua Bolten led the effort to control the administration's late-term administrative rules and regulations. White House personnel staff catalogued and described key administration positions. After the conclusion of the primaries, the General Services Administration began planning with representatives of the two presidential candidates for the creation of transition office space. The Office of Government Ethics spoke informally with candidate representatives as well. The campaign transition representatives also worked with White House officials on developing the memorandum of understanding, the document signed by representatives of the outgoing and incoming administrations that sets transition ground rules.

One of the elements crucial to the success of the 2008–2009 transition was the unprecedented effort by President Bush and his administration to take steps to bring about a smooth transition to power for the eventual winner of the presidential election. John Podesta commented on the cooperation the Obama transition operation received from Chief of Staff Joshua Bolten and the administration. "I think we had a very good professional interaction. I think that was empowered by the President [Bush]. . . . I think it would have been Josh's [inclination] anyway, but I think Bush was mindful of what was going on and . . . said . . . 'Make this thing work right.' It gave us the opportunity to create the dialogue that went back and forth."[4] The early discussions among transition representatives on both teams went beyond anything the White House, departments and agencies, had ever done collectively in earlier transitions.

In past transitions, outgoing two-term presidents thought about their obligations in the final months of their administrations. President Bush departed from his predecessors with his early concern and his instructions to his chief of staff to prepare for a smooth transition. Joshua Bolten discussed the mandate he received about the transition from President Bush in 2007: "I don't recall him talking about the transition until about a year before the end of the administration. And he and I—and I don't have a specific date—had a conversation probably in late 2007 in which he said that he wanted to make sure that his transition was the best, that he recognized that regardless of who won the election, we were still going to be in a situation where the country was under threat. And he basically said, 'Go all-out to make sure that the transition is as effective as it possibly can be, especially in the national security area.'"[5] When asked how President Bush planned on bringing about the goal of the best transition, Bolten replied: "It was up to me. It was not a detailed conversation. It was explicit but not a detailed conversation, which is the way he operated; I set the direction, I set the principles." President Bush told him, "You go work on it, and when you get issues that require my attention, bring them back."[6] With that in mind, Bolten set about fashioning the transition and its timetable for the gathering and dissemination of information as well as developing organizational assignments.

With Bolten responsible for the planning, individuals and agencies took their cues from him. Bolten began early to set the stage for a solid handover on January 20, 2009. He set the dimensions of the transition out of office, assigning specific transition responsibilities to White House and administration officials, issuing orders to administrative agencies, working with administration figures on priorities and timetables, working on national security and domestic policy issue information in preparation for the transition, providing for a smooth personnel process, and meeting with representatives of the Obama and McCain transition teams. All of these actions required coordination of officials and institutions throughout the executive branch. Candidate representatives met with government officials. Everything was on a timetable geared toward getting transition teams up to speed before the election.

To get the transition off to a good start, President Bush arranged a meeting with President-elect Barack Obama at the White House less than a week after Election Day. Other than President Johnson and his White House session with President-elect Nixon, President George W. Bush was the only president in a change of party transition to meet with the incoming president within a week of the election. He did so to make certain that the formal and public part of the transition got off to a swift start. He also wanted to provide the incoming president with information on national security issues in what was a time of a war with fronts in Iraq and Afghanistan and continuing efforts by terrorist groups to establish domestic operations.

TABLE 3.1
Dates Presidents and Presidents-Elect Met about Change-of-Party Transitions

President	President-elect	Date of election	Date of transition meeting
Harry Truman	Dwight Eisenhower	November 4, 1952	November 18, 1952
Dwight Eisenhower	John F. Kennedy	November 8, 1960	December 6, 1960
Lyndon Johnson	Richard Nixon	November 5, 1968	November 11, 1968
Gerald Ford	Jimmy Carter	November 2, 1976	November 22, 1976
Jimmy Carter	Ronald Reagan	November 4, 1980	November 20, 1980
George H. W. Bush	Bill Clinton	November 3, 1992	November 18, 1992
Bill Clinton	George W. Bush	November 7, 2000	December 19, 2000
George W. Bush	Barack Obama	November 4, 2008	November 10, 2008

Note: Transition meeting dates cited in news articles and in presidential statements archived in the relevant volumes for each president in the *Public Papers of the President of the United States.*

White House Actions in Early 2008

Chief of Staff Joshua Bolten set out in early 2008 to turn President Bush's order for a smooth transition into an action plan that covered a broad range of issues, including planning for security crises, gathering domestic and national security information, establishing policies governing the issuance of administrative rules and regulations, and managing the collection of information from departments and agencies.

White House Security Issues

After talking to President Bush late in 2007, Bolten worked with his deputies to plan out their actions. First, Bolten worked with his deputy chief of staff, Joe Hagin, who focused on White House operations and infrastructure. Hagin spent a great deal of his White House time planning and overseeing upgrades to several of the White House suites and rooms, including the Situation Room and the Press Room. Hagin was familiar with the White House physical plant as well as staff operations. Early in 2008 Bolten sought out his expertise.

Bolten's goal was to work through what information they wanted to leave behind and in what form they wanted to leave it: "We wanted to be sure that each of the operating units was leaving behind a good record of how they did business and that required a fair amount of lead time."[7] He commented about the transition discussions he and Hagin had in early spring 2008: "In my early conversations with Joe, we weren't thinking that much about helping the incoming people . . . with their confirmations and that kind of thing, as we were about making sure that we were leaving things in as good and clear . . . [a] position as we possibly could."

While Bolten worked on the contours of the transition and figuring out what the administration wanted to leave behind, Joe Hagin worked on the security piece of the White House transition. As Bolten remembered it, "Joe was especially focused on the security aspects and on emergency procedures that really is one of the tough spots in all of these things in preparing for a crisis. It's very hard to get people who have more than full plates on a daily basis to focus on an event where . . . everybody either thinks or hopes won't happen, to get them to spend time preparing for that is hard." Hagin focused on making sure that others were staying focused on the issue. "So Joe spent a lot of time trying to make sure that we had, before we left, that we had in place the best possible emergency procedures and that we had mechanisms to make sure that people were trained and that there would be continuity between the administrations. So he worked a lot with the military office as well as on the infrastructure, the physical and technological infrastructure that goes with responding to an emergency."[8] The crisis training session they ran early in 2009 comes up later in this chapter.

Disciplining the Issuance of "Midnight" Regulations

One of the things that occurs as presidencies end is the issuance of regulations and executive orders at the end of a term, especially when the election brings a change in party and an inevitable change in political philosophy. What results is a rush by agencies to submit regulations designed to put their priorities in place.[9] On May 9, 2008, Joshua Bolten issued a memorandum seeking to rein in these "midnight" regulations. The memorandum stated: "Except in extraordinary circumstances, regulations to be finalized in this Administration should be proposed no later than June 1, 2008, and final regulations should be issued no later than November 1, 2008."[10] He laid down a process for discipline. Even so, there were enough eleventh-hour exceptions to draw the attention of the administration's critics and news organizations.

Bolten discussed his memorandum. He said the idea for it came from Susan Dudley, who headed the Office of Information and Regulatory Affairs at OMB and Jim Nussle, the director of the Office of Management and Budget. "They came to see me some weeks before, and we talked about it a fair bit, and I was enthusiastic about the notion, worried about the implementation and how it would look, and my fears were justified, I think, in the way it played out." Overall, Bolten thought the memorandum process worked out well. "I think the record of what actually happened was good as a result of that memorandum. But the way it was portrayed politically and in the news I think was maybe mildly damaging."

Joshua Bolten was sympathetic to the idea of tidying up the regulations process at the end of the Bush administration because he remembered the situation that President Clinton and his team left them with in January 2001: "I thought that they [Clinton administration] did a disservice to the process by hustling through a bunch of rules at the end, many of them things that they weren't willing to take responsibility for implementing to justifying during the course of their term. So they thought that they would just dump it on us."[11] Once President Bush came into office, Chief of Staff Andrew Card issued a memorandum "right at the outset, which was an absolute necessity of just freezing everything because they had just hustled an enormous amount through the door right at the end. Much of the stuff was ill considered, and some of it was politically motivated intentionally to cause us trouble."

For Bolten, the sting of the experience lingered long: "I was determined that we avoid that. In other words, I was trying to create a situation in which we didn't recede from what we thought was right, but that we did not intentionally jam or burden our successors. That we go through as much regular order as we could and that we move rapidly to implement the president's agenda while he was president, but that we not do it in a midnight manner with the specific intent of burdening our successors. I just felt like the experience that we had had on the way in shouldn't be standard operating procedure."

The memorandum had the weight of the president behind it. "I asked the president about it before I signed the memorandum, and he confirmed that he didn't want to do business that way," Bolten said. "He wanted to do business straight. So that was the purpose of the memorandum."[12] The Clinton rules and regulations took President Bush's attention when he entered office. Two days after President Bush came into office, his chief of staff declared the administration planned a sixty-day review of all Clinton administration late-issued executive rules and regulations. On the first day they delayed late Clinton rules going into effect until his administration could review them and decide if the new team wanted to go ahead with them. Speaking on *Face the Nation*, Andrew Card said: "We're going to take a look at all of the regulations. We're going to take a look at all of the executive orders. We are going to be responsible about it. This is not a knee-jerk reaction to undo. Instead, it is a responsible review of what has happened."[13]

In the first hundred days, Bush White House officials worked with House Republicans on a list of forty-five regulations the administration and the House members were considering overturning. According to the *Washington Post*, the Clinton rules that House Republicans were considering overturning "imposed stricter energy standards for air conditioners, defined a child as a fetus that is viable after birth, and restricted snowmobile use in national parks. The regulations included on the list touch nearly every major area of government policy, including labor, abortion and the environment, indicating the GOP may pursue a broad assault on policies President Clinton enacted in his last days in office."[14] The Republicans' deputy whip, Roy Blunt (R-Mo.), commented on the Clinton executive actions in the final months of his administration: "This whole move toward midnight regulations is something on which Congress should send a clear message to future presidents. . . . The kind of things you haven't been able to do during your term, you shouldn't try to do as you're closing the door."[15]

What the late Clinton rules and regulations did was make it more difficult for the Bush administration to get off to a quick start with their established agenda and for the issues the orders represented to hold over well beyond the first hundred days of the Bush term in office. Even at the end of eight years, the memory of the Clinton rules was fresh in the minds of those who were in the White House at the time. The rule that gave the new administration its most continuing public attention was one that lowered the acceptable level of arsenic in all water systems, small towns as well as large ones. In late March, after reviewing the Clinton rules, the administrator of the Environmental Protection Agency, Christine Todd Whitman, announced that the administration would cancel the order. "The Environmental Protection Agency announced yesterday it will revoke a Clinton administration rule that would have reduced the acceptable level of arsenic in drinking water, arguing the evidence was not conclusive enough to justify the high cost to states, municipalities and industry of complying with the proposal," recounted the *Washington Post*.[16] After creating a commission to look into the issue and weathering a great deal of criticism from environmentalists, Whitman announced on November 1, 2001, that the administration would in fact accept the arsenic levels recommended by the Clinton EPA regulations.[17]

While Bolten felt establishing standards for administrative rules and regulations was a good move, doing so was sometimes difficult to implement. "I think the record of what actually happened was good as a result of that memorandum. But the way it was portrayed politically and in the news I think was maybe mildly damaging," Bolten said. "It's a little hard to get the cabinet officers to focus on it. . . . One of the reasons that I had as many appeals as I did in October and November and December is that the cabinet officers didn't pay any attention until they realized that they were about to leave office with some important piece, some agenda item that either they thought was important or they thought was important to the president's agenda, [still left] undone. And here was my memorandum saying that if you didn't have it done by X date, it's not happening."[18]

Deputy Chief of Staff Joel Kaplan commented that the real impact of the regulations memorandum was to move the clock back and give those in the White House additional time to consider exceptions to the memorandum. "Josh wanted to be able to identify principled rules by which exceptions would be granted, which really was not fleshed out in the memo," Kaplan observed. "I think what it . . . really was most effective at doing was—I think somebody on our staff coined this phrase—it basically moved midnight to 9 o'clock. . . . You still had a lot of rush at the end, but the end was no longer defined as December 15th; it was now November 1st. We still had a lot of people rushing in and trying [to regulate] but then we had a period to make more rational decisions about where exceptions were warranted. And we did shut down a lot of late rulemaking, much to the chagrin of the agencies, who have a lot of people working on stuff."[19]

From his view, Bolten did not get the cooperation he had hoped for. The department secretaries did not meet the deadlines established in the memorandum, and outside groups were suspicious of his motives. Bolten found the criticism of their effort to slow down the promulgation of regulations unwarranted: "I thought that was a good government thing to do, and I was more than a bit peeved to have had the White House take—it wasn't a lot of criticism, but it was more than trivial criticism—for our supposed midnight regulations, when in fact we were making a pretty serious effort to do the opposite." Some groups were critical of the memoranda, seeing it as an effort to make it difficult for the next administration to change regulations.[20] "In other words, I was trying to create a situation in which we didn't recede from what we thought was right, but that we did not intentionally jam or burden our successors," said Bolten. OMB Watch, a group interested in the operation of that agency, viewed the memorandum in a different light: "In reality, the memo may simply change when the clock strikes midnight in order to insulate potentially controversial rules from disapproval by a new administration. Other rules moving slowly through the regulatory pipeline may be delayed until after Bush leaves office."[21]

Criticism from groups and cabinet secretaries who dragged their feet in following the directions of the memorandum were not the only problems facing Bolten. Because he issued the memorandum, he ended up also being the arbiter of its rules: "It also put me, as chief of staff, in a very awkward position that I had been concerned about when they brought me the memorandum but about which I was uncomfortable as it played out." With more exceptions than he and the OMB team who brought him the memorandum idea had anticipated, he had to decide which rules exception cases to support and which ones to deny. "Because they put me, as the chief of staff, in the position of arbitrating which rules were so important or so much the subject of last-minute development that we could breach the deadlines that I had originally imposed. And that's just not a good position for the chief of staff to be in at the end of the administration."[22]

People came to Bolten with reasons they could not meet the requirements of his memorandum, including that they did not have the information by deadline time or they had not received responses to their exception request from OMB. "Everybody had a really good reason why their rules didn't make it. I would have preferred to have had a system that just said, 'Absolutely not. We set deadlines for a reason, and we're sticking to them.' But a lot of the cases were actually really good cases so I ended up having to make some exceptions and then made everyone else mad, which I succeeded in doing."[23]

Facing opposition both inside and outside of the administration, Bolten was unsure what road another chief of staff should take on this issue at the end of an administration. "I'm not sure how the next chief of staff can fix that but I was uncomfortable with it towards the end, and it's probably worth going back and looking at that memorandum and maybe issuing something like that even earlier to put people more fully on notice that here's the calendar we're going to follow." Furthermore, it would be advantageous to eliminate some of the awkwardness arising from the chief of staff being the arbiter of his own rule. "Maybe having some mechanism that just doesn't rely on the chief of staff saying yeah, the Secretary of HHS has a good point on this one, but a similar point made by the Secretary of Labor, that one just isn't important enough to be breaching the rules. Because those are the judgments I ended up having to make pretty late into the term."[24] He was making such judgments in November and December.

A person familiar with bureaucratic operations pointed out that there is another dynamic at work that makes it difficult for anyone in the White House to control the flow of rules and regulations at the end of an administration. "What matters a lot in government is not necessarily what the chief of staff in the White House does. It's what the regulatory apparatus does," this observer said.[25] Those in the departments and agencies know that it takes a while for a team to set up shop as they want it. Before that happens, those working in the agencies want to make sure that the rules and regulations reflect what they see as important. "So the volume of wanting to get stuff out the door just from an organizational perspective naturally increases, because people at typical career levels are saying we need to do this because this is our job," the observer said. It is difficult for a department secretary to control the flow "short of imposing an I-need-to-see-everything mentality to stop it."

Looking at the issue four years later, however, Joshua Bolten's action was publicly endorsed by an important government-related group. In the summer of 2012, the Obama administration had not released any memoranda relating to the handling of regulations. The Administrative Conference of the United States, an independent federal agency devoted to improving administrative practices, recommended how regulations should be handled in the last year of an administration.[26] These regulations were substantially followed at the end of the Bush administration.

1. Incumbent administrations should manage each step of the rulemaking process throughout their terms in a way that avoids an actual or perceived rush of the final stages of the process.

2. Incumbent administrations should encourage agencies to put significant rulemaking proposals out for public comment well before the date of the upcoming presidential election and to complete rulemakings before the election whenever possible.

3. When incumbent administrations issue a significant "midnight" rule—meaning one issued by an outgoing administration after the Presidential election—they should explain the timing of the rule in the preamble of the final rule (and, if feasible, in the preamble of the proposed rule). The outgoing administration should also consider selecting an effective date that falls 90 days or more into the new administration so as to ensure that the new administration has an opportunity to review the final action and, if desired, withdraw it after notice and comment, before the effective date.

4. Incumbent administrations should refrain from issuing "midnight" rules that address internal government operations, such as consultation requirements and funding restrictions, unless there is a pressing need to act before the transition. While incumbent administrations can suggest such changes to the incoming administration, it is more appropriate to leave the final decision to those who would operate under the new requirements or restrictions.

5. Incumbent administrations should continue the practice of sharing appropriate information about pending rulemaking actions and new regulatory initiatives with incoming administrations.[27]

The Federal Regulation Advisor, a group of professionals following regulation issues, commented on how far behind the Obama administration was on these standards when compared with the George W. Bush administration: "Few Administration instructions have achieved the degree of functional direction and transparency as the Bush Administration's May 8, 2008, memorandum on the

regulatory closing of its second term: 'Except in extraordinary circumstances, regulations to be finalized in this Administration should be proposed no later than
June 1, 2008, and final regulations should be issued no later than November 1,
2008.' The Administration's 'end game' has not been transparent, however, and
the Obama White House could learn from its predecessor."[28] When there is a
two-term administration with a clear end date several years out, it is likely there
will be outside groups interested in having the regulations process adhere to the
Bolten memorandum.

The President's Management Council

Bush administration officials identified early on that to make their transition efforts useful, they needed to get agencies to work together. Clay Johnson began his
work when Joshua Bolten came to him to talk about the executive branch transition: "We first had a conversation about . . . as a leadership community [we] want
to establish as our goals for preparing to receive the new team and get them up
to full governance speed quickly. . . . That began in response to Josh saying, 'Clay,
I want you to handle what agencies do to prepare and separately we'll get the
White House squared away.' That began in say March or April. So that's why we
went through several iterations of what we wanted to define as success for all the
agencies in May and June."[29]

Russell Gerson, who handled transition personnel issues for Senator McCain,
said in 2009 that he had talked to former President Bush about the transition and
Clay Johnson's role in it. "I said how impressed I was with the quality and the
commitment that they gave to the transition effort. . . . He says, 'Yeah, Clay really
focused on this, and this was really important to him.'"[30] Johnson's role had no
publicly identified title. As Gerson said, Johnson's job followed this logic: "What's
Clay's job? Anything he wants." He was a close friend of the president and was
not concerned with titles. Additionally, he was experienced in presidential transitions for George W. Bush through his role as executive director of the 2000–2001
transition. In the spring of 1999, Governor Bush asked Johnson as part of his
duties as his incoming chief of staff to "develop a plan for setting up his new
administration, or as he put it, 'develop a plan for what we should do after we
win.'"[31] From that point on, Johnson did so and continued as personnel director
once the new administration took over in 2001. With a successful transition operation behind him, Johnson, in his assigned role as deputy director for management of the Office of Management and Budget for Management, ran the part of
the transition dealing with departments and agencies through his role as chair
of the President's Management Council.

At the spring meeting of the President's Management Council [PMC], a collection of twenty-two of the key agencies, Johnson talked to agency representatives about the transition. The President's Management Council was established by President Clinton in an October 1, 1993, memorandum and was designed to coordinate the work of the most critical government agencies.[32] Johnson described the Council in the Bush administration as a group that "guided and coordinated all government-wide performance and management reform activities, which would include such efforts as the transition to a new administration."[33] The agencies worked together establishing common agency priorities and templates for their work. Working with what he considered to be a cooperative team of executive branch staff, Johnson discussed the transition with the group in a meeting held on May 14, 2008: "I don't think any previous administration has tried to get the different agencies together and say, 'Let's agree on some common definitions of what it means to prepare.'" By getting agency representatives together, the group could settle on some common ways of gathering and presenting transition information. "It gives people some better perspective about what the agencies are doing so you can pick best practices from all the different agencies and perhaps even raise the bar in terms of what agencies do. . . . People from the agencies loved them [the meetings] because they had just never ever talked to their transition counterparts at other agencies."[34]

On July 18, Johnson sent a memorandum to agencies and departments laying out their transition roles. "The memo was basically the sum and substance of our conversation [in the May 14 PMC meeting] about what we wanted to agree to."[35] The memorandum sets out tasks to be completed by departments and agencies and the deadlines for doing so. The deadlines came on August 1, October 15, and November 1. The memorandum stressed identifying career service leaders within the organization to participate in transition planning and leading the organization when political appointees leave the agencies. By August 1, agencies leaders were to: "Identify a knowledgeable, capable career official to lead/coordinate the transition, and communicate internally and externally."[36] By October 15, "Indentify the career official who will be responsible for acting in place of the departing/departed political official, for each major bureau and office of the department/agency, and communicate internally and externally. Ensure compliance with your agency's delegation of authorities and the Vacancies Act."

The November 1 deadline included information transition career service leaders were to gather and summarize information in the following areas: "Prepare a *brief* summary of the department's basic organization, current mission/function/performance goals, and key personnel. . . . Identify and summarize the 'hot' policy, internal management, legal and infrastructure issues to require immediate attention by the new Administration officials. Ensure the information is approved for release to the intended audience." The career service members were also asked to: "Prepare to provide the work tools and new employee briefings: badges, computers, Blackberries, parking, work spaces, access to secure information and areas, ethics briefings and the like." Their goals should be as follows:

- Work to ensure every program/initiative is as you are proud to have it, as of 1/20/09.
- Ensure all program improvement, high risk improvement and management improvement goals and plans are as all stakeholders are proud to have them, and available to the public, as planned.
- Do transition planning *with* (not *to*) career officials.[37]

In addition to their efforts in helping the new people come into office after the inauguration, the President's Management Council also set deadlines for aiding political appointees leaving office. By August 4, "develop for delivery as needed a briefing on what a departing political can and cannot take with them . . . develop for delivery as needed a briefing on "exit ethics" and post-service health benefit coverage, retirement estimates, etc. Include information about who to contact with related questions after they have left government service."

Johnson's instructions to the agency staff was to focus on priorities: "The way we referred to it was the . . . 'not hot and spicy' items, but the high-priority items or the items, the trend, the specific transactions that the new leadership group will have to deal with and . . . they won't have a choice," Johnson said. "'There's a decision [that] has to be made on this, there's these legal rulings or these regulatory things. There's this world conference that your secretary has to go to in the first ninety days or so.' Focus your assemblage of information on those matters because things are going very, very quickly and they're not going to have time and it won't be appropriate for them to know everything they ever need you to know about the history of the Department of Agriculture and so forth."[38]

Johnson and Gail Lovelace, a career senior executive, who was responsible for the GSA transition effort, discussed getting agency personnel together to discuss the transition as a group rather than simply meeting with agency people individually. "One of the things we had talked about with the PMC was . . . get the senior career transition leads from all agencies together as appropriate," Johnson said.[39] As it worked out, career agency leaders were very interested in meeting as a group. The group met three times, Johnson said. The first session was held on September 23, 2008.

Domestic Policy Memoranda

Chief of Staff Bolten described how they came to create a series of memoranda summarizing what conditions were in several areas of domestic policy, how they responded to those conditions, and how programs and conditions stood as they were at the end of their administration. These memoranda highlighted domestic issues that were important during the time President Bush was in office and ones where they were active in developing policies. Bolten anticipated that there would be memoranda for them when they entered in 2001: "I was a little surprised that when we came into the White House, there was basically nothing that was left behind by the Clinton folks by way of formal memoranda or guideposts and things like that. I subsequently heard that they had prepared some, but they had prepared them for Gore and weren't intended for us."[40] He said when he dealt with the outgoing people one-on-one, he got the information he needed. "The Clinton folks that I dealt with were very cooperative. . . . If you asked a question they were actually forthcoming, but there was no formal mechanism of trying to make sure that successors were informed with the probable exception of the National Security Council."

In part, the White House staff saw the memoranda filling the gap they experienced with a lack of something similar when they came into office in 2001 as well as for the multiple uses the memoranda could serve. The domestic policy memoranda described the state of play on important issues but they were also significant historical documents for their own team to use. "We decided about a year in advance to do those and that was a major undertaking and responsibility from every substantive unit in the White House," said Bolten.[41]

Joshua Bolten worked with Joel Kaplan, the deputy chief of staff for policy, on deciding the purposes they wanted the memoranda to serve: "Joel and I thought that it would be useful both for the Bush administration to make a record for our own purposes, for our own historical purposes, of what had happened and where we thought we left things." The same memoranda would be good for the incoming team. They would have "benefits of our successors, whether they would be Republicans or Democrats that we try to lay out the record as we saw it, not as political documents, but definitely with the Bush point of view in it." He commented further: "If it was a Democratic president, they weren't likely to agree, but they might be able to benefit from at least the factual chronology and the perspective that we had on the problem."[42]

Kaplan was responsible for overseeing the creation of the domestic policy memoranda, and Staff Secretary Raul Yanes collected and distributed them. The goal of the domestic memoranda was different than for foreign policy primarily because domestic policy is transparently in public view. "In the foreign policy area you expect . . . that a lot of issues are just midstream. And the history of the issues and . . . how you engaged with allies or non-allies is important background for the incoming NSC team and the [new] administration and the State Department and Department of Defense."[43] In the domestic policy area, much of the information is already in the public arena. "A lot of those memos would be stuff like [background about the] No Child Left Behind [law] or what we did on Social Security or what we did on Medicare, which the incoming Obama administration already had positions on that tended to be adverse to ours," Kaplan said.

Kaplan described their instructions to agency heads. "What we asked them to do is 'pick out . . . the critical issues that are going to come across the secretary's desk, or should come across the secretary's desk' . . . so [the Obama team could] make sure that in the first ninety days that this does not catch you by surprise," Kaplan said. "Rather than sending them forty different issue papers on things that they would not be interested in . . . and would disagree anyway, what we thought would be most helpful to them would be, 'Here are the things where you are going to have to do something.' It might be because of litigation. It might be because of a statutory deadline that is occurring. It might be because it is just in flux, like student loans."[44]

Working with Candidate Representatives: Summer and Fall 2008

The work undertaken in the winter and spring of 2008 was followed up by increasingly intense work during the summer and fall before and after the party conventions in late August and early September. Under Bolten's direction and the leadership of his deputy Blake Gottesman, who replaced Joe Hagin, the White House organized meetings with representatives of Senators Obama and McCain on the areas where White House transition leaders wanted to take action.

Working with Representatives of Both Presidential Candidates

In earlier transitions between parties, White House staff did not bring in representatives of the candidates, whether separately or together. They waited until after the election to bring in the team of the opposing party. In 2008, White House meetings with candidate representatives were different than earlier practice in two major ways. First, the sessions occurred in the summer, before either major party had had its convention and, second, the candidate representatives came in together for their meetings. Bolten and Gottesman had the candidate representatives come to the White House to discuss how they were planning the transition out of office, what information the administration would provide them, and what their target dates were for getting the information in their hands. The first meeting was in July, and Bolten and Gottesman brought the campaign representatives to the White House on consecutive days. Later they would have meetings on particular topics where representatives would be there together. "Mr. Bolten's office called . . . and asked that the campaign send a representative over to meet with him and his deputy and the White House assistant counsel. I did that. Mr. Podesta, I know, did the same thing, either the day before or the day after," said Will Ball, who represented Senator McCain in these meetings.[45] "That was the official advisory from the White House staff. . . . President Bush had indicated that his administration would be cooperative with the transition process fully, and with both campaigns, and would reach out and establish some procedures and contacts, both at the White House and elsewhere to facilitate all preparations." Once Ball came in to meet Bolten and Gottesman, the two of them introduced Ball to the head of Presidential Personnel [Joie Gregor] and the other White House officials who would be involved.

Sometimes the meetings were with the general representatives for the two campaigns, Will Ball for Senator McCain and Christopher Lu for Senator Obama, and sometimes they brought in others to discuss particular issues, such as matters relating to personnel. Yet another pattern was to bring in people to talk to an official and then have others, such as Bolten, drop by. In their meetings through the summer and fall, White House officials had the representatives work through the personnel issues, including the development of a new software package to handle incoming job applications and the new security clearance procedures. They worked with the two sides on other procedural issues as well. There were also times when the representatives meetings were held outside of the White House.

Bolten met with the candidate representatives on successive days in mid-August. Clay Johnson described the meetings: "'Let us profess our level of commitment to serve you two equally and here are the players you will be introduced to, will be working with, and we want to help you on the presidential personnel front. We want to give you . . . background information on what . . . the person in every one of these PAS [presidential appointment with Senate confirmation required] jobs does statutorily.' . . . So it was the things we were going to do for them and the things that we could help them do: what they needed to do before the election. Then there were very, very frequent communications between their representatives and the White House's representatives just on every conceivable kind of thing."[46] Chris Lu of Obama's team discussed the regular exchanges he had with Gottesman, whom Bolten had tasked to carry out on behalf of the White House the day-to-day transition work with representatives of both candidates. "Blake was the one that was tasked with interacting with the campaigns. . . . Blake and I probably talked every couple days, and I also had regular contact with the McCain people."[47]

When they were discussing personnel matters, the issue came up of the White House personal data questionnaire. Each administration uses a questionnaire as the first point in the personnel process before potential nominees are asked to fill out the SF 278 financial disclosure and the SF 86 national security forms. Ball said that Gottesman and others at the White House talked to them about the personal data statement and the kinds of questions that personnel officers pose to possible nominees. In John Podesta's case, as President Clinton's chief of staff he had authority over the personnel operation and surely would have had the personal data statement the Clinton administration used.

Department of Justice officials held two meetings with the McCain and Obama people. Justice officials discussed the process of submitting names for clearance following the conventions. The IRS described background check procedures covering taxes for those who might be nominated. The associate attorney general for administration assembled both sides. Will Ball, the McCain transition representative at these meetings, described what information the two camps received at the meeting: "As a part of the clearance process, the FBI representatives briefed on the FBI portion of the process. The Justice Department briefed on their role, and how . . . if we had sent names in, what would have been the procedure they would have undertaken, both for interim clearances, and then after the election, for the full permanent clearance process. . . . We had lists of names compiled internally for Senator McCain, but he did not wish at that point to turn names in to begin the clearance process on any individual."[48]

Memorandum of Understanding

Nothing can proceed in a transition without the memorandum of understanding signed by the leaders of the transitions into and out of the White House. The document details how the two sides will deal with one another, what the areas of interactions will be, and how disputes will be settled. The document is signed following the election. But in this transition, the MOU was worked out with both sides before the election so that whatever side won, their agency review teams could get started quickly and begin interacting with the relevant departments and agencies.

The agency review teams gathering information for the Obama transition were large ones. Speaking shortly before a crisis training exercise, Chief of Staff Joshua Bolten described the work they were doing for the sessions. "We've certified nearly a thousand members of the Obama transition team for access to information and briefings at nearly a hundred agencies around the government, and we've expedited clearances for key members of the national security team, so that they're in position to hit the ground running," he said.[49] He explained further why they took these actions. "In the post-9/11 world, this isn't just good-mannered good government; it's a national security responsibility." The MOU is an important part of the process of getting people into the agencies quickly and making certain that everyone who needs to gets briefed at the proper level.

Chris Lu said that "even though the MOU got negotiated out and drafted out from the White House, at the individual agency level there were all kinds of interpretations of it that made it difficult for our folks." When problems arose, the Memorandum of Understanding provided ways for working through them. "Blake Gottesman and I actually had a daily call where we would hash out, 'Okay, X agency, we're hearing from our folks at this agency. If there's a problem, then you would work on those.' And without fail, every one of those problems got resolved in about a day or so."[50]

Postelection Actions

After the election, the Bush administration brought in members of the Obama transition operation on substantive issues as well as on procedural ones. While most actions were planned well in advance, there were also meetings held in response to particular issues arising during the transition period from the election to the inauguration. The most pressing issue during that period was the critical financial situation, including the near-collapse of the American automobile industry.

Financial Crisis: The Auto Bailout

One of the points that presidents make after the election when they meet with incoming presidents is to state that there is only one president at a time. The incoming presidents say that it is the principle they will live by. The reality, however, demonstrates shades of gray. In the Obama transition, his team was required to work with Congress on getting additional Troubled Asset Relief Program (TARP) legislation through, a move that came about because Bolten told them that the Bush people did not have the muscle to get it through. That required the Obama people to get to work on financial issues well before the inauguration.

The automobile industry was another issue the Obama administration needed to grapple with very soon after the election. President Bush talked about aid to the auto industry with President-elect Obama in their meeting at the White House the Monday following the election. As President Bush explained in his book *Decision Points*: "Later that week, I sat down for a meeting with my economic team. 'I told Barack Obama that I wouldn't let the automakers fail,' I said. 'I won't dump this mess on him.'"[51] Bush said that he opposed President Jimmy Carter's bailout of the Chrysler auto company, but he believed that the situation in the autumn of 2008 was different. "Yet the economy was extremely fragile, and my economic advisors had warned that the immediate bankruptcy of the Big Three could cost more than a million jobs, decrease tax revenues by $150 billion, and set back America's GDP by hundreds of billions of dollars." President Bush compared the financial crisis with other periods in his presidency: "The period between September and December 2008 was the most intense, turbulent, decision-packed stretch since those same months in 2001. Because the crisis arose so late in my administration, I wouldn't be in the White House to see the impact of most of the decisions I made."[52]

From Bolten's vantage point as well as that of President Bush's economic and financial advisors, including the secretary of the Treasury, Henry Paulson, the financial crisis of autumn 2008 represented a real threat to the financial stability of the United States. "This was an emergency," Bolten said. "This was a situation where I believe that the economy, not just our economy but the global economy, was on the precipice in September/October. And I think the measures that Paulson put in place, that Bernanke put in place—it's pretty easy now with hindsight to criticize specific details of it but the broad stroke of it was that they saved the world economy and with extreme and unprecedented measures."[53] The depth of the crisis meant swift and decisive action to protect financial markets and to give aid to failing industries.

The automobile industry was a key to saving the system from collapse. "The autos were a part of that," he said. "And the reason why President Bush, as against I guess what would probably be regarded as Republican orthodoxy, stepped in and supported a life raft for the auto companies." Those from whom the president sought advice were agreed on the central role played by the auto industry in our economic system. "The economic advice he was getting, even from some of the most conservative economic advisors on our team, was that the sudden failure of the auto companies, which had we not stepped in when we did, could have been an abrupt chapter 7 and not a chapter 11 filing," referring to a difference in "the bankruptcy code [that] means liquidation and not reorganization."[54]

Since the auto industry affects so many states and involves so many auto parts and supplies businesses, the impact of bankruptcy could have been calamitous. "Either way, an abrupt bankruptcy of the auto companies could have had a cascading affect on the economy that, if they didn't push us over the precipice of that moment, might have made things a whole lot worse than they ended up being."[55]

During that period, Bolten brought the Obama financial team members together with Treasury and White House officials of the Bush administration to discuss the appointment of an auto czar. Although the meeting of November 30, 2008, in Paulson's office at the Treasury Department did not lead to joint action, team members explored the possibilities of how TARP funds could be used and what measures could be taken to deal with the crisis in the auto industry.[56] The session brought together the most important White House players on economic issues—Secretaries Paulson and Carlos Gutierrez (Commerce), Joshua Bolten, Joel Kaplan, Keith Hennessey (director of the National Economic Council), Dan Meyer (director of legislative affairs), and Kevin Fromer (legislative affairs director for the Department of Treasury). The Obama economic team representatives at the meeting included Larry Summers (director designate of the National Economic Council), Mona Sutphen (White House deputy chief of staff designate), Dan Tarullo (leader of the economic policy team), and Phil Schiliro (White House legislative affairs director designate). The team members may not have been able to work out a coordinated policy, but at least the incoming and outgoing officials set a precedent of meeting together to tackle important issues.

In his book *On the Brink,* Secretary of the Treasury Henry Paulson described the meeting held in his office: "After a few pleasantries—and Larry's request to keep these exploratory discussions confidential—Josh opened by saying I wanted Congress to give us access to the rest of TARP, and that would happen only if Obama led the effort." Paulson continued that "other than Larry, Obama's people were quiet and seemed on guard. They asked a lot of questions but offered no suggestions for how we might work together."[57]

In addition to working with TARP funds, officials in the Bush White House were interested in promoting an auto czar to oversee the industry's use of government funds. With the financial world in turmoil and the auto industry at the center, the Bush White House brought together officials from the Obama transition with Treasury and White House officials to discuss the early appointment of an auto czar. Joshua Bolten described their goals in bringing the Obama team in to talk about the appointment of an auto czar. "I had maybe naively hoped and expected that what we could do is actually agree on the czar between us and the Obama administration," said Bolten.[58] "I had even said to Rahm, 'Look, you guys come up with a name, somebody you'll be comfortable with as being the person in charge of managing the government's end of this very, very dicey transaction. And if it's somebody we're comfortable with, we'll nominate him, or we'll just appoint him. And that way there will be continuity of the program.'"

The reason Bolten wanted to work together with the Obama people on selecting an auto czar was, as he said, "because continuity was actually substantively important in that the auto companies certainly and the unions above all were probably expecting that if they waited us out they would get a better deal from the Obama administration." Bolten was worried that waiting it out would be harmful for the recovery of the auto industry. "So for purposes of actually getting them to realize the measures that they needed to take, I thought we were best off showing a united front."[59]

Taking joint action was difficult because an incoming president and his team do not want to take on the problems of the sitting president, especially one as unpopular as President Bush was at that moment. His Gallup job approval rating at that point was 29 percent and his disapproval at 66 percent, among the worst figures for his presidency.[60] Bolten discussed the response of the Obama team: "The Obama folks were reticent to pick it up and I can appreciate that. They're in transition, they . . . didn't want to share in the problem until they were in complete control of the problem, and I think they were just as happy to have us struggle with it until we were out the door."[61]

One of the lessons an outgoing team learns from such gestures is that cooperative actions do not insulate the outgoing administration from criticism on that particular subject. The Obama team criticized the Bush administration for its auto policy in spite of the cooperation they sought. Austan Goolsbee, the chairman of the Council of Economic Advisors, said in an interview on *Fox News Sunday* on June 9, 2009, that the administration had left them with a huge problem: "We are only in this situation because somebody else kicked the can down the road, and that's really an understatement. They shook up the can, they opened the can, and handed [it] to us in our laps. . . . When George Bush put money into General Motors, almost explicitly with the purpose, how many dollars do they need to stay alive until January 20th, 2009? There was no commitment to restructuring, to making these viable enterprises of any kind."[62]

From Bolten's viewpoint, Goolsbee was ignoring the Bush team's attempts to provide early action on the auto industry crisis. Bolten and others felt that President Obama's press secretary, Robert Gibbs, repeated the same line of thinking. Bolten said, "They have a mantra that says the Bush administration kicked the can down the road and left this disaster on their doorstep, which they then had to clean up." The Bush team openly disagreed with the effort to lay blame for the crisis at their doorstep. "Basically we were proposing to them at the end of the administration the same program and in fact put in place the same program that they are now pursuing. We just didn't get their cooperation in it." One of the points that annoyed Bolten and others in the Bush White House about the criticism that they did little to advance a solution for the auto industry crisis is that their work on behalf of the auto industry brought them strong criticism from members of the Senate: "We did put it in place and we did it over the objection of Republicans in the Senate who were fiercely critical of the administration for having taken any measures to use the TARP money to keep the auto companies alive."[63]

Transition Coordinating Council

One of the developments in recent presidential transitions out of office is the creation, by Presidents Clinton and George W. Bush, of a formal coordinating mechanism that brings together the major White House staff and cabinet secretaries involved in transition planning. Both presidents created their councils through executive orders, and both referred to legislation they were carrying out.[64] In most ways the councils were similar in terms of intent and the members they included. The Bush order, however, went farther than the Clinton one did in including people with transition experience who were outside of the government as well as in the breadth of the work they expected from the group. The Clinton order was based on the Presidential Transition Act of 1963 and its amendments, while the Bush one included responsibilities in that act but based much of its orders on the Intelligence Reform and Terrorism Prevention Act of 2004 as well as his authority under section 7301 of the Presidential Transition Act of 1963 to establish regulations for the conduct of executive branch employees.

The difference in the council and the direction of the transition planning was the reality that with wars in Iraq and Afghanistan and a continuing threat of terrorism attacks on the United States, there was an urgency to making transition preparations that did not exist in the 2000–2001 change of power. President Bush signed Executive Order 13476 on October 9, 2008, so that the council could get under way before the election. President Clinton signed Executive Order 13176 on November 27, 2000, three weeks after the election but two weeks before the selection of the president could be determined.

The Bush council was composed of twelve cabinet and White House staff members whose jobs related to the transition.[65] The order was based on the requirements of the Presidential Transition Act of 1963 and called for the General Services Administration to provide the transition directory called for in the Presidential

Transition Effectiveness Act of 1988. It also called on the Office of Presidential Personnel to provide information on presidential appointed positions requiring Senate confirmation, including the statutes creating the positions and their personnel requirements, the Senate committees reviewing the nomination, the congressional committees the people holding the positions regularly interact with, and the names of people the nominees can call upon to answer questions about the posts. President Bush's council superseded the Clinton one. The Bush council convened five times between October 9, when it was created by Executive Order 13476, and January 9, 2009, when the group met for the last time. Members of President-elect Barack Obama's transition team attended the December 4 and January 9 meetings. At those two sessions and one other one as well, Bolten and Gottesman included representatives of a half-dozen outside organizations working on transition issues.[66] While there were a dozen members listed as automatic members of the TCC, the last two sessions had twenty-four and twenty-seven participants, respectively.

The order stated: "The Council shall assist the major party candidates and the President-elect by making every reasonable effort to facilitate the transition between administrations. This assistance may include, among other things, providing information relevant to facilitating the personnel aspect of a presidential transition and such other information that, in the Council's judgment, is useful and appropriate, as long as providing such information is not otherwise prohibited by law."

In the fact sheet accompanying the executive order, the White House emphasized the national security and financial crisis challenges facing the country as the background for the change in administrations. "The peaceful transfer of power from one Presidential Administration to the next is a hallmark of American democracy. With our Nation at war, our homeland targeted by terrorist adversaries, and our economy facing serious challenges, the Administration is committed to establishing and executing a transition plan that minimizes disruption, maintains continuity, and addresses the major changes in government since the 2000 transition, including the Intelligence Reform and Terrorism Prevention Act of 2004, as well as the creation of the Department of Homeland Security, the Director of National Intelligence, and the Homeland Security Council."[67]

Most of what the members of the council did was report on what each member of the TCC had accomplished on transition preparations so that each would know what the other was doing. They did this in some detail. In the fifth and final meeting of the TCC, Gottesman described what it takes for a sitting administration to move out of the White House and for a new team to come in. The Executive

Office of the President, the United States Trade Representative, Office of Management and Budget are 70 percent career, which means that most of them stay. For the White House staff, however, Gottesman noted that the "vast majority are political." "Of those employees, 588 are checked out. Twelve days before the inauguration, they had "cleared out 600 offices, inspected, carpets repaired, and rooms painted."[68] White House staff have worked with incoming people on matters from floor plans to workflow in the offices. They have an office manual for new people and have explained White House operations, including such matters as how to produce the weekly radio addresses. In order to help the incoming designated White House staff check in, staff members from the Office of Administration went to the Transition Office to help with paperwork so that people could check in ahead of time.

In the review of the work of the National Archives and Records Administration, the acting archivist, Adrienne Thomas, reported that NARA had moved documents to Texas that filled thirteen trucks and a plane and had two additional planes and more trucks ready to take more records. Many of these records were in Washington but had already left the White House under the regular Archives process, wherein the agency collects White House records and maintains them in Washington before being taken to a GSA warehouse where they remain until processed by staff for the outgoing president's library. In those trucks were 11,500 feet of records as well as thirty thousand artifacts. The electronic records represented twenty times as much as were created in the Clinton White House. The records went to a warehouse in Fort Worth, Texas, for processing by NARA archivists prior to their release in the forthcoming George W. Bush Library. NARA was also responsible for checking people out of the White House and making sure that proper records procedures were observed.

While most of that Transition Coordinating Council session was taken up with reports from Council members on where they were in getting the tasks completed, there were discussions where people from the Bush and Obama teams worked out issues that could present problems. For example, the issue was raised of the vandalism that was purported to have taken place in the White House compound at the end of the Clinton administration. One knowledgeable member of the Council said that the report of the Government Accountability Office found that the vandalism charges were exaggerated and that only isolated instances of damage took place. Another Council member suggested that the junior people in offices leave first and then put the responsibility on the head of the office to make certain that everything is in good order.

In the fourth meeting on December 4, 2008, an issue came up based on a November 18 *Washington Post* article claiming that the White House was "burrowing in" political appointees into career service posts from which they could not be fired. Mike Hager, the acting director of the Office of Personnel Management, addressed the issues raised by the piece. He went through the process used to review requests to move a position from political to career.

The article, which was written by Juliet Eilperin and Carol Leonnig, called out the administration on the practice with specific examples.[69] Going back several months, the reporters asserted: "Between March 1 and Nov. 3, according to the federal Office of Personnel Management, the Bush administration allowed 20 political appointees to become career civil servants. Six political appointees to the Senior Executive Service, the government's most prestigious and highly paid employees, have received approval to take career jobs at the same level. Fourteen other political, or 'Schedule C,' appointees have also been approved to take career jobs. One candidate was turned down by OPM and two were withdrawn by the submitting agency." The article also pointed out that changing political to career spots is a continuing issue at the end of administrations. Forty-seven positions were switched in the last year of the Clinton administration. There were discussions on each of the positions, some of which were switches from one career spot to another, Hager claimed. Gottesman also denied there were last-minute reclassifications of positions from political to career.

Political appointees came up in the two sessions in another way. An important aspect of preparing for a new administration is cleaning out the offices of political appointees, except for those the incoming administration wanted to hold over or those designated to represent the office temporarily once the offices were cleared. An important aspect of the presidential appointments process is for the incumbent president to terminate the appointments of all of his political appointees. White House staff were in "constant communications with individuals who are behind." They sent out a memorandum in November calling for the resignations of political appointees and subsequently sent out another memorandum saying "we accept their resignations even if they haven't given it."

Developing Crisis Training

Joe Hagin's emergency plans later led to a crisis-training event held on the White House grounds on January 13, 2009. Crisis training among agencies has been done on a fairly regular basis in the post-September 11 world. In discussing the January exercise, Deputy Press Secretary Scott Stanzel described the training practice: "While the federal government has regular exercises of this nature, today's session was the first ever exercise which included both current and outgoing senior White House officials and Cabinet members."[70]

The Obama and Bush White House and national security teams worked together on a manufactured crisis scenario involving improvised explosive devices in several cities.[71] It was an opportunity for the incoming and outgoing officials to sit next to one another and think through possible crisis responses. "Part of it [the crisis exercise] is . . . sobering to the incoming team, and it tells them, 'Here is a bunch of stuff I need to learn about quickly and be ready for . . . on day one,' which is something I think was not the case in the minds of either the outgoing or incoming administration in 2001. . . . I think everybody from both sides appreciated the importance of getting it right," Joel Kaplan commented.[72]

In order to develop a crisis training operation that would run smoothly, the Bush team "ran it on ourselves," noted Steve Hadley. "It was a full-fledged game." They took one of the contingency plans that Peter Feaver, who served from 2005 to 2007 as a special advisor for strategic planning and institutional reform at the National Security Council, was developing as part of the preparations to handle contingencies that they or their successors might face. When they did the crisis plan, they worked through the possible event in several ways: "They spent about three hours getting briefed on how we're organized to do response to a terrorist [attack] or natural disaster, who's in the room, how we relate to state and local authorities, what kind of support is available, how does the communications work."[73] In addition, he noted, "if it's a threat to the president, how does the evacuation of the president work?" In the morning session, the group of incoming and outgoing administration officials "walked through . . . descriptively, how does it work?" In the afternoon session, "we actually put and had a rapporteur, or a facilitator, and we actually put a contingency on the board. And then each of the players explained what they would be doing in response to that contingency over the next six hours." The session involved approximately fifty people. "It was all of the major Cabinet authorities." As secretary of homeland security, Michael Chertoff ran the meeting. In the session, the incoming and outgoing officials assigned to the same post sat next to one another. "Jim Jones sat next to me," Hadley said. "Each pair was doing a little sotto voce communication as we walked through the game. And we thought it gave them at least a sense of what was out there." Many of the Obama officials prepped for the exercise beforehand. Jones gathered some incoming officials in the week before the session took place "so they could begin to organize themselves; so that they would be able to participate effectively in this session."[74]

The Bush team valued crisis training because they knew from 2001 and Hurricane Katrina how difficult it was for personnel across the government to work together in situations where they did not know one another. In his role at the Office of Management and Budget, Clay Johnson was involved in the development of training for crisis management. The idea for such a plan came from what they learned in Hurricane Katrina about the operation of the government in crisis. You need to have a history with people in other agencies; otherwise it is difficult to make the initial contacts work if they are getting to know one another for the first time in a crisis. Johnson observed that the need to have regular contacts among those in departments and agencies across the government arises from the fact that "we do way more things that are government-wide now than we did ten years ago. . . . So one of the things that came out of Katrina was an initiative to train our people, orient and train and groom people . . . such that they are used to working with their counterparts in other agencies." This is important in settings where conditions are not optimal for decision-making, such as situations "where they never have enough information about what's going on, where there's no clear recipe for success."[75]

Conclusion

President George W. Bush had a historic transition out of office. He started earlier than his predecessors and called for a greater variety of preparations as well. Serving in his last term and with two wars under way, the president began early for the change in power, with the administration gathering information from across all its departments and agencies. As they did so, those working in government systematically developed and reported information. The Transition Coordinating Council and the President's Management Council set out frameworks for the gathering of information and materials that administration people working in the departments and agencies would use. Having the heads of the departments and agencies work through what was important for a new team provided a framework to ensure consistency in the information they reported and in the presentation of their findings.

For the first time, White House officials brought together both sides to provide them with information the incumbents believed would be useful in understanding the rhythms of an administration. Sometimes the transition teams came in individually; at other times the people representing Senators McCain and Obama met with officials together so that everyone could work through issues relating to personnel and computer software and the memorandum of understanding governing the contacts between the president-elect's team and the officials working in the departments and agencies. Finally, the groups came in to work through with incumbents on how to handle a tabletop crisis exercise.

The processes used for the Bush administration transition out of office will be used again as the templates provided information that any new team will need. Yet some of their work was fairly unique, especially the handling of the financial crisis, because it came into being with a set of circumstances that are not likely to reappear in the same way at the same point in an incumbent's presidency. Even though the financial crisis is not likely to reoccur in the same way, the pattern of handling a crisis and working through with each side on how to manage it is important as an example of what two sides can accomplish together. Though the two sides cooperated, there were limits in what they could achieve. No incoming administration wants to buy into what they see as the problems remaining at the end of an earlier one.

CHAPTER FOUR

Coming into the Presidency

Entering the White House without your ducks in a row, in terms of policy and decision agenda, is no longer an option. With increased attention to the vulnerability of the United States during a change in presidential power, in 2008 the outgoing president and the major-party candidates had a shared commitment to an informed process preparing for the coming transfer. Lisa Brown, who led the early preparations for the agency review teams that would go into the departments and agencies following the November election, commented on the shared interests of the outgoing Bush and incoming Obama administrations. "The incentives aligned, because 9/11 dramatically changed the cost of not doing it for everybody," Brown said. "Part of that was nobody wanted any glitch on the national security front. So there was an incentive to be really forthcoming . . . [because] the country's too important. . . . My sense is that that was one part of the reason that it worked as well as it did."[1]

While it would seem that early planning is a natural part of a candidate's preparations for an office he expects to occupy in a few months, the record of such planning is uneven. As recently as the Clinton administration early planning sometimes meant getting ready once you came into office, not several months ahead of time. A January 30–31 Clinton staff retreat gives us a good sense of the implications of the result when proper sequencing of decisions is not followed. With President Clinton choosing his White House staff less than two weeks before his inauguration, a retreat brought fifty staff members together to talk about the term ahead. The topics focused mainly on policy and priorities: President Clinton and Vice President Gore discussed "Goals and Agenda/How We Will Work," "Toward a Shared Vision," "Priorities: 100 Days;" "U.S. Economic Context—Budget," "Congress/Communications Strategies."[2] In the two administrations that came after the Clinton years, these and other topics were discussed and an agenda settled in a period beginning several months before the president-elect took the oath of office. If a chief executive is discussing the way forward after he is already in office, he is, in fact, well behind where he needs to be to get a good start to his presidency. When someone comes into the White House as chief executive, he needs to have his plans laid out and his decisions sequenced for maximum impact. The public is watching, as are governmental officials and others in Washington institutions looking for signals from the new chief executive on policy and his priorities. They are ready for action, and he needs to be as well.

Timelines for an Upcoming Transition

Whether the incoming president is a Democrat or a Republican, a liberal or a conservative, he will need to get a grasp on key positions in his administration and who might fill them, policies and their relative priorities, and the organization he will need in his White House and throughout the executive branch to develop his policies and to implement the laws. In most ways, the needs remain the same from one presidency to the next.

Transitions have a rhythm to them that involves a defined number of people, activities, and decisions to be made. There are four traditional transition phases. The first stage occurs during the primary campaign phase when most presidential candidates designate a person to gather information on personnel and decision timetables. The second period follows the party nominating conventions when government institutions, such as the Office of Government Ethics, get involved in the transition process in a limited way. Following the election, when the winning candidate has been designated president-elect, the formal seventy-five-day transition period into office forms the third stage. The fourth and final period is the transition into governing that takes place following the inauguration.

In 2008, there were five stages in the transition, not the traditional four. An additional period emerged in 2008 and is particularly important in the pre–major-party convention period. There is a point when many of the primaries are in the past and both major parties have presumptive presidential candidates. When that happened in 2008, officials in government institutions informally talked to the candidates' representatives with baseline information on what help agencies can provide and what the candidates would need to do in order to meet the requirements associated with presidential appointments, record-keeping, financial disclosure, and national security clearances. They did not wait until after the election or even the post-convention period.

Those candidate-government talks took place about two or three months prior to the last of the major-party conventions in early September. And in a break with tradition, those talks included ones held at the White House with senior staff members. The critical date for the evolution from the first to the second stage in 2008 is June 7, when Senator Hillary Clinton pulled out of the Democratic presidential contest, leaving Senator Barack Obama as the presumptive nominee. Once clear candidates were apparent for both of the major parties, government agencies and the White House could, and did, begin the process of establishing contacts with them.

The remainder of the stages for the Obama transition played out as earlier ones have. Stage Three followed the formal party convention nominations for Senators Obama and McCain, Stage Four took place with the November 4 presidential election when Senator Obama became president-elect, and Stage Five began with the inauguration of President Obama. At that point, all of the transition planning work on presidential appointments, White House and administration organization, and policy moved into the implementation stage. We will discuss the Stage Five, implementing transition plans and campaign promises, following the inauguration in chapter 5.

Stage One: Early Transition Stirrings

The early stirrings involve the presidential candidate settling on a person and a process for gathering transition information. The next step is for that person to assemble transition-related material and to talk to people who were involved in earlier transitions. Senator Obama began that process by having discussions with his Senate staff members in spring 2008.

Choosing Transition Leadership

Settling on one person to run the transition operation is important because it is necessary for an operation that is responsible to the candidate and that coordinates with the campaign. The Obama staff was aware of the effectiveness of George W. Bush's preparation for presidential transition. Bush's early transition operation paid off handsomely because the task of information-gathering took place early and was administered by one person, Clay Johnson, a close friend of George W. Bush who handled the appointments process when Bush served as governor.

Having one person serve as the wrangler gathering and processing transition and appointment information allows for clear responsibility for the process. Senator Obama knew from past examples that someone known to the campaign should handle the operation in order for the relationship between the campaign and the transition to operate with a minimum of conflict. The primary person to handle the early process was Chris Lu, Senator Obama's legislative assistant and friend from their law school days. He was responsible for transition work in the late spring and early summer before John Podesta came on to lead the effort in late July. "I think there were conversations happening very early on largely between Senator Obama and Pete Rouse [chief of staff of Obama's Senate office], probably in the spring. . . . I will tell you that from my perspective I was asked to start thinking about the transition in probably mid-May, so before the primaries were actually over," said Lu. "I suspect Pete Rouse had been thinking about it even longer than that."[3] Rouse, who served President Obama as senior advisor, acting chief of staff, and counselor before leaving the White House in 2013, worked for and was very close to Senator Obama.

Lu explained his transition assignment. "It actually came about in kind of a funny way. I was the legislative director in the Senate office under Pete Rouse, who was the chief of staff. As Pete spent more and more of his time on the campaign, I became the acting chief of staff, and I was fine doing that role, because it was an important role. But I remember having a conversation with Obama. It was probably March or April, and I said, 'Look, I'm happy to continue doing this and holding down the fort in D.C., but if there's a better use of my time in the campaign I'd be interested in that as well, even if that meant moving to Chicago.'" Senator Obama said he needed him in Washington but "if there's something you can think about that you could do here in D.C., I'd be open to it." Lu suggested the transition. "He mentioned that to Pete—and he had really wanted Pete to be the main guy." But as Rouse devoted more time to the campaign, there wasn't sufficient time for him to handle transition work as well. "So I was basically Pete's designated person on the transition efforts, and then at a certain point, Pete . . . backed out and let me handle it."[4] By spring, the transition work was in the hands of Chris Lu.

Information Gathering in the Early Obama Operation

When Chris Lu set out to gather information, he did so in a broad way. He searched for transition materials and also for people who had experience with earlier presidential transitions. Some information was public and some rested with those who kept records of transition planning they had undertaken for other presidential candidates. Lu explained the importance of casting a wide net while gathering information for a transition. The process must start early because there is so much to look for even though not all the material will be used. "No matter how much time you spend, there's never enough time. So you might as well start as early as you possibly can, and even if you know a certain percentage of the work that you do is going to be unnecessary, you might as well do more of that work rather than less and, hopefully, that increases the utility of what you're doing," Lu said.[5]

One of the difficult aspects of the information-gathering process is having a sense of the information that will be relevant at the time the transition takes place, many months after the assembling begins. "When you're trying to cover every policy issue under the sun, not only areas that we've talked about on the campaign, but just general areas we haven't talked about and what we ought to do, what the federal government's role is on different issues, who the different people you want to fill [are], there's no end in sight to all of the work you could do. So you might as well start early."[6]

In addition to starting early, gathering information means anticipating the issues that might develop into important presidential concerns and focusing on ones that are currently under discussion. Lu talked about the financial collapse and the difficulty of planning to handle that issue several months out. "If we were to redo the 2008 transition, we would have had a hundred people working on economic plans and job creation messages on day one. . . . Whether it's different tax cuts that might spur the economy, whether it's a big job program, but we just didn't know that's the world we'd be in. . . . All you can do is cover everything and then hope that something sticks."[7]

In the spring and early summer, Lu read all transition materials available from earlier administrations as well as public government materials and academic studies. Some of the materials he received came from former vice president Al Gore (2000) and Senator John Kerry (2004) transition operations. In the latter transition effort, Jim Johnson, who was the transition director for Kerry, gathered and organized the information. Lu read those materials as well as articles and books on past transitions. "There was not a long time that was pre-Podesta. And, during that time it was basically just me talking to as many people as I could, and me talking to David McKean [co-chair of the Kerry transition], Alexis Herman [co-chair of the Kerry transition], and to Jim Johnson, talking to Harrison [Wellford], talking to a lot of the good government groups on the outside, just pulling together as much information as I possibly could for John [Podesta]," said Lu.[8] Johnson and McKean led the 2004 Kerry transition effort. Harrison Wellford, who was one of the leaders of the Carter transition out of office, handled the White House staff structure piece for the Kerry transition. He did the same for the early Obama effort working with a PowerPoint presentation he had developed for Senator Kerry in 2004 and updated in June and early July 2008.

The work the Obama transition team did in the early months was similar in some ways to what the George W. Bush operation did in 1999 and 2000. The Obama operation, however, started perhaps six months later than the Bush team did for the 2000 election. For the Bush preparations, Governor Bush tasked Clay Johnson with transition planning in late spring 1999. According to Johnson, Bush instructed him as follows: "As we focus on this campaign, I want you to figure out what we do after November 7 or 8 when we win, what's involved in a transition, what are we trying to accomplish, how do we organize to get it done. I suggest you talk to the likes of George Shultz and Jim Baker and read what you need to, talk to who you need to, and develop a plan. It ought to be separate from the effort required to get elected. Develop a plan for after the election."[9] Johnson gathered the names of notable people sent in and also went out and talked to people they knew in policy areas. "Then I called a lot of people in the state of Texas, in the environmental area, and said, 'Who are the prominent people in the environmental area nationally and the HHS [Health and Human Services] world, who are the well-known HHS people either from prior federal administrations or in other states who are the people of note.' . . . There was a list of about a hundred names."[10]

In the period since John Kennedy won the presidency, there were seven presidents who came into office through election and had a normal transition. Of those, Presidents Carter, Reagan, George H. W. Bush, and George W. Bush designated people to work on transition issues substantially before the party nominating conventions. It may not have worked out equally well for all of them, but they did all realize that one person needed to begin the transition work and set the course before others came in to share the growing responsibilities and the volume of work.

Campaign Policy Teams

During the campaign, there were policy committees that later morphed into early preelection transition operations. Dan Chenok, formerly a career official in OMB who served as branch chief for information policy and technology, worked on a campaign technology policy team that easily led into a pre-transition policy group dealing with the same subjects. "What made the transition so effective was that the way the campaign was architected to address policy issues from a merits perspective," Chenok said.[11] Because they were working on issues that would be relevant for governing, the move from the campaign to preparations for governing was not a difficult one. Getting together through occasional conference calls and virtual meetings, the group "came up with themes and issues that we thought were important for the campaign to know about." A benefit of the early policy groups was their recruitment of people to support the technology issues that came up in the campaign. The campaign was also organized, Chenok said, to address issues "from a community building perspective, creating support among different constituencies and communities." The very tech-savvy campaign operation attracted support from the technology community that remained as their operation changed its emphasis from campaign to pre-transition planning. They were able to take their campaign work and use it in the pre-transition period.

While the transition was closely organized once it got under way, that was not the case with the policy groups in the early phases of the campaign. They were to some extent self-starter groups that came up with recommendations. "I thought the interesting thing about the campaign is that they didn't feel the need to have control over every aspect of all of the elements of the campaign," Chenok noted. Other groups operated on their own, including ones interested in specific transition issues. A legal team was preparing executive orders so that they could come in ready to take charge. Lawyers Todd Stern and Greg Craig, veterans from the Clinton years, were most closely associated with the executive orders. The executive order rollout began the day they came into office; the first executive orders touched on ethics pledges and the closing of Guantanamo Bay prison. "There was a whole separate process that ran on that," Lu commented.[12]

Organizing and Planning for a President McCain

While the Obama operation geared up, so too did those working with Senator McCain. In the early stage of the pre-convention period, the McCain operation was low-key. The veterans working on transition and campaign issues persuaded McCain to allow people to begin work gathering information even though he was reticent. As Will Ball explained, "He permitted those of us who were working in this area . . . to go forward rather aggressively and start to make plans. He did not want to initiate it too early. . . . Through Rick Davis, his campaign manager, and Charlie Black [McCain friend and campaign advisor and a veteran of the Washington lobbying community] and others, he recognized early on that this is a complicated process, and so he permitted this activity to begin."[13]

Beginning in the early period, the McCain transition team was composed of five people who were close to the senator. They were Rick Davis; Trevor Potter, the campaign counsel; John Lehman and Will Ball, close friends of McCain and former Navy secretaries; and William Timmons, a veteran of four Republican presidential transitions. Russell Gerson, who handled personnel for the transition, was brought in at the end of June while the others were working together earlier, most of them as part of the campaign. The integration of the campaign and the transition operations were built into the way they set up their operation. That was quite different from the organizational setup of the Obama transition operation, where there were two separate campaign and transition operations following Rouse's departure to the campaign.

Senator McCain assigned the job of early information-gathering to Will Ball. A close associate and friend to McCain, Ball quietly set about to assemble materials on earlier transitions. Interestingly, the campaign and the transition operations were initially integrated through both location and personnel. The two organizations were located in the same office building in Crystal City, Virginia, a few minutes from downtown Washington. When the transition people needed to talk to the political people, it was easy to do so and in the process make certain that there were no misunderstandings between them. At the same time, though, having to organize their meetings around the availability of campaign manager Rick Davis meant that sessions were difficult to schedule.

Ball met with people who served in earlier transitions as well as those studying the patterns of transitions. "In April, I was simply gathering. I was reading your articles and going to Max's conference up in New York, and having conversations with Andy Card and Clay Johnson. . . . I was collecting information." Once the full group began meeting, they would meet "typically every two weeks," Ball said.[14] "I'd put together an agenda, we'd [go] through a list of next steps for the next phase. What our planning would focus on." Ball was one of the participants at the transition conference described in chapter 2 that Max Stier, chief executive of the Partnership for Public Service, held at Pocantico Hills sponsored by the Rockefeller Foundation.

Ball said that after the conference, "we started with the idea of developing objectives for the transition and goals. We had a concerted effort to distill the lessons learned from previous transitions and identify what some of the agreed upon mistakes had been."[15] They particularly concentrated on same-party transitions or "friendly" ones because if McCain won it would mean no change of party even though there would be significant changes in personnel.

Tapping into the Collective Memory and Knowledge of the Washington Community

Washington is a community of people with experience serving in Congress and others who work on the Hill or did so at one time, those who served in the White House and in executive branch positions, others who work in groups outside of government but are focused on the policymaking process. While there are partisan differences and during most of the stages of a transition those divisions are clear, within political parties people in the community give aid to their presidential candidates and those working for them, including the people preparing for a transition.

Some people associated with the Obama transition effort represent the institutional memory of several Democratic presidential transitions. Harrison Wellford was one of them. Senator McCain also had people on his team experienced in multiple transitions. Having worked in the Carter administration on both the transitions into and out of office, Wellford is typical of the partisan institutional memory. His specialty was the organization of the Executive Office of the President. In addition to his work on the Carter transitions, he prepared transition information for presidential candidates Walter Mondale, Bill Clinton, and John Kerry. As the person who kept preparatory transitions documents, Wellford was the go-to person for materials and recollections of participants' activities. For example, Wellford worked on the project with Jim Johnson, who ran the 2004 Kerry transition operation. "Afterwards—and it was Jim Johnson's idea—we pulled together all the material that we had done, volumes and volumes of it, and organized it so that it would be available the next time around. And when Jim met with Obama, he took all the stuff out there."[16] Chris Lu said that he received the materials in late May or early June.[17]

Wellford's role was to take the 2004 materials on the Executive Office of the President (EOP) and update them, taking into account organizational developments in the EOP. "And what I had done is that we gave him all of the Kerry material as it had been produced, and then what I did was to do an overview memo . . . that drew on that material but then adjusted it to the current [EOP organizational structure]." After his meetings on the 2004 materials and his updates to them, "we would get through Chris and to some degree through [Tom] Daschle, and then, until his problems, Jim Johnson." Following those discussions, "we would get follow-up questions from Obama. . . . We would do additional memorandums in response to that."[18] Chris Lu said of Wellford: "Harrison is another one of these folks who has such incredible institutional memory about transition, so he was a valuable asset." Wellford was also involved in early Obama team discussions with the General Services Administration. "And then Harrison did a lot of outside consulting with John Podesta on a variety of issues," said Lu.[19] Wellford did the latter work during the second and third transition stages.

In addition to the work that Wellford was undertaking on the organizational structure of an Obama administration, he also participated in a regular one-hour meeting of several Washington hands that was led by former Senate Majority Leader Tom Daschle. "There was a meeting every two weeks that Daschle chaired, sort of a Washington strategy meeting. . . . It was basically to get a report from the key people on the campaign about what was going on and then to answer Washington's related issue that came up and then to do troubleshooting for the campaign when they needed us to do it. And that was clearly a Tom Daschle show." The kinds of issues they got involved in were "mainly political issues; questions, for example, whether or not the farm state senators had a misinterpretation of something Obama said in a speech. Could you go get that fixed? . . . There was somebody at the meeting could quickly get in touch with whoever was the right reference point on any issue that came up."[20]

Questions did come out of the meetings that dealt with governing matters. Wellford explained some of the issues he was asked to work on: "And from time to time we got other requests for information; or somebody's speaking for him. Some . . . staffer of his that was working someplace else would call us up and ask for help. . . . They would be things that were sort of out of the mainstream sometimes, like questions about contracting out and how you stop the outgoing administration from burrowing in and questions about regulatory freezes." These were questions important for transition preparations and came throughout the period when the Daschle sessions were regularly taking place. These meetings took place during the spring and summer until John Podesta came on board as the leader of the transition effort. The meeting size varied depending on whether a session was before of after Senator Clinton dropped out of the presidential race. The early meetings had under ten people but after June 7, when she ended her candidacy, the group reached numbers as high as forty. It was important to bring in those Democrats even if they had opposed Senator Obama. "Then there was an effort pretty soon after that to reach out to the Hillary people and bring them in," Wellford commented. The atmosphere of the meetings inevitably changed. "That changed the whole nature of the group. From then on it was not quite the same, because you had sitting around the table people that you were fighting against just the other day."[21] The membership also shifted depending on who was available at meeting times. Members of Congress participated in the sessions—Senator Kerry, for example—and their schedules could be election-dependent.

Daschle's advantage in holding such a meeting was that he was a natural coordinating point for the Chicago and Washington people. He was tied to both the Obama campaign and transition people and had information on the happenings in many segments of the Washington community. "Daschle was the most influential sort of all-purpose Washington advisor," Wellford said. "He had more of his people in key positions than anybody. . . . His people were all over the campaign and then later all of the transition."[22] Having coordinating mechanisms that bring together campaign and transition people is important because of the problems that can develop if there is little contact between the two organizations. Coordinating with those in the Washington community is an important aspect of building on the knowledge of others. Candidates need a transition operation that begins early but is in regular contact with the political operation and with the candidate. Competition between the campaign and early transition operations can derail early transition work and build in a kind of competition the candidate will want to make certain to avoid. The one recent operation where an early transition operation worked cooperatively with the campaign was that of President George W. Bush.[23]

Stage Two: Presumptive Major-Party Candidates Set Up Their Organizations

Major organizational and policy transition work in 2008 started after the June 7 declaration by Senator Clinton that she was no longer a presidential candidate. Her exit had a substantial impact on the transition-building efforts of Senator Obama because it signaled that he was now the presumptive Democratic candidate for president. Senator McCain reached that point in the Republican party on March 4 with his accumulation of the necessary delegates pledged to support him at the party nominating convention.

The second stage ran until early September following the conclusion of both presidential nominating conventions. During the months from June to September, the relevant government agencies and the candidates established their relationships and lines of communications with one another and the candidates' staffs gathered more information on what preparations they would need to make following a win on election night and what help they could expect from government.

The major work during this period for government agencies and officials is letting the candidates know where the government is involved in transition operations and then encouraging the candidates to plan. During this period, the candidates must work on shaping their organization operations with separate groups considering executive branch appointments, policy initiatives and priorities, and then beginning to assemble agency review teams to assess ongoing government programs and operations. Both candidates had active operations prior to the conventions at the end of the summer.

In part, the decisions by both camps to begin transition work prior to the major-party nominating conventions grew out of necessity. Government agencies wanted to meet informally with representatives of the two candidates in order to explain to them what their roles would be. The federal government agencies featured in chapter 2 began their work with representatives of the two candidates once the two presumptive candidates were set. The General Services Administration controls decisions on the location of the government transition headquarters and then tailors the office design to one preferred by each candidate. By informing the candidates at an early point of decisions they will be required to make for a transition, GSA can get a jump on the process. The Office of Government Ethics can give candidates early warnings about the ethics process and how it works. Knowing the rules makes it easier to develop a recruitment and appointments process for nominees for executive branch positions. The White House put pressure on the candidates to name representatives to work with officials there to develop a solid early appointments process as well as to get started on the security clearing of transition workers.

John Podesta's Corporate Style

The exit of Senator Clinton from the presidential race made a great deal of difference to the organization of the Obama transition operation. Many people who supported her came over to the Obama operation to help the presumptive nominee organize for governing. One of the most important people to make that move was John Podesta. In July he came in to run the transition as part of a three-person group that included him, Valerie Jarrett, and Pete Rouse. Lu took the position of executive director and became the daily contact with the Bush White House on transition issues.

In commenting on the Obama transition operation, Joshua Bolten observed that the seeds of success in the Obama transition organization lay in its corporate rather than family structure. "Obama's campaign was corporate by the end. . . . To take somebody like Podesta who had been Clinton's chief of staff and . . . had a good relationship with Obama but not a family member, and to basically subcontract to him."[24] It worked well because Podesta brought to the transition the resources of a cadre of people with experience appropriate to transition and governing tasks as well as the financial resources to fund his own operation during the early months before government funding begins. As the founder and head of the Center for American Progress, Podesta had a wealth of resources to draw on as he prepared for his transition role. The organization has 180 employees and a yearly budget of $25 million.[25] Founded in 2003, the organization has almost daily presentations of experts and practitioners on domestic and foreign policy and national security issues.

Through the Center's many sessions, Podesta got to know the talents and interests of a broad range of people in a variety of policy circles. He estimated that by late spring 2009, approximately forty people from the Center had gotten jobs in the Obama administration.[26] When Senator Obama brought Podesta to his team after Hillary Clinton left the race, he welcomed an advisor with experience building an organization and with a reputation around Washington as an effective person who knows how to make things work. In commenting on Podesta and Bolten, Steve Hadley observed: "They're both very substantive, and they're kind of low-key. They've got their egos in line."[27] That style worked well for Podesta in the transition and for Obama, because his transition chief kept out of the limelight and focused on the tasks of preparing to govern.

Part of the reason the Podesta operation worked well was that he was not a member of the coterie of aides around the candidate, nor did he want a job in an Obama administration. Chris Lu indicated the Obama transition operation was mindful of the need to staff the transition with people who were not angling for a job in the coming administration: "You don't want them jockeying for their future jobs, so we looked for people who either didn't have a vested interest in who was going to staff certain jobs or could be seen as honest brokers. . . . In many ways, that was the perfect pick, because John Podesta made clear fairly early on that he had no desire to go into the administration, at least at the outset, so people saw John as an honest broker."[28] These were lessons learned through the experiences of those serving in earlier transitions and administrations and reinforced in the writings of Clay Johnson.

The agency review team operation was in a formative stage during the pretransition period. Lisa Brown began work as one of the organizers of the agency review team operation. The groups worked with the administration gathering basic information about the agencies. Chenok, who served on the OMB and technology review teams, discussed their work. "We wanted to create a record that they [the postelection agency review team] could pick up so that they wouldn't have to create that record on their own," he said.[29] They prepared short pieces on the basics of the agencies, such as what the duties of the agencies are and how processes work. "It was more to create a record so that the transition team and people coming in wouldn't have to . . . say 'How do I do this?'" They gathered information on what past administrations had done in the early months and a timeline of when they took particular actions.

Once there were presumptive major-party candidates, others were informally involved in early behind-the-scenes preparations for the candidates. The General Services Administration had its transition website up that those working on the preparations for the candidates could use to gather information. Additionally, officials from GSA and the Office of Government Ethics met with people dealing with the Obama and McCain operations so that those working for the two candidates would know what information they needed to gather and what to expect from their agencies once they were formally candidates and began thinking about their appointments.

John McCain's Transition Operation

As an operation of six people, the McCain operation was small. Joshua Bolten observed that whereas the Obama operation was characterized by its corporate structure, the McCain operation had a family feel to it, with many decisions closely held.

John McCain had a group of six people handling transition issues, two of whom were also central people in the campaign operation. Rick Davis and Trevor Potter served as the campaign manager and campaign counsel, respectively. Trying to work meetings around their schedule was not easy, especially in the fall. Two of the six, John Lehman, former Navy secretary and 9/11 Commission member, and Russell Gerson, who has a professional personnel search firm in New York, were based in New York and were not in Washington full-time. Will Ball was based in Washington, as was William Timmons, a lobbyist with strong ties in the Washington community. Joshua Bolten discussed the differences in dealing with the two organizations: "I invited both campaigns to send a transition designee and the Obama camp seemed much more organized. . . . They had groups and sub-groups and the desk in charge who knew everything. The McCain campaign was a little slower on the uptake and was a little more ambiguous about who was actually in charge."[30] Ball represented the McCain transition operation in meetings at the White House and the Department of Justice, but there was no publicly designated leader among the transition group board members.

In the early stage of the pre-convention period, the McCain operation was low-key. The veterans working on transition and campaign issues persuaded McCain to allow people to begin work gathering information, although he was reticent to do so. Ball explained the start up of the operation: "He permitted those of us who were working in this area . . . to go forward rather aggressively and start to make plans. He did not want to initiate it too early. . . . Through Rick Davis, his campaign manager, and Charlie Black [McCain friend, campaign advisor and a veteran of the Washington lobbying community] and others, he recognized early on that this is a complicated process, and so he permitted this activity to begin."[31] Ball spent April and part of May gathering information reading about past transitions and having conversations with people such as Andy Card, former chief of staff under President Bush, and Clay Johnson as well as others in the Washington governing community. As summer began, he met with Davis and Russ Gerson, who was handling the personnel search, to discuss transition preparations.

Stage Three: Transition Operations after the Convention

President Obama's transition planning operation brought together people knowledgeable about and experienced in government operations and policy as well as those who knew the candidate well. The operation had a well-organized process for gathering information and making decisions. It had a personnel operation that brought in people with expertise and a background in government service. The transition board, the agency review teams, and the policy teams during the transition successfully brought together people, process, and policy as the Obama teams gathered information on department and agency operations and prepared to govern. The policy teams prepared initiatives for the new administration-in-waiting to share with the Democratic congressional leadership, such as the economic stimulus bill, state children's health insurance, and the Lilly Ledbetter Fair Pay Act. The transition teams also prepared executive action for the president to set the tone of an active chief executive swiftly and decisively moving in a different policy direction from his predecessor.

Transition and Campaign Operations

While the McCain transition operation was entwined with the McCain campaign, such was not the case with the Obama operation. "We very much separated the work of the campaign from the work of the transition," said Lu. "If there was an hour of time that the senator could spend either on planning the transition or helping to win the election, we wanted him to win the election. So we very carefully did not put our campaign people onto the transition, and they were actually sort of cordoned off from it."[32] With two separate operations, there was a need for a person who could coordinate them at least as far as letting each know what the other was doing. Pete Rouse took on that role. "Pete has always been seen as an honest broker on things, and Pete was really the conduit of information back and forth," said Lu.[33]

There was overlap with campaign policy people when the transition operation needed names of appropriate policy experts. "I had worked closely with our campaign policy director, Heather Higginbottom, so when I wanted to say, 'We're looking for somebody to help us on education policy to balance out the team, who would you suggest?' she would give me names of people she thought were good who the campaign wasn't using. . . . I think the communications people were coordinating to some extent." There was crossover on scheduling as well, Lu said. "We did not want to take up Obama's time in the last . . . month or so. . . . And in retrospect it obviously was the right decision."[34]

Creating Agency Review Teams

One of the most important transition preparations undertaken in the pre-convention period is setting up agency review teams. These are groups made up of policy specialists and former government employees who know the department and some outsiders who have dealt with the agencies and departments being studied. The groups explore the elements of the organization, its programs, and its people.

Transition operations are confronted with the decision of whether to create task forces to deal with government policies and programs and then how to compose them, for instance to decide how many people they should include. Task forces have a somewhat rocky history because they are difficult to control and and because the quality of their studies has varied. The Reagan transition organization had forty-eight task force operations that proved to be of less value than originally envisioned. In his study of presidential transitions, John Burke commented on the problems resulting from the work of the Reagan teams: "Some veterans of past administrations were particularly unhappy with the work of their assigned team, including Caspar Weinberger, Terrell Bell, and Alexander Haig. The relationship of transition teams to the independent regulatory agencies was especially rocky."[35] The George W. Bush transition eschewed larger task forces composed of lobbyists or those seeking appointments in the administration. Instead it opted for "small teams to prepare briefing books for, and interact with, each cabinet department" said Clay Johnson. Once the transition was under way, Johnson said that they created "large advisory groups and let them advise the department policy teams as they saw fit but did not let them interface directly with the departments."[36] They did not have the same difficulties directing the groups as the Reagan transition operation did with their larger operation.

The Obama transition operation planned early for extensive agency review teams and set them up early. There were two stages to the agency review process, said Lisa Brown, who coordinated the process: (1) preelection collection of publicly available information, and (2) postelection official transition visits to the agencies, all aimed at compiling the information that would enable the president and his cabinet to begin actively governing immediately after the inauguration.

The postelection agency review teams received memoranda that were prepared before the election. "We were very clear to the teams going in—first of all, to the teams preelection—here's what we want from you that you can hand to the team that will be going into the agency so that they have X information," Brown said. "Here's a template that lays out how we want you to focus your work: What are the strategic priorities/opportunities for the agency, and what are the key issues that are going to be coming down the pike—legislative, regulatory, litigation, budgetary, and personnel."[37]

Brown continued, "The work of the Obama agency review preparation team began in late August, and by very early September we . . . had our templates ready for . . . folks to use. . . . The real work started in early September. That August we spent putting together the teams of people (with some additions thereafter). So you had essentially two months to put together information that would prepare the agency review teams to go into the agencies quickly and effectively after the election."[38]

The teams had information ready for the larger agency review teams that would go into the departments and agencies. For the Obama team setting up the agency review teams, "the first real deadline for everybody was to compile information on agencies to be ready on Election Day," Brown said.[39] Looking for information on agencies "involved collecting publicly available information, and relying on people who were knowledgeable about the agencies." These were people who had a mix of experiences. Some of them had worked there before, though they did not bring in people if they "were appearing before an agency in some way."[40]

The Obama team developed a pledge they had ready for those coming in to serve on any of their policy and review boards. Anyone working for the transition operation had to sign a pledge that included these main components: "I will disqualify myself from involvement in any particular Obama Transition Project matter which to my knowledge may directly conflict with a financial interest of an immediate family member, partner, client, or other individual or organization with which I have had a business relationship within the past 12 months." In addition to disqualifying themselves for working in the Obama transition for a conflict of interest involving business relationships, participants had to be free of any relationships with interest groups where they lobbied government. The pledge provided: "I will disqualify myself from involvement in any particular transition matter if I have engaged in regulated lobbying activities with respect to such matter, as defined by the Lobbying Disclosure Act, within the previous 12 months."[41]

In peopling the agency teams, they were very selective. "We didn't take random people and assign them to an agency. We chose very carefully a group of educated people so that they came in ready," Brown said. "The group that came in was very knowledgeable to start with about what the issues were, what the agency was dealing with, and so I think that . . . probably made a big difference, too, in terms of helping to inform [people using the materials]." In the first part of their reviews, they used only materials that were publicly available. Then they collected information on people knowledgeable of agency operations. "One of the things we asked the agency review teams to do was identify people that should be spoken to very soon after the election," she said. They looked for people on the Hill and others to form a small group that could be helpful after the election: "The teams were considerably smaller preelection. They got bigger as they actually went into agencies."[42] Before the election, those working on the small agency review teams did not contact anyone, opting instead to wait until the election results were in.

The preelection agency review information was important for more than merely informing those who were going into the agencies and departments as administration appointees. They provided significant information for President-elect Obama as he prepared to govern. As part of their preparations for governing, the group provided Obama with information he could go through on his trip to Hawaii to see his grandmother, who would die less than ten days later. "We gave him two-pagers for that trip. We were asked to make sure that we had them . . . because that was when they were . . . making some personnel decisions," Lisa Brown said.[43] Knowing what the agency functions were was an important component in figuring out which person to choose for what job. On the same trip, Obama had material on White House staff and what the functions were of the various offices and how people in the past had organized the White House.[44]

McCain Organization Focused on Personnel

The McCain transition operation focused on the transition budget and on developing the personnel list. Late in June, Rick Davis and Senator McCain recruited their personnel chief, Russell Gerson. Gerson heads his own New York personnel recruitment firm, The Gerson Group. He spoke with Reagan transition personnel chief and professional recruiter Pendleton James, who told him that before he accepted the job, he needed to commit himself to the job well into the administration. "The first thing he said to me [was], 'Russ, you understand that basically you have just given up your life for the next eighteen months. Assuming he wins,'" he noted. "He took me through all of the work that he had done, and one of the things that was impressive about the Reagan transition personnel [operation] is, they started in January," Gerson recounted.[45] Gerson came to Washington two days a week and on weekends and assembled a team of outside experts in seven different policy areas who could develop a list of possible job candidates.

The personnel operation focused on building a database of possible nominees.

Ball recounted, "Russ Gerson came down from New York each week and pulled together a team of volunteers." Ball explained that as Gerson shaped the team gathering names for personnel suggestions, Senator McCain encouraged him to search broadly. McCain said to "pull people in from beyond the beltway . . . who would have some fresh ideas, and who were leaders in their respective fields, and who could help . . . develop a broad-based list."[46] That was in June or July, Ball said.

Most of the McCain transition volunteers were not professional personnel search experts but rather professionals who knew policy. Some were close friends of Senator McCain. "We had a woman from the faculty of Yale medical school, who was an M.D., who led our health group. We had financial [people] from New York, and one from Texas. We broke it down by different disciplines," Ball said. McCain also tapped some old friends, Ball added. The team "had a retired admiral [from] Florida, who came to help with the Defense Department, who Senator McCain had known years ago. So it was an eclectic mix."[47] Ball said the guidance given to him and Gerson was "to identify people without ties to Washington to be the initiators of this process in compiling prospective [candidates for nomination]. . . . This was to simply compile a list of prospects." They never advanced to the next step of calling people and asking if they would be willing to serve.

McCain's team prepared to submit a budget consistent with the candidate's campaign agenda. Ball pointed out that the transition would have been different from a Bush-to-Obama transition: "In our case, had we won, it would have been a same-party to same-party transition. . . . Clay [Johnson] had done a pretty good job of laying out the objectives and goals [for the internal administration transition]. We tried to focus on the policy side and the budget side, specifically getting a budget team together that would anticipate the fact that this budget process was so front-loaded."[48] They also had a team that worked on the federal budget. Ball was referring to the fact that within his first month in office, a president has to submit a preliminary budget to Congress, which is followed later by a more complete document.

The transition group worked on schedules and goals. "And so we had a similar budget group assembled," said Ball. "So personnel, budget, planning in the broader sense, goals and objectives, we would discuss, and a timetable. We'd . . . take a timetable and break it out into phase one, phase two, phase three, with . . . pre-convention planning, which was, for lack of a better term, fairly covert, it was underground, so to speak." The periods broke down for them in this way after the pre-convention period: "Then convention to Election Day was a much broader effort, involving more people and more engagement with our broader personnel team and policy teams. And then, Election Day in Phoenix, we had our [three] books ready and our plans ready."[49]

The meeting schedule for the group of six was dominated by the need for at least two of the participants, Rick Davis and Trevor Potter, to put their attention on their campaign responsibilities "We tried to meet every week. . . . But as a practical matter, since Rick Davis was integral to this process and he was the campaign manager, we couldn't nail that down every week." With John Lehman and Russ Gerson in New York for much of the week, the group needed to convene via a weekly conference call through August and September rather than in person. "In October, we started trying to meet every week. And then down the home stretch of the campaign, we pretty much had our plans ready. The last two weeks of October, we had a lot of communication, but we didn't have any meetings."[50]

It was during this period that Senator McCain assembled his group of people tasked with transition preparations. For most of the transition team members, working on transition issues meant adding tasks to the work they were already doing for McCain. Rick Davis was already serving as campaign manager and Trevor Potter as the campaign lawyer, while John Lehman and Will Ball, both former Navy secretaries and longtime friends, served as advisors. As we saw, Ball began his work gathering transition information in May.

Stage Four: After the Election

Incoming presidents have an opportunity to establish their agenda early in their term, but this requires that the president integrate his campaign policy priorities with a knowledge of the world he is about to enter.

Bringing the Transition and the Campaign Teams Together

Once Obama won the election, then the campaign people who had focused on the election goal came into the transition operation. "A lot of our planning got changed from November 4th to November 5th. We largely hadn't talked to people on the campaign before we did any of these things, and then once we won, we then had those conversations," Lu said.[51] "People like [campaign spokesman] Robert Gibbs, [campaign strategist] David Axelrod, who we largely had not interacted with at all during the transition, had very strong ideas on what we should do." Once the campaign people got into the transition and went through the recommendations, there were changes: "There was probably a mixing of ideas, and so I'm sure we used a lot of stuff that had been preplanned. A lot of it was changed based on the input of people who had been on the campaign."[52]

As executive director of the transition, Chris Lu stayed in Washington during the campaign. "John [Podesta] had conversations with Senator Obama every single week, a short call . . . where they discussed things, but we largely didn't want to take up the candidate's time at all." After the campaign, Lu was in Washington while the president-elect spent most of his time in Chicago. "The first month was just meeting after meeting with Podesta, Rahm [Emanuel], president-elect, vice president-elect [Joe Biden], and a couple other people. . . . There were mostly personnel-related meetings. Rahm initially did not get involved really in the transition. . . . There came a point at which John started passing more of that stuff off to Rahm."[53]

In most presidential transitions, after Election Day the campaign team worries about missing an opening to get a Washington job with the new president. The Obama team sought to allay the fears of campaign staff members. Lu recounted: "There were a good number of folks on the campaign who just needed some time off and didn't want to help on the transition. . . . The message was sent to them that, 'Look, if you take time off, this is not going to disadvantage you in getting a job,' and it didn't, because lots of folks that didn't participate in the transition got wonderful jobs." At the same time, the senior people on the campaign wanted to participate in the transition. "I think virtually every senior-level person who wanted to participate had a chance to participate. And Pete Rouse was the main person helping to facilitate that."

Handling the Unanticipated

In a transition, it is wise to start up early because, though they will differ in size and complexity, there will always be unanticipated obstacles in the road that will slow down a presidential candidate's progress or divert his path. He can count on personnel selections going sour and organizational structures requiring adjustments. In the 2008 transition, there were diversions that impacted both the personnel and policy areas.

The first crucial decision a candidate has to make in assembling a transition operation is pulling together the people to direct it. Early in the transition preparation process, Senator Obama had to deal with the unanticipated when the person who was prepared to lead the transition had to bow out. Jim Johnson, who had run Senator Kerry's 2004 transition operation, ran into difficulties over questions raised about a favorable below-market mortgage rate he received from Countrywide Financial CEO Angelo Mozillo. Countrywide Financial was a major player in the sub-prime mortgage crisis, which was still a live issue at the time. He bowed out of the early planning, although he did provide materials from Senator Kerry's 2004 transition preparations.

For President-elect Obama, the most significant work he had to do during the postelection period was to focus on the financial crisis and see possible responses in the period before he took office to stabilize the situation and get up to speed on what he would need to do and what positions he would have to fill once he came into office. The priorities they may have established at an earlier time were no longer at the top of the priority list. "No matter what the promises we made were, a lot of that was turned on its head by the fall of 2008 when we had the financial crisis," Lu said. "When you're in the middle of the greatest downturn since the Great Depression, whatever else you said you were going to do, you now have to focus on the economy."[54] The new team also encountered other unanticipated issues, as they entered office with "a nuclear crisis in North Korea and a Supreme Court vacancy," Lu said.[55] As Dan Pfeiffer, deputy in the Office of Communications, observed without risk of overstatement: "There was a lot on our plate."[56]

One of the most important ways President-elect Obama kept up to date on unanticipated events was through briefings. During the time between the election and the inauguration, President-elect Obama got his information from principals handling particular issues for the George W. Bush administration. Ed Gillespie, counselor to President Bush, wanted this to be a time when they would provide the incoming team with information about the important crises they were facing. President Bush sought to "make sure—and especially because we are at war—and then with the economic crisis in the financial markets, that we had domestic policy concerns that we knew this next president was going to have to confront, that we make sure that they are able to fulfill the responsibilities of the executive branch from the moment the president takes office, regardless of party, and that was ingrained in us here."[57]

Briefings with cabinet officers were the key way to keep President-elect Obama up to date. In the foreign policy area, Secretary of State Condoleezza Rice led briefings. "There was a lot going on. We were trying, for example, to get the war in Gaza over before President Obama came in, and Condi briefed President-elect Obama on that issue fairly frequently. And on some other foreign policy issues as well." That was not the only issue on which he received briefings from cabinet officers, though not from the president. "Hank Paulson was briefing President-elect Obama on the financial crisis. But I think the number of times that the two presidents talked was very few," Hadley said.[58] Most of these briefings with the president-elect were by phone.

Prior to the election briefings were "largely to be done through staff people. Joel Kaplan [deputy chief of staff] had a counterpart in each campaign that he would communicate with," said Hadley. "I would talk to Randy Scheunemann [McCain's foreign policy advisor], and I would talk to the current deputy national security advisor [Denis McDonough]. When there was a specific issue that came up, a candidate might get in touch with a White House person. Senator McCain, for example, called NSC advisor Hadley to discuss the leadership crisis in Georgia. Hadley said that most often he talked with representatives of the two candidates: "I talked with him [McCain] on Georgia [formerly part of Russia], but I continued to work through Randy, and I continued to work through Denis McDonough. I never talked to candidate Obama. I never talked to President-elect Obama. Secretary of State Rice did that because she knew him. . . . He was on the Foreign Relations Committee, and he actually voted to confirm her, which she thought showed a lot of courage."[59]

The Financial Crisis

While there is a long-held rule that there is only one president at a time, the 2008 transition demonstrated a need for some modifications to that view. The financial crisis came up late in the presidential campaign and required immediate action. That was something President Bush understood, and so too did President-elect Obama as well as the congressional leadership. Dan Pfeiffer, who worked on the Obama campaign and the transition and then came into the White House as a part of the communications operation, noted how quickly they had to move into governing. "We didn't really get to transition because we were in a quasi-governing mode almost from the moment we got there. You know, when we tried to pass the Recovery Act, and auto companies are failing, and the markets were crashing, the American people were looking to the next President and not the current President for guidance," Pfeiffer said.[60] "So we jumped in." "Jumping in" meant gathering information and taking action.

Initially, they had decisions they needed to make and issues that needed the attention of the president-elect. Learning the dimensions of the financial crisis was made easier by the access the Bush administration people gave them to information and to people. Additionally, the Bush people brought the president-elect and his team into many crucial decisions. "John Podesta did an amazing job and queued up all the necessary decisions," commented Chris Lu. "That was incredibly important, because this transition was unique in so many ways." In such an environment, "the last thing he [Obama] wanted to think about was all the day-in and day-out stuff with the transition, and he didn't have to," Lu commented. "That was one of the advantages of having a very smooth transition. . . . [Obama] obviously had more important issues on his plate."[61]

The financial crisis provided a window into areas where an incoming president and his team are involved in governing decisions. Treasury Secretary Henry Paulson spoke regularly with both presidential candidates: "I would, in fact, get to know Obama better over the course of the fall, speaking to him frequently, sometimes several times a day."[62] For the auto bailout, the Bush White House was most interested in making certain that there would be stability. We saw in chapter 3 the difficulties inherent in trying to have the outgoing and incoming administrations work together to decide issues. The sitting administration, for example, wanted to work together with the incoming one on naming an auto czar. The problem in such situations is the perception that once an incoming team agrees to joint action, they own not only the decision but any problems related to it.

Effective Governmental Relationships

One of the interesting aspects of a transition into governing is establishing relationships that will serve the president and his team. In the case of the Obama transition, there were some interesting relationships that had to be worked out among the branches of government. Members of Congress, the vice president, and members of the White House staff have to work out their relationships with the president after the election and once they come into office as well.

One of the first relationships requiring definition is the one between the president and vice president. On the campaign trail, the role of the vice-presidential candidate is pretty much at the will of the president and his campaign team, who decide where his presence would be the most useful and when they need him at a particular location. They work off of his strengths and the needs of the campaign. Once the president wins and considers his own roles, the role (or roles) of the vice president need to be hammered out. In practice, whatever commitments they make are not written down. Instead, their agreements are more in the form of tacit understandings than legal commitments.

In Vice President Biden's case, he discussed his roles with the president in terms of his preference in his approach to his job and then where he saw himself fitting in the national security area. Ted Kaufman, his chief of staff during his Senate career and then his successor in the Delaware Senate seat, spoke of Biden's discussion with President-elect Obama. Kaufman said Biden talked to former vice presidents and "essentially said there are two kinds of models. . . . There's the portfolio model. . . . He didn't want a portfolio."

Instead of taking a whole policy area to be his domain, as Vice President Gore had done with executive reorganization initiatives in the Clinton years, what Biden was interested in was working on individual projects. "What he wanted to do is work on a project, get it done, look around for what is the best use of his time and move onto the next project."[63] Biden has worked on a variety of projects through the six years of the administration, beginning with Iraq and the American Recovery Act.

Vice President Biden also wanted to be the last person in the room, to put himself in a position to give the president his views. Kaufman said, "The single most important thing he wanted out of being vice president was . . . he said, 'Look, I'm coming here. I'm willing to help any way I can. What I really want to do is be able to be the last person in the room. I'm not saying you have to listen to me or anything else, but I want to be the person at the end that you talk to.'"[64] Kaufman continued on Biden's biggest role: "On all these important decisions, at the end, the president says to him, 'Joe, what do you think?' And he tells him. And the president makes his decision. And that's the big thing." Biden got what he wanted there as well. While it would seem to be a given that a vice president would be in the room when decisions are made, it is not always the case. When Lyndon Johnson served as vice president, he had little role in policy decisions and their implementation. Johnson biographer Robert Caro detailed a very minimal role for the vice president, even in matters relating to the Senate.[65]

Former vice president Cheney's shadow came up in more than one way as the new team sought to establish their relationships within the White House and on the Hill. "Vice President Biden wasn't interested in making the vice president's office into what Cheney had. He said that right at the beginning," Kaufman said. Biden saw a difference in his organizational role and that of Vice President Cheney. In national security operations, Kaufman said that Biden told the president: "I don't want to have our national security staff and your national security staff . . . the way Cheney had it. I want one national security staff, and as long as you promise me that my people can go be involved . . . as long as I am getting the paperwork and what's going on, then we're just going to have one national security staff."[66]

Another area where Cheney came up as a model for government relationships was for the vice president's role in Senate party meetings. Vice President Cheney regularly attended the Republican caucus meetings for the Senate and the House. In early December, Majority Leader Harry Reid had an interview with a reporter from the *Las Vegas Sun* who asked the Senate leader whether Biden would be invited to weekly Senate Democratic caucus meetings as Cheney had with his caucus during his years as vice president. Reid's answer: "Absolutely not."[67] When asked about the vice president's role in Senate meetings, his spokeswoman Elizabeth Alexander stated: "Vice President-elect Biden had no intention of continuing the practice started by Vice President Cheney of regularly attending internal legislative branch meetings—he firmly believes in restoring the Office of the Vice President to its historical role. He and Senator Reid see eye to eye on this."[68]

With the depth of the financial crisis, Reid adjusted his meeting rules to accommodate the need of Senate Democrats to hear from President-elect Obama's senior advisors who were coming into the administration. As toxic as Democrats regarded the Cheney model to be, the vice president was well received among Republicans when George W. Bush was declared president-elect. One of the early Bush initiatives of the transition team was to work on their relations with Congress and with those they chose to be cabinet secretaries. "Everybody talks about the importance of reaching out to the Congress," observed Clay Johnson, executive director of the Bush transition.

> We use the phrase a lot, "Doing it *with* them, not *to* them," doing it *with* Congress, not *to* Congress and doing it *with* the subcabinet, *with* the cabinet secretary, doing it *with* them, not *to* them. That general theme, I think, is an important one during a transition. I would suggest that nobody had more credibility with the Hill than Dick Cheney. So as the Congress is all concerned about who these new people are, no one was better suited to be the administration's senior person on the ground in the Washington area than Dick Cheney. . . . And then Dave Gribbin came in and set up the legislative affairs operation very quickly. So getting connected with all the Republican leadership, the congressional leadership was overseen by Dick and he did it very, very well. So we didn't have unnecessary fights to pick or unnecessary credibility problems to deal with because of who he was and how involved he was in the transition.[69]

Senator Biden came into the vice presidency with a great deal of goodwill and respect in the Senate chamber that worked to the benefit of the administration. The extent of his importance to the president and his administration was signaled by discussions of the stimulus bill. Ted Kaufman, who was the director of Biden's transition and later took his place in the Senate, told of the support the stimulus bill received as a result of Biden's presence in the administration. "We'll go for it as long as Joe is in charge," was a sentiment Kaufman heard from several senators.[70] They told him that with Biden in charge, "This is going to work right. We're going to have transparency. We're going to do this right." So they told Kaufman, "We'll vote for it, but we got to know . . . Joe is going to be in charge of this thing." Kaufman continued: "That's the reason, primarily, why the president assigned him the stimulus bill. It was part of the deal with the senators that signed on to it."

A president either establishes good relationships early on or pays dearly later when there is no support from the Washington community for administration proposals. President Carter never had the Washington relations that are so important for developing support for a president among those in the governing community, and it meant he did not have a bench of supporters known to the Washington community who could attest to the worthiness of his actions and plans.

One of the reasons that putting a great deal of emphasis on the Congress is so important during the transition is that presidents spend far more time than they anticipate dealing with members of Congress. The way needs to be prepared during the transition.

The Transition Board, Agency Review Teams, and Policy Working Groups

Presidential candidates have followed a variety of patterns in organizing their official transitions after Election Day. A transition operation has to decide on a central organization to guide the preparations for governing. "One of the things that we did very early on after John Podesta came on was to sit down and figure out how we wanted to organize the transition," Lu said.[71] John Kerry, for example, used three people who formed a board that together served as co-chairs. In the Obama transition, there was also a board with three co-chairs, each of whom represented three important facets of Obama's political persona. Valerie Jarrett is the close friend from Chicago, Pete Rouse his trusted mastermind from the Senate, and John Podesta the wise survivor of the Clinton years who could navigate Washington and the three branches of government.

Lu described the transition leadership operation of twenty-eight that included the three co-chairs John Podesta, Valerie Jarrett, and Pete Rouse, which had twelve advisory board members active in the operation and a senior staff of thirteen members. The team's senior staff members later came into the administration, all but three of them in the White House. This was the group that provided direction to the transition operation and its policy work. "Each person was in charge of a certain [policy] area, and they would manage that part on a day-to-day basis." During the campaign period, Lu described how they worked: "And then we would have board meetings . . . report on what was going on." After the election, however, the pace stepped up and the group "met multiple times a day."[72] John Podesta chaired these sessions. The structure brought together people from Barack Obama's political career, those who had long experience in government, and a few who were new to governing. "There were a lot of folks who came out of

TABLE 4.1
Policy Areas and Composition of Policy Working Groups

Policy working groups	Leaders	Members	Total
Economic	1	10	11
Education	1	12	13
Energy and environment	1	9	10
Health care	1	11	12
Immigration	2	8	10
National security	2	41	43
Technology, innovation, and government reform	3	32	35
Total positions	11	123	134

Source: Office of the President-elect, "Policy Working Groups."

'Obama World': people like myself, . . . Pete [Rouse], . . . Michael Froman, Julius Genachowski, Don Gips; people like that who are Obama people. And then there are people who had had previous experience in government, people like . . . Jim Steinberg, Carol Browner."[73]

Some people on the board, such as foreign policy specialist Susan Rice, had experience in the Clinton White House and with Barack Obama as well. Others, such as Sonal Shah of Google, had public and private sector experience but were new to the Obama world. Lu talked about the blend: "I thought it was a very useful process to get cross-pollination of ideas." The board experience also gave the senior staff, almost all of whom came into the administration, a feel for working together as a team in the Obama White House and throughout the executive branch.

An important element of the transition structure was the policy working groups that coordinated with members of the transition board and the agency review teams. The policy teams worked through the issues in seven areas: economy; education; energy and environment; health care; immigration; national security; and technology, innovation, and government reform. From the reviews, the teams prepared initiatives for the administration to undertake once President Obama took office. Ranging from eight members for the immigration group to forty-one for the national security group, in all there were 134 positions in the working groups, including the eleven leaders of the individual groups.[74] The groups worked together with the transition board as they facilitated a swift start for the administration on January 20.

While the Obama transition board and policy working groups discussed policy and strategies, Obama's separate agency review operation was designed to gather information to support individuals nominated and appointed to the administration. The Obama team defined the tasks for the ten teams. As stated on the campaign website change.gov, the ten teams organized around issues and agencies were charged to "provide the President-elect, Vice President-elect, and key advisors with information needed to make strategic policy, budgetary, and personnel decisions prior to the inauguration. The Teams will ensure that senior appointees have the information necessary to complete the confirmation process, lead their departments, and begin implementing signature policy initiatives immediately after they are sworn in."[75]

The specific nature of the agency review tasks helped organize what could well have become an unwieldy operation. The agency review teams structure was headed by three co-chairs—Melody Barnes, Lisa Brown, and Don Gips—and fifteen working group members who led the ten review teams. The review teams were organized around the following ten government agency groupings: economic and international trade; national security; justice and civil rights; energy and natural resources; education and labor; health and human services; science, tech, space, and arts; executive office of the president; government operations; and transportation. Each team had a group of lead people ranging from six for transportation to twenty-one for economics and international trade. The teams themselves varied from ten for the government operations team to seventy-five for the national security team. In all there were 365 team member positions, 134 team leads for the ten teams with a leadership of fifteen working group members and three agency review co-chairs.[76] That made an agency review team operation of 517 positions.

Though there were what appeared to be a multitude of people working independently in the agency review operation, it was closely guided by John Podesta. As a former staff secretary in the Clinton administration, Podesta was experienced in bringing together mission and method. He described the operation as "much more highly disciplined process than at least the past Democratic transition. . . . People had very specific assignments about what to produce in what form and at what lengths. So they didn't just wander all over the place producing reams of useless information."[77] There were templates for the teams to use, rather than having each one decide how to produce information. "You know, a template for the budget, a template for particular management challenges. People reviewed all the most recent IG reports, the GAO reports on the agency," Podesta said. "I think that what was most specific, what was most helpful probably was to try to marry the agency mission . . . and those elements of where there were problems, . . . with . . . what the budget looked like, where there [were] looming

TABLE 4.2
Agency Review Teams

Agency review team groups	Team leaders	Team members	Total leaders and members	Departments reviewed by group	Agencies reviewed by group
Economics and international trade	21	50	71	1	12
National security	12	75	87	3	4
Justice and civil rights	16	35	51	1	4
Energy and natural resources	11	42	53	3	3
Education and labor	13	34	47	2	5
Department of health and human services	12	56	68	3	2
Science, technology, space, and arts	12	23	35	1	3
Executive office of the President	21	27	48	0	8
Government operations	10	10	20	0	4
Transportation	6	13	19	1	1
Subtotal	134	365	499		
Agency review co-chairs			3		
Working group members			15		
Total			517		

Source: Office of the President-elect, "Obama-Biden Transition: Agency Review Teams."

decisions that would need to be taken early on by a cabinet secretary, with a mission coming from the campaign."[78]

Podesta commented that the agency review teams produced what they were asked to do. "People actually came through and executed . . . [which is] what really made the effort worthwhile." The protocol they set up stressed gathering similar information from all the agencies they were assessing. "You could take a program, an agency, the budget, [and say] 'These are the challenges, how do you move forward and produce the results Obama had promised, both during the campaign and then fleshed out in the transition and into the early parts of governing?'" Cabinet secretaries and White House staff found the information they received from the agency review teams to be useful, Podesta said. "They got strategic product that was more digestible, [a view of] both opportunity and challenge from the perspective of what Obama was trying to accomplish coming into office, as . . . it was coming from the campaign. So there was alignment between what these review teams were producing and the way the now-transition team was thinking about the project of governing. That gave the review teams the opportunity to surface particular problems in the agency, but not just wander all over the place and . . . start making it up from scratch." He added, "In my conversations with the incoming cabinet secretaries, they very much appreciated that they were getting focused, well-written, reviewed third-draft thirty-page memos, not five thousand pages of junk, [as] had been practiced in the past."[79]

The agency review teams produced a "top line two-pager," says Brown, who was one of the three directors of the agency review process, along with a twenty-page "roadmap" on key issues facing the agency. They also compiled a "database of documents . . . that included everything from . . . what are all the programs that this agency runs, what's the statutory authority for [the programs] . . . what's the personnel situation been like, what's the budget been like, which gave you a lot more information," Brown said. The review teams were also asked to find cost savings that "could possibly be reallocated to other priorities."[80]

The reviews included as well a look at Bush executive orders and current regulations of the departments and agencies. There was a "separate work chain looking at executive orders. What were we bound by? What would we want to change early on?" Brown said.[81] That was true for regulations as well.

The agency review documents, both the early short ones and the more developed ones, were important for other purposes as well. "They were used initially in part to inform the president and the transition teams about selection. What type of person do you need to be running this agency? So when he was appointing people, he could look at it and see, the Agriculture Department is going to have these six issues coming up," Lisa Brown said. The materials were important in the confirmation process as well. The materials "helped to frame the conversation . . . and [were] used when there was a nominee who was preparing for confirmation hearings."

Although there were overlaps of people working on more than one review team and perhaps working in a policy area as well, including the three areas of the advisory board and the central leaders (28), the policy working group operation (134), and the agency review teams (517), there were 679 positions filled on the teams, including its leaders and members.

Presidential Public Presence in the Postelection Period

The most important transition a president-elect needs to make is from candidate to president. In a sense, a major part of that transition is made by not being present in Washington, where much of the transition is taking place. Presidents-elect need to leave behind their candidate persona and come to Washington, D.C., as the leader of all the people, and remaining out of sight helps. Of the seventy-five days of the transition, President-elect Obama was in Washington for part of one day before coming to Washington on January 4 for the final seventeen days of the transition. He came early to enroll his children in their new school and to work with his Washington transition team. At that point, he wound down the Chicago transition operation space provided for him by GSA. Most presidents-elect have similar schedules where they spend most of their time in their home city or town as well as vacationing.

Public opinion surveys have shown, presidents-elect are generally quite successful in this regard, as early in their term in office their Gallup poll ratings are considerably higher than the percentage of the electorate that cast their vote for the winning candidate. President Obama, for example, received 52.9 percent of the vote and had a 68 percent favorability rating in his first weeks in office. Presidents-elect George W. Bush, Bill Clinton, and Ronald Reagan all chose a mixture of home time, vacation, and a few days in Washington before arriving for good in January.

During the period they were out of Washington, they assembled their White House staff, nominated their cabinet and selected department and agency officials, worked through their agenda, and made some public announcements about their appointees. President-elect Obama had a limited number of appearances between the election and his arrival in Washington on January 4. Most of the work they did was out of public view and done through staff, such as statements and announcements of nominations of administration officials. President-elect Obama held few press conferences, even so most presidents-elect use those occasions for personnel announcements, not for major discussions of their agenda.

When the president-elect did come into view, it was often for interviews presenting the new President-elect Barack Obama and his wife Michelle Obama, with an emphasis on who they are and what they intend to do once they get to Washington. Obama did interviews with CBS's *60 Minutes* and a Barbara Walters special, both times with Michelle present, and then individual interviews with NBC's *Meet the Press*, ABC's *This Week with George Stephanopoulos*, CNN, CNBC, and Univision. He had print interviews with *Time* magazine, the *Wall Street Journal*, the *New York Times*, and the Tribune newspapers (the *Chicago Tribune* and the *Los Angeles Times*) and met with the editorial board of the *Washington Post*. Rather than sending an overall message uniting his campaign agenda with his plans for action once he came into office, he responded to questions that interested the news organizations and the actions he was taking on that day. His press conferences and short question-and-answer sessions most often had to do with his appointments.

Assembling a team and setting up the early actions for his presidency generally consume the time a president-elect has during the seventy-five days along with a limited number of his public appearances. Sometimes a president can create time for a conference on a primary issue, as George W. Bush did in Crawford, Texas, for his education initiative. He brought in a dozen congressional leaders from the House and the Senate on December 21, 2000, to discuss his first initiative and then held an education conference when he was in Washington on January 11, 2001, shortly before he came to office. Clinton also focused on an issue with a two-day economic conference in Little Rock on December 14 and 15, 1992. He followed up on his economic discussion with a broader issue agenda during his trip to South Carolina for Renaissance Weekend, an annual event featuring political and social discussion. Both Bush and Clinton spent some time focusing on what would be their first initiatives, though Clinton did so at the expense of putting together his White House staff, which he did not assemble until six days before he took office.

With the separate tasks that a president-elect has to accomplish—readying and sending out his agency review teams, staffing up his transition headquarters in Washington and in his home town and state, creating the rules that will apply to those working in the transition and in his administration, making his White House staff and cabinet selections, organizing his White House and his administration, making the move to the White House, organizing his family, meeting the Mexican president and the Canadian prime minister—there is little time to create a general narrative for the administration. For many presidents that is not a problem because they campaigned on a limited number of items that were articulated over a period of time. That was true for Ronald Reagan, for example, as he discussed his notions of privatization of government tasks, military buildup, the struggle against the Soviet Union, budget cuts, and tax cuts to the point that everyone knew what he would do when he came into office. President George W. Bush had an agenda that was fairly well known during the campaign. He highlighted his first presidential initiative with the education conference he held during the transition.

For Barack Obama, the transition period required tending to the various tasks in the previous paragraph as well as addressing the critical financial situation. That meant that when Obama arrived at the White House and continued to deal with the financial situation, he did not have a clear agenda that he had worked through with the public other than items mentioned in his basic campaign speech and his eighty-three-page booklet defining his priorities and policy ideas, *Blueprint for Change*. The public was aware the idea of change was central to what he would bring to the presidency, but the shape change would take remained to be seen.

CHAPTER FIVE

Transition Plans and Campaign Promises

In his early weeks and months, President Obama's agenda only partially reflected the order the president thought would be his guide for his time and attention. While he was making choices of people, policy, and priorities, he was also responding to unfolding events and the actions of others. The financial collapse and the legislative machinations that lasted throughout his transition required his response and initiatives at the same time that he was lining up people in positions. Overseas, terrorist attacks in Mumbai shook the Indian political and financial system, while at home the financial collapse deepened, with Congress reluctant to support more Troubled Asset Relief Program funds. All required the attention of the president-elect. Even at the sub-national level, President-elect Obama had an unanticipated issue over his Senate seat to deal with as he headed for Washington. Governor Rod Blagojevich, whose responsibility it was to fill the seat, was under investigation for attempting to "sell" the soon-to-be-vacant Senate seat. As reluctant as he was to do so, the president-elect had to weigh in on the issue in mid-December, including speaking with federal prosecutors.

At the same time, the incumbent president is chief executive until the new president takes the oath of office. "Tomorrow I stop being President," noted President Reagan in his diary for January 19, 1989.[1] Nothing brings that home like a look at the activities of a president's last day in office. President Clinton was distributing pardons until the last hours of his presidency. Reagan too was thinking through pardons on his last full day. In his diary, President Reagan noted in his entry for January 19: "Dick Thornburgh [attorney general] came in to see me about pardons. He doesn't believe I should pardon Patty Hearst, [Oliver] North, [John] Poindexter, and [Robert] McFarlane. I'm afraid he's right."[2] On his final day, President Reagan was in his office even though it was only a couple of hours before the change in power. Ken Duberstein, chief of staff for President Reagan in his final year in office, told of an incident that happened during Reagan's final two hours in office. Duberstein and Colin Powell, then NSC advisor, were with the president as he readied to leave the Oval Office. President Reagan took a card out of his pants pocket and offered it to the two men. "Here, fellas, I don't need this any more"; the card listed the top-secret, presidential codes for missile launches. "We both said, 'No, Mr. President! It'll be deactivated at noon! Put it back in your pocket!'"[3] A president is chief executive until the end, but everything has to be readied for the next president.

As the president moves into his office, he wants to get off to a fast start and begin the rollout of the agenda his transition team has been working on. In this chapter we will look at five basic areas. First is the move into the White House, how it is organized and what is involved on moving day itself. The second order of business is bringing in the White House staff. President-elect Obama made his choices and announced them well before Christmas and before his cabinet selection announcements. Once he is settled in his office, with the staff working on unfolding his agenda, then we can see just what the president had in mind for his priorities. The third subject for the chapter is the nature of the office as the outgoing president left it. In most two-term presidencies where the incumbent is not running for reelection, no matter what party they represent, presidents leave office with a decided downturn in their activity. After the final off-year congressional elections, the energy and attention of the media and the Washington community move to the race for the next president, including those in the president's party. During the final year and, in most presidencies, much of the year before as well, the sitting president loses the attention of the public and his party except for the work he does in foreign policy. That leaves a gap in domestic policy that is waiting to be filled by a new chief executive. That is the situation that awaits any incoming president.

The fourth area to be explored is what the new president does when he comes in with a policy agenda to unveil as the public follows his moves. In his first months, he will put forward his proposals, release executive orders and memoranda for executive branch departments and agencies, and respond to events occurring during the early weeks and months. The way ahead in those weeks depends to a great extent on the campaign and what the president promised he would do and his commitments about how he would work. The fifth area we will investigate is the way in which President Obama and his team shifted from campaigning to governing, including some of the problems they encountered as they made the shift from making promises to attempting to deliver on them.

Moving Out and Moving Into the White House

When a presidential candidate wins the November election, he has a to-do list that confronts him with items ranging from packing up the family belongings and moving to Washington to setting up a list of priorities on the appointments and policy fronts. The White House comes first in terms of family and, on the governing front, for his order of appointments. A president needs to be as sensitive to where his children will go to school as he is to which of his campaign staff are coming into the White House, what his team's governing priorities will be, and how much time they will have to react to the events unfolding around them. All of these were considerations as President Obama entered the White House.

During a four- to five-hour period on January 20, 2009, the family belongings for President and Mrs. Bush were packed into a moving van and taken away, while arriving at the residence were the items that President and Mrs. Obama, her mother Marian Robinson, and their daughters, Malia and Sasha, chose to bring into the White House residence. During that short period devoted to the move, the belongings of the outgoing family are first moved out before those of the incoming family are brought in. In addition to the personal items an outgoing president takes with him, the White House residency staff conducting the move also need to take out any items the first family had on loan from the White House collection or had borrowed from museums. In between the two moves, the General Services Administration staff at the White House complex send cleaning crews into the West Wing, and the residence staff works on freshening up the residential areas on the second and third floors of the White House. The National Archives and Records Administration does a final sweep of the remaining presidential records from the Bush administration.

As personal as the Obama family's move into the White House was, it had the same mixture of people, resources, and institutions that characterized the transition as a whole. Among the groups we have seen as important in transition preparations who were key to the Inauguration Day move were Laura Bush and her staff, the West Wing staff, Chief Usher Stephen Rochon and the White House residence staff, the General Services Administration, the National Archives and Records Administration, the National Park Service, and the transition and incoming White House staffs of President-elect Obama.

During their visit to the White House the Monday following the election, President-elect and Mrs. Obama received a wealth of information from Mrs. Bush and her staff and from Chief Usher Stephen Rochon, who headed the residence staff. The National Park Service and General Services Administration provided information on their operations maintaining, respectively, the outdoor grounds of President's Park and the inside of the properties on the compound, including the West Wing. Anita McBride, chief of staff for Mrs. Bush, prepared briefing books about the East Wing operation. Those books went to Mrs. Obama and her team along with another set of books with information on White House resources available to the First Family, including furniture they might want to use. When a president and his family come to the White House, they can choose to use furniture and decorative arts from the White House collection and some items from local museums as well as their own furnishings they bring from their homes. Rochon gave them the books identifying the items in the White House collection available for them to use in the family quarters. Rochon and McBride gave the Obamas the briefing books that they had prepared when President-elect and Mrs. Obama came to Washington on November 10 to meet with President and Mrs. Bush. There are three areas to furnish, including bedrooms as well as three sitting room areas, plus a rooftop solarium floor.

First families do avail themselves of items from the White House collection, and some come to the White House with few furnishings. When President and Mrs. Bush came to the White House, for example, they brought with them one piece of furniture, a chest belonging to George Bush's grandmother.[4] Anita McBride noted that the only additional items the Bushes brought to the White House beyond their personal belongings and the chest were "their personal pictures and some books." In leaving the White House after eight years, Laura Bush planned a gradual transition that would leave little to move in the last days. "She had, over the summer of 2008, started moving some things home to the ranch and started clearing things out," said McBride. "She didn't want the residence staff . . . so overwhelmed unnecessarily because she knows how hectic it is moving in."[5] Thus, in those final days there was no major move out of the White House because the Bushes brought few household items with them when they came in, and they sent home those items and others they acquired while in Washington during their eight years.

On Inauguration Day, as President and Mrs. Bush hosted the traditional coffee in the Blue Room for President-elect and Mrs. Obama as well as the outgoing and incoming vice presidents and their wives, the move begins with furnishings moved by executive residence staff who have White House security clearances. With the Bushes ready to go with their few remaining items, the 2009 move was focused on the Obamas' move in. The chief usher is the one who manages the move. Gary Walters, who served for thirty-seven years as chief usher or as a deputy, commented on the goal for the day: "They walk in, . . . and more than their house, it's their home."[6] In order to get to that point, the move out of and into the White House begins when the presidential entourage leaves for the Hill at approximately 11:30 a.m. In addition to those moving the furnishings out of the residence areas, NARA staff go through West Wing offices to make sure that computers have clean hard drives and that any remaining records from the Bush staff are saved for shipment and storage in the warehouses holding materials for the forthcoming presidential library. Each administration starts with a clean computer slate without any records in those computers from the outgoing staff.

Assembling the White House Staff

The process of assembling a White House staff involves bringing together people with a variety of experiences and areas of knowledge. Staffing needs to be balanced between governing and campaign people, as the needs of governing are different from those of campaigning. That is one of the most difficult issues a president-elect deals with because everyone who worked on the campaign wants to be in the White House close to the president. How to spread them around the administration is one of the most challenging tasks a new president faces. Once a president wins, he needs to focus first on setting up his White House staff. The reason is that a decision-making system has to be in place before the cabinet secretaries are chosen or other important decisions are made.

The chief of staff appointment is usually announced in the first few days following the election because once he is in place, the president can work with the new chief on setting up the way in which he wants to make decisions and the types of information he requires before he regards an issue to be ripe for a decision. In addition to a chief of staff, the president requires having a staff secretary, personnel director, counsel, press secretary, communications director, national security and domestic policy advisors. He also needs a budget director, who is responsible for assessing the costs of presidential initiatives and preparing the budget for a broad overview in early February and a spring delivery. The reason these constitute the front line staff for a president is that they represent the types of information and processes he will need to put in place to gather substantive information on policy initiatives; to check to make sure he has touched the bases around Washington that should be consulted, such as members of Congress; and then to have procedures in place to make public what it is the president is doing and what his initiatives mean.

The chief of staff is the center of the staff system, which is there to reflect the president's choices; he or she is responsible for recruiting those who fill the needs that come up early in an administration. If the president is going to bring in someone close to him as a counselor or senior advisor, that person will be chosen in the early wave of White House appointments. Setting up a decision-making process is the first order of business, and it is established with the president, his chief of staff, and his staff secretary, who disciplines that process by keeping track of material coming to the president for decisions and then following the implementation of decisions once they are made. Appointments to administrative posts come second. The personnel director and the White House counsel are crucial for recruiting and then vetting the appointees a president will make in his term. The president and chief of staff weigh in on the types of people he wants as well as name specific people to fill department and agency vacancies, and then the personnel and counsel teams work on getting them in place. The basic policy people need to be in place, including his top domestic and national security advisors as well as his director at the Office of Management and Budget. The general outline of the budget is due about a month after the president comes into office, and his budget person needs to be lined up well before the president comes into office. In addition to the process people (chief of staff, staff secretary, personnel, counsel) and the policy people (budget, domestic policy, national security policy, economic policy), the incoming president also arranges to bring in at the outset those who will handle his relations with the world outside the White House, such as those in charge of handling legislative affairs, communications, and his press secretary.

Having the White House staff in place is crucial for getting the policy right and laid out in the order that the president decides is best for his agenda. In the chart below, we can see that President-elect Obama appointed his key White House staff and OMB director well before his predecessors made those choices. President George W. Bush, however, was quick to appoint his staff and then his cabinet once Vice President Gore conceded on December 13, 2000. Both Bush and Obama picked most of their senior White House advisors before the end of the month they became presidents-elect had ended.

With time to work through process choices, Obama's team worked on decision-making procedures starting in the transition period. Lisa Brown, who came into the White House as staff secretary, discussed how they developed the ways in which the paper briefing and decision-making process would operate. Part of their decision-making strategy was to let the process evolve, and another part was to rely on what they had learned from their predecessors "in the staff secretary post and part was to begin working and adapt to the president-elect's style," said Brown. The staff secretary's office oversees the paper flow to the president, including organizing it and ensuring that all of the appropriate bases have been touched

TABLE 5.1
Presidential Naming of White House / OMB Key Senior Staff

	Reagan (1980–81)	G. H. W. Bush (1988–89)	Clinton (1992–93)	G. W. Bush (declared President-elect on 12/13) (2000–2001)	Obama (2008–2009)
Election date	11/4	11/8	11/3	11/7; 12/13	11/4
Chief of staff	11/14	11/17	12/12	12/16	11/6
Senior advisor / counselor	11/14; 12/17	No such position	1/14	12/17; 1/4	11/15; 11/16
National security advisor	11/23	11/23	12/22	12/17	12/1
National Economic Council (position created in 1993)			12/10	1/3	11/24
Domestic policy advisor	12/17	1/11	1/14	1/5	11/24
Counsel	1/30	11/9	1/14	12/17	11/17
Personnel	1/13	11/9	1/14	12/29	1/5
Press secretary	1/6	11/28	1/14	12/28	11/22
Communications director	3/27	12/22	1/14	12/17	11/22
Staff secretary	1/14	12/16	1/14	1/5	11/19
Legislative affairs	12/17	12/22	1/14	1/4	11/15
OMB director	12/11	11/21	12/10	12/23	11/26

Source: Contemporaneous news accounts in the *Washington Post* and the *New York Times.* John P. Burke, *Becoming President*, 42–49.

before the materials go to the president. "We started during the transition to be effectively serving like the staff secretary in terms of the information that was provided to him," Brown said. "Rather than going from zero to 100 the day after inauguration, we began working on the process during the transition, and it evolved."[7] The practices of earlier administrations in setting up their decision-making process were important for Lisa Brown and her White House colleagues. "We built very heavily on . . . staff secretaries from Republican administrations, Democratic administrations," she said. "Everybody was very generous in terms of sitting down without regard to politics and sharing what works, what doesn't work, . . . here are things to watch out for."

Balance in a White House staff is a key to its success. The balance comes with five different types of knowledge and experience.[8] The types of knowledge are: substantive policy; the rhythms of a White House; the campaign; the knowledge of the president-elect; and the Washington community, including the press and Congress. In order to benefit from what people in these groups bring to a White House, staff members with these backgrounds need to be spread around the White House in such a way that what they know can be used throughout the building rather than in particular warrens.

A president benefits when he brings in people who know how a White House works. Having people appointed early and including people in the new White House staff who have previously served in a White House is important because of the gradual dwindling of people who were on the staff through many administrations. Particularly in the operational offices, many staff members who had once served under several presidents left during the 1990s from such offices as the correspondence unit, the travel office, and the office of administration. With them left an institutional memory of how those offices functioned under the long series of twentieth-century presidents and what issues they dealt with. McBride recounted that the person who trained her when she came into the correspondence office in the Reagan White House was a staff person who had come in during Franklin Roosevelt's administration and knew the mail process well. When she returned during the George W. Bush administration to handle personnel for the White House itself, she found a very different situation: "People who had been there twenty and thirty years that were training all the new administrations coming in weren't there. . . . And not having the go-to people that I was used to in the past just to help you get started" made the start particularly difficult.[9] In the broader office functions, there was at least one additional factor that made it difficult in recent years to get information from people who have served multiple administrations, especially those in operational spots. "The people that we would need to depend on for personnel and other functions, even IT functions, were . . . very subpoena-wary. They had been through a lot, and so they were not as forthcoming as I had experienced in the past." Finding White House staff with a long institutional memory is not as easy as it once was.

For President Obama, having Rahm Emanuel as chief of staff gave the new president a good start in his dealings with the Washington community, especially with Democratic members of the House of Representatives who knew Emanuel as a colleague. Additionally, he had served in several posts in the Clinton White House and knew its rhythms too. What Emanuel did not have was a history with the president himself, something that most—but not all—chiefs of staff have in their backgrounds. The president had a large number of people who came in with him who had worked with him on the campaign trail. David Axelrod, Robert Gibbs, Dan Pfeiffer, Pete Rouse, and Greg Craig all came into the White House off of the campaign trail or one of its policy support teams. Having people who know the issues the president focused on in the campaign is a key to keeping an emphasis on those priorities.

At the same time, it is important to have someone in a senior post, Valerie Jarrett in this case, who knows the president well and has his back. Because so many presidential initiatives come out of the White House, it is equally important that an incoming president have people with backgrounds in substantive policy on his staff as well. That is particularly true in recent years because it is difficult for a president to get his nominees to departments and agencies through the Senate confirmation process. One of the ways the Obama White House brought on people with knowledge in the issue areas at the heart of the president's policy agenda who were ready to implement the president's policies was to bring them on as staff with a broad portfolio in a particular issue area. Carol Browner, for instance, who dealt with energy and climate change issues, came in with a background in environmental regulation issues and covered the area of energy. Their portfolios cut across several agencies and allowed them to coordinate what the White House was doing as the president began his tenure. Such positions were not new to the Obama administration, as President Bush and his predecessors had appointed officials to deal with particular issues and events requiring someone to work with several agencies and governmental institutions at all levels.

At the beginning of the administration, there were several people with wide portfolios who quickly went into action on issues that required immediate attention and that cut across several departments and agencies. In addition to Browner, three examples of those with such assignments were General Douglas Lute, the president's representative on Iraq and Afghanistan; Ron Bloom, the president's advisor who headed the automotive task force; and Edward DeSeve, who was responsible for the implementation of the American Recovery Act. But as time went by and more appointees were confirmed and departments and agencies took over more of the initiative, those posts ended when their original occupants, such as Browner, left the White House.

In the days leading up to their entry into the White House, staff and cabinet secretaries also set up the staff structure in ways that suit them. In general, the White House staff structure has shown considerable continuity in government operations, as there have been few changes in the shape of the organization chart over the years. The offices that exist, such as the Press Office and the Office of Communications, remain structured in a similar way because of the continuing nature of the work they do and the constituents they serve. At the same time, there are always pressures to create a new office, to add on to the responsibilities of existing ones, or to reshape who is involved in office operations. In the preparations for an Obama White House, all three pressures were at work. John Podesta spoke of his effort to handle the issue of energy through the creation of a council that could work across agencies. "I argued very strongly, given the president's position on energy and energy transformation and climate change and its importance and relevance to the economic program going forward, and the national security program going forward, that having someone in the White House who could work with . . . a large number of agencies who had something to do with this was critical," Podesta said.[10] With the importance of the issue and the lack of specific and prominent coverage of energy in White House organizations, Podesta argued for one of two alternatives. "I pushed for either the creation of a national energy council along the lines of the NEC, or at least an office that coordinated that work." He argued his case with incoming chief of staff Rahm Emanuel. "I think for a variety of reasons, Rahm was convinced that the latter was better than the former and . . . reached out and hired Carol Browner to do that."

John Podesta was not the only person recommending that energy be a significant part of a White House energy portfolio. General Jones was also interested in the issue as an aspect of the National Security Council. He wanted to set up a separate energy directorate within the NSC. Some of the other changes they made included creating some new areas: "We included things like global development, the economic piece run by Mike Froman. We brought in cybersecurity." Energy was the area where their reorganization failed to bring in an area Jones considered important: "I tried and failed to bring in an energy senior director because I think . . . energy security is a critical function of national security now." Carol Browner controlled administration energy and climate issues through her position as director of the White House Office of Energy and Climate Change Policy. As the staff person who would coordinate energy issues across the administration, Browner had control of those issues within her portfolio.

Although he lost on the issue of creating an energy directorate within the NSC, Jones continued to believe that the energy issue merited directorate status: "I had so much on my plate that I let that go reluctantly because I still told the president on the day I left that I thought that not having a senior director for energy and an organization that dealt with energy security inside NSC was a mistake when you look at how diffuse the energy portfolio is in our government. And the different departments all have a major say in energy, and as a result—if everybody has got a say in it, nobody has got a say in it."[11]

What fits one senior official may not suit others. In their book *HRC: State Secrets and the Rebirth of Hillary Clinton,* Jonathan Allen and Amie Parnes relate that James Steinberg, who worked on national security issues for the Obama campaign and who served as a deputy in the National Security Council in the Clinton administration, hoped that he would be appointed national security advisor. "Disappointed that he wouldn't become Obama's national security advisor, Steinberg asked for one concession from the president: Give me a permanent seat at the National Security Council meetings," Allen and Parnes relate.[12] He wanted to be part of the policymaking process, and this arrangement would give him a seat at the national security table even if he was not associated with the NSC. "It's okay with me, if it's okay with Hillary," the authors quote the president-elect as saying. "Hillary liked that idea because Steinberg's presence would mean State had two seats at the national security table, and Steinberg was an acceptable number two because of his long-standing ties to trusted Clintonites."[13] From the viewpoint of General Jones, members of the principals committee did not appreciate having one department represented by two officials. "It was a little awkward because that was the only department where the secretary and the deputy were on the principals. And the other secretaries weren't too thrilled with that because that meant that Clinton had two people at the table," Jones said.[14]

Tom Daschle and the White House Staff: A Staff without Its Leader

One of the curious aspects of the Obama White House is the way in which it was set up to work effectively with a top White House official who never came into office. It provides a good case study of the difference individuals make in shaping what can go wrong. When President-elect Obama nominated former Senate majority leader Thomas Daschle as his secretary for health and human services, he also said that Daschle would be his White House advisor on health care issues. "I've asked Tom to serve not just as my secretary of health and human service but also as my director of White House . . . office of health reform. As such, he will be responsible not just for implementing our health care plan, he will also be the lead architect of that plan," Obama said. "Tom brings more than just great expertise to this task. He brings the respect that he earned during his years of leadership in Congress. He knows how to reach across the aisle and bridge bipartisan divides. And he has the trust of folks from every angle of this issue—doctors, nurses, and patients, unions and businesses, hospitals and advocacy groups, all of who will have a seat as we craft our plan. And once we pass this legislation, I know I can rely on Tom to implement it effectively. A gifted manager, Tom is the original no-drama guy known for speaking softly but leading bolding [sic], always treating his staff with respect while demanding excellence and empowering them to deliver."[15] John Podesta, who served as a counselor to Daschle when he served as Senate majority leader and knew the former senator well, commented on Daschle's ability to develop and implement policy: "For those of us who really knew and respected Tom, he was uniquely qualified to be both an administration leader in the development of [health policy] and run the agency."[16] Podesta believed that Daschle would have been confirmed if he had not chosen to withdraw his name after tax issues arose during the confirmation process. "I think that was Tom's decision," he said. "I think he would have been confirmed."[17] Once President Obama lost Tom Daschle as his HHS nominee, he had a top White House staff that had spent more time with the nominee than they had serving the president-elect.

Several top White House advisors once worked for Daschle and also worked for Obama during his Senate years. Denis McDonough, the current White House chief of staff, served as a foreign policy advisor in the Obama campaign and then as deputy to Tom Donilon in the NSC, had also worked for Tom Daschle. Additional Daschle veterans include Dan Pfeiffer, deputy campaign communications director and post-inauguration deputy White House communications director, and Anita Dunn, who served as communications chief for the Hope Fund, Obama's presidential campaign effort from early 2006, the predecessor of Obama for America. Three months into President Obama's administration, she became communications director. Her husband, Robert Bauer, also a Daschle veteran, became White House counsel when Greg Craig, a non-Daschle person, resigned in November 2009.

Nancy Hogan became director of the Office of Presidential Personnel when Don Gips left less than six months into the administration. She worked for Daschle when he was minority leader and then at Alston and Bird, the Washington law firm where Daschle worked after his Senate reelection defeat in 2004. Mark Childress, a longtime Daschle aide, came into the White House from a post in the Department of Justice, where he had begun his administration service. He served as deputy chief of staff for planning when Jack Lew was serving as chief of staff.

For all of these people who worked in the campaign and in the transition, former Senator Daschle was an important touchstone. They could easily work together no matter what their geographical distance was. They knew and trusted one another. Losing Daschle shook the team. "With Daschle, everything kind of stopped. It stopped and went off the rails, and they lost confidence," a person familiar with the Obama staff operations observed. "It was also the key people in charge of it [who] lost confidence. You know, everything had gone so well, and then all of a sudden it didn't." Daschle was important to all of those who were coming together to form the new White House team. "It's not like Tom was a cabinet level person who didn't make it. Tom was their mentor and their friend. Half the people there had had some connection with Tom, so it was a personal disappointment, a cruel personal disappointment, because people loved Tom Daschle, and he would have played a huge role," the person continued.[18] It is hard to imagine that with Daschle's political acumen, his knowledge of the health care industry and its politics, and his relationships in the Senate that the administration would have had the problems it has experienced developing and then releasing its health care plan.

The Daschle people came into the White House without the person under whom they had worked for years. The time spent working for President-elect Obama was far less than that spent with Daschle. Such a situation caused headaches for those coming into the White House without the common Daschle experience. No recent president has as many chiefs of staff as President Obama, who in January 2013, the start of his fifth year in office, named his fifth chief; one of the five, Pete Rouse, served only as interim chief of staff. At a comparable point in their presidencies, President Bush was still on his first chief, Clinton his third, and President Reagan his second. Of the Obama chiefs of staff, three of them—Rahm Emanuel, Bill Daley, and Jack Lew—did not have a background working with Daschle. Pete Rouse, the interim chief of staff who did not want the job, and Denis McDonough, the most recent chief, had Daschle connections of long standing. Both have had an easier time than did Emanuel and Daley in terms of their dealings with White House staff members. One of the reasons Daley had a tough time was his absence on the 2008 campaign trail. As a Daley person told journalist Paul Starobin for a Daley profile: "'I think coming in late [to the White House] and not being part of the original Dream Team is a hard nut to crack' . . . because 'the folks who got the president elected' always have the inside track."[19] And they also were the people who were close to Daschle.

In the long run in the health care area, the president felt the absence of Tom Daschle in his administration as his primary health care advisor. President Obama struggled in the health care battle as legislation moved through Congress in 2009 and 2010 and then during the implementation process for the following three years, which has proved a technical and political problem for the president. Between the hostile reception it continues to receive five years after its introduction and the poor rollout of the healthcare.gov website, the president's signature measure proved a flashpoint for his critics. Would the situation have been different with Daschle guiding it? He was knowledgeable in the area of health, had strong relationships with his former colleagues in the Senate as well as in the House, where he also served. He understood health care issues and was also familiar with people in the health reform community. Because health care was one of his policy specialties, he had the background to serve in the dual posts of head of the White House health care office as well as serve as the secretary of health and human services.

The Campaign Team Moves Into the White House

The transition from campaigning to governing can be very difficult. First there is the inevitable concern during the campaign that the early transition people are working off on their own and dividing up the jobs among themselves. It is important for campaigns to want to prevent this kind of talk from starting. As outlined in chapter 4, the Obama operation made it clear that taking time off after Election Day would not disadvantage campaign staff who were looking for administration positions.

One of the difficult aspects of the transition into the White House is establishing an official relationship with the president to replace the more informal campaign one, especially for those staff members who have been with the candidate for the duration of the campaign. "One of the challenges . . . was more with the campaign staff who came into the White House, who didn't understand [that] all of a sudden, there's somebody between me and the president when I've had direct access for so long," commented a senior White House staff member in the first term.[20] Another person described the campaign relationship and the need to replace it with the more professional one. Speaking in 2012, the staff member said: "Candidly, I think it's still evolving. I think it gets hard. When you . . . come off a campaign and you have people who have either worked closely with a candidate or people who have a preexisting relationship with the president, it is natural when the president says, 'How are you? What's going on?' to say, 'Hey, I'm working on X,' and . . . to try to get some feedback on the things you're doing," the staff member said of the difficulties making the switch to a White House staff decision process.[21]

The stakes involved in getting used to a White House decision system are high in that an established process is the only way a president can avoid chaos. "You have to learn you might be able to get away with that once or twice, but . . . [it] is really frowned upon. I'm not going to say people don't do it, but it's really frowned upon when people do it," commented a White House official familiar with the maneuver. "Discipline takes a while , [but] . . . discipline makes sense. . . . Otherwise [the decision-making system] becomes chaotic," the same aide commented. "It's a discipline that it took people a lot of time to really internalize, and I'm not going to say that everyone followed it, and I'm not going to say that people didn't do end runs because I know people did do end runs."[22] With the Obama administration, the end run opportunities were greater than those in earlier administrations.

As Chris Lu noted, today the challenges of establishing a disciplined process are more challenging than they once were. "We also had to deal with the situation where for the first time a president carried a BlackBerry and had email. People who have email access to the president are specifically advised, 'You don't use this as a way to go around the process.' . . . The staff secretary process protects us," Lu said. As a senior aide commented: "I look at memos that other people are sending in, and for every memo I send in where people disagree with what I'm doing, I have the ability to weigh in on other people's memos. So I think it protects all of us at the same time. . . . And if you play by the rules, I think it works for everybody, and you win some and you lose some, but I do think it's a struggle that we constantly have around here."[23]

General Jones gave his assessment of the stakes in making the shift from campaigning to governing and the difficulty the president's staff had in making the transition. "The biggest challenge, I think, overall in an administration is the newly elected administration has to very quickly understand that there is a difference between campaigning and governing. And the longer it takes for an administration to realize that, the worse it is for the administration and the worse it is for the country." The decision-making process is different, and the stakes in getting the process and decisions right is even higher and more difficult than in a campaign. "Most of the problems that I thought we faced had to do with people who used to enjoy tremendous access to the president when he was campaigning, daily access, walk in and talk to him, sit down and get your marching orders." For someone who was part of the governing rather than the campaign process, the situation impeded good governance. "Now, faced with new jobs, the campaign is over, you're trying to govern, but that—tendency to huddle around the candidate, in this case, the President, and keep that kind of access that they—especially the younger they are, the more they don't understand this, is actually harmful. And that has been a problem in this administration."[24]

Coming into the White House: Executive Action in Early 2009

Modern presidents take inauguration tips from President Reagan. While presidents traditionally held their inauguration ceremonies on the east face of the capital, Reagan chose the west side. On that side was a vista with the Washington monument and Lincoln memorial in the background. The scene made a perfect backdrop for television. Reagan did not stop there in setting the presidential scene in the early hours and days of his presidency. He made his priorities clear very quickly through orders he signed. His successors, including President Obama, have followed this pattern. He too wanted to issue a stamp symbolizing the goals and procedures of his presidency.

President Reagan's first official act was to follow through on a campaign promise and set the stage for his economic priorities. It was a simple act of signing an administrative order to put a freeze on hiring in the federal government. He explained his action: "This—for the benefit of the oral press—this is an order that I am signing, an immediate freeze on the hiring of civilian employees in the executive branch. I pledged last July that this would be a first step toward controlling the growth and the size of Government and reducing the drain on the economy for the public sector. And beyond the symbolic value of this, which is my first official act, the freeze will eventually lead to a significant reduction in the size of the Federal workforce. Only rare exemptions will be permitted in order to maintain vital services."[25] In the order itself, he said: "Imposing a freeze now can eventually lead to a significant reduction in the size of the Federal work force. This begins the process of restoring our economic strength and returning the Nation to prosperity."[26] President Reagan followed his first memorandum with a second one two days later. That memorandum laid out in specific terms what additional cost-saving measures would be taken in the federal government.[27] President George W. Bush also issued a hiring freeze at the beginning of his administration. Presidents Clinton and George W. Bush signed memoranda dealing with standards of conduct. After issuing memoranda and executive orders related to their policy goals, presidents move to their legislative agendas, which will take longer to accomplish.

In addition to standards of conduct and government spending issues, recent presidents have used the early days to signal their social policy preferences. Two days after Clinton's inauguration, for instance, Clinton administration officials rescinded federal regulations adopted by the Reagan and Bush administration dealing with several women's health issues related to abortion services. In a series of presidential memoranda, President Clinton directed governmental agencies to rescind the prohibition on importing the abortion pill RU-486; to reverse the ban on privately funded abortions at military hospitals; to remove the restrictions on the Agency for International Development involving the use of funds for family planning services; to remove the rule disallowing family planning clinics from giving abortion information, counseling, or referrals to low-income patients; and to remove restrictions on using fetal tissue from induced abortions for federally funded research.[28]

President Obama followed up on the revolving social and work-related issues where Democrats take one position and the Republicans another. When there is a change in party, each new president reverses orders his predecessor issued relating to the interests of specific constituent groups of the incoming party. The

TABLE 5.2
Presidential Executive Activity: January and First 100 Days

	Eisenhower		Nixon		Carter		Reagan	
	January	100	January	100	January	100	January	100
Executive orders	1	20	2	15	2	16	2	18
Memoranda	1	4	1	5	0	17	4	12
Proclamations	0	8	1	19	2	22	0	26
	G. H. W. Bush		Clinton		G. W. Bush		Obama	
	January	100	January	100	January	100	January	100
Executive orders	1	11	2	13	2	11	9	19
Memoranda	0	2	7	10	2	11	10	23
Proclamations	1	30	2	28	1	28	1	24

Source: Public Papers of the President, as found at American Presidency Project, www.presidency
.ucsb.edu/ws/.

nine executive orders and ten presidential memoranda President Obama signed
in his first ten days in office covered a broad range of subjects, including ethics
standards for administration employees, labor regulations, the economy, detention policies and the future of Guantanamo Bay, reproductive rights, energy, a
White House pay freeze, and a review of agency regulations. The group of memoranda and executive orders represent a combination of President Obama's campaign commitments to communities interested in particular issues, particularly
labor, women, and transparency groups, and reflect his earlier statements about
the processes his administration would use to do business. They also reflect his
oft-stated campaign commitments to bring about policy redirections, such as reviews of Guantanamo Bay prison detention and military trial policies.

The nineteen executive actions fit into three basic categories: Guantanamo
Bay prison policies, government operations, and those responding to particular
constituent groups. Women's rights groups are important for Democrats and
right-to-life groups are a key element in the Republican coalition, as the two groups
represent opposing interests on reproductive rights issues. The reproductive
rights issue has been a flashpoint with each change-of-party administration following that of President Reagan. Presidents Clinton, George W. Bush, and Obama
have all promulgated orders on the issue within days of assuming the presidency.
In August 1984, President Reagan issued an order halting aid through the State
Department and its Agency for International Development to nongovernment
organizations that "engage in a wide range of activities, including providing advice, counseling, or information regarding abortion, or lobbying a foreign government to legalize or make abortion available."[29]

One can get a quick feel for the way in which this issue bounced from one point of view to its polar opposite at the time of a change-of-party transition. Not three days passed for the last three presidents before each dealt with the issue. President Obama's memorandum of January 23, 2009, included the following language:

> Accordingly, I hereby revoke the Presidential memorandum of January 22, 2001, for the Administrator of USAID (Restoration of the Mexico City Policy), the Presidential memorandum of March 28, 2001, for the Administrator of USAID (Restoration of the Mexico City Policy), and the Presidential memorandum of August 29, 2003, for the Secretary of State (Assistance for Voluntary Population Planning). In addition, I direct the Secretary of State and the Administrator of USAID to take the following actions with respect to conditions in voluntary population planning assistance and USAID grants that were imposed pursuant to either the 2001 or 2003 memoranda and that are not required by the Foreign Assistance Act or any other law: (1) immediately waive such conditions in any current grants, and (2) notify current grantees, as soon as possible, that these conditions have been waived. I further direct that the Department of State and USAID immediately cease imposing these conditions in any future grants.[30]

By this action, President Obama unwound the policy begun by President Reagan that was nullified by President Clinton, an act that was followed by a revocation of the Clinton order by President George W. Bush. President Clinton issued his revocation of the Reagan policy on January 22, 1993, and President George W. Bush undid the Clinton policy on January 22, 2001. All saw the policy as a central one to their constituents.

Labor and business often receive early consideration from a new president when he replaces a chief executive of the opposing party. On January 30, 2009, President Obama issued Executive Order 13495 Nondisplacement of Qualified Workers Under Service Contracts. If a contract expires and the same services are needed at the same place, the order provides for a continuation of those workers who were employed by the first contractor. As the executive order reads, "The Federal Government's procurement interests in economy and efficiency are served when the successor contractor hires the predecessor's employees. A carryover work force reduces disruption to the delivery of services during the period of transition between contractors and provides the Federal Government the benefits of an experienced and trained work force that is familiar with the Federal Government's personnel, facilities, and requirements."[31] That order revoked President George W. Bush's Executive Order 13204 of February 17, 2001, which permitted businesses to choose employees without restrictions on who to hire. The Bush order nullified Clinton's Executive Order 12933, which was issued on October 20, 1994. Each is responding to the needs of constituents who were key to their presidential victories.

Early executive orders and memoranda deal with governmental process as well as with key policy interests. Government process is a campaign issue, especially the issue of standards of ethics for White House staff and government officials appointed by the president. While there are ethics laws in place for federal workers, recent presidents have added their own sets of post-employment restrictions as well as conflict of interest rules. The day after his inauguration, President Obama issued his order relating to a ban on hiring people who had lobbied for any organization, whether profit or nonprofit. On Inauguration Day itself, President George W. Bush issued his ethics order as a memorandum on standards of conduct. President Clinton released his Executive Order 13490 on ethics commitments by executive branch officials on January 20, 1993, while President George H. W. Bush had one on April 12, 1989. President Carter advocated for an Office of Government Ethics and issued his own orders, as did President Reagan after him. Neither issued their ethics rules during the first hundred days, as the four most recent presidents have done.

All incoming presidents are interested in the review of regulations and rules promulgated by their predecessor. President Obama was no exception with his Executive Order 13497, which revoked earlier Bush orders on rules and regulations that were in the pipeline.[32] On January 21, 2009, President Obama carried through on his promise of "open government" with memoranda on "transparency and open government" as well as the Freedom of Information Act.[33] At the same time, with Executive Order 13489 he revoked an unpopular order issued by President Bush in November 2001 that provided for a White House review before a presidential library could release documents.[34]

While most of the government-related issues among presidents are ones related to domestic decision-making and the rules surrounding them, there was a group of issues that caused a flurry of discussion and years to debate. President Obama issued three orders on January 22, 2009, related to interrogations and to detentions of terror suspects held at Guantanamo Bay (Executive Orders 13491, 13492, 13493) as well a memorandum on the same day relating to the detention of one individual.[35] Controversial executive orders relating to hostilities are not unknown. The day following his inauguration, President Carter issued Executive Order 11967 relating to his proclamation of the same day that granted pardons to those who had violated the Selective Service Act between mid-1964 and the end of March 1973.[36] His pardon was for those who resisted the draft for service in the Vietnam War, which ended before his presidency.

Bringing in the Legislative Agenda

In addition to preparing the executive orders and memoranda President Obama rolled out once he came into office, his transition staff also worked on signature items Obama introduced in his first hundred days in office. As we saw in the leadup to the inauguration, the only way for the American Recovery Act to get passed was for the Obama people to come in and work with members of Congress to get it enacted. Obama worked too with the Senate and House Democratic leadership on the passage of the Lilly Ledbetter Fair Pay bill through the two legislative chambers. The bill came to the White House during his first week in office, and he signed it on January 29. It was the first bill President Obama signed, and it was one he has heralded as a signature item of his presidency. In his first term, Obama mentioned the Lilly Ledbetter Fair Pay Act in proclamations, statements and remarks sixty-five times, with twenty-four of them coming during 2012, when he was running for reelection. A president's early actions have resonance throughout his tenure in office.

When he made his electoral argument for his first-term accomplishments, President Obama used additional examples from his administration's hundred-day agenda, including efforts to save the automobile industry through government loans, such as the one to Chrysler that he announced on April 30, 2009. He also regularly referred to the American Recovery and Reinvestment Act of 2009, signed February 17, and the Children's Health Insurance Reauthorization Act of 2009, signed February 4, as well as his education reform proposals of April 24 that sought reform of Pell Grants for students. In a typical and oft-repeated speech at a Democratic fundraiser in 2012, Obama drew on his early legislative proposals and victories. "And so there's an enormous amount at stake. And we're going to have to make sure that in this election, we are describing clearly what's at stake. And we shouldn't be afraid of this debate, because we've got the better argument," Obama said. "It's not just a matter of being able to say the change that we brought about in lifting the auto industry back, that's something we're proud of. It's not just the 4.3 million jobs. It's not just the fact that 2.5 million young people have health insurance that didn't have it before. It's not just the fact that, as a consequence of our policies, millions of young people are getting Pell Grants and have the capacity to go to college who didn't have it before. . . . But it's also the fact that when you look at our history, America has not grown, it has not prospered, it has not succeeded with a philosophy that says, 'You're all on your own.'"[37]

On April 14, 2009, President Obama laid out several priorities to which he would return throughout his first term. In a speech on the economy, he cited five pillars as being important to American prosperity, including health care reform. All are ones he revisited throughout his time in office as key elements of his presidency. He explained:

> It's a foundation built upon five pillars that will grow our economy and make this new century another American century: number one, new rules for Wall Street that will reward drive and innovation, not reckless risk-taking; number two, new investments in education that will make our workforce more skilled and competitive; number three, new investments in renewable energy and technology that will create new jobs and new industries; number four, new investments in health care that will cut costs for families and businesses; and number five, new savings in our Federal budget that will bring down the debt for future generations. That's the new foundation we must build.[38]

All of the work the Obama transition teams did was aimed at getting their policy agenda under way as soon as possible with all of the above elements at the core of his administration.

Management Takes a Back Seat

Legislative initiatives are the focus of most incoming administrations, with management issues taking a backseat. Yet it takes a strong management team to gather information to support the legislation and to administer the laws that result from the initiatives. No agency is more important as a management support system for the president than the Office of Management and Budget, which has a government-wide perspective on the development of policy. It is traditionally the agency that establishes practices and oversees all of the federal government through its role preparing the administration's budget, approving agency regulations, and establishing management practices.

Obama imagined an enhanced management role for the agency through the creation of the position of chief performance officer for OMB. On January 3, 2009, in announcing that Nancy Killefer would be his appointee for the post, Obama detailed his promises for the personal impact she would make. "I will be instructing members of my cabinet and key members of their staffs to meet with Nancy soon after we take office. And on a regular basis thereafter, to discuss how they can run their agencies with greater efficiency, transparency, and accountability," he said. "In order to make these investments that we need, we'll have to cut the spending that we don't. And I'll be relying on Nancy to help guide that process."[39]

As a former Treasury Department official in the Clinton administration and an executive at McKinsey and Company, Killefer was well qualified for the position. When asked about the management agenda, John Podesta reflected on her import-ant role: "Nancy was well positioned to carry forward" the management policies the president-elect articulated during the campaign. "The president wanted to put some effort into that."[40]

Less than a month later, on the same day that Daschle withdrew his name from consideration for the two posts for which he was named, Nancy Killefer withdrew hers from consideration for the OMB post. Both nominees had tax is-sues, although hers involved a small sum that she had already paid. Three months later the president nominated Jeffrey Zients, a management consultant from the private sector, to the position; he was confirmed in mid-June. Now that six months had gone by, it was difficult for Zients to establish the performance criteria when the department secretaries had already been in place for some while. "Jeff Zients did a good job, but I think it was always . . . lower profile," Podesta commented.[41] He also noted the administration was doing things related to management, "but in terms of messaging, none of that came through."

It was difficult for the president himself to focus on management as an issue at the beginning and also later in the administration. "On the domestic side, the engine of the White House was really about churning out big legislative achieve-ments," Podesta observed.[42] Not being able to focus on a domestic management agenda in those early months was also a product of the severity of the financial crises the administration were dealing with as the president came into office. "Some of that I think has to do with just how deep the hole was in the economy and . . . how much policy work there was. The focus was really in the legislative arena, whether that was health care, the American Recovery Act, Dodd-Frank; and there was a fairly important education bill passed," Podesta said. Manage-ment was an important consideration, however, on the national security front. "I would say that it was different on the national security front versus the domestic front. On the national security side, he was consumed with execution of deci-sions that he had made. I think he was comfortable and quickly took control of what you'd think of as the execution side."

Over the more than six years since Obama's first inauguration, the adminis-tration has not succeeded in establishing a stable top-tier leadership structure for OMB. Since the time of Killefer's nomination problems, OMB has struggled to confirm their officials in the top posts. For the director's post, over one-third of the time President Obama has been in office, there has been an acting director of OMB rather than someone confirmed by the Senate. This state of affairs has continued to the present day. Jeffrey Zients served two stints adding up to just under twenty months. His second tour of fifteen months conflicted with the terms of the Federal Vacancies Reform Act of 1998, which provided that officials cannot serve in an "acting" status longer than 210 days.[43] Under the terms of that act, Zients's tour expired at the end of September 2012; he lost the title of "acting" even if he continued to perform the functions of the office. He continued to serve in his post as deputy for management as well as his role as chief performance officer, using those positions to do the work of director of the agency even if he no longer had the title. Zients left the OMB post on April 24, 2013, when Sylvia Mathews Burwell was named to head the agency.

While as president-elect Obama had planned to organize management of the administration out of OMB, as the administration unfolded the agency became a talent pool for other positions the president cared about. There was little continuity in OMB in the leadership spots, aside from the many hats Jeff Zients was obliged to wear. Zients was first person called in to fill the director's seat on an acting basis because the president had moved two of its three confirmed directors to other positions in the administration. Jack Lew, Obama's second OMB director, was tapped after fourteen months in the job to serve as the president's chief of staff and then as secretary of the Treasury. Sylvia Mathews Burwell headed the agency for less than a year before the president announced her departure to become secretary of health and human services. Zients moved over to deal with health care when the president asked him to unravel the problems with the healthcare.gov website and, following that stint, to become director of the National Economic Council. He formally left OMB on May 1, 2013; his assistant, Shelly Metzenbaum, who worked on performance issues, left on May 3.

In addition to the management, budget, and performance areas of OMB that saw so many occupants of those top chairs, the regulations part of OMB suffered from a vacancy as well. Cass Sunstein headed the Office of Information and Regulatory Affairs from September 2009 to early August of 2012, when he announced he would be returning to Harvard Law School. An acting official preceded him, and another one following him. His eventual successor, Howard Shelanski, was not nominated until the end of April 2013 and was confirmed three months later. In an environment where executive action, including rules and regulations, was to be a central part of Obama's second-term agenda, OIRA was a key agency in the president's plan to accomplish his goals.

The vacancies occurred because the officials were tapped for a variety of presidential assignments. While the first director, Peter Orszag, returned to private life, his successors were enlisted by the president to take other positions. The second

OMB director, Jack Lew, was tapped for White chief of staff and then, two years later, for secretary of the Treasury. Jeffrey Zients, the OMB acting director and Mr. Fix-It for health care, moved to the White House as head of the National Economic Council. The third director, Sylvia Mathews Burwell, was in the position less than a year before she was chosen to be secretary of health and human services. The agency accumulated a great deal of management knowledge and experience, but it was outsourced rather than used to establish a continuing management team working out of the Office of Management and Budget.

The environment at OMB has suffered from the continuing management changes. While most government agencies have found employees dissatisfied with their workplaces because of sequestration and stagnant salaries, OMB has suffered more than most. The Partnership for Public Service surveys of the "Best Places to Work," a government-wide look at employee satisfaction in federal government agencies, annually query people about life in their agencies. Orszag emphasized the importance of the survey as a management tool when the 2009 figures—reporting their 2008 findings—were released early in the Obama administration. Orszag remarked at a May 2009 awards ceremony honoring OMB and others with high survey rankings. "This survey is an excellent resource . . . [that] offers useful metrics that should be incorporated into how we manage government."[44] In the latest survey based on data on employee satisfaction from 2013, OMB ranked 23 out of 29 small agencies. Using metrics dealing with leadership empowerment, work-life balance, employee skills and their match with OMB's mission, training and development, OMB ranked lower than 20 out of the 28 agencies measured for this part of the survey. The three surveys prior to the 2009 one all had OMB with a high management satisfaction rate. Only one—2012—of what would become annual surveys using data collected between 2009 and 2013 ranked OMB above the satisfaction level of the agencies in the survey.[45] The fall in morale at OMB was matched by the public's poor marks for the president on his management of government. In a June 2014 poll, the public rated President Obama at 39 percent in the category "can manage government effectively."[46] While the initial problems with the health care signups certainly had more to do with the perception of the president's management accomplishments than the vacancies at the Office of Management and Budget, the lack of a continuing leadership core in the central management agency dedicated to government-wide management issues is important, as officials throughout the government depend on OMB for guidance and coordination.

The reality of presidential politics is that at the beginning of their terms in office, few presidents want to invest a great deal of energy in management issues.

While they come in with management items they want to pursue right at the start—open government for Obama, faith-based offices throughout the federal government for George W. Bush, and government performance review for Clinton—more pressing items come to the fore that drive out broad management issues, whether it is a financial crisis, a national security crisis, or a crowded legislative agenda. Presidents often spend little personal energy on management because they see inadequate rewards coming from their efforts. President Clinton had limited personal involvement in the national performance review initiative in his administration, tasking it instead to Vice President Gore. Jonathan Breul, who worked on several presidential management initiatives in his position as a senior career staff member at OMB, noted Clinton's efforts. "He understood instinctively that this management stuff didn't get him one vote, and he wasn't going to waste any effort in trying to change that." That did not mean that he placed no value on management issues, but the benefit was more in a matter of preventing problems where the blame could be placed at his door. Breul continued, "He still saw a need and a value in it, but it wasn't political. . . . It was prophylactic. It was protective of everything because it ensured that he wouldn't get criticized if there was going to be a problem. But he wouldn't get any points for having done it."[47] Management may be significant for presidents to reach their goals, but it is difficult to get them to pay attention. At the same time, one can see the cost it can have for a president in both having programs, such as the introduction of the Affordable Care Act gone awry, and in the public's view of a president's management achievements.

Selling the Agenda: Increased Pressures on Modern Presidents

Presidents need to explain and elaborate on their initiatives. Presidents with an aggressive agenda coming into office have accordingly increased their public appearances consistent with the high number of early policy actions. The following chart looks at the increase in actions and public appearances from President Eisenhower's early days to those of President Obama. There are two time entries for each of the presidents in the chart. The first one is for a president's activities in January (that is, the first eleven days) and the second for the entire first hundred days in office.

From a slow public start-up in Eisenhower's first eleven days and then through April 29—which marks the end of the hundred-day period—to today, presidents increase their public remarks consistent with their increase in executive and legislative policy action. Eisenhower gave twelve speeches and remarks and held seven solo press conferences, while in the same period President Obama's numbers

TABLE 5.3
Presidential Activity: January and First 100 Days

	Eisenhower		Kennedy		Nixon		Carter		Reagan		G. H. W. Bush		Clinton		G. W. Bush		Obama	
	Jan	100	Jan	100	Jan	100	Jan	100	Jan	100	Jan	100	Jan	100	Jan	100	Jan	100
Addresses to Congress (inaugural and joint session)	1	2	2	2	1	1	1	2	1	3	1	2	1	2	1	2	1	2
Address to nation	0	0	0	0	0	0	0	2	0	1	0	0	0	1	0	0	0	0
Radio addresses	0	0	0	0	0	0	0	0	0	0	0	0	0	12	1	14	2	14
Remarks	0	10	3	32	9	88	14	79	15	57	9	101	8	75	16	124	11	126
Remarks & Exchange	0	0	0	0	0	0	0	5	0	1	1	8	4	26	11	43	1	16
Addresses/Remarks Total	**1**	**12**	**5**	**34**	**10**	**89**	**15**	**88**	**16**	**62**	**11**	**111**	**13**	**116**	**29**	**183**	**15**	**158**
Press conferences	0	7	1	10	1	5	0	6	1	2	1	11	1	13	0	5	0	12
Solo	0	7	1	10	1	5	0	6	1	2	1	9	1	4	0	2	0	6
Joint	0	0	0	0	0	0	0	0	0	0	0	2	0	9	0	3	0	6
Short Q&A (Exchanges with reporters)	0	0	0	0	0	0	0	8	1	7	2	10	10	82	11	53	1	18
Interviews	0	0	1	2	0	0	0	4	0	16	1	12	0	9	0	19	3	46
Interchanges with Press Total	**0**	**7**	**2**	**12**	**1**	**5**	**0**	**18**	**2**	**25**	**4**	**33**	**11**	**104**	**11**	**77**	**4**	**76**
Travel days out of U.S. / countries visited	0/0	0/0	0/0	0/0	0/0	8/6	0/0	0/0	0/0	2/1	0/0	6/4	0/0	2/1	0/0	4/2	0/0	13/9

Note: Information categories are the ones used by the National Archives for presidential addresses and remarks as well as interchanges with reporters. The Short Q&As are instances where the president answers one or two questions from reporters in less formal settings than press conferences.
Source: Public Papers of the President, as found at American Presidency Project: http://www.presidency.ucsb.edu/ws/. National Archives, The Compilation of Presidential Documents found at: http://www.gpo.gov/fdsys/browse/collection.action?collectionCode=CPD. For presidential travel, Office of the Historian, Department of State, https://history.state.gov/departmenthistory/travels/president.

were 158 addresses and remarks with twelve press conferences, six solo and six joint. In Eisenhower's time, solo press conferences were a major element of a president's public appearances (35%), but in Obama's first hundred days, only seven percent of his appearances were press conferences, joint and solo.

Patterns presidents establish show up in their early days in office and often remain throughout their tenure. That is true with the interactions with reporters that President Obama had in his first five years in office. While his recent predecessors George W. Bush and Bill Clinton spent time in short question-and-answer sessions with a pool of reporters, President Obama eschewed such sessions right from the start of his administration. He was more reluctant than his immediate predecessors to use such a venue, where he would often be called on to respond to unfolding current events.

Taking the figures above, we can see that President Obama preferred to do his questioning with reporters in interview settings in his first hundred days, and throughout his first five years he maintained the same pattern. Interviews come first, short question-and-answer sessions a distant second on the preference scale, and press conferences last. This pattern mirrors a consistency of preferences found in the practices of President Clinton and George W. Bush. In both periods—at the hundred-day mark and at five years—the two presidents favored short question-and-answer sessions. At least in the area of presidential exchanges with reporters, the venues a president prefers at the beginning of his administration will most likely remain the preferred pattern.

Today a president has a six- or seven-day week with a Saturday address, an element that came into the contemporary presidency in Ronald Reagan's second year. All of his successors, except for George H. W. Bush, gave weekly radio/television addresses from their first days in office. Their public appearances serve as support for their active policy agendas. Eisenhower did not have initiatives to announce in his early weeks and months on a scale of current chief executives. The growth from Eisenhower's time in presidential appearances responding to reporters' queries is related to the modern growth in government activity and the president's role in presenting initiatives in domestic policy areas that now include, to name a few, clean air and clean water, aid to education, consumer protection, and women's health issues. When presidents act in these areas, they need to elaborate on what they are doing and then reinforce their actions with further explanations for as long as it takes to reach their goals.

Most modern presidents now begin their tenure with executive action, including executive orders, memoranda to executive branch agencies and departments, and proclamations relating to issues, institutions, and noteworthy dates. Part of

TABLE 5.4
Presidential Interchanges with Reporters at 100 Days and Five-Year Mark

	Clinton	G. W. Bush	Obama
100 Days			
Press conferences	13 (12.5%)	5 (6.5%)	12 (15.8%)
Short Q&A	82 (78.9%)	53 (68.8%)	18 (23.7%)
Interviews	9 (8.6%)	19 (24.7%)	46 (60.5%)
Total	**104**	**77**	**76**
Five-Year Mark			
Press conferences	154 (13.9%)	124 (15.9%)	99 (10.1%)
Short Q&A	742 (67.1%)	391 (50.1%)	123 (12.5%)
Interviews	210 (19.0%)	266 (34.0%)	761 (77.4%)
Total	**1,106**	**781**	**983**

Source: Public Papers of the President, as found at American Presidency Project, www.presidency.ucsb.edu/ws/. Short Question and Answer sessions are categorized by the National Archives for the *Public Papers* as "exchanges with reporters." Interview information gathered from internal White House sources for each of the three presidents.

the public appearances of the early days in office for a president is travel abroad. Eisenhower followed up on his 1952 campaign promise by traveling to Korea, but he did so before he became president. Once he took office, he did not travel abroad until after the hundred-day period. President Obama, on the other hand, traveled to nine countries in the early period, taking up thirteen days of the first hundred. In large part, the trips were tied to the global financial issues that were part of the financial collapse Obama had been dealing with since he was elected. Together, we have a portrait of a contemporary president active from his earliest days in office. That level of activity is now what presidents have to prepare for during their pre- and postelection periods.

Campaign Commitments Limit Presidential Actions

Campaigns affect a president-elect's transition into office through promises that have an impact on how he shapes the administration. Some management and policy commitments limit what a president will be able to do when in office, while a clearly articulated policy agenda during the campaign makes it easier for a chief executive to establish from the start the direction of his administration. With presidents who waged campaigns with a broad range of commitments rather than a targeted agenda, commitments have almost as many negative points as positive ones. That is particularly true when the candidate has an umbrella theme, as Senator Obama did with "hope and change." Unfulfilled promises can haunt candidates because they are so difficult to back away from and end up enraging critics and disappointing allies. In addition, news organizations now take the candidates' promises, break them down individually, and then maintain an updated progress report on where a president is keeping them.

Campaign Agenda as a Governing Agenda

While campaign commitments can limit the options a president-elect has at the point when the incoming chief executive is organizing the administration, they can also serve as the center of his governing agenda when he comes into office. The president-elect can organize policy priorities around campaign commitments and adjust the emphasis he gave them over the period of his candidacy. One of the reasons President Bush had an unexpectedly smooth start to his administration after the contested election is because the candidate and his team saw their campaign agenda as their governing one. Clay Johnson said of Bush: "He said our priorities will be what we campaigned on. We want education, we want a strong national defense. . . . We said they were our priorities, and they are."[48] Once he came into office, President Bush took the basic issues he campaigned on and laid out his plans for them in a sequential fashion. His first week in office was devoted to education, followed the next week by faith-based initiatives and the creation of that office, then his tax cut program and strengthening defense through increased spending.

In the age of the Internet, campaign promises are easily tracked, followed, and assessed. In the 2008 campaign, Bill Adair, Washington bureau chief for the *Tampa Bay Times,* created a political fact-checking website, PolitiFact, that featured an "Obameter" that was used to weigh the commitments Senator Obama made as a candidate with what he did during the transition and the early days of his administration. He tracked how Obama's promises included in *Blueprint for Change* as well as in separate promises made in speeches were handled during the transition and as the administration came into office. The online document was there for people to compare. In 2009, Adair received a Pulitzer Prize for his project. While he left the paper in 2013, there are others who do similar work. In the "Fact Checker" column at the *Washington Post,* Glenn Kessler continues to invoke Obama's promises as a candidate to track his current performance.

Ethics Pledges and Transparency Commitments

Many candidates make statements during their presidential campaigns that are popular on the campaign trail but prove limiting once they become president. The ethics pledges and transparency commitments of the 2008 cycle are good examples of the continuing difficulties a president can have meeting standards laid down in strong, declarative campaign pledges. For our purposes here, we will focus on the ethics pledges President Obama's transition staff and administration officials were required to sign.

Senator Obama promised in a 2007 campaign speech that he would not have anyone in his administration who was involved in lobbying. "When I am President, I will make it absolutely clear that working in an Obama Administration is not about serving your former employer, your future employer, or your bank account—it's about serving your country, and that's what comes first. When you walk into my administration, you will not be able to work on regulations or contracts directly related to your former employer for two years. And when you leave, you will not be able to lobby the Administration through the remainder of my term in office."[49] As we saw in chapter 4, when they worked in the transition, anyone working on Obama's behalf in the agency review teams, the policy teams, or elsewhere in the transition, were required to sign pledges limiting their transition activities depending on the conflicts laid out by the Obama team.

Ethics continued to be a key matter when Obama came into office. One of the executive orders he issued on his first full day in office was designed to carry out his campaign ethics pledge limiting who could work for his administration. Executive Order 13490 on "Ethics Commitments by Executive Branch Personnel" called for three lobbying bans: a lobbyist gift ban, a "revolving door" ban providing restrictions on those entering government, and "revolving door" restrictions on where and on what subjects those leaving office are allowed to work. The commitments include: "I will not accept gifts from registered lobbyists or lobbying organizations for the duration of my service as an appointee. . . . I will not for a period of 2 years from the date of my appointment participate in any particular matter involving specific parties that is directly and substantially related to my former employer or former clients, including regulations and contracts."[50] If an appointee was a lobbyist two years before the person came into office, he or she is restricted for two years following the election from participating in "any particular matter on which I lobbied within the 2 years before the date of my appointment." As strong as the pledge was, the president and his team wanted to provide a way to bring in people who they believed were important additions to their administration but who did not meet the restrictions. For that reason, the executive order provides for the director of the Office of Management and Budget to grant waivers from these restrictions.

It did not take long for the administration to grant its first waiver, an act that caught the eye of news organizations both because of the timing and the nature of the waiver. The day after the president issued the order, Senator Carl Levin, who as chair of the Senate Armed Services Committee was presiding over the confirmation of William J. Lynn III to be deputy secretary of defense, called for a review of Lynn's nomination in light of the president's executive order.[51] Lynn came into the administration from his position at Raytheon, a corporation that sells billions of dollars' worth of military equipment to the Pentagon. Among its products for the Defense Department are the Army's Patriot Missile and the Tomahawk missile used by the Navy. More than any other official in government, the Pentagon procurement officer makes purchasing decisions that rank in the billions of dollars. The waiver, signed by Peter Orszag, reads: "After consultation with Counsel to the President, I hereby waive the requirements of Paragraphs 2 and 3 of the Ethics Pledge of Mr. William Lynn. I have determined that it is in the public interest to grant the waiver given Mr. Lynn's qualifications for his position and the current national security situation."[52] There was no further elaboration on his qualifications or what the conflicts were. The conflict of interest was evident through the 2008 lobbying registration filing of the Raytheon Corporation with Congress listing William J. Lynn III as one of the corporate officers lobbying on defense department authorization and appropriations issues.[53] The Raytheon form submitted under the Lobbying Disclosure Act of 1997 (LDA) listed its congressional lobbying interests as "provisions related to acquisition policy, force protection, military space and intelligence, command and control, simulation and training, self-defense systems and decoys, missile defense, sensors and radars, missiles, munitions and artillery, and advanced technology programs."[54]

The *New York Times* editorial board praised the executive order on ethics and condemned the Lynn waiver: "The new president's actions provided a burst of executive sunshine that Washington badly needs. Unfortunately, Mr. Obama already wants to make an exception for William Lynn, a former lobbyist for the defense contractor Raytheon, to become deputy secretary of defense. Mr. Lynn, a respected Pentagon official in the Clinton administration, has the right resume—except that he was a lobbyist until last year. This clearly violates the mint-new standard, especially since the Pentagon job is so wide-ranging that recusal on specific issues is impossible."[55] Nor did other news organizations let the contrast between the pledge and the waiver slide. In one of its news blogs, for instance, ABC News ran a story with a headline "Two Days after Instituting Ethics Rules, President Obama Waives Them for Deputy Pentagon Secretary Nominee."[56]

The difficulty of these kinds of pledges is that while they might garner some votes for your approach, they are much more likely to put the candidate at risk for comparisons for actions during his administration once he enters office. For President Obama, there have been continuing comparisons between his statements about transparency and openness and the way business has been conducted during his administration. The ethics pledge has led to a continuing conversation with groups over the unintended consequences of the ethics requirement.

President Obama touted his administration's ethics rules in his 2010 State of the Union message, but a significant group of organizations did not share his enthusiasm for the ethics pledge or how it had worked in the president's first year. He spoke of the administration's ethics commitments: "To close that credibility gap, we have to take action on both ends of Pennsylvania Avenue to end the outsized influence of lobbyists, to do our work openly, to give our people the Government they deserve. Now, that's what I came to Washington to do. That's why, for the first time in history, my administration posts . . . our White House visitors online. That's why we've excluded lobbyists from policymaking jobs or seats on Federal boards and commissions."[57] From the viewpoint of some nonprofit groups, the intersection of the administration's ethics rules and the administration's lobbying rules did not produce a good result.

Six days before the president's 2010 State of the Union message, thirteen nonprofit organizations that focus on issues on transparency and ethical conduct in government wrote to the president. They complained that the order was unduly harsh on those with experience at nonprofit organizations, as the order applied equally to those in corporate and the nonprofit worlds. The order led, they claimed, to an increase in people who lobbied to deregister under the LDA. "One year later, it is clear that the Order as currently structured has yielded some unintended consequences that undermine your goals of open government and broad civic participation in the public interest."[58] They pointed out that the ethics rules based on the LDA has the "perverse result of decreasing transparency and driving real influence peddlers into the shadows and out of the sunlight. By using the LDA, the Ethics Order is substantially over-inclusive, actually harming the public interest more than special interests. Thus, countless charities that have no actual or perceived financial conflicts of interest are treated as 'collateral damage' and discouraged from much-needed policy involvement." The groups signing the letter included Citizens for Responsibility and Ethics in Washington (CREW), Common Cause, Consumers Union, Human Rights Watch, and the Center for Lobbying in the Public Interest.

The following year, the Center for Lobbying in the Public Interest conducted a survey based on interviews with representatives of nonprofit lobbying organizations that called into question the impact of the lobbying restrictions based on those who registered under the Lobbying Disclosure Act of 1997. The study reached the following conclusion: "After two and a half years of experience, it is clear that these public service restrictions have done little to curb special interest influence in Washington, while unintentionally harming public-interest advocacy and undermining the Administration's efforts to promote transparency and good government."[59] The lobbyists for many nonprofit organizations have deregistered under the LDA so that they could become eligible two years for an administration position later. The study noted: "The Administration's restrictions have introduced a new phrase into the American political lexicon: 'getting clean.' This is how several nonprofit leaders describe the situation where a public-interest advocate stops lobbying at their nonprofit or leaves altogether for two years waiting to become eligible for relevant service in the executive branch."[60]

The study found that since 2009, 42 percent of the survey respondents said they had released people covered by the LDA.[61] Of those who released their personnel, "57% reported that the decision to terminate was influenced by the Obama Administration's restrictions. About 32% disagreed with that assessment."[62] Other organizations focused as well on lobbying. A report by the American Bar Association arises out of a 2009 study by that body's Task Force on Federal Lobbying Laws and the subsequent adoption of resolutions by its House of Delegates on August 8–9, 2011. The report discussed the deregistration problems: "To the extent that lobbyists may have responded to this [deregistration and nonregistration] incentive, the result has been reduced transparency in government, as well as the unhappy consequences of leaving people who comply with the LDA worse off than those who bypass it, either lawfully or otherwise."[63]

Declarative pledges inevitably lead to cases where it is difficult to understand the criteria the White House Counsel's office could have used to determine who needed a waiver, what issues would be included in their review, and how the rulings were made. While it took seventy-three words to waive William Lynn as procurement chief at the Pentagon, General James Jones required a waiver of 839 words to be allowed to introduce former president Clinton at a luncheon hosted by the Atlantic Council. General Jones received no compensation for his work with the Atlantic Council when he worked there and none for his introduction, which White House Ethics Counsel Norman Eisen assured "will be brief."[64] Among the waivers Eisen signed included one for Counsel to the President Robert Bauer.

Those who received waivers were among the most important of members of President Obama's White House inner circle. Of the fifteen ethics waivers issued for members of the Obama White House, in addition to Jones and Bauer the list includes Obama's chief of staff, William Daley; terrorism advisor John Brennan; senior advisor Valerie Jarrett; and the director of intergovernmental affairs, Cecilia Munoz.[65] Others, such as Biden's counselor and then chief of staff,

Steve Ricchetti, did not require a waiver to take his post though he formed and headed an organization, Ricchetti Inc., that continues to do a substantial amount of lobbying of Congress.[66] The waivers are only required for those who were registered to lobby Congress under the Lobbying Disclosure Act of 1997. Ricchetti deregistered as a lobbyist in late 2008 and thus was not required under the Obama administration rules to register when he came into the White House in 2012. In addition to the waivers the White House granted to White House staff and administration officials, the Office of Government Ethics has the forty-two waivers granted at the department level that are in addition to the ones granted by the White House.[67]

President Obama is not the only chief executive to find it difficult to make campaign pledges into policy. Believing that they needed to demonstrate their willingness to make cuts in the government workforce, Presidents Clinton and Carter got into difficulty by promising to make deep cuts in the White House staff. Clinton's cuts, such as those in the career staff responsible for telephones and correspondence, turned out to be unpopular.[68] President Clinton got into additional difficulties over campaign ethics promises. One of his early actions was to issue an executive order calling for stiff post-employment regulations requiring appointees to make the following promise: "I will not, within five years after the termination of my employment as a senior appointee in any executive agency in which I am appointed to serve, lobby any officer or employee of that agency."[69] Additionally, they would not be allowed to work for a foreign government for life. Some groups focusing on public administration viewed a lifetime ban on certain kinds of lobbying and a five-year limitation on all kinds of lobbying relating to the agency the person served in as too stiff. "It's generally believed this executive order was much too burdensome and that a five-year ban went much too far," said New York University Professor Paul Light.[70] Stephen Potts, head of the Office of Government Ethics, commented that the order "was more restrictive than need be and it was going to have an inevitable chilling impact on their ability to recruit."[71] Near the end of his administration, on December 28, 2000, President Clinton revoked the order.[72]

As difficult as the rules are to administer, the Obama administration has held with the rules tied to the ethics pledge. One member of the White House staff argued for the pledges based on the impact they have on public trust in government. "They give you a basis to talk about changing the culture within the government on ethics and compliance matters," he said.[73] "If you don't really treat ethics and compliance matters as if they're just as important as what you're trying to accomplish, ultimately you'll lose the public's trust because the public loses trust every time they see ethics scandals." From his vantage point, he could see a difference in how people in the government viewed ethics issues and the need to be responsive to the guidelines. "The culture [has changed] inside government about how people treat these rules, and people pay more attention to them because we've been able to drill in that these things matter more than just as speed bumps on the way to somewhere else."[74] The staff person said that rather than waiting until a problem arises and saying "Oops, what do we do now?" people come forward to question whether they are complying with the rules.

The Last Months of Two-Term Presidencies

Two-term presidents know that they are leaving office and therefore spend their final year in a way that differs from what recent one-term presidents have done. Other people and institutions also are well aware the incumbent is soon leaving and turn their focus to the candidates and then to the president-elect. Of the ten presidents who served while the two-term limit applied to their presidencies, four presidents (Eisenhower, Reagan, Clinton, George W. Bush) served two full terms. In the case of the three one-term presidents (Ford, Carter, George H. W. Bush), each ran for reelection (although in Ford's case it was his first presidential election). Two of the remaining three presidents—John F. Kennedy, Richard Nixon—did not complete their terms. Of those who did win a second term (even if after a shortened first term), only Lyndon Johnson did not run for reelection. What this means is that in an eight-year presidency, the chief executive is not focused on his own election and, in most cases, has a limited domestic agenda for his final year and sometimes two years, especially if his party suffered significant losses in the last mid-term congressional elections. Unless there is a critical situation that arises at the end, as there was in George W. Bush's presidency with the financial collapse, two-term presidents have few policy initiatives in their final months.

When presidents take office after a two-term president, as Barack Obama did, they come in to an office where the incumbent has most often been preparing to leave office and not been active on the policy front, except in the areas of foreign policy and national security. When the sitting president in question did take action, it was most likely through executive action, in particular executive orders, memoranda, and pardons. These are actions a president can take alone, although his actions may of course meet with a critical response from those within and outside the branches of government. Such was the case, for example, when President Clinton left office and was criticized by Republicans for his executive orders and by officials of both parties for his pardons.

Some presidents come into a situation where their early actions are going to include responses to the actions of their immediate predecessors, such as with executive orders issued by an outgoing president of the opposing party. Of the four two-term presidents who have held office since 1953, only Ronald Reagan turned the White House over to a successor from his own party. This means that in their final months, presidents are going to think through their final actions, particularly in the event of a president from the opposing party coming into office following them.

In chapter 4 we saw the particular sensitivity of President George W. Bush over executive orders issued at the end of the Clinton administration that Bush believed did damage to the Clinton administration. No matter what actions a president takes at the end, the incoming president starts off his presidency by ordering a stop to whatever executive actions are in the pipeline but have not yet been approved. If there is a change of party, presidents and their staffs begin their tenures by deciding which of those late actions that have yet to be published in the Federal Register should remain as policy. Publication in the Federal Register is the final step before they become operational.

Additionally, with few initiatives to put forward and with increased attention placed on his potential successors, the president gradually becomes less of a presence in public life in terms of his public appearances, including his remarks, press conferences, and events where he responds to reporters' queries. During the last six months of his presidency and sometimes even a year before his departure, a president is seen and heard less than was the case in his earlier years. He is less relevant to the news organizations, people in the Washington community, and his party, especially when the results of the last mid-term congressional elections before he leaves office bring in a wave of elected officials from the opposing party. Except where foreign and national security policy is concerned, he winds down the number of remarks he gives as well as the number of times he speaks with reporters. What he does ramp up, however, is presidential travel, especially if his party has just lost a large number of seats in one or both houses of Congress.

President Eisenhower faced such a loss in 1958, when Republicans lost forty-seven seats in the House and thirteen in the Senate and so too did Lyndon Johnson in 1966, when Democrats lost forty-seven House seats and four seats in the Senate. In the congressional elections of 1986 during the Reagan years, Republicans lost control of the Senate when they lost eight seats, though they only lost five seats in the House. President Clinton was in a different position as Democrats neither lost nor gained Senate seats in the 1998 election and gained four in

TABLE 5.5

Party Control in Final Off-Year Congressional Election for a Two-Term President

	House seats before		House seats after		Senate seats before		Senate seats after	
	D	R	D	R	D	R	D	R
Eisenhower (R) 1958	234	201	283	154	49	47	64	34
Reagan (R) 1986	253	182	258	177	47	53	55	45
Clinton (D) 1998	207	227	211	223	45	55	45	55
G. W. Bush (R) 2006	201	232	233	202	44	55	49	49
Barack Obama 2014	201	234	188	247	53	45	44	54

Source: Stanley and Niemi, "Table 1-10: House and Senate Election Results, by Congress, 1788–2004," *Vital Statistics on American Politics, 2013–2014*, 30–31; 2014 figures from contemporary news accounts.
Note: After 2006 and into 2015, two Senate Independents caucused with the Democrats.

the House. For President George W. Bush, the pattern was a repeat of earlier eras in which the incumbent saw his party lose enough House seats for a shift in control to the Democrats. Republicans lost thirty House seats, while the Democrats took over control of the Senate with a gain of six seats, bringing the Democrats to a 49–49 split, with two candidates who ran as independents, Joseph Lieberman and Bernie Sanders, promising to caucus with the Democrats.

With fewer initiatives to talk about, outgoing two-term presidents hold fewer press conferences in their last year than they did, on average, in their first seven years. With fewer policy initiatives to discuss, solo press conferences are less important, as they primarily serve the purpose for chief executives of demonstrating how conversant they are with important issues and persuading the public to back their initiatives, especially their domestic ones. President George W. Bush, for example, held fifty-one solo press conferences during his eight years, but only five of them were held in 2008–2009.[75] For President Clinton, the same decrease in solo press conferences was a pattern of his last year in 1999–2000. He held three of them in his last year in office, and none after June 2000. President Reagan had forty-six solo press conferences, with four in his last year. With foreign travel at the fore, many of their public appearances and press conferences, whether at home or abroad, were events with foreign leaders, except for Reagan, whose press conferences were all solo ones.

Presidents facing significant congressional losses with two years left in their presidencies focus on foreign policy, including a great deal of foreign travel. The template of a president as a world traveler in his final year starts with President

Eisenhower, the first president to finish his second term in office with the knowledge that he was not permitted to run for a third term. During his eight years, President Eisenhower entered a foreign country thirty-seven times (some countries are counted multiple times; France, for instance, is counted four times).[76] When the visits are broken down by year, twenty-eight of President Eisenhower's thirty-six visits (77.8%) took place between February 1959 and October 1960. Once the 1958 congressional elections results were in and the Democrats captured control of the House and retained the Senate, President Eisenhower adopted a lower profile because he knew that his legislative agenda would meet a hostile Congress.

The speeches he gave during this period reflected his trips abroad and his foreign policy and national security goals for the United States. Lyndon Johnson took to foreign travel as well, entering twenty-seven countries in his five and a quarter years, with seventeen of those (63.0%) in his last two years. Presidents Clinton and George W. Bush were the biggest travelers of them all but still fit into the pattern of loading a large amount of their foreign travel into their final months. President Clinton had 133 country visits, with fifty-one of them (38.3%) in the period following the 1998 congressional elections. President George W. Bush's travels closely mirror those of President Clinton, with 140 country visits and fifty-four (38.6%) in the almost two years following the off-year congressional election.[77] Reagan represents a departure from the pattern, with forty-nine country visits in his eight-year presidency, but only eleven of them (22.5%) occurred in his last year and a half.

With our recent two-term presidents on the road and visiting with foreign leaders in Washington for much of their last two years in office, there is less of a presence for them among the American public than was the case earlier in their presidencies. The result is that an incoming president following a two-term president works in an environment where a president in his last two years in office has made fewer appointments than was the case in earlier years and put forward fewer policy initiatives. He comes into office with an expectation among the public that there is much to be done in many areas of government action.

Moving the Campaign into the White House

A president moves into the White House with an agenda that runs from the immediate to the long-range and from the personal to the public. The first order of business for President Obama was to settle his young family in their new home and schools while also broadcasting the initial signals of his brand of leadership. An attentive Washington audience of elected officials, public servants, and those interested in furthering—or halting—particular policies search for clues in a president's initial offering of executive orders and memoranda to executive branch departments and agencies while also mining his speeches and remarks for indications of where he wants to go in the days and weeks to come. President Obama's agenda was a combination of items he cued up for his entry into the White House and ones arising from the financial collapse. Before he could attend to policy, though, his appointments took center stage. While he got his White House staff in place without incident, several of his cabinet choices did meet with resistance. Blown off course by the depth of the financial crisis and the problems his nominees presented, Obama spent more time than he wanted responding to issues not of his choosing.

We can see from President Obama's actions in his early days in office that the choices he made at that time on policy, personnel, and process are the same ones that have continued to be prominent during his tenure. In his case, the issues he laid out in his "Five Pillars" speech at Georgetown University in April have continued to be top priorities during his first six years in office. His White House staff is composed of many of his campaign people, a pattern that has stayed intact more than is true in most administrations at the six-year mark. His chief communications advisor, Dan Pfeiffer, is now a counselor to the president, and his senior advisor and friend, Valerie Jarrett, as well as his chief of staff, Denis McDonough, are people who came in from his Senate and campaign days. They continue to form his inner circle.

The move into the White House is not an easy one, as the pressures come from so many directions that it is hard to change course at such high speeds. The choices a president-elect makes during his transition into office are especially important because once he comes into the White House, the agendas of others and the exigencies of the time crowd out less immediately essential matters. He travels with what he brings with him and that includes the choices he made during the transition and what he learned then as well as what his core staff learned during their campaign and transition days.

CHAPTER SIX

The National Security Council Transition

Providing Continuity in a Bipartisan Environment

Perhaps the most important organizational and policy element of a contemporary presidential transition is the national security piece. The stakes involved in having a smooth organizational transition could not be higher. In fact, continuity in national security and foreign policy from one administration to the next, in a post-September 11 world, is key to a safe and smooth transition. The transition teams for President George W. Bush and President-elect Obama understood this very well. Since the creation of the National Security Council in the National Security Act of 1947, the National Security Advisor has been a critical figure synthesizing military, intelligence, and foreign policy information for the president and his White House team.[1]

In addition to demonstrating how a crucial area of transition planning is organized, the national security piece of a transition into the White House demonstrates other important aspects of the passage of power. One can see how the most significant area of a presidential transition is fashioned and what the differences are between a transition out of office and one coming in. In viewing the preparations out of office made by President George W. Bush's National Security Advisor Stephen J. Hadley and his National Security Council [NSC] staff, we see what the opportunities are for making a good exit and how it can be done in a way that serves the interests of both administrations. We also see the not-so-easy questions that require an answer before the policy issues can be addressed as well as the organizational issues, including personnel matters, that one has to deal with coming into the White House as head of the National Security Council staff.

Steve Hadley was in an excellent position to run the NSC transition out of office because he understood well the past patterns of transition preparations. He had served on the NSC staffs of Presidents Ford, Reagan, George H. W. Bush, and George W. Bush as well as a brief period in the Carter White House. The experiences of General James L. Jones Jr. provide us with a sense of the stack of decisions the NSC advisor, or any senior White House official with organizational responsibilities, has to consider during the transition and in the early months of an administration. General Jones did not have previous White House experience, but he was well versed on foreign policy and military issues and had dealt with national security officials in the Clinton and Bush administrations through his positions as commander of the U.S. European Command (EUCOM) and as Supreme Commander Europe (SACEUR) and earlier as Commandant of the Marine Corps.

The outgoing administration is in a favorable position planning its transition out of office because there are few rules governing the terms on which it leaves. The incumbent president and his team have the choice of how much time to devote to the transition and the power to choose when to begin and what information to provide. As they do their planning, those in office have the advantage as well of having settled relationships with the incumbent president and the senior White House staff. In conjunction with the president, the national security advisor decides what information to provide. There is no downside to early preparation because providing assistance to the incoming administration, no matter the party, is in the national interest and also works to the advantage of the outgoing president. The information the NSC gathers for the incoming team works well for the legacy of the outgoing president because the materials provide a wrap-up of what the administration faced while in office and what the administration's responses were. When you are leaving office, you can work far ahead of time on preparing information with several purposes. You can make your own administration look good, make the incumbent president look good, and help the incoming national security advisor, which is a good government move. The result is aces all around for the departing team.

For the incoming national security advisor, there is no smooth road.[2] Time is tight, and within weeks initial decisions on organization, policy, and personnel have to be made. An NSC advisor is going to be chosen and begin work sometime after the election. In General Jones's case, it was around Thanksgiving when he signed on to the new administration and December 1 when his appointment was formally announced. The outgoing team can work effectively coordinating information because the advisor has established relationships around the federal government that he can call on to help him gather the information he needs. When the NSC advisor enters, he or she does so without a clear road map of how to make the office reflect and support the incoming president. In a short time, the NSC advisor needs to set up a decision-making process that reflects the chief executive's interests and stated preferences. Organizationally, the NSC advisor works through personnel, budget, and structural issues relating to the office as he or she tries to establish his or her agenda and to tee up his or her initiatives. With a staff of approximately two hundred policy people, there is a great deal of organizational work to be done in the short space of seventy-five days.[3] Together, Steve Hadley and General Jones provide good studies of the advantages and perils of leaving and arriving in the West Wing office.

Particularly in 2008, both incoming and outgoing officials recognized the vulnerability of the transition period. "At a time of war, you don't want there to be any gaps, but particularly any extended gaps in having knowledgeable people [in office]," commented Joe Hagin, deputy White House chief of staff for a good portion of the final year of the George W. Bush administration.[4] From a national security point of view, continuity in government is crucial. Transitions represent periods when the government is changing hands and is thus more vulnerable than usual. Those preparing for the 2008 transition had sobering examples to consider as they prepared the way for a new administration. As I pointed out in 2008: "In June 2007, for example, three days after Prime Minister Gordon Brown took office in the United Kingdom, there were terrorist attacks in Glasgow and London. The March 2004 Madrid train bombings that killed 191 people came three days before that country's general election. With wars in Afghanistan and Iraq underway, continuity in governing was essential."[5]

Even before the September 11 attacks, the early months were vulnerable ones for a president. Sometimes presidents have had to deal simultaneously with multiple national security issues in their early months. President Clinton had to deal with several threats within his first two months in office. Two incidents were domestic terrorist attacks and a third, eight months later, involved attacks on our troops in Somalia stationed there for humanitarian purposes as part of a United Nations operation begun late in the presidency of George H. W. Bush. Initially viewed as a simple plan to alleviate starvation caused by environmental factors, the action led to a situation where U.S. soldiers were attacked by the forces of local warlords early in the Clinton administration. It took the president more than a year into his administration to bring the U.S. troops home, by which time forty-four of them had died.[6] On the domestic front, February 26, 1993, President Clinton was in office barely a month when there was a terrorist bombing under the North Tower of the World Trade Center. Two days later, four Alcohol, Tobacco, and Firearms agents were killed in a gun battle in Waco, Texas, where they were trying to serve a warrant on religious cult leader David Koresh. The Federal Bureau of Investigation then took over the law enforcement effort, which lasted fifty days. On April 19 a second assault resulted in a fire that destroyed the Branch Davidian complex; the raid resulted in the death of seventy-five people. Janet Reno, who would oversee the FBI and its efforts, had been sworn in as attorney general on March 11, barely a month before the siege at Waco. When a president and his cabinet secretaries come into office, they must prepare for uncertainty both at home and abroad.

In their book *Difficult Transitions: Foreign Policy Troubles at the Outset of Presidential Power*, Kurt M. Campbell and James B. Steinberg discuss the critical national security issues incoming presidents have faced. "The option of postponing decisions until the new president takes office is often unavailable when it comes to unfolding national security problems," they wrote.[7] Whether it was the Korean War, the Vietnam War, or Iraq and Afghanistan, presidents-elect have had to be ready to cope with conflicts that are under way during the transition period. Some incoming presidents also had to consider national security plans that are under way as the new chief executive came in. In looking back at the failure of the Bay of Pigs invasion for which President Kennedy provided the green light, Kennedy explained the dilemma confronting a chief executive in the national security area. "If someone comes in to tell me this or that about the minimum wage bill I have no hesitation in overruling them. But you always assume that the military and intelligence people have some secret skill not available to ordinary mortals," Kennedy said.[8]

The only antidote to a situation where the president or president-elect lacks the intelligence and the tools to cope with a given event or crisis is information and a knowledgeable staff. The outgoing Bush administration provided information to the incoming administration of Barack Obama, who in turn made early appointments decisions that allowed his national security team to get information from the incumbent administration well before the inauguration. Throughout the preparations for the 2008 changeover of power between the outgoing and incoming administrations, three key elements facilitated an effective start for the National Security Council as well as other administrative units.

First in importance for the NSC were the face-to-face briefings and conversations of those leaving office with the people coming in. In these principal-to-principal sessions, the outgoing people openly discussed with their incoming counterparts what they considered to be central points about how their operations worked and also responded to the inquiries posed by those coming in. Those sessions took place at the presidential level right down to the senior- and mid-level staff ranks. Underlying the success of the principal-to-principal meetings was the second element of the transition, a series of memoranda informing the principals about the status of issues and recent events in particular geographical areas, including contingency plans for possible events requiring quick responses prepared by the outgoing NSC staff. The third element, which developed out of the first two, was a White House decision-making system tailored to the president-elect's requirements. That system took into account how Obama wanted to receive information as well as the ingredients he desired in order to reach mature national security decisions. As the two teams prepared to change places, bipartisanship was a key ingredient in the success in the development of the principal-to-principal meetings, the memoranda prepared for the Obama team, and the overall decision-making system.

The Principal-to-Principal Part of the Transition

Principal-to-principal contact is a central aspect of a transition. Memoranda are important, but for questions to be answered and officeholders to speak with relative candor about their tenure, a setting without the inherent restrictions of paper, pen, and recording device is required. That was the case with the 2008 transition.

President Bush and the National Security Briefing Process

President Bush shaped important aspects of the White House briefing process as well as served as the official to brief the president-elect. Steve Hadley explained the role that President Bush played in the briefing process. President Bush controlled the chain of intelligence knowledge by deciding what information candidates and the president-elect would receive, who would receive it, and when they would get it. "I know the one thing that the president wanted neither of the candidates to get, nor the president-elect to get, was operational detail about CIA activities, operations . . . sources and methods issues," Steve Hadley said. According to Hadley, President Bush said, "When the man comes in and is president, sitting in this chair, that's time enough."[9] Operational "sources and methods" details should only be available to a person when he formally becomes president. That includes who and what the sources of intelligence information are and what methods were used to get it.

While he did not discuss sources and methods when he met with President-elect Obama, President Bush did discuss confidential programs with him. Hadley commented, "The most sensitive things we were doing, the president briefed President-elect Obama on himself, before he became president." That briefing took place on November 10, the Monday after the presidential election; it was the only postelection meeting the two men had alone. As to what they discussed, Hadley said that "the president wanted control over that."[10]

On certain issues, President Bush did not want his staff or administration officials to brief the incoming president; he wanted to go through a specific list of priority issues and programs he had singled out for discussion: "In their meeting, President Bush and President-elect Obama went through substantively some of these issues, where President Bush . . . transitioned some of these most important issues to President Obama personally."[11] President Bush set three issues as priorities in his discussion with President-elect Obama. While Hadley did not elaborate on what those issues were, *New York Times* reporter David E. Sanger has revealed two of the administration programs President Bush brought up in that session. The first dealt with Iran, and the second was the administration's drone program.

In his book *Confront and Conceal: Obama's Secret Wars and Surprising Use of American Power*, Sanger elaborates on a "worm" program that attacked the computer system associated with Iran's nuclear program: "Versions of the worm were deployed through the end of the Bush presidency and . . . before the handover, the forty-third president of the United States invited the forty-fourth to the White House for a one-on-one talk, in which Bush urged Obama to preserve two classified programs, the cyber attacks on Iran and the drone programs in Pakistan. The Iranians, Obama was told, were still clueless about why their centrifuges were blowing up."[12] While the worm program and the details of the drone program were not publicly known at the time the two presidents met, both projects have subsequently been the subject of a great deal of media and congressional attention.

According to a former administration official, in addition to these two issues President Bush brought up a third subject, "the importance of maintaining a strong relationship with Saudi Arabia."[13] In the post-September 11 world, Saudi Arabia is important for the United States not just because of the enduring oil relationship the two countries share but also because the country serves as one of the United States intelligence bases in a turbulent Middle East. Late in Obama's first year in office, the United States began construction of a drone base in Saudi Arabia.[14] Drones from that base were used to target and kill enemies in Yemen working with al-Qaeda, including Anwar al-Awlaki. On all three subjects—Iran cyber programs, the drone program, and the Saudi relationship—President Obama built on what President Bush talked to him about that day. Their conversation was an important example of the possible long-term impact of what takes place in a brief transition period. Actions taken during this period can set the table for what comes next.

In addition to deciding what information candidates and the president-elect would get, President Bush also was involved in determining who else could get information. Hadley noted that the "second issue that comes up is who and how many people does candidate Obama and then President-elect Obama get to have in the room when he gets briefed, and we had a lot of back and forth about that, and President Bush really tried to limit the number of people." As President Bush told Hadley: "These briefings are for the president-elect, not for all the staff at this point." Not all transition staff members come into a new administration, so many do not need to be informed about the most sensitive issues. Ultimately "we worked out a compromise that had him having two or three folks in the briefing."[15]

The director of national intelligence (DNI), Michael McConnell, was the person who worked with President Bush on questions relating to intelligence briefings and the person who handled the access negotiations. "Mike McConnell worked all of this between [President Bush and President-elect Obama]," Hadley said. McConnell "would bring the issues to the president, the president would make his decision, he would convey it to the president-elect. If the president-elect didn't like it, Mike would bring it back to the president." Hadley continued: "I would play in this a little bit, too, but Mike was the person who was handling that as the DNI at the time."[16]

Principal-to-Principal Briefings at the Cabinet and Staff Levels

Steve Hadley was particularly concerned to have principal-to-principal contact because of the shortened transition of thirty-seven days the Bush national security team experienced when they came into the White House prior to the inauguration in January 2001.

Hadley thought that principal meetings and exchanges of information would be particularly useful because, if the transition process was limited to memoranda prepared by lower level staff, key gaps would result, since outgoing cabinet secretaries had information those lower down in the organization did not have. "Memos would capture second-order issues better than first-order issues because a lot of the bureaucracies would not really know what the outgoing principals were doing on the most important issues," Hadley explained.[17] Issues of first importance, such as the status of key programs and discussions about them with the president and his White House staff, might not have filtered down to those lower in rank. When Bush officials were coming into the White House in 2001, there were few principal-to-principal sessions held in the national security area. "The only issue I know that was briefed outgoing principal–to–incoming principal was a deal that the Clinton administration thought they had with North Korea on ballistic missile production and testing," he recalled.[18] "Sandy [Berger] and Madeleine Albright sat down with Condi Rice and Colin Powell about the week before the inauguration and briefed them on it." The meeting was held outside of the White House. "That briefing got people's attention," Hadley said. Once they got the information about the missile issue, "it was briefed to the president. We looked at it. In the end of the day, we thought it wasn't real. They, I'm sure, will have a different view."

The experience of not having more extensive principal-to-principal briefings as they came into the White House in 2001 convinced Hadley that the Bush team needed to do it on the way out: "One of the things we did is we agreed we would try to have some face-to-face conversations with the new team to talk about the key issues that were transitioning—and that came about." Secretary of State Condoleezza Rice hosted a two-hour dinner at the State Department approximately ten days to two weeks prior to the inauguration. "Jim Jones and Hillary Clinton and Tom Donilon were on one side," said Hadley, "and Condi and I—and she had someone from State—were on the other." At the dinner, the group "went over in detail North Korea and Middle East peace." The session gave the Obama team a "starting point on where we were."[19]

In addition to the State Department and NSC principals transition meeting, the Bush team was interested in giving the Obama team a good sense of the direct dealings between the secretaries of defense and state. As secretaries of defense and state, respectively, Robert Gates and Condoleezza Rice dealt directly with one another. Hadley said, "They were dealing directly on a whole host of issues, which I very much encouraged, rather than putting it all through the interagency process. It's faster if you can get agencies to deal directly."[20] Hadley wasn't concerned that such direct meetings would be going around him: "I had known Bob and Condi forever. And I knew that they would let me know what was going on in that channel, which they did. I wanted to see if we could encourage the new team to have a similar kind of relationship." As the outgoing and incoming secretary of defense, Robert Gates met with Hillary Clinton and Condoleezza Rice on dealing with one another as principals.

From the viewpoint of General Jones, the earlier contacts made a difference as well: "I was very fortunate. First of all, having Steve Hadley there and knowing him before, and also Condi Rice and having known her and worked for her a little bit before," Jones said. "These are two extraordinarily decent, thoughtful people who went out of their way, especially Steve because he was the national security advisor, to prepare a glide path where I think the transition was—if it wasn't close to ideal, it was pretty darn close to being ideal."[21]

The largest and perhaps most important incoming and outgoing meeting occurred on the morning of the inauguration. The two national security teams met in the Situation Room. While the major order of business was the possible disruption of the inauguration, the incoming and outgoing secretaries in the national security area discussed two other matters as well.[22]

According to Hadley, one of the subjects under discussion was the status of U.S. efforts and activities in Afghanistan: "We also talked about the Afghan strategy review, something we had completed. . . . We basically transitioned it to the new team, and it became the basis for the review that they did." Hadley explained that they did not talk publicly about the Afghan review: "We were not comfortable touting it because we wanted the new team to be able to accept it and make it their own." The issue of ownership of the review was important because a new team from the opposing political party does not want to appear as if it is simply following what the outgoing administration did. They would naturally want to "create their own review. And if we claimed this one as ours, it would make it harder for them to accept."[23]

The principals also discussed Iran, according to Hadley: "We talked about Iran, and some very sensitive things we were doing in Iran." Iran was a priority for President Bush when he met with President-elect Obama in their postelection session at the White House. One of the topics would likely have been the "worm" program attacking Iran's computer system that David Sanger discussed in his *New York Times* article and in *Confront and Conceal*.[24] The White House team wanted to make sure that they had briefed the incoming senior people on the national security issues where it was important to get information correct. "So we had thought that on the most sensitive issues, we had better do a principals to principals handover," said Hadley.[25]

Briefings at a middle level in the National Security Council were an effective complement to the printed and electronic information that staff members received. After General Jones was appointed around Thanksgiving, selected staff members who would be coming in as part of the new team came into the White House to sit with their counterparts. What they found was that the mix of printed material and conversation with their counterparts made for a very useful combination. From their discussions, the incoming staff learned much more about why the Bush administration had made the decisions they did. Two senior administration officials discussed the benefits of such information sessions: "Should Canada be part of the Europe directorate because it's part of NATO, or should it be part of Western Hemisphere Affairs? You know, it changed at one point. And they [the Bush officials] said, we would recommend you keep it part of Western Hemisphere affairs. But here's the argument on the other side."[26]

Another person commented on the kinds of the responses they received from staff members. They were "very frank," this person said. "We said, 'Here are the two questions we're thinking about.' [They would say,] 'Here's how we solved it. We think it'll work for this reason structurally.' They would say, 'We recognize this seems weird when you look at it from an organization chart perspective. But here's the reason why we did it, and here's why we think it works.'" One official said the frank discussions made a difference for those coming into the administration. "So that a lot of it [the discussion] was this kind of back-and-forth conversation, which I found was very useful, just because you could have more give and take. You got a better understanding of where they were coming from."[27]

Principal-to-principal contact was invaluable because the incoming team got the thinking of those who already had thought through the issues in their time in the office. The incoming team posed questions to the Bush people about the choices the outgoing team made. One example would be the position held by Lieutenant General Douglas Lute, who in the Bush administration held the title of assistant to the president and deputy national security advisor for Iraq and Afghanistan. The new team needed to think through whether "General Lute keeps Iraq in his portfolio or not. That's a big decision to make bureaucratically. It's a big decision to make symbolically," said the two senior administration officials. "One of the reasons why the Bush administration had created that job several years earlier was because they wanted to send a message to the interagency [units] and to the world that Iraq was so important to that president that they wanted someone sitting in the West Wing of the White House who only thought about Iraq."[28]

The new NSC team could have decided "to migrate Iraq away from Lute. . . . We could have decided to do that, and politically it could have become an issue. . . . We really sought their advice and counsel on how to make this work and how to make the right decision here in terms of how to just structure our [office]."[29] The Obama team kept General Lute in essentially the same position, except that gradually his focus switched to Pakistan instead of Iraq while maintaining the Afghanistan portion of his portfolio. His title indicated the changing administration emphasis from Iraq to Pakistan: It would become special assistant to the president and coordinator for Afghanistan and Pakistan. Having people who had already thought through the same issues they were cutting their teeth on was crucial to a successful startup for the NSC.

Briefing General Jones on Outstanding Decisions

In addition to the meetings that brought together the chief executives and the sessions with cabinet officers and some senior White House staff members, there were additional briefings given by the national security advisor. One of the most important briefings was the one Hadley had with incoming NSC advisor General James Jones, Jones's deputy Tom Donilon, and White House counsel designate Greg Craig. Hadley accumulated current information to prepare for this meeting: "I had been for about two months, been keeping a stack of paper, which were actions that I had either taken that I wanted to explain to Jim Jones personally, or actions that had come in to me, that I could either take or hold for him, depending on what he wanted to do."[30]

This session was different from the other meetings in that Hadley wanted the thinking of the others in order to take action himself. Here we have an instance where the principle of "one president at a time" is not as nearly clear-cut as officials and citizens might think. With the election behind them, the outgoing president and his staff are most often careful about talking to the new team before acting themselves. Hadley explained what information he provided and what he sought from his successor: "In the last week before the inauguration, I made a copy of that [the four- or five-inch] file for Tom Donilon and for Jim Jones." Hadley sketched out how he dealt with the files and the issues they involved: "I went through them one by one, and said, 'Here's what this is. Here's what I probably would do, if left to my own devices. Do you want me to take that action, and have it off your plate, or do you want to take it yourself?'"[31] His questions to the new team were not simply idle ones. Once Jones gave him an answer, Hadley would adjust his future actions: "I invariably took his advice." Presidents and their staffs may be in office and make decisions up to January 20, but many times they prefer to let those who won the election have the final say on a lingering issue.

On the issue of French participation in NATO, the outgoing and incoming administrations talked through what each wanted to do. "We had set up the whole drill for getting France back into the military side of NATO, which got no public commentary," said Hadley. "And yet when it was tried in the past, and I was part of the effort in 1990, it was a huge issue in Washington, and it failed."[32] There had already been efforts in 1997 and 1998. The Clinton administration was working with President Jacques Chirac. "And it leaked prematurely, and it failed again." The George W. Bush national security and foreign policy teams worked on it as well. "We actually had gotten it done working through the military side with Mike Mullen in the lead, and a very small group," said Hadley. Hadley told the Obama group: "This is all done. Do you want us to get it announced and get it done before you come in, or do you want to do it on your watch?" The Jones team responded: "We'll handle it." From Hadley's view, that made sense as General Jones had served as commander of the U.S. European Command (EUCOM) and as Supreme Allied Commander Europe (SACEUR). "He was very comfortable with it." In addition, Jones was fluent in French, and "that, of course, helps with the French."

In their meeting, the advisors also went through the Afghan strategy review that the Bush administration had developed. Hadley explained what they intended to do unless Jones and his team warned him off of the actions. "I said very clearly, 'This is what it finds. I think you can build on it. It's designed to have you build on it. There are ten things that we're going to go ahead and do. They'll be below the public radar screen, but they will give you options early on in your tenure that we think you're going to want. So unless you tell me otherwise, we're going to do those ten things." As to the other aspects of the review, the Bush team gave the Obama staff a choice: "Do you want us to go public on it, and start talking to the allies, or do you want to just give it to you, and you can use it as an input to your own strategy review?' And they elected to do the latter, which was a smart thing to do."[33]

When asked about what seemed like a "green light" for drone strikes during the period after the election and before the inauguration, Hadley would not acknowledge that there was such a campaign. "If we were doing that kind of thing, we would probably be doing it pursuant to covert action authorities. And, of course, one of the things about covert action authorities is you don't acknowledge them." If the drone strikes were done, "they would have been done by the book. They would have been done based on the CIA determining that they had intelligence there was a terrorist there that needed to be dealt with. . . . If this program were ongoing, this is not something we would have rushed through for political reasons, either to get it done before we left office, or to box in the new team."[34] The briefing for Jones, Donilon, and Craig also dealt with specifics on the covert action operations and the process through which covert action decisions were made.

"We gave them a set of briefing slides, and then backup materials that covered three things," Hadley said. "We gave a set of briefing slides of how the covert action process worked, how the findings are developed, what are the guidelines under which the CIA operates for doing covert action." Then they went over each of the covert action findings "so that they knew what was ongoing." The second area of the covert action briefing dealt with military operations that "were being done clandestinely, not covert action, but clandestine. That is to say, non-public, and both the authorities that had been given to the secretary of defense by the president, and how the process for getting those approvals worked," said Hadley. They gave the three Obama advisors "a binder on each so that they had the documentation on what those authorities were, both on the Defense side, and then of course, the CIA covert actions." There was a third area where the outgoing NSC team discussed sensitive operations, "We also briefed them on the process by how we determine some strategic intelligence operations that we do."[35]

While Hadley and senior staff members in the NSC did the national security briefings for those coming into office, those were not the only national security issues, and they were not the sole briefers. For example, information about what cases were in courts created under the Foreign Intelligence Surveillance Act and what court-approved surveillance operations were under way was not within the NSC's purview. Hadley commented, "The FISA court stuff is really done as a Justice Department, FBI matter. And that would have gone to Greg Craig directly in his transition [briefings] from the Justice Department and from [White House Counsel for President Bush] Fred Fielding."[36]

Briefings on Specific Subjects

Some briefings were devoted to particular subjects. One of the controversial programs briefed by Hadley to Greg Craig, the incoming counsel, was the CIA interrogation program of persons suspected to be terrorists plotting against the United States. Hadley and White House Counsel Fred Fielding had a December meeting with Craig "where we walked through the history and current status of the CIA's high value terrorist interrogation program, where it had been and its evolution over time, and where it was at the time that the new team came in. We made available to them all of the supporting documentation."[37]

Rather than coming in blind to the specific issues of the program, Hadley and Fielding made sure that Craig knew what they were doing. Hadley said, "So Greg Craig knew where that stood, and I walked through with him all of the issues they were going to face about what to do with military commissions, all the efforts we'd made to get the population out of Guantanamo, that we'd gone from about 850 to roughly 250, the problems about getting other countries to take people back, either getting assurances they wouldn't torture them or also assurances they wouldn't just let them go and some of the political problems associated with that." From Hadley's viewpoint, Craig "had a pretty good idea of the issues he was going to have to deal with, and has had to deal with, when he walked in the door. . . . I wanted to walk him through that personally, which I did do."[38]

When President-elect Obama received his briefings after the election, he learned more about the issues of Guantanamo and interrogations from the director of the Central Intelligence Agency, General Michael Hayden. General Jones attended some of these Chicago sessions. "The times I came out there, I listened to the morning briefing that the CIA director, General Hayden, gave," Jones said. "There was an intensity, an intense focus on terrorism. It was really the underlying threat of what's the wolf that is closest to the door, and we were going through a lot of briefings on Guantanamo Bay, interrogation, [what constitutes] torture."[39]

General Jones described these briefings: "And I remember General Hayden was really passionate about what the rules were for how you could interrogate people. There's a lot of, not only explanations, but also demonstrations about what constituted torture."[40] In a briefing held while President-elect Obama was in Chicago, General Hayden "had an assistant come in and say, 'This is what you can do; this is what you can't do.' How you touch prisoners and . . . what you can do in terms of food deprivation or isolation or things like that." In Hayden's briefings during the early transition days, "he wanted us—he wanted the president to have a clear understanding of what the rules of the road were on interrogation. He had his own views on—the most notorious one, of course, was waterboarding. . . . I would say that overall, the majority of the focus was on terrorist-related incidents [and] issues and Guantanamo Bay and those kinds of issues."[41] There was also an underlying concern in these briefings about the vulnerability of members of the CIA to charges relating to torture. "The director of the CIA at the time was probably concerned about the possibility that some people in the CIA might be prosecuted, and so he was properly concerned about it."[42] Hayden wanted to protect his people from possible prosecution, a subject then being discussed by Democrats in the House of Representatives. In June 2008, fifty-six House Democrats wrote Attorney General Michael B. Mukasey requesting that he appoint a special prosecutor to investigate whether "aggressive interrogation techniques" advocated by administration officials had violated U.S. and international law. The CIA was specifically mentioned in their letter as employing such techniques during questioning of the detainees.[43] General Hayden wanted to protect those in the CIA who were involved in conducting interrogations by having the incoming Democratic administration sign off on their activities.

Briefing NSC Staff during the Transition

The transition team coming into the NSC began to get its briefings after the election and at transition headquarters. The briefings dealt with both policy and issues of organization; usually four or five people were present. In both areas the briefings were important. Mostly it was policy people who received the briefings, but sometimes people from the agency review teams came in as well. One person who had served in the Clinton White House and now was entering the Obama administration eight years later found a far different world in 2008 on intelligence processes: "I remember there was one on the national intelligence priorities framework, which is the big process the Intel community undertakes to give general guidance to the IC [intelligence community] on collection and analysis . . . the government was dramatically different in 2008 than in 2000 when many of us had left."[44] There had been many changes in the administrative structures since 2001, and "we were being introduced to it for the first time. The Homeland Security Council did not exist when we had all been in government under the Clinton administration. So some of it was learning" about whole new areas in the national security world. "In 2001 when Bill Clinton left, Dick Clarke was here, and he had a little CT [counterterrorism] directorate. But the CT universe is totally different now than it was then."[45] With no Department of Homeland Security or director of national intelligence when several of the people coming into the NSC had last been in the White House, there was a great deal to learn about how the structure worked.

Briefings on policy issues probably had less impact because those coming in had worked on the issues of their expertise, and there were already policy recommendations they had worked through from the campaign and within the transition. The incoming team was working on "what the U.S. should or shouldn't be doing on a particular issue."[46] The briefings on process served as an important complement to the internal policy sessions the incoming people were conducting.

Organizing Personnel for the Transition Out of Office

In order to do the briefings, the Bush NSC operation needed to assemble a team that combined people staying through the latter weeks of the administration with those remaining into the next administration. A situation in which many people are leaving the White House with the incumbent president makes it difficult for the new team to get a complex process up and running in a knowledgeable way. Steve Hadley recalled the transition from the Gerald Ford administration to the Jimmy Carter administration: "Bill Hyland, who was deputy national security advisor, came around after President Carter had been elected and basically met with each member of the staff and told them that their services were not needed and they should leave, and there were only initially three of us who were asked to stay, of the whole policy staff of the NSC."[47]

The transition from President Clinton to George W. Bush was especially problematic. Hadley remembers that the Bush team's late start meant that their "first two, three weeks was spent getting to know the people, and telling Sandy [Clinton

NSC advisor Samuel Berger] who we wanted to stay and who we want to go, which was a lot of time and effort."[48] Their time was spent managing people rather than dealing with policy. Policy could be addressed only after the initial organization was well in hand.

When it came time for the Bush people to leave, Hadley and the NSC staff organized the personnel transition differently from their earlier experiences. They made the assumption that the senior people in the office would leave and that the junior ones would stay. "Our assumption was that they would want all the senior directors and all the deputy national security advisors to leave. So we told all of them that they should expect to be gone on the 20th of January."[49] If the Obama NSC team wanted them to stay, they could contact the former Bush staff people and let them know. "But their assumption needed to be that they would be gone." The nonpolitical people in the office, most of whom were there on a temporary basis from the state or defense departments or from an intelligence agency, received a different message. Those who "were not senior directors, not national security advisors, and were all state department people, intelligence people, military people, very nonpolitical, we told them the assumption ought to be that they would stay."[50]

Hadley and his deputies chose one of the nonpolitical people in the office to serve as a senior director for each of the directorates. "We had one among the junior people designated as senior director, so that pending whatever decisions the new national security advisor made, from the moment they walked in, they had a staff that would allow them to operate."[51] The Obama team "accepted that, thought that was a good idea." A skeleton crew for each of the directorates—of which there are sixteen in the Obama NSC—meant that the Obama team could start managing substantive issues from their first day in office. Having General Lute and others continue their service meant that the staff had people close by who could provide the reasoning behind national security actions made in earlier years.

Transitioning the Documentary Record: Files and Memoranda

In addition to the principal-to-principal briefings in the national security area, the 2008 transition was different from earlier ones because of the extensive information the George W. Bush White House team left behind for their successors. While the Presidential Records Act of 1978 establishes rules for the treatment of the incumbent president's papers that leave with him, there are hardly any rules about what information can or must remain. Steve Hadley and his team left sets of records in the NSC and also created a series of forty memoranda about the status of the national security issues they were dealing with and about countries and geographical areas important for an understanding of U.S. security policies. In addition, they gave the Obama team a series of contingency plans for possible events that could confront them.

Providing Sets of Documents

Incoming White House staff members are confronted with empty shelves where documents were once kept. Steve Hadley reminisced about the status of NSC records at the end of President Gerald Ford administration: "I remember going around the offices on the last day. We all had filing cabinets—two of those big black filing cabinets. They were all empty. . . . All the working documents, papers of all the staff went."[52] The only documents held by the executive secretary of the NSC were the "institutional documents," Hadley said. "The presidential directives [NSC policy instruments] would have remained, but not much else." The documents went with President Ford for their eventual review by archivists working for the National Archives and Records Administration and then for their later release to the public through the Gerald R. Ford Library.

Accumulated White House materials are important for the record of an American presidency as well as for the new team that will soon be making important decisions. Though the Presidential Records Act requires papers of an administration to leave with an administration, there is no restriction on copying files and leaving the originals behind. Hadley worked at filling in some of the document holes in White House files and then left behind a set of documents that would be useful to the new team. One such example is a series of agreements between the United States and Israel. At the end of the administration and at the end of his tenure, the Israeli ambassador to the United States, Sallai Meridor, met with Hadley and his deputy, Elliott Abrams. They discussed agreements between the United States and Israel over a period of forty years. Meridor referred to a 1969 agreement. Hadley turned to Abrams, who was keeping track of U.S.-Israeli relations: "Elliott didn't know about the agreement either. So I said to Meridor, 'Give me a set of these agreements,' which he did. I'm sure the State Department would spend weeks trying to find them . . . our continuity of documents in the White House stinks, and, in any event, is not very user-friendly."[53]

There were additional sets of documents NSC officials left behind. Hadley said they left a complete set of national security presidential directives with an index of them as well. There was also a set of executive orders. There were other documents as well. "And we also gave them a volume of what we call the SOCs," meaning the "'summary of conclusions' from all the National Security Council meetings and all the Principal Committee meetings."[54] These are summaries because no transcripts were ever made of the sessions. "We did not have a verbatim transcript of either, but what we did do after each of those meetings was [generate] a summary of conclusions that summarized the main points and actions to be taken."[55]

Another document set that the new team received was one supporting the work of the staff members designated to fill the directorate positions. "We had a different approach [than earlier administrations], which was, since people were going to stay to staff the new administration, they needed to have the working papers required for the work they were doing," Hadley said.[56] "We allowed all of them to select out and copy those documents that they thought they would need to do their jobs under the new team, and that process was supervised. So there wasn't over-inclusion or under-inclusion, and . . . copies were left so that there wasn't any disruption of the integrity of the presidential documents process."[57] The document copying process was supervised by Bill Leary, who has been responsible for NSC documents over several administrations.

In addition to leaving paper records of what actions President Bush and his staff had taken, the NSC team prepared a calendar of events that would take the NSC advisor through the first nine months. In fact, almost all offices related to the White House brought together information on the year ahead. "We gave them a calendar of key events they would face in the first nine months so that they could get the planning started," said Hadley. Those key events included such things as "elections overseas that mattered, summits and other meetings that the president would have to participate in and that they would need to get interagency planning started."[58] They did not elaborate on the individual items on the calendar because both General Jones and his deputy Tom Donilon were very familiar with the various annual checkpoints in the calendar year.

Presidential Memoranda on National Security Issues

President George W. Bush took an interest in the memoranda developed by the National Security Council as they organized to leave office. This process commenced in the fall of 2007, and President Bush took a personal role in the preparation of the documents. Chief of Staff Joshua Bolten discussed the president's interest in the memoranda: "Especially on the national security side, the president read a lot of those and made his own comments . . . because he wanted to see them. He was interested in something of a recap on his way out the door."[59] While President Bush left most of the transition preparations to his senior staff, the creation of the memoranda was an area where he was consistently involved, and the final product represents his thinking and priorities.

Forty Presidential Memoranda on Issues and Countries

One of the most important projects the National Security Council undertook to prepare for the change of power was a series of memoranda dealing with issues and countries important for an understanding of what the administration had done and containing information a new team would need to know about the status of foreign and national security affairs. "We identified forty topics, which we thought were the major policy initiatives, or issues with which we dealt," said Hadley. "We asked each of the relevant directorates to prepare what we called a presidential memorandum. And the form was a memorandum for the record."[60]

The memoranda served several functions. First, the memoranda created a history, based on government-wide information, of Bush administration actions and policies in important national security areas. With so little information being maintained from one administration to the next and remaining in the NSC files, the memoranda would fill out the institutional memory on issues the Bush administration found to be the key subjects arising during their eight-year tenure. Second, and more directly pertinent, the memoranda provided important information for the new president and his national security team. Since the memoranda were organized along priority lines, the staff coming in could get a quick reading on what issues they needed to know about to function well from their first day in office. Third, the memoranda provided President Bush and his key senior national security advisors a record of what they did. That record will be important to scholars and others using the administration's records in the George W. Bush Presidential Library. People will be able to see the issues as Bush administration officials viewed them.

The memoranda were referred to as presidential ones because President Bush was very involved in their creation. "The outgoing president of the United States read each one and made changes on them," Hadley commented. "It was going to be a resource for him recording what had happened in his administration. But it was also going to be what he wanted and was comfortable telling the new president in these varying policy areas."[61]

The senior directors of the NSC made suggestions for memoranda selections after Hadley made an initial effort at isolating the issues that had been important during their tenure. "I took a cut at it," he said. "We circulated it to all the senior directors. They did pluses and minuses, and we ended up with what the senior leadership, the senior management of the NSC staff thought were the most important issues."[62] Once they settled on the subjects of the memoranda, the whole staff set to work on them: "I asked the senior directors to personally take responsibility for them and to review them. And they in turn had one or two people in their directorates who did the drafting."

Hadley explained how he constructed the list of foreign policy and national security memoranda: "They were both country focused, and they were also functionally focused, so China policy, Iraq policy, Afghanistan policy, Pakistan policy, our policy with respect to Iran, all the country-specific big issues. . . . And similarly, we would have the functional issues—war on terror, proliferation. We would go through and have trade issues, Doha [the Doha Development Round of World Trade Organization negotiations] and related issues. So it was both issues driven by our relations with particular countries but also the functional issues that we were dealing with that cut across geographic areas. There were a number of them in the defense area, what did we do about cybersecurity, for example."[63]

A few of the issue memoranda cut across units within the White House. Hadley said, "A couple of these memoranda—the one on HIV/AIDS, the one on trade issues for example—we did jointly with the Domestic Policy Council or the National Economic Council, other White House councils who had an interest and who had part of the story." The AIDS initiative of the administration, known as PEPFAR (President's Emergency Plan for AIDS Relief), was both a domestic and an international initiative. The domestic policy staffs also did a set of memoranda "along the same lines that they also got into the president [and] that they passed to their counterparts of the incoming team as well," said Hadley. The NSC memoranda "became the prototype for a process that became government-wide."[64]

The memoranda process took most of 2008, beginning in February and ending in December. At the end of the year, the Obama national security team began receiving them. After Thanksgiving most of the memoranda were completed, and "we probably started passing [them to the Obama people] the first week in December." A few came in later, as the issues were still live, and "you couldn't really close on them. For example, like Iraq, we didn't actually get the [Status of Forces and Strategic Framework] agreements until the last week in December, first week in January. . . . The last couple memoranda were passed shortly before the 20th of January."[65]

Steve Hadley discussed the common structure of the memoranda with General Jones and Tom Donilon. Hadley established a consistent structure for the memoranda, with each having four sections: "The first section will be what we found, then what our strategy was, then what we think we accomplished, and finally what was left to do, what was going to hit the new team early on." While the memoranda were fairly short, there was supporting information for each demonstrating what people had said and done on the various issues and region-specific situations: "We supported that with tabs, where we had all the relevant policy documents; SOCs of NSC meetings or principals' meetings, or in some cases deputies' meetings, where major policy decisions were made; the key presidential speeches, or my speeches, or Condi's speeches; and 'memcons' [memoranda of in-person conversations] of meetings the president had, and the telephone calls the president had [known as "telcons"], especially with other leaders." Certain documents were removed before the information set was handed over, but it was made clear that staff members could get them if needed. "In the end, we actually pulled out of the set memcons and phone call transcripts, but the index showed what they were. And I said to the new team, 'If you decide you need any of these [memcons and telcons], call us, and we'll get you a copy.' And they have, and we have."[66]

Toward the end of their tenure in office, the memoranda took into account what was then happening. "To the extent the forty memos didn't capture particularly late-breaking stuff, we had a notebook of additional short memos of a similar format to cover those issues as well," Hadley said. The senior directors had two and sometimes three memoranda to deal with, and each had one or two writers at his or her disposal. "Directorates who did not author the memo but had an interest in [it] . . . would get a chance to see it and comment on it." In the end, the project "involved virtually the whole staff, policy staff, and that amounted to around 200 people."[67]

Together the memoranda and supporting material "fill three or four files drawers," said Hadley. One set was for incoming NSC advisor Jim Jones and his deputy Tom Donilon. The other set "they can break apart and give the relevant memos to the relevant senior directors or deputy national security advisors. So they would have our view about what the situation is that they find as they come in, what we did, what we think we accomplished, what is left to be done, and all the relevant documents that would tell them the story. And that was new."[68]

The Memoranda for President Obama's NSC Team

Members of the NSC team working in the Obama administration found the memoranda useful in several ways. The memoranda presented a set of facts that reflected the Bush administration's thoughts on what happened in important national security areas. "I think actually this is a case where a historian may look at these and [say,] 'This is a gold mine.' And it is a gold mine because it's one cut of what they inherited [from] the Bush team, and what they did about it," said one administration person speaking about the documents.[69] Another administration official described them as useful but in a limited way: "The documents were useful because I think, in one sense, that they were like just-the-facts in some ways of all this stuff. But they also slowly morphed into kind of legacy documents. But in terms of folks coming into jobs here, taking those documents and reading them, and saying, 'Okay, got it, now we know what we should do'—I don't know that people did that."[70]

These two administration officials believed that there were two reasons people in the NSC did not see them as revelatory documents. First, the documents were designed as a rendering of what happened and what the Bush administration did. They were documents that made the case for the Bush administration's policies rather than ones with time spent focusing on where things went wrong. In describing the documents as legacy-oriented, another administration official said: "There wasn't a lot in the documents that was, 'We screwed this up. We screwed that up. We should have done this differently. Here are things we didn't finish.'"[71]

In writing the memoranda, some Bush administration officials were concerned that the documents would be used by the Obama administration to criticize them for their actions. Hadley believed that this would not be the case, nor should it be a concern. The Bush administration had the opportunity to make the case for their policies in the memoranda, and it seems that the Obama team did not use them as a basis for criticizing the administration. "There were a number of people . . . on our staff, who were very concerned about the memos from that vantage point, that they would be used by the Obama administration to discredit Bush," said Hadley. "The Obama administration went out of their way to bash the Bush administration every chance they could, but I thought that we could write the memos in such a way that it would make it hard for them, because we had a case to make for our policies." Hadley did not find instances where the memoranda were used to argue against the Bush policies. "I don't recall any case where there was something done by the Obama administration that I thought it was traceable to the memos."[72]

The work that Democratic national security policy people had been doing in the eight years they were out of the White House is a second reason that incoming staff did not view the documents as ones from which they could learn a great deal that they had not already known. Democrats interested in national security policies had spent a lot of time on the outside during the Bush years working on the Hill and in think tanks exploring the issues covered by the memoranda. One administration official observed, "Those of us who worked on the outside for years or on Capitol Hill during that time had developed a fairly robust critique of the previous administration's policy."[73] He went on to explain that by 2008 party policy experts had spent a great deal of effort on beefing up their national security credentials because that was an issue they had been beaten on in 2004. The same official noted, "We Democrats on the outside had spent probably more time than any Democratic administration or incoming Democratic administration than ever before because we had been beaten in 2004 [because there] was a sense that we were weak on national security." In the "post-9/11 world [there was] the understanding that this [national security] was so important."[74] Democrats were preparing in the national security area in many different ways. "There had probably been more preparation done, whether through the campaign or think tanks or things like the Truman National Security Project that helped . . . prepare people to serve in government. There was obviously information they didn't know." Yet at the same time they had specialists who knew their policy or country areas and also had plans ready for the incoming officials. An administration official said, "Our guy who did China, Jeff Bader, who is one of the foremost experts on it, he knew what he wanted to do, what the president-elect, Tom Donilon, General Jones wanted to do."[75]

At the same time, the memoranda have a purpose after a transition has taken place as part of an institutional memory for the office. "It's certainly useful looking back. Right? And it's a useful exercise to take stock of what we've accomplished, like what we've done and what we're leaving, and the rationale for certain decisions that were made because those of us in office can learn from that, that's useful," said one knowledgeable administration official.[76] Learning takes place after the transition, not just at the beginning. "But sometimes that's learning that occurs over time. It's not just part of the transition. . . . Even today, we may look back and say, 'Huh. How did our predecessors deal with a certain set of problems, to help inform us going forward?'" Having the memoranda serves many different purposes from historical documents to background for decision-making.

Preparing Crisis Contingency Plans

An area where outside recommendations became an important part of the 2008–2009 transition planning was the 9/11 Commission recommendation calling for an administration to provide national security threat information to the incoming team as soon as possible after the election: "The outgoing administration should provide the president-elect, as soon as possible after Election Day, with a classified, compartmented list that catalogues specific, operational threats to national security; major military or covert operations; and pending decisions on the possible use of force."[77] While the initial impetus for contingency plans for the transition may have been the 9/11 Commission, such plans are useful for any administration to develop and maintain on an ongoing basis. In 2007–2008, Steve Hadley worked with a new NSC unit to develop contingency plans.[78]

On December 4, 2008, at the final meeting of the Transition Coordinating Council established by President Bush to oversee the transition, Hadley reported that the national security transition staffs for the outgoing and incoming administrations had met to discuss the Afghanistan policy review the Bush team had under way as well as broader terrorism issues.[79] In addition, Hadley discussed a series of seventeen contingency plans. "If the worst happens, here are some responses," he told the assembled two dozen Bush administration officials as well as representatives of the Obama transition operation and representatives of groups involved in transition issues.[80] Joshua Bolten commented on their contingency plans: "We put a lot of effort in towards the end of the administration into making sure that those [were] updated, in place . . . ready to hand over in good shape. . . . Our impending departure . . . really helped focus our minds on making sure those things were right before we left."[81]

The contingency plans project was organized by the NSC's Office for Strategic Planning and Institutional Reform. The unit was developed in 2005 and worked under the leadership of Duke University political scientist Peter D. Feaver, who stayed through 2007. The project focused on bringing together information from inside and outside the government on possible crises the administration might have to confront. The group gathered information from various sources in the administration and at think tanks about possible crises that might arise. "And they in turn started to work with the policy planning people at treasury, state, and DOD, to start addressing issues . . . three to five years out," said Hadley. "And we asked them to develop a list of contingency plans, things that might happen. We started this in 2007 for our own purposes. But I also thought it was going to be useful, something to give to the transition team."[82]

According to Hadley, the group developed the plans by going to relevant agencies throughout the government: "We tasked these papers out, some of them to the intelligence community through the NIC [National Intelligence Council], some of them to individual agencies, some this little inter-agency group did by itself, some the NSC did."[83] They would be useful particularly in the early days of the new administration, but the plans had their limits. Hadley explained that the set of plans was "not interagency-coordinated; it has not been reviewed by the principals, and it has not been reviewed by the president of the United States as the forty memos had been."[84]

Hadley told them the plans were "a level down—or two down—from the forty memos." Jones indicated that he wanted them, so the Bush White House provided them.[85] Hadley went on to describe the plans: "I don't put a lot of stock in these contingency plans. I think they were useful, but they were only supposed to be kind of the first draft. They were not full-up—not contingency plans like the Department of Defense does with huge plans and annexes and assignment of responsibilities." Instead, the pieces represented a preliminary thinking through of a number of situations. "If X were to arise, in four or five pages, frame it and tell people what they need to think about it and what the first questions are going to be, . . . something you could read in about fifteen or twenty minutes that would get you sited on a problem. They weren't full-up contingency plans. I want to be clear about that."[86]

The distribution of the contingency plans was more restricted within the incoming NSC team than the memoranda on issues and countries. As one of the administration people familiar with the memoranda but not the contingency plans observed: "I think there was a lot of contingency planning, but just due to the nature of intelligence, I think they were the things that they were really worried about happening, but were more broad-term think-tanky, [such as] what were some general trends? Those are things that would be written in a memo like that."[87] In fact, Hadley did put out a call to think tanks to see if they were working on issues that would fit into what the NSC was doing. Some of the contingency plans "were farmed out into the think tank community, because we wanted them to be separate from the government, and some of them the inter-agency strategic planning group did." The division within the NSC that did the planning was small and worked with the resources of others. There "were probably three professionals . . . and a couple of support staff, but we had set up this inter-agency policy planning group which they chaired, and they could task that group."[88]

Perhaps the most important use of the contingency plans was the use of two of the plans in tabletop exercises after the election and prior to the inauguration; this was the IED threat simulation described in chapter 3. Another mock crisis was taken from the contingency plans. A training exercise that did not receive as much attention took place in Chicago in early December 2008. General Jones used it to work through the processes that the council would use to consider terrorist events and then to consider what action the government should take in response to the new situation. Additionally, it was used as a way of working through their decision-making process.[89]

Establishing an Organization Reflecting President Obama's Interests

An incoming president has to set up his decision-making process and organizational structure. Through one-on-one meetings with General Jones, the president created a flatter White House organization than the earlier hierarchical structure. In the national security area, bringing information to the president through a structure he wanted meant folding the Homeland Security Council into the National Security Council. It also meant not having competing national security organizations, such as in the George W. Bush White House with Vice President Cheney having his own organization and personnel.

Additional changes involved bringing in a couple of divisions within the NSC to reflect new global economic and cyber concerns. In some ways, though, the NSC organization remained similar to the structure it had had when George W. Bush was president. Most of the senior director positions, for example, stayed the same through the transition. The president and Jones chose to retain some of the people who had worked in the Bush national security operation, such as General Lute, so that they would be guaranteed continuity in some areas at a time when a new administration is most vulnerable. General Jones focused on budget and personnel issues as additional ways to make the organization reflect the president's needs. There were wins and some losses in these areas.

Establishing a Decision-Making Process with the President-Elect

For General Jones, the key to establishing an effective National Security Council was to work early with the president-elect to create an organizational structure that would reflect his interests. The first big challenge is making sure that "whoever the national security advisor is going to be can really get the information that he or she needs to understand how the president wants this to work, how he likes to work. And if you can get that done early, then it can drive everything. But if you get that wrong, then you really will have a problem."[90] So it was that he worked during the transition period on establishing the shape of the organization.

"I think he clearly wanted the NSC to be collegial," said General Jones about President Obama's plans for the National Security Council. "He didn't want NSC issues played out in the press. In other words, he didn't want rogue cabinet members pontificating in the press. I mean the 'No drama Obama' thing was probably a pretty fair representation. And he . . . wanted the issues to be fully vetted and debated and wanted to be sure that everyone who had equities at the table was at the table and was consulted at every level."[91] Knowing President-elect Obama's manner during the transition period allowed Jones to set up a process that reflected the styles and interests of both men.

"He worked very hard to do that even when we knew, when everybody agreed. He'd still go around the table and call on every principal to make sure that this was the way it was going to go, whatever the outcome was," Jones remembered. "The president had a very good habit, I thought, of calling on everybody." In addition to seeking out the opinion of those in the room, the president came to meetings fully engaged. "He did two things I thought were good. One is if you gave him papers to read before the meeting, he'd read them and remembered them. And so he'd always be fully prepared. And he made sure that everybody at the table had an obligation to say something, to participate." The result of using this process was that participants did not publicly complain when they lost an argument. "I never saw it in print where a principal had his or her nose out of joint because they were not consulted or a decision was made on something that they had equities in that they were not asked to participate. That just didn't happen. That had a pretty good community effect, I think."[92]

The president-elect also wanted an operation where decisions percolated up through a system where new issues that had arisen in the recent past had their own focus. The practice for bringing up issues was characterized by its disciplined process for topics related to countries and subjects related to the responsibilities of the senior directors as well as keeping track of subjects currently in play. "So I think process, I think collegiality, building a team and vetting the issues academically, intellectually and always making sure that you're taking care of the really hot ones," said Jones. "I used to have about ten or eleven, maybe twelve issues that we're always watching 24/7. . . . And the senior directors knew where their issues were in the overall pecking order. . . . And we also had . . . people who were just looking down range at the approaching storms and trying to figure that out."[93]

Taking Issues to the President

One of the key arrangements the national security advisor needs to settle is the process for taking issues to the president when the advisor and the group decide that the president needs to hear a given subject. Jones developed a procedure for bringing information to the president and having his staff involved as a key part of those briefings. "My sense of how to do the job, my view was that I could . . . run a big organization and . . . deal with a lot of people around the world. . . . But

I couldn't do all of those things and at the same time be at the president's shoulder every single time. And so I talked to him early on, and I said, 'Look, if you don't have any objection, this is how I'm going to do this job' and told him that I really hired the best people we could find to be the senior directors and that they do the work and as a reward they get to brief their work." That was the way Jones did his briefings with the president. "When I went in to talk to the president about an issue, there were very few times when I went in by myself. There were some times when I did, but the old image of the national security advisor being solo, one on one with the president whispering in his ear, was not me," Jones said.[94]

The way he and his staff prepared for meetings was to do run-throughs with the senior directors. "I gave great faith to the people who were doing the work," Jones said. "They would come into my office maybe the day before. We'd talk about going to see the president on subject X the next day, generally talk about the main issues." The idea was to make the presentations very focused, with few extraneous tangents that strayed from the central briefing points. "I found that rehearsals were always good, because it gets rid of the excess stuff because you only have thirty minutes, [there's a risk that] you can get off on tangents. If you rehearse it briefly once, and you know what is going to be said and what you have got to cover, the next time it is more efficient. And so that is the model that we used." Jones was not reluctant to have others brief the president, including his deputies. "Many times when I was doing things that involved other countries and there was a briefing going on in the Oval Office and it wasn't essential for me to be there, the senior directors and the deputy national security advisor would go in, and they'd do the briefing. And I had full trust and confidence that they were doing the right thing."[95] Even if he was not present, it was General Jones who established the direction and the contours of their presentations in the meetings with the president.

While Jones's approach of having deputies present information to the president gave those staff members a good opportunity to interact with the president, the world outside of the White House sometimes interpreted the practice as a weakness. The same was true inside the building, where some presidential aides took shots at the new national security advisor for what seemed like flimsy reasons. Less than four months into the administration, Jones was criticized by anonymous sources for not making known his own opinions in a principals meeting with the president. In an Afghanistan strategy meeting in March 2009, General Jones, "although seated next to the president, seldom voiced his own opinions, according to officials in the room. Instead, he preferred to go around the table collecting the views of others."[96] In reality, seeking and listening to the views of others was something the president himself consistently did in meetings. In the same article, staff members complained that Jones "went home early," but in fact he was spending twelve hours at work each day. As Bob Woodward makes clear in *Obama's Wars*, the sniping did not subside in the months to come.[97]

When it comes to White House operations, bipartisanship has its limits. General Jones's case demonstrates how difficult it is for someone with no party or personal ties to a president to operate at the senior level in a White House, especially if the person wants to bring about procedural or organizational changes. In his government service prior to his White House years, General Jones had not played a political role. His appointments came from President Clinton, who appointed him as commandant of the Marine Corps, and President George W. Bush, who chose him to serve as NATO commander. He interacted with White House officials but was never associated with a particular president or party.

In 2008, with the United States in two wars, both Senators McCain and Obama were interested in having a person with military and foreign policy experience as their national security advisor. Both were interested in General Jones. A longtime friend, McCain talked to Jones about the national security advisor job. Jones recounted his conversation with McCain: "'Look, if I am elected,'—this is way early on—'would you consider it?' I said, 'Yeah, of course I'd consider it,'" Jones said.[98] The McCain personnel operation thought about Jones for other spots as well. Russ Gerson, who ran the appointments recruitment operation for the McCain campaign, did not want to speak on the record about the specific jobs for which Jones was being considered: "You can mention that Jim Jones was one of the people considered for numerous jobs."[99] In addition to the White House post, Jones was also on the "top tier" list for positions in the Department of Defense and in the Department of Homeland Security.

When both sides approached Jones, he was working at the Chamber of Commerce, whose policy required that employees steer clear of electoral politics. Jones said, "The Chamber of Commerce had a policy of not interfering, not playing in presidential campaigns. So because I worked for the Chamber, I . . . couldn't endorse, advocate, do anything. That's not my nature anyway because I like to stay out of the politics thing . . . by nature, I am not political, so I am not a Republican. I am very independent. And I explained all of that so that there was no misunderstanding."[100]

His political independence in a partisan White House world was a break with the usual practice of appointing senior aides, including the national security advisor, from the president's coterie of advisors. "I think that, to be honest, that when I did sign on with President Obama to be a national security advisor, which I would have done for McCain if he had asked me—if he had been elected—I think there were quite a few people who did not understand that." Jones was selected for his ties to the military community, the accomplishments in his military service, and his knowledge of a volatile world that the new president coming into office in 2009 would need to understand. Once he was in the White House, Jones's independent status and lack of close ties to Obama world prove to be hurdles he had to navigate in his work on national security issues and organization.

Restructuring the NSC as a Coordinating Unit

One of the early issues to settle was centralizing national security processes so that the national security and homeland security units could come together as one. The president "likes process," Jones said. "We had in mind to create, to try to create a National Security Council that, first of all, meshed with the Homeland Security Council. I thought that the logic for bringing them together was very clear. We did a study for a couple of months to make sure that that's what we wanted to do before we did it," Jones said.[101] "Being able to combine the staffs into a national security staff was a good thing, and I think for this president, it worked very well."

Jones indicated that the idea behind the restructuring was to facilitate the coordination required among so many government organizations dealing with issues touching on national and homeland security: "What we're trying to do is recognize that in this twenty-first century there is probably no single agency that controls any major issue all by itself. And if there were such a case, you could deal with that single agency almost in a special way. But because all of the major issues span multiple agencies and departments, the job of the NSC and it's bottom-up approach, is to bring the players together so that . . . all boats can rise at the same level."[102]

There were some "bumps and bruises and clashes" below the senior level, but at the top level people met often to coordinate issues they all were working on. "I used to meet with the cabinet people individually once a week, certainly with Clinton and Gates and others to make sure that we all stayed on the same sheet of the music where the issue was concerned," he said. "We divided up the responsibilities and said, 'Look, here's the piece that the State Department is going to work. You're going to work this piece. Defense Department and Treasury, you're going to work this.' When you're dealing with an effort, for instance, to impose sanctions on Iran, . . . that's a whole different community that has to involve."[103]

Whoever formed the new national security team, Jones indicated, needed "to understand how the president wants—visualizes the NSC working." Part of that is making sure that the NSC had no competing organizational centers. "I went to the vice president because I knew that there was the Cheney National Security Council and Bush National Security Council. I have known Senator Biden for a long time, Vice President Biden." Jones stressed that the planned structure for the NSC was to be one organization, as it had traditionally been. "I said, 'I want to make something clear up front. You should have your own guy to talk to you, but I'm also your guy. And your guy is welcome to any meeting we have, my morning meeting, anything else. And this is your national security council, so if you want something done, we're here for you as well. You're the number two guy in the country.' And he bought that. And as a result, we didn't have a competing organization, which I thought was useful for the president."[104]

Vice President Biden was very mindful of the point of a competing national security operation. Ted Kaufman, longtime chief of staff to Senator Biden and later his replacement in the Senate, recounted that the vice president discussed with the president the same issue of his role in the national security council organization as he had with General Jones: "The vice president said to the president, 'Look, I don't want to have our national security staff and your national security staff . . . the way Cheney had it. I want one national security staff, and as long as you promise me that my people can go be involved in whatever is . . . [happening], as long as I am getting the paperwork on what's going on, then we're just going to have one national security staff.' And that's what they did."[105]

In addition to bringing homeland security into the NSC, they also reorganized the internal operation. "When I looked at the previous administration's organization charts, I came to certain conclusions about how the National Security Council, to support the next president, had to be reorganized. And what we did was, we organized it along the lines of geography." The question that arose was the philosophy behind the geographical divisions various groups were using. "One of the things that always mystified me about the government is that everybody had a different map. . . . If you look at the Unified Command Plan of the Defense Department, they had a map of regional commanders, and that's what I grew up with, so I was very comfortable with the Unified Command Plan. But if you look at the State Department, it was completely different," Jones said. "So I just made a command decision early on that we were going to try to look at the map the same way. I never did get the State Department to go along with it, but at least the NSC and the Department of Defense were kind of in sync. And with a couple of exceptions, we reorganized the world so that it fit into a more understandable matrix as to who was responsible for what. And we built a series of senior directors that had geographic responsibilities, and we had a group of senior directors that had functional responsibilities."[106]

When General Jones left the White House, President Obama talked about the multiple major issues and crises the administration had had to deal with in its first two years in office. After listing a dozen critical issues from the Middle East to Iraq to Afghanistan and Pakistan, President Obama praised Jones's "steady voice" and the reform of the national security structure to modernize the directorates. President Obama said of Jones: "Through these challenges, Jim has always been a steady voice in Situation Room sessions, daily briefings, and with meetings with foreign leaders, while also representing our country abroad with allies and partners in every region of the world. At the same time, he has led an unprecedented reform of our national security staff here at the White House. Reflecting the new challenges of our time, he put new emphasis on cybersecurity, development, and climate change and made sure that homeland security is fully integrated into our efforts."[107]

Working through Decision-Making Practices

For the Obama team, getting ready for the coming national security transition meant preparing for the unexpected and setting up a decision-making system. For the first exercise using the contingency plans, the president-elect and all principals for an NSC meeting were present. It was a good opportunity to establish how the president wanted his decision-making process to be organized. The session, led by General Jones, took place in Chicago in early December shortly after Thanksgiving: "I'm not sure everybody was there because I think all the positions hadn't been filled, but certainly the Sec State was there, Sec Def was there, all of the intelligence guys, the DNI was there, chairman of the joint chiefs. I think the attorney general was there, the vice president and the president-elect."[108]

The session was a good opportunity to work through the decision-making process with the principals who served on the council. Furthermore, using a crisis scenario allowed everyone to work through what needed to be done in handling an event. One message from the meeting was that when such meetings took place, all principals were required to attend: "It basically was the first time everybody had come around the table. And one of the key points that we wanted to make was what the process would be for meetings of the NSC. Those meetings were generally to be attended by the principals when there is a principals meeting." General Jones said that he and the president "established the rules of the road [for the NSC] clearly up front that when it's a principals meeting, it's a principals meeting, and only by exception should the principal not be there. And I think I used the line that if you're not at the table, you're probably on the menu, so you might want to be there."[109]

Before the exercise, the group talked about how their decision-making process would work. "Before we played this scenario game, we talked about process and how we were going to tee up issues," Jones said. "And we talked about the primacy of the bottom-up approach and the working groups and tried to tell them that the people you send to the working groups should be empowered, they should be empowered to do certain things and to move the football along."[110] Discussing the roles of the deputies and principals committees was critical to the exercise in order for the group to work through what should happen at both of those levels.

The deputies level was important as the location where the ground work would be done. General Jones explained what would happen at the two basic levels: "We're not looking for solutions at every level, but we're looking for people to be more than just note-takers. And we established that the deputies committee was probably going to be the engine that really drove the process. And that's where the really tough work would be done."[111] That was a decision that echoed Obama's predecessors, as all of the administrations since President George H. W. Bush have worked through deputies and principals committees.[112] The "deputies then principals" model was first set up as it is today by the national security advisor at the time, General Brent Scowcroft, and the configuration has been known since then as the Scowcroft model.

The principals would focus on the issues that could not be decided at the deputies level. Jones said, "then the principals would tackle the issues that deputies couldn't agree on, and then the full NSC with the president and the vice president would be the last bastion of discussion."[113] Hadley pointed out that in most administrations "if important enough, principals would review even if deputies agreed."[114]

Reorganizing the Internal NSC Structure

Budget and personnel changes within a White House unit are an area where many senior staff experience restructuring difficulties. In the case of the National Security Council, there are anomalies that prove difficult to work through at the beginning of an administration. Its budget is a small one, and the bulk of personnel comes from outside the White House. "One of the things that I didn't get done, that I tried to do in the transition, was to fix the . . . essentially broken nature of the NSC as an institution," said Jones.[115]

As a statutory office, he thought that it should have its own budget. He explained some of the quirks of the NSC budget with a personal illustration: "Any time any national security advisor or foreign minister or defense minister, sometimes even head of state came to my office and I offered them a cup of coffee or anything, I got a bill for it at the end of the month. You know, it was out of personal funds to the tune of about $400 a month out of pocket."[116] That was something that did not change. Part of the reason for the need to have the NSC advisor pay out of a personal account was the budget troubles of the agency. "When we took over on January 20, 2009, the budget for the NSC was $6 million annually."[117]

In order to figure out what their needs were, General Jones did a study of the unit's requirements in terms of personnel and budget. "I did a study immediately, as quickly as possible, to figure out, what does it take to run this organization, to do everything that we want to do, to fund travel, to attend conferences and to be relevant, to be able to be the machine that drives the interagency process that brings people to the table and runs this thing? And I came up with a figure of about 325 people total." Many of those people are ones on detail from the Department of Defense and the Department of State, and in those cases the home department picks up their salaries. Changing the ratio of detailed personnel to salaried NSC employees—a 70 percent detailees to 30 percent permanent NSC personnel—proved difficult to change as well.

At the same time, Jones did make gains in the effort to increase the NSC budget. "So I came up with $12 million, and when I left, we got it up. That caused shockwaves around the White House, because they didn't want any one particular organization around the White House to be bumped up when everybody else was going to stay pretty flat."[118] Though the budget was increased, the added funds were not sufficient to deal with the issue of the detailed personnel. The detail issue is an important one because it means there is a constant flow of new people coming into the NSC.

General Jones explained that the detailing system is an organizational weak point that they weren't able to resolve: "It's really one of the weak links. It's not that the detailees are bad, but it's just that it creates this revolving door of people who are just always coming and going to do their year or two at the NSC and then go back to their agencies." While the detailees are important for the operation, having roughly two-thirds of the staff on detail "is not good for the organization. And we felt that within a year because after a year people started leaving, some very key people started leaving. . . . They walk out one day, and their replacement shows up maybe sometimes two weeks later, and it takes them a long time to come up to speed. So that's definitely a weakness."

Interestingly, in the Bush administration, Hadley viewed detailed personnel as a benefit to the NSC because he worried about the presence of a entrenched staff if the office did not have regular turnover. From his viewpoint, there were ways to hold over detailees when he wanted to, and doing so mitigated against building a staff structure that would become its own entrenched bureaucracy. "We sought to avoid creating a 'permanent' NSC policy staff of career NSC policy people," Hadley said. "Such a permanent staff would soon develop its own bureaucratic prejudices and interests and reduce the NSC to just one more government agency." The NSC is charged with synthesizing information that staff gathers from departments and executive branch agencies. Hadley explained his thinking: "The NSC is supposed to integrate across the stovepipes of the federal bureaucracy, coordinate issues across many agencies, and have reach-back into those agencies based on the NSC staff members' ties with people in those agencies and their experience serving there. All of these functions become harder and are in some sense compromised if you develop a permanent NSC policy staff."[119] Even in a bipartisan environment there are differences in interpretation of what kind of staff is needed. Both men had strong and contrasting arguments for their viewpoints on detailing staff from other agencies. Their disagreement gets to the reality of White House organization that the structure one adopts reflects the interests of the current president. There is no one way to organize any unit of the White House staff, including the National Security Council.

Listening to the Voices of the Past

One of the practices General Jones had was to create a sounding board using people who understood well the problems he faced. He regularly brought in those who had served in his position in earlier administrations to get some sense of what had gone before him and to find out what rhythms the office has that have weathered several administrations and those that have not. Jones said that the sessions were sparked by his calls to Hadley following the transition: "He was very, very willing to help in any way possible. As a matter of fact, one of the things that that relationship triggered in my mind was to periodically bring in all former national security advisors for regular consultations or briefings. And most of them came, the Kissingers, the Brzezinskis, the Scowcrofts, the Powells, anybody who was a national security advisor was invited."[120]

With seven or eight people regularly around the table, the sessions were "a good give and take . . . completely bipartisan . . . [and] all about the current issues." Jones said that the meetings were popular ones with President Obama and Vice President Biden who "used to really look forward to the national security advisors coming in because they felt they could talk freely and they wouldn't read about it in the press the next day." The group discussed "all of the top issues . . .

the Middle East, Afghanistan, Iraq, Pakistan, India, all of the hot-button issues at the time. There was nothing that was off the table."[121]

Having an outside sounding board is a practice through the years that many senior White House officials have had. It is sometimes difficult to have a sense of how actions appear outside of the White House and Washington as well as if there is something that those inside the building and in the departments have overlooked as they develop their policies. In some ways, having a group to talk to extends the cooperation a new team receives when they prepare for office.

Conclusion

The national security transition in 2008 was the most important aspect of the presidential transition out of office and the one into the White House as well. In both instances, the preparations went well because of the efforts of a cadre of people inside and outside of government committed to making the transfer of power operate well. The most important of these people to the success of the transition planning were President Bush, who supported a strong national security transition, and President-elect Barack Obama, who devoted attention and resources to thinking through the decision-making process and the organization of the National Security Council. Also critical to the success of the transition were the two national security advisors, Steve Hadley and General Jones.

There are myriad choices for an outgoing president and his national security advisor for organizing their transition out of office. If, as in the case of the 2008 transition, the incumbent chief executive is not running for another term, then there are great opportunities for fashioning a detailed transition out of office. A good transition out provides continuity in government, benefits the functioning of the NSC, and becomes a part of the legacy of the outgoing president. Steve Hadley and President Bush went out of their way to make certain that they could be helpful to the eventual winner of the presidential election by starting early and providing complete information on NSC programs, organization, and personnel. They had a choice of what they did and what information to give to the winners of the November election.

For their part, President Obama, General Jones, and their national security staff had a great deal to do in a short period of time. They had to gather information, learn about the world they were entering, and make decisions on programs, people, and policies. At the same time, they could not get started until their basic national security team came together after Thanksgiving, when General Jones was appointed and when cabinet officers were getting named to positions. Through a variety of discussions during the seventy-five-day transition period as well as the first few months of the new administration, the president and his team put their stamp on the reorganization of the NSC.

It is difficult to make organizational changes in the White House at the beginning of an administration because when a new team comes in, its policy agenda is usually its first priority. Organizational work requires a great deal of preparation of a kind that is difficult to do before coming into the White House. The staff in most White House offices accepted the White House structure they found when they came into the West Wing on January 20. Some of them, such as the Office of Communications and the Press Office, rearranged their organizational structure later in the first term, but not in their first year in office, as the NSC did. President-elect Obama and General Jones decided to restructure the national security offices in the White House and bring in additional subject areas they thought needed to be represented in the NSC. While there were many structural changes and additions, it was also clear that it is difficult to make the changes one wants. There are always going to be others who have made their own portfolio arrangements that limit the flexibility of those in other offices who are seeking change. The surprise is that there was as much change brought about as there was in the transition and in the early months of the administration.

CHAPTER SEVEN

Presidential Appointments

If national security is the most important policy area of a presidential transition, then presidential appointments is the operations area that is most crucial for a president-elect in terms of governing. It is also the most troublesome aspect of a transition because the hazards are omnipresent and can derail, at least temporarily, a smooth start to an administration. The angst a president-elect feels coming into the process stems from the knowledge that the appointments are going to be crucial to policy successes; he can plan out the process and recruit the best people in the knowledge that something will almost certainly go awry. What isn't known from the outset is how, when, or where the trouble will strike or how bad the damage will be.

For President Obama, it didn't take long to feel the sting of an imperfect appointment. Even before he came into office, Timothy Geithner, his treasury secretary nominee, came under fire for unpaid taxes that he owed. After President Obama was in office, trouble struck full-force on February 3 when two of his nominees for top administration posts—former Senator Tom Daschle, nominated for the position of secretary of health and human services, and Nancy Killefer, slated to fill the new position of chief performance officer at the Office of Management and Budget—were forced to withdraw their names from consideration, also over the issue of unpaid taxes. That evening, President Obama did interviews with the anchors of the NBC, CBS, and ABC evening news programs with the same message about the withdrawals. "I'm here on television saying I screwed up," President Obama said to NBC's Brian Williams. "I'm frustrated with myself, with our team. But ultimately . . . my job is to get this thing back on track, because what we need to focus on is a deteriorating economy and getting people back to work."[1] In an effort to right the ship that day, he announced the nomination of Senator Judd Gregg to the commerce secretary position—only to have Gregg pull out nine days later because he had decided that "this will not work for me as I have found that on issues such as the stimulus package and the census there are irresolvable conflicts for me."[2] Former governor Bill Richardson of New Mexico had been nominated for the commerce secretary position in early December but bowed out a month later because of a federal investigation into state contracts that may have gone to his political supporters.

By April 2009, President Obama was still feeling the sting of his appointments gone awry, though not all by the tax route. At the end of the hundred-day mark, an aide asked the president what had surprised him so far. He responded, "The number of people who don't pay their taxes."[3] Some departments were particularly hard hit by the swirl of controversy, Treasury being one of them. With the positions of deputy and undersecretary vacant (including a withdrawal for the undersecretary for international affairs) this department, so vital to the economic recovery and our commitments abroad, was struggling to govern in some areas. British cabinet secretary Sir Gus O'Donnell, who was involved in setting up the G20 summit in London that year and also met with U.S. Treasury officials in the international affairs area, complained to his civil servants that it was difficult to find anyone to talk to at the U.S. Treasury Department. "There is nobody there," he said. "You cannot believe how difficult it is."[4]

Why Focus Early on Appointments?

Appointments matter at the most critical ends of the policy process—development and implementation. They involve assembling a team with an emphasis on carrying out the campaign policy agenda as well as making clear a president's governing intentions and priorities before he enters office. Appointments cut across management, policy, and leadership. Without a functioning political level of executives at the departments and agencies, there is not much that career people can do on their own to develop the information needed for presidential decision-making or to carry decisions out once they are made. Both policy development and implementation depend heavily on having experienced cabinet secretaries with an effective support staff of their choice at the deputy, assistant, and undersecretary levels. It makes a difference if those political positions at the sub-cabinet level go unfilled, because they are the people who can conduct policy reviews for the new administration, work on implementing the existing laws according to the president's preference, and develop the policies the president wants to see put into place.

Career people and the secretary's personal staff, being a chief of staff, deputies, lawyers, and communications people, are appointees that do not require Senate confirmation, and they cannot do the kind of work that the deputy, assistant, and deputy assistant secretaries can do with their confirmed status. Paul Light, an authority on presidential appointments, explained the cost of having departmental assistant and deputy assistant secretaries unfilled in the treasury department as well as in other ones. "That's the real problem here, that you have this de facto sub-cabinet that operates out of the secretary's office, but you don't have your true sub-cabinet in place because it's stuck on Capitol Hill or it's still being audited," he said. "So you don't have the middle vertebrae, the neck, if you will, of government. You've got the head of the Treasury Department. You've got the career people. It's kind of neck-less government, if you will. You just don't have those vertebrae in place to transfer information on down and to move policy ideas on up."[5]

In addition to their being a distraction and halting the momentum of a good entry into office, appointments missteps can be costly for a president-elect in a personal way because they rob him of the people he had anticipated would be key participants in his administration. That was the case with the loss of Tom Daschle as Health and Human Services secretary and Nancy Killifer at OMB.

While the Obama personnel start was rocky, the outgoing administration provided materials and help smooth some aspects of the personnel transition. In explaining his emphasis on appointments in his dealings with the representatives of Senators Obama and McCain, Joshua Bolten commented on why he made personnel the primary agenda item. "I thought the most important thing for them to focus on was the personnel side and that they really needed to get that going early," he said.[6] Many major-party candidates have shared Bolten's emphasis on personnel, especially in cases where an electoral victory would mean a change in the party in the White House and hence a need to quickly fill a large number of vacancies. Among recent presidents who took office from the opposing party and who had early appointments operations were Ronald Reagan and George W. Bush. Both men benefited from their early appointments work when they came into the presidency. On the other hand, President Clinton suffered from not having a similar operation in place.

One basic lesson about presidential personnel operations from the 2008 transition is that the information learned from past transitions that will help achieve an effective start—begin early on personnel, appoint one person to oversee the operation, and start with appointing White House staff—is important but still not enough to overcome the natural obstacles that are currently in the path of a smooth and quick transition into the White House. Following the lessons of the past is an important and helpful approach, but it does not determine the overall results on its own. The appointments process has been one of the most difficult aspects of transitions for President Obama as well as most of his recent predecessors. For decades observers have described the process as broken. First, the positions to be filled have long been vacant, and their agencies have been without leadership at the undersecretary, assistant secretary, and agency head levels. To this, add that a presidential personnel operation takes time to get up and running, and once again the result is more weeks and months without executive branch leadership. With increased efforts to bring transparency to government operations and to its officials, the demands on potential nominees for detailed personal and financial information have grown dramatically in the last forty years. Once nominees fill out the paperwork of the White House personal data statement, the SF 86 on national security and the SF 278 on financial disclosure, the information goes from the White House to the Senate, where it languishes in committees. Meanwhile, executive branch nominees must put their lives on hold for an undetermined period of time, and the same is true of government agencies in terms of their own policy leadership. There are some ways of moderating the depth of the problems presidents face as they set up their administrative teams, but they need help that far outstrips what their transition personnel operation can provide.

What difference does it make if the positions are filled, either at the end or the beginning of an administration? When looking at the product of the branches of government, one can see the demands on the executive branch agencies to implement legislation and court orders and on the president to issue executive orders. All three branches need the executive branch agencies to write the rules and regulations associated with the legislation passed by Congress. In the 111th Congress (2009–2011) there were 10,621 bills introduced in the Congress, of which 338 were enacted.[7] The enacted ones require implementation, and the ones that are introduced often require a response from the president, the White House staff, and others in the administration, such as in a statement of administration policy on the bill. President Obama had to put forward administration policy in several Statements of Administration Policy (SAP), four of which came out during the first hundred days and forty-seven in his first year.[8] It is difficult to put together SAPs without political people in place in departments and agencies. Executive orders (EO) require implementation by those in the same departments and agencies. With strong planning including the writeup of specific EOs during the transition by a legal team of Todd Stern and Greg Craig, President Obama got off to a quick start with nineteen in his first hundred days and thirty-nine in his first year.[9] A president gives directions to departments and agencies through other instruments as well. Presidential memoranda cover executive branch issues such as ethics guidelines. In his first hundred days, President Obama issued twenty-four presidential memoranda and seventy in his first year, including six memoranda classified as Presidential Determinations.[10] The nation's foreign policy is a continuing area of meetings, agreements, and choices. Treaties and executive agreements with foreign nations require implementation as well. In 2009–2010, President Obama had to deal with eleven treaties that were concluded as well as 422 executive agreements.[11] In his first hundred days he went to nine countries and visited twenty-five nations in his first year; in addition, six foreign leaders came to visit him.[12] His secretary of state, Hillary Rodham Clinton, visited twenty-two nations in the first hundred days of the administration, all of which required Obama's instructions to her, as she was his emissary to the governments and the officials she would meet. With pressure to make and enforce decisions, executive branch agencies cannot afford to have the kinds of vacancies we have had in the late stages of our recent two-term administrations.

Candidates focus early on the executive branch appointments process for two additional reasons. First, the Senate confirmation process has become a protracted, contentious, and partisan one that requires early and constant attention. Second, starting in the Reagan administration, appointees have experienced increased demands to provide personal and financial information about themselves and their families and to divest holdings that represent a conflict of interest with the nominee's new posts. While much about the transition process has become easier with institutional support from Congress and the executive branch, the appointments process has headed in the opposite direction, with senators placing holds on lower-level political nominees until they can extract promises from the fledgling administration to support the senators' wishes, most often ones dealing with local rather than national issues. For a year, Senator Kit Bond (D-Mo.), for example, in 2009 held up the nomination of Martha Johnson for the top post at the General Services Administration because he wanted the federal government to commit to building a $175 million complex of buildings in Kansas City, Missouri.[13] He did not question her qualifications for the position. When her nomination came to the Senate floor ten months later, she was confirmed 96–0.

Gradually, even at the secretary and deputy secretary levels, the opposing party has increasingly refused to go along with some scheduled votes, though usually not at the beginning of an administration. The major problem that surfaces at the beginning of an administration is its own difficulty in putting forward nominees for all of the vacant positions. In 2008 the cumbersome nomination process required nominees to fill out a sixty-three-question personal data statement, to submit to an FBI background check, to fill out the SF 86 national security background form, and to sign off for the IRS to release their tax returns for Senate committees (and sometimes the White House) to review, and to fill out the SF 278 financial review form to uncover conflicts of interest for the Office of Government Ethics.[14] If the person requires Senate confirmation, there are committee forms as well. All of this tells a nominee to begin early—or, alternately, to refrain from getting involved at all.

With all of the demands on their nominees from a variety of institutions inside and outside of government, a presidential candidate can expect a contentious appointments process. So it is not surprising that the personnel part of President Obama's transition into office was uneven. On the plus side was the growing number of vacancies he had to fill and his ability at the end of the first hundred days to register higher percentages than Presidents George W. Bush and Bill Clinton had achieved at the same point. It was not the same story at the end of the first year, however. By that juncture President Obama had the lowest percentage of confirmed executive branch positions of the five most recent presidents.

Some of the problems they experienced resulted from their failure to adopt practices that have worked in the past, particularly having one person lead the process of recruitment. Other reasons for the relatively low percentage of nominees confirmed relate to the layers of inquiry that have accrued with each presidential election cycle. Increased scrutiny and increased partisanship mean more areas of inquiry, more questions to answer, more media attention to appointment problems. Once a problem nomination surfaces at the cabinet level and then another follows with perhaps a few additional ones at the subcabinet level, the media outlets generate a storyline about the administration's problems. Interest groups come in and circle around the nominees they want to see voted down or withdrawn, and others come to support nominees.

We will look at the appointments process for President Obama from several vantage points. First we will get a sense of the challenge a president faces in appointing nominees to executive branch positions. We will explore the number of vacancies available for a president to nominate officials in 2008 as well as discuss the urgency in getting people in place to fill a leadership vacuum preceding his arrival in office. A second area for us to study in the 2008 personnel process is the way the process was different from ones used in earlier years. The 9/11 Commission suggested changes to the security clearance process for presidential transition teams, and Congress enacted legislation instilling those changes starting with the 2008 presidential election. Through the work of his chief of staff, Joshua Bolten, and the rest of his White House staff, President Bush made significant efforts to smooth the process. Third, President-elect Obama clearly learned from past changeovers of power in how to create a personnel selection organization and how to establish priorities. What are the lessons he learned, and how did they come into play in 2008? Fourth, what personnel selection structure did presidential candidates Senators Obama and McCain establish and how did that process work once President Obama came into the White House? Finally, what did the personnel process yield? What were the successes and failures, and what did they mean in 2008 and for the future? We will include in this discussion appointments to the court system.

The Universe of Executive Branch Appointments

The statistics on presidential appointments make the case for the importance for a new administration of getting a quick hold on the process to achieve a significant policy impact. First, there are several thousand positions to fill. If a president and his team don't think through their priorities in filling them, they will soon be swamped by the vast dimensions of the task of getting new people into all of the executive branch positions. Second, when most modern presidents come in after a two-term incumbent, there are more vacancies in the higher reaches of the outgoing administration. Officials know the end is in sight, and they want to make sure they leave well before the election. With months to go to the conclusion of a president's second term, many of those positions inevitably remain unfilled. The result is that a new administration faces a leadership vacuum in many departments and agencies. Third, once a new president does take office, he faces the inevitable difficulty of filling those thousand-plus vacant spots. Both the nomination and Senate confirmation processes slow down a new president's efforts to get officials into those positions, even the ones in the executive branch that don't require Senate confirmation. These three realities of the modern appointments process make it difficult for an incoming administration to get the early start it needs to hit the ground running.

The Number of Vacancies

The appointments universe is vast. In his book *Inside the White House Staff: Continuity and Innovation,* Bradley Patterson lays out how long the appointments list is.[15] There are the following categories of presidential appointments that in 2008 added up to a total of 7,840, including approximately 400 judicial vacancies. There were 1,177 presidential appointees requiring Senate confirmation (PAS), including cabinet secretaries, their deputies and assistants, ambassadors, district attorneys, and U.S. marshals. The White House personnel operation has control over the PAS positions, but it also has a role in approving noncareer positions that the agency heads select. Patterson lists 1,428 Schedule C positions and another 796 noncareer positions in the Senior Executive Service in 2008. Not all of the positions are full-time ones. In 2008, there were 3,088 part-time members of boards and commissions a president could name, 579 of which require Senate confirmation. The president can also appoint another approximately 790 White House staff members, Patterson calculated.

Protracted Vacancies during Transitions

When a president starts off his administration, there is an urgency to get the appointments process started because so many of the positions have been vacant for a protracted amount of time, especially the mid-level ones in the departments and agencies. That means that there has been no leadership in those areas for a substantial time. In her study of presidential appointments based on information from the Office of Personnel Management, Anne O'Connell points to an urgent problem that confronts presidents in the appointments area.[16] Particularly when a president is at the end of two terms and the election is near, many offices empty out.

While cabinet positions are filled fairly constantly with Senate-confirmed appointees, below that level departments and agencies struggle with a continuing vacancy problem, especially at the end of a two-term presidency. Knowing the end date and wanting to be well situated somewhere else before that time arrives, political appointees leave early. In the two eight-year administrations for which O'Connell had complete figures, as shown in table 7.1, the Reagan and the Clinton administrations, there was an average of only 0.14 days in the Reagan administration and 12.93 in the Clinton administration for which there was a vacancy in a Senate-confirmed cabinet secretary position.[17] The numbers for the deputy secretaries were similar, but at level of the agency and deputy agency heads, the assistant secretaries and undersecretaries, positions often go unfilled for several hundred days at the end of an administration.[18] As positions empty out, the work of the agencies and departments comes to a standstill. At the end of President Reagan's administration, there were fewer vacancies at the senior level as they were able to hold over people from one Republican administration to the next. In the early days of both the Reagan and Clinton administrations, there was a change of party that increased the need to get their own senior-level people into the administration as soon as they could.

With little leadership at the end of an administration in executive branch agencies, a new administration suffers its own difficulties in getting people into those vacant spots. Inevitably, an incoming administration suffers long waits before those positions can be filled. The depth of the problem in filling the leadership

TABLE 7.1
*Numbers of Days without a Political Appointee in Place at the End of the Reagan,
G. H. W. Bush, and Clinton Administrations*

	Reagan	G. H. W. Bush	Clinton
Cabinet secretary	0.14	9.31	12.93
Deputy cabinet secretary	0.67	93.94	3.29
Agency head	142.71	23.96	204.90
Deputy agency head	94.69	114.70	239.59
Assistant secretary	100.23	69.81	256.13
Under secretary	357.95	81.74	340.88

Source: O'Connell, "Let's Get It Started," 8.

TABLE 7.2
*Average Number of Days to Fill First Appointments to PAS Positions in the Reagan,
Clinton, and G. W. Bush Administrations*

	Reagan	Clinton	G. W. Bush
Cabinet secretary	13.21	4.86	4.50
Deputy cabinet secretary	75.86	153.57	132.79
Agency head	165.95	200.35	237.71
Deputy agency head	270.71	457.14	347.28
Assistant secretary	188.95	249.56	234.91
Under secretary	101.82	209.33	183.64

Source: O'Connell, "Let's Get It Started," 7.

positions is clear from O'Connell's figures for the above spots. The departments and agencies may soon have cabinet secretaries in place, but the subordinate positions do not get filled nearly as quickly. The agency heads, their deputies, the assistant secretaries, and the undersecretaries are crucial to establishing the direction of the executive branch units.

In looking at the appointment confirmation figures in the light of whether the president's party controls the Senate and by how much, there is a growing slowdown in the confirmation of first appointees at the deputy secretary and agency head levels. Party can be an important factor, but it is not the only one. President George H. W. Bush, for example, followed a Republican president for whom he had served as vice president and felt no need to move swiftly to fill vacancies, as Bush had been part of the earlier administration.

Legislative and White House Actions Strengthening the Nomination Process

Realizing after September 11 the increased importance of an administration's first months, Congress and the Bush administration took actions in the 2001–2008

TABLE 7.3
Senate Political Party Control, First Two Years in Office, in Number of Majority Seats

Reagan (R)	G. H. W. Bush (R)	Clinton (D)	G. W. Bush (R)	Barack Obama (D)
Republican (53)	Democratic (55)	Democratic (57)	50 Republicans, 50 Democrats	55 Democrats plus 2 Independents who organized with the Democrats

Note: Under George W. Bush, Senate composition had been 50–50 when Sen. James Jeffords (VT) switched parties from Republican to Independent. He pledged to caucus with the Democrats.

period to set up an incoming team for a solid start in 2009. The 2008–2009 transition was the first one in which the incumbent administration gave the transition teams of both major-party candidates information on the executive branch positions a president could fill as well as provided details on what the posts involved. The appointments process was a primary focus for Joshua Bolten as he carried out the planning for the Bush administrations transition out of office. With the appointments process defined by its risks, what have those in office done to prepare the way for a new team and to help them fill those vacancies? The appointments area is one where a sitting administration at the end of eight years has traditionally given little aid to the opposing major-party candidate and sometimes rather little to their own party's candidate. Additionally, the incumbent has come in late into the personnel process, well after the election. Some have provided substantial help to their own party candidate, but not to the opposition.

The Bush administration broke that pattern in three ways. First, the administration implemented the Intelligence Reform and Terrorism Prevention Act of 2004 that called for candidates to submit the names of their transition staff well before the election, permitting the FBI to do their clearances before the election so that the new team could get started right after the election. Second, White House officials provided personnel information to both candidates, not just Senator McCain, the candidate representing the same party as President Bush. Third, they invited representatives of the two candidates to come to the White House and work together on several issues, including the development of a personnel software package. Through their actions, Joshua Bolten and his personnel team were able to get the two candidates to focus early on getting their transition operation prepared to make appointments decisions for their transition operation, with the result that when Senator Obama won the election, he had his transition team in place and was ready to get started on his formal transition duties.

Implementing the Recommendations of the 9/11 Commission

Other than the Presidential Transition Act of 1963 and its amendments, the most important piece of legislation for the 2008 transition was the Intelligence Reform and Terrorism Prevention Act of 2004. While the act was designed to deal with intelligence issues in the wake of the attacks on the United States on September 11, 2001, the bill is important in that it addresses the issues stemming from the large number of appointments an incoming president has to make in a short time.

The groundwork laid by government officials in the area of national security helped make the 2008–2009 transition smoother and better thought out. The Congress and the president viewed a smooth transition as a national security necessity, and both branches took action on issues related to getting a new administration up and running as soon as possible. The impetus for much of their preparatory work was the events of September 11, 2001. The attacks on the United States that day had a substantial impact on the shape of the 2008–2009 transition. In two subject areas discussed here, the National Commission on Terrorist Attacks Upon the United States, also called the 9/11 Commission, recommendations shaped the course of the 2008–2009 presidential transition. Congress and the administration took action on both security clearances for administration nominees and contingency crisis plans. Other transition security issues were at stake as well, such as ensuring a smooth first transition for the Department of Homeland Security, but our discussion here is focused on the examples of security clearances and contingency plans.

The government adopted the Commission's recommendations to improve the national security clearance process and to gather and provide information on security threats. In recent transitions, security clearances have consistently been an issue because they represent a major pinch point in getting presidential appointees from announcement to confirmation. The appointments process itself is notoriously slow, with the result that it takes several months to get a new government up and running with a president's political employees in place. Effectively gathering and sharing security threat information was an important concern after the September 11 attacks and was a central feature of the 9/11 Commission report to Congress.

The 9/11 commissioners criticized the lack of a full complement of presidential appointees in national security positions at the time of the September terrorist attacks. One of their recommendations to Congress and the president was to install future national security teams sooner than was the case in 2001:

Since a catastrophic attack could occur with little or no notice, we should minimize as much as possible the disruption of national security policymaking during the change of administrations by accelerating the process for national security appointments. We think the process could be improved significantly so transitions can work more effectively and allow new officials to assume their new responsibilities as quickly as possible.[19]

Congress and the president responded to the commission's recommendations for a smooth transition by passing the Intelligence Reform and Terrorism Prevention Act of 2004, which implemented changes in the security clearance process for nominees to executive branch positions. In the section on presidential transitions, the act calls for the president-elect to submit names for clearance as soon as possible after the election results are affirmed:

The President-elect should submit to the Federal Bureau of Investigation or other appropriate agency and then, upon taking effect and designation, to the agency designated by the President under section 115(b) of the National Intelligence-Reform Act of 2004, the names of candidates for high level national security positions through the level of undersecretary of cabinet departments as soon as possible after the date of the general elections held to determine the electors of President and Vice President under section 1 or 2 of title 3, United States Code.[20]

At the same time, the act provides that the two major-party candidates begin setting up their organizations for the transition by submitting names for national security clearance prior to Election Day: "Each major party candidate for President may submit, before the date of the general election, requests for security clearances for prospective transition team members who will have a need for access to classified information to carry out their responsibilities as members of the President elect's transition team."[21] This section of the act was useful for the presidential candidates in that they could submit names to the FBI for security clearances, ensuring that the eventual victor would be prepared for national security events soon after the election.

The White House was particularly interested in having the transition teams for the presidential candidates make effective use of the new legal provision allowing the candidates to clear their names early. Joshua Bolten talked about his discussions with representatives of the candidates whom he wanted to understand the importance of getting personnel right. Since those decisions needed to be made early, Bolten said he let them know: "We were there, ready to use the authorities from the legislation to get them clearances and that we wanted to put in place a mechanism that would permit them, without fear of compromise either on the general issue of being presumptive and sort of arrogantly starting to name people, or on just the specific side of names getting out." The question for Bolten was how to create a way for the transition teams to submit names without leaks to reporters and others. "We were keen to put in place a mechanism and a commitment that they would face no risk from us, the White House, in pushing that process forward," said Bolten. "Both sides were, I thought, naturally reticent about taking a political ding for naming people too early, and I think the Obama people might have been nervous that if they gave us names that we would leak the names. But we were able to assure them that we were not going to make the situation any worse for them."[22]

Pre-Convention Personnel Meetings with Candidate Representatives

The legislation calling for early clearance of transition officials was based on a recommendation of the 9/11 Commission, which was written in vague terms with no recommendations for how many people a candidate could put forward for clearance and no indication of whether the transition team needed to put names matched up with possible positions they could be appointed to. The act provided the following:

> (2) IN GENERAL.—Each major party candidate for President . . . may submit, before the date of the general election, requests for security clearances for prospective transition team members who will have a need for access to classified information to carry out their responsibilities as members of the President elect's transition team.

> (3) COMPLETION DATE.—Necessary background investigations and eligibility determinations to permit appropriate prospective transition team members to have access to classified information shall be completed, to the fullest extent practicable, by the day after the date of the general election.

Bush administration officials interpreted the provision in the broadest possible way. They put no limit on how many people a candidate could submit to the FBI for review for service in his postelection transition operation. Nor did they impose a requirement calling for the transition team to name one or more positions the person might hold during the transition period. Additionally, there was no reason for the campaign organizations to state whether the names being submitted were intended for the transition or for administration positions. There was no effort at any of the points of contact on the issue to put restrictions on what the transition teams could ask for in getting their people cleared for transition work. The process the administration set up called for bringing in the representatives of both campaigns to discuss the specifics of security clearances and the information the candidates' transition representatives could get from the Department of Justice. Senator McCain's transition representative on personnel issues was Will Ball, a former Navy secretary and a close personal friend of the candidate. Ball talked about the meeting the representatives of the McCain and Obama transition teams had in July at the Justice Department. "That particular meeting was at the Justice Department, and the associate attorney general for administration had assembled all components there," he said.[23] "The IRS representatives were there to brief on the IRS check procedure, which is a part of this. . . . The FBI representatives briefed on the FBI portion of the process. The Justice Department briefed on their role, and how they—and that if we had sent names in, what would have been the procedure they would have undertaken, both for interim clearances, and then after the election, for the full permanent clearance process."

Providing Information on Executive Branch Positions

Starting early to gather information that would be useful to a transition, Clay Johnson, deputy director for management of the Office of Management and Budget, assembled a list of more than one hundred positions that were important to fill as soon as possible in a new administration; eventually the number reached 150 positions. Don Gips, who headed the personnel operation, spoke about how they used the list: "The Bush administration gave us their view of it, and then we added and added. The whole transition board looked at it, and based on what we saw in the agency review [from the agency review teams]," he said. Then they had their specialists look at the lists. "Carol Browner looked at the energy stuff, and . . . wherever people had expertise, which we had pretty broad expertise on the board, we added and subtracted from that list."[24]

Putting together a short list of executive branch positions takes time, which can result in the list of positions becoming somewhat stale by the time they had to be implemented. That happened in the 2008 transition because the financial collapse that became such an important part of the transition came up too quickly for the need to be adequately reflected in the list of the most important jobs. By the time the Obama personnel operation was putting together their list, the financial meltdown was under way, and it took a primary position. John Podesta said, "They began that work at a time when their mindset was we've got two active conflicts going on, and we've got the threat of terrorism out there. We have homeland security challenges. That was their principal focus," Podesta said.[25] Even if the list required adjustment, it was a starting point for the Obama team to use as they thought through how to piece together an administration.

Four personnel briefing books assembled by Joie Gregor, director of the White House Office of Presidential Personnel, served as a complement to the list of the most significant positions. With a background in corporate personnel with Heidrick and Struggles, Gregor placed emphasis on the development of information on the individual positions in the federal government. The books contained the positions requiring Senate confirmation and the positions a president can appoint as political appointees as well as the noncareer Senior Executive Service ones. "We all decided, 'Let's take all eight hundred and some high-level positions and put what the actual statute would say about it and put what we think the competencies are and then a process under it, unique skill sets,'" Gregor said.[26] The information they prepared did not come to the Obama team until after the election, but Chris Lu was able to see the materials in his White House meetings. Lu described how he saw them: "You can come and . . . peek under the curtain. But we didn't really have physical access to it until after the election. . . . They had a brief for each of the PA [presidential appointee without Senate confirmation] positions."[27]

In addition to those materials, they also provided information on the personnel books they regularly presented to President Bush. "We showed them what a book would be like, would go to the president and this whole flowchart and all of these templates were there, including the questions to ask low-level, mid-level, and high-level people. And we wrote them out, and we had White House counsel double-check offices, ethics," Gregor said.[28] In both the early view of the detailed personnel information and the templates they used for presenting information to President Bush, the White House staff were giving material to representatives of the two campaigns as no White House staff had ever done. In previous years, the information that was provided—not nearly as detailed—came from the Office of Personnel Management and the Congress in the form of what was known as the Plum Book, which traditionally came out after the election.

In reality, after the election is too late for the president-elect to receive a list of presidentially appointed positions. A transition operation needs to work with a current personnel list, and it needs it early. In their willingness to prepare early for the transition, the Bush White House operation in July gave personnel information to the representatives of both candidates. Joie Gregor oversaw the collection of information about the most important presidential appointments. She laid out the markers important to particular positions and then had her staff collect information of individual appointments that indicated what specialty a person would have to have to fill the position, what responsibilities there would be, and the history of the agency.

Software Development

Along the same lines but earlier still, in June 1999 Governor George W. Bush picked his appointments specialist and friend, Clay Johnson, to handle transition issues and to focus on appointments issues including the recruitment of nominees for executive branch positions as well as the selection of an appropriate software package to handle resumes for a president-elect. Johnson handled the processing of appointments for Governor Bush as well as recruitment. It is with the George W. Bush administration that considering how to handle recruitment for positions a president could select became an important component of the appointments process. Johnson used the same basic software package for President Bush as he had for Governor Bush. By the end of the eight Bush presidential years, Johnson and the people in presidential personnel in the White House decided that it was time to design a new package. Knowing that it would be costly and need several months lead time to prepare, White House staff decided to get ahead of the process by contracting with a software company to develop a new package to meet the current personnel needs.

The way White House officials dealt with the upcoming need for a new personnel software program was to bring together the designated representatives for the McCain and Obama operations and discuss the issue with them. In the past, in the rare cases when candidates dealt with White House or administration officials, they did so one by one, not together. Bush White House officials wanted to have the agreement of both candidates on their software package needs. The incentive for reaching an agreement with both sides was the offer from the White House to purchase the software package—but only if both sides could agree on its contents. Chris Lu described the process: "They wanted to contract out for a new system that would be in place by January 20th. So they sat down with us. We had meetings here at EEOB [Eisenhower Executive Office Building] with the McCain campaign where we all discussed what we wanted in a system. And we basically came up with the specs for it, and we agreed on it. The White House contracted it out."[29]

The discussion was not easy during the session. Blake Gottesman, the deputy chief of staff handling the day-to-day operation for the transition out of office, intervened. Gail Lovelace, who attended the session for the General Services Administration, explained Gottesman's role: "It was a software issue, and I won't say too much more than that. But we got them in a room together and all the people from the White House were there and a bunch of people. And I'll tell you, Blake took a situation that I felt could have blown out of proportion, and he calmed it right down. He was a class act. He was unbelievable in that meeting."[30] Lu said, "Once they got the software vendor, the vendor gave the system to us and to the McCain campaign people to tinker with as we wanted, so that whoever won November 5th would have it the way they wanted it. And that was really facilitated by the Bush administration."[31]

Earlier administrations did not deal with this aspect of the appointments process because computer software to handle nominations was a new way to manage the recruitment process in 2000. Even as late as the Clinton administration, the process was done without a computer program managing the resumes of the thousands of people applying for jobs. At the same time, the number of resumes they were working with was not anything like the numbers of those that came in during the thirty-seven days of the George W. Bush transition or the seventy-five-day transition of Barack Obama.

Clearing Out Political Appointees

Before a president can appoint administration officials, those working for the previous chief executive need to be cleared out. One of the most important actions a president can take to help his successor is to take a strong hand in clearing out political appointees and to use a restrained hand in last-minute policy commitments. On December 1, 2008, Chief of Staff Joshua Bolten sent a memorandum to all of the administration's political appointees with the message that they were expected to quit their posts before the new administration came into office. "To provide the President-elect maximum flexibility in assembling his Administration, and consistent with past practice, President Bush is requesting letters of resignation from all non-career appointees except Inspectors General and those individuals that hold termed positions." Also given exceptions were those non-career Senior Executive Service and Schedule C appointees at independent regulatory commissions. The Bolten memorandum included language that a political appointee could use in his or her resignation letter to the president. It read, "Dear Mr. President, I hereby tender my resignation as [title]. I anticipate that my last day of service will be January 20, 2009, and I understand that you will act on this offer no later than noon, January 20, 2009. Sincerely, [name and title]."[32]

Clearing out executive branch offices is not easy because people often want to stay where they are. If there is a change in parties, though, it is easier to get people out of their posts. On the other hand, when there is a same-party transition, people often feel they are entitled to continued service if they so choose. That has been one of the problems of those transitions where a sitting vice president wins the presidency. President George H. W. Bush followed a president who did not clear out the offices, and so he had to do it himself. Shortly after Bush's victory, President Reagan requested resignations of all of his top political appointees.[33] But he did not force people to resign, and Bush and his cabinet officers were left to clear out people who remained after Bush took office. Louis Sullivan was confirmed as Secretary of Health and Human Services in March 1989. Three days after assuming office, Sullivan "acting under standing orders to department from the White House, . . . sent notice to HHS' approximately 100 Schedule C political appointees that their employment would be terminated as of April 1. The White House . . . told secretaries to take such action on political appointees in order to make way for new political appointees selected by the Bush Administration."[34] It was difficult for President Bush to start fresh when he had to clear out President Reagan's appointees. President Clinton ordered his political appointees to leave before he left office and then on January 19th fired the people who had not yet left.[35]

Getting People in Place Early

One initiative did not work for Bush officials. The Bush administration tried to reduce the time needed to perform a national security investigation in advance of the transition period. Clay Johnson, the deputy for management at the Office of Management and Budget, used several approaches to reach the goal of getting presidential appointees requiring Senate confirmation (PAS) into office earlier than was true in 2000–2001. Johnson said his focus was twofold: "Expand the capacity to do the work and shorten the process, the elapsed time."[36]

There were three ways the Bush administration sought to increase capacity. First, require the FBI, the agency conducting many of the national security clearance investigations, to reduce the amount of time it takes to conduct an investigation and, second, have the Office of Personnel Management (OPM) undertake investigations as well. Johnson explained how the government determines how many clearances need to be done and then asks the FBI to figure out what resources it needs to reach that goal: "You go to the FBI, and you say you need to figure out what sort of staff you need to be able to do this in thirty days, maximum. It used to take sixty days on average, including filling out the paperwork for the applicant. Sixty days average is not satisfactory. We expect thirty days maximum. So the FBI goes back, and they have to figure out how many extra agents to hire and how to change their processes and so forth. So they were charged to go do that." In addition to increasing the funding for the FBI to hire a sufficient number of agents or personnel to conduct the investigations, Johnson also recommended using other agencies to do investigations, especially OPM. "We looked at alternative organizations to do the investigations. We determined that it is conceivable that if the new administration wanted to . . . with no real impact on quality of the investigation, [it could ask] OPM to do a lot of these investigations," Johnson said.[37] Yet no one chose to do it.

Third, the Bush White House took an additional step to get needed presidential appointees in place early in an administration. Their effort was aimed at reducing the number of presidential appointed positions requiring Senate confirmation. The effort failed in the short term but bore fruit after the administration left office. The idea was to reduce non-policymaking positions requiring Senate confirmation from PAS (presidential appointee Senate confirmed) to "PA" status, which denotes presidential appointments not requiring Senate consultation. With Clay Johnson leading the internal effort to streamline the process in 2001, White House officials came up with a list of positions that the Bush administration believed could be dropped from the list of approximately 1,200 Senate-confirmed ones. "The actual letter we ended up sending to the Congress, and I think it was over 100, maybe 140 or 150 positions that weren't policy positions, they weren't high-level operational positions, they were support positions," explained Johnson. "Leg [legislative] affairs, government affairs, public affairs, intergovernmental affairs. . . . We recommended all the general counsels, all the CFOs, those kind of positions."[38]

If the designated positions were converted to presidential appointees without Senate confirmation, the officeholders, as Johnson observed, "would still be presidential appointed positions, and they could still testify." The group also included part-time board and commission positions that are Senate-confirmed. "Some of them are important, like the Broadcasting Board of Governors and some of these things can be sensitive, but others . . . there's no apparent reason why they need to be Senate confirmed." The idea was not to change the posts but "just streamlines the process a little." The response of the Senate leadership was not positive. "They looked at it, and they disagreed with our definition of what was critical or not. They came back and had whittled the list down to eight positions. . . . We got the message that they weren't interested and said thank you." In preparation for the 2008 transition, White House officials tried rekindling the discussion with Congress and thought about "going back up with such a list, but nothing ever became of it," Johnson said.[39]

Joel Kaplan, deputy chief of staff under Joshua Bolten, viewed the effort as "a bit of tilting of windmills. . . . To me that falls into the category of good govern-ment that is probably not worth spending a lot of high-level time on it because it is unlikely to happen. I did not use up a whole lot of my time and effort. I had been through a similar effort early in the administration. . . . Congress just does not like getting rid of PAS positions."[40] Johnson said that the "issue is not whether they need to confirm somebody or not to ensure that America is having the best and the brightest in these positions. That's not the thing that drives their think-ing." Senators of both parties are interested in having leverage with administra-tion officials. "Every appointee is a bargaining chip. . . . The more power and lever-age they have over an administration, the more they like it. Remove the number of leverage points, the number of Senate confirm positions . . . it removes some power from them."[41]

Senators want the lower-level positions to retain their PAS status, as lower-level positions are more realistic bargaining chips than are cabinet secretaries. "They wouldn't dare try to bargain with somebody who is going to be Secretary of Education . . . because that's high-profile. They would rather do their bargain-ing with some lower-profile people because it's sort of a nuisance, and you try to get rid of the nuisance."[42] Johnson's chief staff aide, Robert Shea, pointed out that political appointees who have managed to get through the confirmation process enjoy the added legitimacy Senate confirmation provided them and are often just as reluctant as senators to see positions converted to PA ones.[43]

With all signs pointing against any action on reducing the number of positions requiring Senate confirmation, the initiative saw a sudden change in fortunes in 2011. The Senate developed the Presidential Appointment Efficiency and Stream-lining Act of 2011 (actually signed into law in 2012), which reduced the number of PAS positions. The affected 163 positions were not high-level ones but rather unpaid boards and commissions as well as nominees for departmental positions for public affairs officials for the departments and agencies.[44]

Senate Holds

A persistent problem in the appointments process has been the practice of indi-vidual senators placing holds on the nomination of individual nominees for exec-utive branch positions and on judgeships as well. The rise in holds has profoundly slowed down the process of confirming assistant secretaries, undersecretaries, and agency heads. The likely nadir of the process arrived in February 2010, when Senator Richard Shelby, a Republican from Alabama, placed holds on all of Pres-ident Obama's nominees then pending for consideration.[45] At that point, there were over seventy nominees on the Senate's executive calendar. He placed the holds on February 5, and it triggered such a buzzsaw of criticism that he lifted them two days later. His spokesperson, Jonathan Graffero, explained Shelby's holds: "The purpose of placing numerous holds was to get the White House's attention on two issues that are critical to our national security—the Air Force's aerial refueling tanker acquisition and the FBI's Terrorist Device Analytical Center (TEDAC). With that accomplished, Sen. Shelby has decided to release his holds on all but a few nominees directly related to the Air Force tanker acquisition until the new Request for Proposal is issued."[46] Both projects were ones related to Alabama and had nothing to do with the appointees under consideration or the positions to which they were nominated. The issues of such concern to Shelby involved sizable amounts of money to Alabama. The tanker contract was for $35 billion and the explosives testing center related to a $45 million earmark that had been provided for in 2008 but had not been built.[47]

Lessons Learned From Past Transitions

Because all presidents begin their administrations with the same problem of filling vacant slots, there are some lessons to be learned about the ways a presidential candidate and then president-elect should set up his appointments process.

Choose One Official and Start Early: The Reagan and George W. Bush Precedents

A benefit that both the Reagan and Bush examples have taught those interested in the appointments process is that a well-established set of ground rules and a single person responsible for the appointments process will lead to the benefit of fewer nominations blowing up. With almost eight thousand positions that can be filled by a president and his White House team, an important part of the personnel process is reducing the appointments that turn sour to a bare minimum. For both of those presidents, few nominees derailed their appointment rollouts and the good feelings that invariably accompanied their announcement. No cabinet posts derailed the smooth nomination process for Reagan, and even with his thirty-seven-day transition, the George W. Bush administration had only one, the secretary of labor, and they quickly got the nominee, Linda Chavez, to withdraw and within nine days had sent a nominee, Elaine Chao, to the Senate. She worked out well as a nominee because she was guaranteed of a quick review and, as the wife of Senate minority leader Mitch McConnell, certain confirmation.

Because a president-elect needs to get an early jump on staffing his administration, as a candidate he needs to task someone close to him to head the recruitment and appointments processes. Most candidates have understood this. One of the areas where there is an established transition pattern that has worked is the area of presidential appointments. The appointments process is very much at the heart of the early work of a transition. All recent Republican presidents have assigned a person knowledgeable in appointments the task of gathering information on appointments.

Between the number of positions to fill and the steps in the confirmation process an appointee must navigate, presidential candidates and their staffs focus first on those appointees who are most important to their agenda. For President Reagan, his agenda of appointments emphasized his interest in the economy as an issue, as there was a building recession when he came into office. Pendleton James, who handled the personnel operation during the transition and in the White House, detailed how they identified the positions they were interested in: "So I and my group went through and said what are the key economic policy-making jobs? Those are the ones we want to address first because, until that person is sworn in, confirmed or appointed, that desk is empty over at Treasury or over at Commerce. Economic policy goes from State Department, Commerce, Treasury; it goes through everybody. It's not just Treasury Department. You want to make certain in the early days to work filling those appointments crucial to your initiatives of the first hundred days."[48]

Having spent eight years as Ronald Reagan's vice president, President George H. W. Bush did not have the same kind of urgency to fill vacancies as Reagan had following a chief executive of the opposing party. President-elect Clinton did not have a narrow range of issues he wanted to influence through appointments. Instead, he focused on the whole of the cabinet and agency heads and only later filled senior White House posts. Following the Reagan example, however, Governor George W. Bush had Clay Johnson gather information about the positions he would be able to fill if he was elected. Once Andy Card became chief of staff, he knew from his experience in the Reagan and Bush administrations that they would benefit from sifting through possible appointments with an idea of what they wanted their early achievements to be. According to Johnson, "Andy had suggested that we focus on, in addition to the deputies [of the department secretaries] the legislative affairs, the public affairs and the general counsels. Let's get them a good lawyer, a good PR person, and a good relationship person with the Congress."[49] Those positions combined account for around seventy-five appointments. Filling these positions early meant the departmental secretaries could get off to a solid start.

One of the keys to the success of their transition effort was that the work was under the wing of one person, Clay Johnson, an old friend of George W. Bush and someone well known to all of the campaign staff. No one viewed Johnson's operation as a competing one because campaign officials knew that Bush had asked Johnson to gather transition information and they also knew that politics had never been within his ken. Johnson met occasionally with the campaign leaders as well as with the candidate to give them a sense of what he was doing and finding. That way, there was no conflict among them. The second part of that process is to have clearly established public rules to govern the process and apply them strictly. With rules to deploy when trouble comes, a president and his team can easily rid themselves of problem nominations.

The first part of a transition takes place during the primary season, when the candidate designates a person to gather information. The person looks for information on personnel, past transitions, and upcoming decisions points. One needs a sense of the decisions made by the incumbent administration, dealing with governing and noting their timing. Expecting transitions where a change in party would be in store, the Reagan and George W. Bush administrations created an early operation with an emphasis on personnel and gathering information from past transitions. The effective practices developed by Clay Johnson for George W. Bush as candidate, president-elect, and president were described in detail in chapter 4.

Setting Up the Personnel Operation for Senators Obama and McCain

There is a partisan dimension to how major-party presidential nominees set up their personnel operations. Of the five recent presidents, only Presidents Clinton and Obama did not have one person heading the personnel recruitment process from the early spring. During the transition phases, Governor Clinton had at least five people who identified themselves as heading the process. The personnel portfolio for Senator Obama had many hands as well. All of the Republican presidents had one person handling personnel recruitment. That goes for Senator McCain as well.

The two candidates began their appointments work around the same time, but with an important difference. Both operations got their start in June and had many similarities, but the organizational structures were different in terms of how many people handled the portfolio. Senator McCain chose one person to develop the process, while the Obama operation had several. Russell Gerson, who has a New York executive recruitment firm, the Gerson Group, joined the McCain operation in late June after campaign manager Rick Davis and then Senator McCain talked to him about leading their personnel effort, which he did through the election. In the event that McCain were elected, Gerson committed himself to continue in the position through the whole process and to serve as personnel director for at least the first year of a McCain administration. Gerson spoke with Pendleton James in early July, and James stressed the importance of committing oneself to an eighteen-month tour in the personnel spot, which he did.[50]

Senator Obama had several people head his recruitment of executive branch employees at the early point and later on as well. The main people were Michael Froman, a friend of Obama's from law school and a Citicorp executive, and Federico Peña, former secretary of transportation and secretary of energy under Clinton. "Mike [Froman] probably came on in June or July. He was one of the very early people. . . . Don Gips was very early. Federico was very early. Pete Rouse was very early."[51] When Froman came in, he and Peña ran that personnel process, Lu said. The two "took the universe of potential jobs and winnowed it down. . . . They had done slates . . . but [the process] was also notionally more the order in which you tee these things up."[52] In the McCain personnel process, the same winnowing process took place.

John Podesta spoke about the organization of the personnel operation. Because Peña was out campaigning, "the lion's share of the duty of establishing how the structure would work fell on Froman's shoulders. . . . He then built out cluster teams that largely functioned through the inauguration." The structure Froman established continued in place, but he did not. "It was clear Froman wasn't going to be the personnel director. At some point, we settled on [Don] Gips." That had not been the intention of the Obama team when they first planned out their transition organization. Podesta said, "The one thing that we had wanted to do in the early planning was to have a personnel director settled early on in the process who could run it and take it into the White House. It was . . . a lesson from Clinton and Bush." For practical reasons, it didn't happen. "Mike was doing a good job. He had built out the team, and it made sense for him to continue with that."[53]

Senator Obama had clear thoughts on what he wanted in his personnel process, but his early operation was one part of an overall information-gathering operation. Chris Lu explained what Senator Obama was thinking about early in the transition in terms of people he would want to bring into his administration: "Senator Obama in probably our first or second transition meeting with him was very, very clear, that he wanted us to build an administration that just was not the usual suspects, . . . the inside the Beltway people. He wanted people that not only had a diversity of race and sex, but . . . folks that actually had private sector experience, state and local experience, people from academia, people from all parts of the country."[54] That was an interest he later communicated to his personnel director.

Senator McCain was also interested in recruiting people from the private sector. He wanted a search process that went beyond those who normally come into politically appointed positions in the executive branch. Gerson recounted a conversation with Senator McCain who did not like a list he had given the senator: "Russ, I hired you because you're from the private sector. I can get all the government people I want, and I'll hire people that have government experience. But I want you to focus on bringing in private sector people in the government."[55] Gerson said that McCain "wanted a demonstrated track record of success in getting things done."[56] When Gerson and his team of volunteers assembled, along with a group of young people who did some of their Internet searches, "we said this is the criteria: demonstrated track record of success, a deep understanding of a particular sector, whether it's the economy, whether it's health care, whether it is energy, but a demonstrated track record of success, . . . whether it's building a company or whether it's a reputation for success."[57]

Each operation depended on experts who could help in the process of gathering names for specific issue areas. Yet the people selected to organize each area and to come up with names were quite different in the two preelection transition operations. Each operation had a little over a half-dozen people working on gathering names for positions in specific issue areas, but the people they chose to do the hunts had different backgrounds. The McCain people were specialists in their policy areas, many of whom worked outside of Washington and none of whom had a politics background. The Obama operation had people with previous governing experience to fill in names for their areas.

Both transition personnel operations worried about leaks of possible names for executive branch posts. In the summer months, the personnel operation was dominated by a fear of leaks. Lu discussed their fears: "We weren't . . . asking potential nominees for their tax returns. We were basically having our folks run Nexis searches on people. . . . We were very conscious of the leaks, and in the summer of 2008, at the end of the summer, we were very, very careful about this 'presumptuous arrogance' label that McCain's campaign had started throwing at us."[58]

The result was that work that perhaps needed to get done was not getting done. Lu continued: "Could we have done more work? Yeah, we probably could have done more work on that front, actually. But the idea was that we did not want to be thrown off by leaks coming out of the transition about X person being named for a certain job."

While there were notable problems with several nominations at the beginning of the process, especially with three cabinet secretaries—Treasury, Commerce, and Health and Human Services—as well as the management deputy at the Office of Management and Budget, the process settled down once the administration got their clearance process working so that they were better able to recruit nominees for positions and to sense trouble on the horizon. The administration had to provide waivers to several nominees who did not meet President Obama's ethics regulations, but the bad publicity such waivers generated had a short life. By the hundred-day mark on April 29, the administration was ahead of Obama's recent predecessors in terms of nominations announced and confirmed by the Senate.

Assembling a Rubik's Cube

Once the election was behind them and the Obama team filled out the personnel puzzle for the new administration, personnel director Don Gips likened the task of personnel selection to creating a Rubik's Cube. "I call this the Rubik's Cube of personnel," said Gips about the way he and his staff approached their work putting together the Obama administration team.[59] "Because you really are trying to put together a meld of the right skill sets, some new blood, some old blood, geographic diversity, gender diversity, racial diversity. And you've got to balance that whole cube to put together the right thing. And then you've got politics, senators, congressmen, governors, mayors . . . who did what in the campaign. All those things go into this black box or Rubik's Cube that we've got to sort out for each, across the board. I mean, we have to look at, how's HUD doing on diversity, are they picking. . . . Is it all people who Shaun Donovan's known his whole life, or does he have a lot of people who did a lot on the campaign and live, breathe, and sleep Obama?"

President Obama and his team, aiming for a Rubik's Cube of diversity, selected a team for the fifteen-member cabinet that was made up of eleven men and four women, with less than half (40%) making up the traditional white male grouping. In looking further at the diversity of the original team, the appointees break down this way: eleven men (73%) and four women (27%); of which one appointee was African-American (7%), three were Asian-American (20%), and two were Latino (13%). These numbers seem low for African-American secretaries but represent the largest tallies of women and of Asian-Americans in a president's original cabinet. Eric Holder became the first African-American attorney general and Senator Hillary Clinton the first woman to be appointed secretary of state at the beginning of an administration. Other women who served as secretaries of state, Madeline Albright in the Clinton administration and Condoleezza Rice in the George W. Bush one, were appointed in their presidents' second term.

Of the first picks in the Reagan administration, only men were selected for the thirteen cabinet positions that existed at the beginning of that administration (the Departments of Education and Energy had been added during the Carter years), none of whom had a Latino or Asian background. In his cabinet of 92% white men, he had one African-American member, Sam Pierce at housing and urban development. President Carter brought two women into his eleven-member cabinet, one of whom was an African-American and the other a Latina. Otherwise his cabinet was composed of nine white men (82%). President George H. W. Bush's cabinet portrait was more similar to Carter's than Reagan's. President George H. W. Bush had one woman, two Latino men, and one African-American in his original cabinet of fourteen positions (Veterans Affairs being added during the Reagan administration) making it a 71 percent white male group. Presidents Clinton and George W. Bush brought in a more diverse group of people into their fourteen-member cabinets than their predecessors. President Clinton was the first president to appoint a cabinet in which white men represented less than half of the people who served (43%). He chose three women, two Latino men, and four African-Americans for cabinet posts. His nominee for attorney general, Janet Reno, represented the first time a woman was chosen for that position. In his second term, he broke the gender barrier at the State Department by naming Madeleine Albright to be the first woman to serve as secretary of state.

For his fourteen department cabinets, President George W. Bush moved forward from the model of his father but with less diversity than President Clinton's cabinet. Bush brought in Asian-Americans, which his predecessors had not done. Half of his cabinet picks were white men, but President Bush filled the other half with people of a variety of backgrounds including three women, two African-Americans, two Asian-Americans, and one Latino. His choice of Colin Powell as secretary of state represented the first time an African-American served in that position. A comparison of recent presidents demonstrates a solid pattern of presidents reaching out to a diverse group of people to serve in their cabinets. When counting his first selections for cabinet posts, President Obama's choices continued a trend of opening up the top spots to people other than the white men who until recently formed the cabinet core.

To round out their Rubik's Cube, the Obama personnel team pursued numerous paths to recruiting a diverse pool of applicants, indicated Gips, "including extensive outreach both through the Internet and through outreach of groups around the country." One of the ways the administration broadened the pool was by allowing cabinet secretaries to bring in their own staffs when they took their posts. "Our cabinet's pretty diverse in where they've come from, so Ken Salazar [secretary of the interior and a former senator from Colorado] has people from Colorado . . . and Gary Locke [secretary of commerce and former governor of Washington] has brought people from Washington state. Those help . . . broaden the pool of people we're looking for."[60] Most administrations encourage cabinet secretaries to accept political appointees White House officials have vetted and selected for the departments. The president's team usually worries about the divided loyalties and differing values of those who serve cabinet secretaries instead of their real boss, the president. As it turned out, there was a real benefit in appointing people who have held elected office.

The person designing the system was the president. Don Gips discussed the president's role in the appointments process: "He's been very clear that he's hired these secretaries to run their agencies, so he's really counting on them to make their selection. He wants to make sure that they believe in his vision . . . they're diverse, and that they are representing America well." Gips discussed how they worked with department secretaries on appointments. "We'll work with them to make sure they're consistent people. And every single candidate goes through this vetting process. . . . 'Do they share our views, are they a good fit for what we're trying to do?'" Cabinet secretaries have the expertise appropriate for selecting specialists. "Secretary Chu [secretary of energy] is going to have a much better idea than any of us are going to have about . . . nuclear safety, what does he need to have." While department secretaries are important in choosing their own deputies, White House staff are important in those selections as well. Of all the department secretaries, the one with the greatest latitude in choosing her deputies was Secretary Clinton.[61] White House officials with a particular portfolio will know what kinds of people they want in department positions. Gips explained: "Phil Schiliro [White House legislative affairs] has a very good idea of the type of people he wants to see representing us, or for public affairs, Dan Pfeiffer [White House communications deputy] does."[62] From John Podesta's viewpoint, there were "checks and balances" in the process, and "it was pretty efficient. I think that that reflected back on Clinton. He was probably too engaged at too junior a level, which meant that the process slowed down."[63]

Many Chefs Stirring Obama's Personnel Pot

The three personnel rules learned over the course of several administrations are (1) hire one person to shepherd the personnel process; (2) have that person work on personnel from the early days of the campaign through the first year of the administration; and (3) have a settled White House personnel staff before beginning cabinet selections. Looking at the personnel process of the Obama transition,

President Obama did not follow any of these three rules learned through past positive and negative experience of the five administrations preceding the Obama one. The person who did some early transition work, Pete Rouse, turned over the portfolio to Chris Lu, who then focused on the transition process as a whole. Others who then worked on personnel were Michael Froman, Federico Peña, Jim Messina, and then, as they were about to enter the White House, Don Gips. Up to that point, Gips was one of a group of three leading the agency review teams, and Jim Messina was director of personnel for the transition. Both were appointed to those positions on November 6. His deputy for the transition personnel operation, who came into the White House as political director, not in the personnel operation, was Patrick Gaspard. Ten days later, on November 16, Messina was named deputy White House chief of staff. Having many people handling the one portfolio and then one person designated as personnel chief and incoming deputy chief of staff split the pie into many slices.

Thus the personnel portfolio went through many hands prior to settling in the hands of Don Gips, who then served as personnel director for not quite six months. He was appointed on January 5, 2009, by which time cabinet positions had already been announced, including Treasury, State, and Defense as well as the attorney general. Gips served in the role of personnel director until June 2009, when the White House announced his nomination as ambassador to South Africa. In the same June 4, 2009, press release, the White House also announced that Gips's deputy, David Jacobson, was also leaving the Office of Presidential Personnel. In his case it was to become ambassador to Canada. With so much shuffling around in the personnel operation, there was little institutional memory.

What difference does it make to have continuity in the personnel position? There are at least four reasons that it benefits an incoming president to have one person lead the process for an extended time. First, the person can start early and line up what needs to be done to gather names for the positions a president can fill. Second, with exclusive rights to the personnel area, the person can deal directly with the presidential candidate on what qualities and background he wants of his nominees. Third, the person can establish the process and rules for handling nominees. The principal benefit of having one person head the process is there need to be rules about what the appointees bring and when they don't measure up, a solid process can provide a fast exit. A personnel process needs a person in charge of setting up the procedures for handling all the hundreds of thousands of resumes that will come in. Coordinating all of the pieces means too that the personnel director can implement the rules he or she has established with the candidate as governing their process for filling executive branch posts.

TABLE 7.4
Obama Administration Nominations That Ran into Difficulty, 2008–2009

Position	Appointee	Announcement	Difficulty	Withdrawal	Hearing date	Confirmation date	Vote
Treasury secretary	Timothy Geithner	November 24, 2008	$31,356 tax owed in amended returns for 2001–2002 and 2004–2006		January 21, 2009	January 26, 2009	60–34
Attorney general	Eric Holder	December 1, 2008	Role in Clinton's Marc Rich pardon while Deputy AG at DOJ		January 15–16, 2009	February 2, 2009	75–21
Commerce secretary	Bill Richardson	December 3, 2008	State contracts involving political supporters	January 4, 2009			
Commerce secretary	Senator Judd Gregg	February 3, 2009	Disagreed with Obama stimulus program and census plans	February 12, 2009			
Health and Human Services secretary	Thomas Daschle	December 11, 2008	Filed amended tax returns; paid $128,203 in back taxes and $11,964 in interest.	February 3, 2009			
OMB chief performance officer	Nancy Killefer	January 7, 2009	2005 DC government lien on house for $ 946.69 since paid	February 3, 2009			

Source: Contemporaneous news accounts of nomination difficulties in the *Washington Post* and *New York Times.* Nomination dates are found at "Barack H. Obama Cabinet Nominations," available at http://www.senate.gov/pagelayout/reference/six_column_table/Obama_cabinet.htm.

In looking at how the departments fared in their first year in filling out the posts requiring Senate confirmation, it is striking how much damage is done when there is a controversy selecting the cabinet secretary. Out of the fifteen departments, the ones with the lowest percentage of Senate-confirmed people in place were ones where there had been a controversy over the person appointed to the position. Both Commerce and Health and Human Services suffered from having nominees who were withdrawn and only later getting a confirmed person in place. For commerce, Gary Locke's name was sent to the Senate as the first nominee for that position sent to the Senate. Locke's two announced predecessors, Bill Richardson and Senator Judd Gregg, withdrew their names from consideration. Two months elapsed before Locke's name went to the Senate for the Commerce position on March 18, 2009.

Tom Daschle was announced on December 11, 2008, for the Health and Human Services position and nominated on January 20, 2009, with the full slate of nominees formally presented following Obama's inauguration. After two months of controversy, Daschle withdrew on February 9, and the White House sent Kathleen Sebelius's name to the Senate on March 17. Their late arrival into office took its toll on both eventual cabinet secretaries because their initial energies were so strongly focused on the confirmation process. The result was that only 48 percent of Commerce and 5 percent of Health and Human Services positions requiring Senate confirmation were filled a year after Obama came into office. Two secretaries whose nominations drew controversy, Timothy Geithner at the Treasury Department and Eric Holder for attorney general, also slowed down the process of filling Senate-confirmed vacancies. At the one-year mark, Treasury had 52 percent of its slots filled, and Justice 46 percent. Whereas the four departments with the lowest percentage of Senate-confirmed positions filled were also the ones where a controversy had surrounded the nominees for the post, the four posts that had the highest percentage of positions filled demonstrated an important pattern of their own. The four—Transportation, Interior, Agriculture, State—were all departments headed by officials who had left elected positions to join the administration. Representative Ray LaHood, Senator Ken Salazar, Governor Tom Vilsack, and Senator Hillary Rodham Clinton brought important assets to their positions. Because they were allowed to bring their own deputies of their own choosing, they brought with them a staff that had already been vetted by them as well as a political nose for trouble. Senator Clinton recruited as deputies people who had served on her staff in her time in the Senate and in the Clinton White House and administration. In all of these cases, they were able to recruit people who had faced vetting at an earlier point, with the consequence that the people selected had few problems—tax or otherwise—in terms of achieving Senate confirmation.

The White House Is Crucial to the Process

One of the consequences of the protracted Senate confirmation process and the multiple forms appointees have to fill out is an additional need to focus on the White House first. Getting the White House organized and staffed up at the senior level is particularly important because only after putting a decision-making process in place can a president-elect begin to make his executive branch choices. He must first lay out what the qualities are that he is looking for in his nominees and then establish the filtering process for recruiting people. He must decide as well what the priorities are for filling administration positions.

Organizing the top tier of the White House is a central task of the transition, as is lining up the budget operation. How the White House is organized and how the president makes decisions about the selections of aides are matters of great importance to the direction of the government. In December 2008 ABC reporter John Cochran asked President Bush about the qualities required to be president: "You've been in office for seven years now. You must have some pretty strong opinions about what it takes to sit in the Oval Office. What is important to you?" The president went on to discuss how important the White House is to what a chief executive does and how significant the structure of the decision-making system is. "How do you intend to get advice from people you surround yourself—who are you going to surround yourself with, and what process will you have in place to ensure that you get the unvarnished opinion of advisors? Because whoever sits in that Oval Office is going to find this is a complex world, with a lot of issues coming into the Oval Office—a lot—and a great expectation in the world that the United States take the lead. And so my question would be, how do you intend to set up your Oval Office so that people will come in and give their advice?"[64] He did not say whether he came in with that view or it was something he learned through his years in office.

In order to pick cabinet secretaries, the president needs the White House chief of staff, personnel director, and counsel in place. Assessing potential administration appointees requires the work of several White House offices. Personnel staff sift through possible appointees and gather the material on each, but presidents consult their relevant policy people, the chief of staff, and his counsel before making a choice. That means the major White House staff members need to be in place. Not having them in place can be costly: When President Clinton chose Zoë

Baird as his nominee for attorney general, he did not have his White House staff in place or a personnel operation set up and in coordination with the incoming White House counsel. Having a legal opinion is important in weighing nominations, because had Clinton had such an operation in place, he might have understood the cost of putting forward Baird's nomination in spite of her and her husband having employed undocumented workers. Her problems were a front-page story for over a week, including the days of his inauguration. When the George W. Bush staff made aware that their nominee for labor secretary, Linda Chavez, had a similar undocumented worker situation, she withdrew within two days. Those handling the personnel vetting process for George W. Bush were people with previous White House experience. Fred Fielding had served in the Nixon and Reagan years as White House counsel, and Tim Flanigan had been in the Justice Department during the Reagan years; both were familiar with the Senate confirmation process.

Getting budget officials and White House policy staff in place early is important as well. The budget prepared by the outgoing president will be submitted early in February. If the president-elect is to have an impact on the budget, the incoming chief executive will need to choose top budget officials and then ask the sitting president to have the outgoing budget team provide their figures to the new crew. That way they can figure out how they want to handle the budget document, which is necessarily more general than the one they will submit in April. "The issue," commented Clay Johnson III, "is how much will a new President's budget reflect his/her priorities."[65] The budget is the bottom line for presidential policy, but by the time the president submits one, there are few appointees below the departmental secretary level who have made it through the confirmation process at the hundred-day mark.[66]

With so few people in place in the departments, the policy people in the White House and those in OMB take on a special importance. "Another reason it is important to start early [picking White House staff and budget officials] is that at that point there are very few appointees," commented Jonathan Breul. "Even by June, very few got through [in Bush's first year]. So you don't have a government in place that can function that well, so you have OMB director and policy folks to decide how to move forward. It is a thin group. That is how OMB directors [David] Stockman pulled things together for Reagan, [Leon] Panetta for Clinton, and [Mitch] Daniels for Bush."[67]

How did President-elect Obama measure up to earlier practices and expectations? With one very important exception, President Obama was able to fill out most of his White House staff structure well before he came into office. The exception, however, was one of the most important White House officials for an effective personnel appointments process: the personnel director. The January 5 appointment of Don Gips to be personnel director was quite late for that position. We have already seen the benefits that coming in early provided the National Security Council staff, namely that individual staff members were able to talk at length over a course of a month to their counterparts prior to coming into office.

Incoming staff had time to have a conversation or two with their predecessors but little else. They received some briefing materials as well, but not long before they came in. While Rahm Emanuel was named as chief of staff on November 6, two days following the election, the transition and agency review teams were the focus of the first week's announcements. Except for the national security team announced on December 1, all of the White House senior and even some mid-level staff were named to their posts in the period between November 15 and December 1. The top staff members for Vice President Biden, Michelle Obama, and Jill Biden also were named before Thanksgiving. Of the twenty-one White House staff members who had the top salaries in 2009 and who came in at the beginning of the administration, eighteen were announced by December 1. Don Gips was not hired at top salary and was named very late in the selection process. That reflected the trouble the Obama team had settling on a personnel director in the first place, a clear signal of trouble for the cabinet selection process. Following the inauguration, they had difficulty getting their personnel team settled in the White House.

The Obama Personnel Operation by the Numbers

Even if there was early delay once they arrived in the White House, the transition gave the incoming Obama administration a relatively quick start on nominations. Despite having many cooks involved in the process, President Obama had a good record in getting his nominations in during the first hundred days of his administration. While a president can appoint several thousand people during his term, a White House team focuses first on executive branch appointments to the departments and agencies at the leadership level. Appointments to part-time boards and commissions come well after the early round of nominations. Independent regulatory boards and commissions, such as the Federal Communications Commission, are first-tier jobs and get the attention of an administration personnel operation, particularly for vacant commission chairmanships. Federal district and court of appeals nominations come once a president has gotten well under way in nominating his executive branch officials. Usually at the end of the first hundred days, the personnel operation broadens to include a group of less critical positions. The second wave of appointments includes U.S. attorneys, marshals, and ambassadors. All are part of the appointees list requiring Senate confirmation.

For the first hundred days, filling the top executive branch positions is the focus of the presidential personnel team. For the early appointments to executive branch positions, there is a study of appointments using the authoritative and pub-licly unavailable figures of the Office of Personnel Management, the institution where federal employment information is gathered and retained.[68] University of California law professor Anne O'Connell tracked the progress of the nomination and appointments process from Reagan through Obama's first year. Comparative figures give us a sense of the speed of the early appointments in terms of their nomination and confirmation. One also notes the more complicated political en-vironment a president is in when making his appointments. A point to remem-ber as we look at these figures is the growth in executive branch positions that a president can fill between the Reagan years of the 1980s and Obama's time of 2009. The difference in scale shows up in the number of positions to fill. In look-ing at one year of the administration, she has 295 positions for Reagan to fill, 317 for George H. W. Bush, 361 for Clinton, 336 for George W. Bush, and 422 for Obama. Since Reagan's first year we have the addition of two cabinet depart-ments: Veterans Affairs and Homeland Security.

The positions studied are those most important in cabinet departments and some executive agencies; the author excluded ambassadors, U.S. attorneys and marshals, and federal judges. The latter four categories of positions typically are filled after the central executive branch positions are filled: cabinet secretar-ies, deputy secretaries, assistant secretaries, undersecretaries, agency heads, and deputies to the agency leaders. These are the positions that drive policy and its implementation in the first year of an administration, so they take top billing when positions are lined up. O'Connell's figures demonstrate the early successes and the later slowdown of the Obama administration to fill its vacancies.

First, the aggregate figures at the hundred-day mark for executive branch nominations. The Obama administration did relatively well, especially given the increase in important executive branch policymaking positions that a president has to fill. Their early efforts, though somewhat scattered in terms of how many people were working on executive branch appointments, did look good by the numbers. The problem for the administration was getting their people through the process. At that stage, each misstep can prove costly because of the lost mo-mentum it generates for the president and his White House staff; inevitably the

TABLE 7.5
Presidential Executive Branch Nominations and Senate Confirmations
at 100-Day Mark

	Nominations	Confirmations (%)
George H. W. Bush	77	45 (58.4)
Bill Clinton	138	45 (32.6)
George W. Bush	126	32 (25.4)
Barack Obama	164	62 (37.8)

Source: O'Connell, "Waiting for Leadership," 9.

participants have to talk about problems rather than looking forward with their policies and initiatives.

Second, the figures demonstrate some important political realities about the appointments process. It makes a great deal of difference to have a same-party transition, as George H. W. Bush had when he followed the eight years of the Reagan administration in which he had served as vice president. President Reagan substantially smoothed the path for his vice president in the fall of 1988 by appointing Bush's preferred candidates for secretary of the treasury (Nicholas Brady), attorney general (Richard Thornburgh), and education secretary (Lauro Cavazos). Once he came into office in 1989, he kept all three and spared himself and his team the time and energy it would have taken to fill these spots. In a same-party transition, Bush did not feel the immediate need to change departmental leaders under the secretary level because as vice president he was involved, at least tacitly, in their selection and could easily make the case for them to sign on to his priorities. Thus, Bush could afford to wade more slowly into the appointments process than a president who comes into office after administrative control by the opposing party.

President George W. Bush, Bill Clinton, and Barack Obama did not have the luxury President George H. W. Bush had in adopting a personnel pace that fit in with what else he wanted to focus on in his administration. As the vice president in the Reagan administration and as a person involved in some of the president's personnel choices, Bush could afford to adopt a slower pace in choosing appointees because those in place were in part his own choices. The three most recent presidents entered after the opposing party had occupied the White House and therefore had no opportunity for such a transition in any of their cabinet secretary positions. In Obama's case, though, he did elect to retain Robert Gates as secretary of defense, although he made some changes as the deputy level.

The Reagan numbers demonstrating a fast confirmation process bring to mind

TABLE 7.6
*Percentage Filled for Senate Confirmed Positions in Departments and Agencies,
One Year into Term*

	Confirmed positions	Available positions	Percentage confirmed
Ronald Reagan	255	295	86.4
George H. W. Bush	254	317	80.1
Bill Clinton	252	361	69.8
George W. Bush	248	336	73.8
Barack Obama	272	422	64.4

Source: O'Connell, "Waiting for Leadership," 8.

another complication that now faces a president as he composes his cabinet. When Ronald Reagan selected his thirteen cabinet secretaries, gender was not a prominent issue for him, nor was ethnicity aside from race, which was preferable but not required. He had one African-American secretary—Samuel Pierce at Housing and Urban Development—but as he came into office, his first appointments included no women or Hispanics to head departments. Today a president has to create a more complicated mosaic as he puts together a cabinet. The process of searching for appointees as well as convincing them to run the gauntlet of the personal date statement, the national security form, and the financial disclosure questionnaire followed up by Senate committee forms is a daunting one. The pileup of hazards confronting an administration results in a slow process that is hard for an incoming administration to get purchase on.

In part the lower numbers for Obama reflect the "Rubik's Cube" that Donald Gips described. At the same time, the numbers reflect the state of the nomination process at the time of a president's first year. When compared to the political landscape President Reagan inherited, there are now more positions to fill, more questions for nominees to answer, more institutions to navigate.

The percentage of departments of executive branch positions filled at the one-year mark indicates the difficulties of filling positions when there is a delay in the confirmation process. The protracted hearings cost the president in terms of having people in place in the departments and agencies to work on the issues that were central to his new administration. There were many empty chairs in key departments, such as the Treasury Department, where decision-making for the financial crisis was centered.

Judicial Nominations

Executive branch positions are not the only ones that a president has to tend to when he comes into office, nor are they necessarily the ones with the most im-

TABLE 7.7

Percentage of Executive Branch Confirmations by Department, One Year into Term

	Reagan	G. H. W. Bush	Clinton	G. W. Bush	Obama
Agriculture	92.9	66.7	75.0	80.0	81.3
Commerce	86.4	70.8	43.3	87.0	48.0
Defense	89.7	80.0	57.4	93.3	64.0
Education	94.1	78.6	70.6	64.7	72.2
Energy	81.8	68.8	82.4	71.4	69.6
Health and Human Services	92.9	66.7	93.8	80.0	55.0
Homeland Security					66.7
Housing and Urban Development	100.0	90.9	100.0	61.5	60.0
Interior	93.3	100.0	68.8	69.2	88.2
Justice	65.0	75.0	62.5	88.0	46.2
Labor	85.7	92.3	87.5	73.3	61.1
State	91.3	96.2	80.6	72.7	74.4
Transportation	93.3	82.4	76.5	77.8	89.5
Treasury	100.0	94.1	84.2	65.0	52.2
Veterans Affairs	100.0	90.9	75.0	75.0	57.1

Source: O'Connell, "Waiting for Leadership," 8.

pact. When President Obama was talking about the appointment of a chair of the Federal Reserve, he gave priority in importance to filling in vacancies in the Supreme Court and the Fed as important decisions a president makes. "That person presumably will stay on after I'm President," he said. "So this, along with Supreme Court appointments, is probably as important a decision as I make as President."[69] As with the Supreme Court, successful nominations for district and circuit courts of appeal last until the judge decides to step down, unless the person is deemed by the Senate to have violated the mandate in Article III of the Constitution that the person serve a term of "good behavior."

Both Obama and Bush put special attention on court nominations, enlisting both the White House Counsel and the Justice Department for the recruitment and vetting processes, not the Office of Presidential Personnel. Traditionally presidents hold back on nominations for district and circuit courts of appeal until they have gotten through the first wave of appointments to executive branch positions. Those nominations generally begin going down to the Senate in the spring. Studies of President Obama's judicial nominations demonstrate the same patterns found in executive branch ones. The nomination process has been slower than was true in earlier administrations. An important part of the judicial nomination process is the opportunity President Obama had in his first term to make two nominations to fill Supreme Court vacancies. Supreme Court nominations put all other court nominations to the back of the line. Those nominations took a great deal of preparatory time, as one of Obama's nominees, Elena Kagan, had worked in Clinton White House and also served as solicitor general, so there were many records of hers to go through before and during the Senate confirmation process.

The White House counsel is the point person for handling the selection process for court nominations. In March 2009, Greg Craig, White House counsel during President Obama's first two years in office, explained to the Senate Democratic caucus the process the administration was using for court nominations. The *New York Times* reported Craig's description of their process: "In a closed meeting on Capitol Hill two weeks ago, Craig told Democratic senators that the White House would rely on their recommendations to fill the district courts. But he said that while Obama would welcome their advice, he warned that filling the appeals courts was largely a presidential prerogative, participants said." Some Democratic senators were unhappy; an aide interviewed by the reporter noted the established continuities governing the nomination process: "One senior aide briefed on the meeting said that such an effort to limit Democratic senators' role could create friction. But the aide said that every White House tried to impose such an understanding at the beginning only to become flexible when it needed a senator's vote on some unrelated issue." Republicans were less willing than Democrats to support the president and gave their own warning "to block his judicial nominees by filibuster if they were not consulted on vacancies from their home states."[70]

In a Brookings Institution study of court nominations for Obama's first three years, Russell Wheeler found that President George W. Bush had a faster process for nominating people to fill court vacancies: "Just as Obama made fewer district nominees than Clinton or Bush at this point [three years], he's taken longer to make them, in terms both of the average number of days and the median number (the midpoint in the range). Bush's comparatively quick district court nominations—272 days on average versus 366 and 399 for Clinton and Obama—speak again to his well-oiled nomination machinery."[71] Of the five most recent presidents, George W. Bush among the group had the largest percentage of district court nominees confirmed during their first terms. According to a Congressional Research Service study, the percent of district court confirmations for the five are as follows: Reagan 90.3%; George H. W. Bush 76.9%; Clinton 85.9%; George W. Bush 95%; Obama 82.7%.[72]

President Obama was quicker with his circuit court nominations than with his district court ones, for which he took an average 198 days to fill vacancies, as opposed to Presidents Clinton at 336 and George W. Bush at 146 days. While Bush was swift to announce nominees for all court vacancies, the process slowed down for his circuit court nominations once the names reached the Senate. The CRS study found the confirmation rates for the five presidents in their first terms to be Reagan 86.8%; George H. W. Bush 79.2%; Clinton 73.2%; George W. Bush 67.3%; Obama 71.4%.[73] The internal dynamics of the Senate confirmation process account for much of what happens to a nomination once it arrives on the Hill, including whether senators decide to "slow-walk" a president's nominations through the process.[74] Compared with President Bush, President Obama benefited from the Senate process in terms of timing. The following are the number of days that nominations took in the their first three years before hearings were held on the nominees: President Clinton, 58 for district court and 81 for circuit court; President George W. Bush, 101 for district court and 258 for circuit court; President Obama, 79 for district court and 65 for circuit court.[75] Thus, Obama was able to make up in the Senate process some of the time it took for nominations to reach the Hill. One element in that process is that President Bush did not seek an evaluation from the American Bar Association (ABA) on a nominee's fitness to serve in the judicial post for which he or she was nominated. Once the nomination got to the Senate, however, Democrats on the Senate Judiciary Committee required ABA evaluation. President Obama includes the ABA evaluation as part of the information package sent to the Senate.

The Obama nominations have made a strong impact in the partisan breakdown of those confirmed for circuit court judgeships. When President Obama took office, there were more Republicans as active circuit judges on the bench than Democrats by 55 percent to 37 percent with 8 percent of the judgeships remaining vacant. At the end of three years of the Obama administration, the percentage of Democratic nominees to judgeships rose to 44 percent (the 8 percent vacancy rate remained constant).[76] In mid-2014, nine of the thirteen circuit courts of appeal have a majority of Democratic judges, whereas in 2009, that figure was three.[77] President Obama had a strong impact on the court system with his two Supreme Court appointments as well as those on the circuit and district courts. What has made a difference in confirmations in Obama's sixth year is a Senate decision to change its confirmation procedures.

On November 21, 2013, Majority Leader Harry Reid announced that he was seeking a change in Senate rules, specifically a reduction in the number of votes needed to break a filibuster on presidential appointments, except for nominations to the Supreme Court, where current practices applied. While it is too early to tell how this change is going to work out in terms of the response of Republicans to executive branch and federal court nominees, in the first seven months President Obama got through more court nominees than he had when the sixty-vote filibuster was still in place. In the seven months after the rules change, the Senate confirmed fifty-four court nominees, while only thirty-six were confirmed in 2013 before the voting alteration. In 2012, a total of forty-nine judges were confirmed.

The Stakes on Appointments

Managing government has become more difficult over time. Expansion in the number of federal programs the executive branch implements has meant an increase in the number of confirmed and non-confirmed appointed positions. There is simply more for government to do and more appointees to do the work in 2009 than there was in 1981, when the confirmation process was easier in terms of both nomination and confirmation. Then too the increased demands for transparency in the information process have put greater demands on those interested in presidential appointments to executive branch positions and to judgeships. None of this is likely to change in the future, and the same is true of calls for appointed and elected officials to eliminate any possible conflicts of interest.

While President Obama had a difficult time getting his appointments process under way, much of the problem had to do with the system itself and its growing complications and partisanship. As quarrelsome as the nomination process appears to be, it is not difficult to find incidents that transcend the partisanship than appears to saturate every corner of the process. As we saw in the 2008–2009 nomination process, the outgoing administration made substantial efforts to prepare information for whichever side secured the presidency. Then, too, in its effort to establish a smooth transfer of power, Congress created procedures that candidates could use to prepare for their entry into government. Congressional efforts continue to reduce the number of appointed positions requiring Senate scrutiny, but for those posts that are Senate-confirmed, the scrutiny is as intense as it has ever been.

CHAPTER EIGHT

The 2008 Transition

Lessons and Challenges for Future Transitions

With its early planning on both sides, the 2008 transition established new rules for us to add to those we learned in the prior period, which starts with the 1952 transition in which President Harry S Truman sought to use White House staff and his administration officials at an early point to make the transition to a new president a smooth one. We have come a long way since that time. The 2008 transition reflects a level of cooperation of the president and president-elect that we have not seen in earlier change-of-party transitions. After Eisenhower met with Truman, he wrote about the presidential meeting in his memoir: "This meeting . . . added little to my knowledge, nor did it affect my planning for the new administration, but I did thank the President sincerely for his cooperation."[1] President-elect Eisenhower's assessment of his meeting with President Truman is a good reminder of the acrimony that has existed in many transitions as well as the "he doesn't have anything to tell me" attitude of some incoming presidents.

Contrast that meeting with the one between President George W. Bush and President-elect Obama. President Bush kicked off transition preparations in late 2007 when he discussed the organization of the transition with Chief of Staff Joshua Bolten. After the election, Bush let it be known to staff that he planned to brief the president-elect on what he considered to be the key national security issues the new president would face rather than have staff members or administration officials do it. President Bush wanted to signal the importance of these issues, and personally briefing on the issues was an ideal way to drive home their significance. The three issues—drones in Pakistan, U.S. policy toward Iran, and our relationship with Saudi Arabia—proved as crucial for President Obama as they had for President Bush. A great deal of President Obama's foreign policy time has been spent on these issues.

In 2008, President Truman's vision of major-party presidential candidates who would be informed about executive branch programs and positions finally came about with the early work the White House staff did with the involvement of representatives of Senators McCain and Obama and the behind-the-scenes efforts to gather and assess information that might be useful to whichever man won the presidential election. At the same time, Senator Obama paid early attention to transition issues and assigned preparations to his senior campaign and staff aides, Pete Rouse and Chris Lu. In the early summer, Obama assigned the overall transition task to John Podesta, who deployed his staff in the Center for American Progress to gather the necessary information and then recruit people to work on developing the organizational teams to review agencies and to create policy initiatives.

With the efforts of both the outgoing and incoming presidents, the presidential transition was a very effective one in meeting the president-elect's basic needs. More than earlier transitions, when President-elect Barack Obama came into office, he had a White House staff structure in place, a personnel operation up and running (even if problems were persistent), his priorities were established, and his legislative and executive action initiatives were ready to introduce. Once he became president-elect, Obama and his staff were well informed by those in office throughout the government about the status of issues, programs, and positions. While the financial crisis in the late autumn reordered their priorities, the transition team was able to keep up with their immediate governing needs.

The outgoing government facilitated their path to power through early actions by President Bush and his staff intended to make certain that there would be a smooth handoff from the Bush team to the Obama team. It took a series of legislative and executive actions to lay the groundwork for it by easing the clearance process for appointments so that people could begin working on the transition as soon as there was a president-elect. The path to governing was smoothed by the increasing amount of information available in the public domain as well as data available from earlier transition preparations of presidential candidates and outside people and groups. A great deal of the credit for the smooth passage to power in 2009 belongs to Barack Obama and the experienced group handling his transition as well as the actions of the outgoing administration transition operation authorized by President Bush and headed by Chief of Staff Joshua Bolten.

Principal Lessons from 2008 for Those Planning Future Transition Operations

Inside and outside of the government, the 2008–2009 transition is regarded as an ideal template for how to plan future power changes, whether a same-party

one or one involving a change of party. Some of the reasons include the importance of transitions in the post-September 11 world combined with technological
developments that make it easier to coordinate the materials of governmental
units and give those inside of government as well as outside of it the will to "get
it right." Add the fact that the country was at the end of an eight-year presidency
and on the brink of an inevitable transition; all parties understood the need to
prepare for the change. Additionally, the vice president was not running for the
presidency, which is the first time that that situation has existed at the end of a
two-term presidency since the advent of the two-term limit for presidents. Without a vice president as a presidential candidate, President George W. Bush would
not be handing over power to a president-elect who had been part of his administration.

In light of the new seriousness that Bush brought to the presidential transition process, there are practices and lessons that those working in future transitions should consider adopting. These lessons come from what worked in the
2008–2009 transition as well as those areas where the new team had trouble. Any
transition is going to experience problems, and this one was no exception. At the
same time, the 2008 transition provides as close a model of the planning outgoing and incoming administrations should adopt that it is worth looking at the
lessons we learn from the handoff of the presidency from George W. Bush to
Barack Obama. We also will look at some of the challenges transitions present to
the effective functioning of government.

Lesson 1. Leverage the Resources of the Incumbent President: The Quality of a Presidential Transition Depends on It

The 2008–2009 transition taught us that all benefit when a president directs early
and thorough preparations for the change in administrations. Never have we had
a transition where the sitting administration prepared so much information
across its administration and began the process so early. At the direction of President Bush, Joshua Bolten guided a government-wide effort to define and then
meet the needs of the new administration.

The September 11 Attacks as an Impetus for Changes in Transition Preparations.
The attacks on the United States on September 11, 2001, occurred early in an
administration well before the administration was fully staffed up in depart-
ments and agencies, including such critical ones as Defense and Commerce.
Presidents today cannot afford to let preparations wait until after the election.
Through legislation, executive direction, and individual effort, the Congress,
President Bush, and career and political officials in the departments and agencies

all worked hard to prepare the next president and his team for the responsibilities of governing. They made certain information was available on government programs and positions to ensure continuity in governing with career staff assigned to fill the posts of political appointees as they left the Bush administration.

Transition Changes Established in Law. Future presidents will be expected to lay a solid groundwork for their successors, especially when an incumbent president has served his maximum of eight years. When a president is running for reelection, it is natural to expect that transition preparations will be minimal, so some preparations are now required by law. Following the major-party conventions, the Pre-Election Presidential Transition Act of 2010 calls for the services to the candidates provided by the General Services Administration to include office space, communications equipment, printing, and funds for briefings and workshops. In 2012, the Obama administration worked with the Mitt Romney transition operation headed by Michael Leavitt. Chris Lu, who was the executive director of the Obama transition in 2008 and who later served for four years as the cabinet secretary, and Lisa Brown, the deputy director of OMB, both went over the reports of what GSA provided. But the White House was not involved in the work itself. Most of the work they did went through GSA as part of their effort to provide resources and materials to the Romney team. We can expect that only at the end of an eight-year term will an incumbent president develop the types of materials that President Bush did in 2008.

The Outgoing Transition Is Part of a President's Legacy. A good transition out of office benefits the outgoing chief executive, as a smooth passage of power becomes an item in his legacy. That was true for President George W. Bush, as the transition he oversaw was the most effective since the two-term limit was imposed on presidents in 1951. There are two ways the transition preparations benefit a sitting president. First, the knowledge that he is leaving provides a president serving eight years an opportunity to use his final year to prepare for his successor by instructing his team to gather information and manage his own administration at the end in a way that reflects good management of the changeover. In other words, they get to leave on a high note. Additionally, the work that the aides do provides a summation of a president's time in office that he can use as he leaves to remind the public of what he has accomplished. Then the detailed information they pulled together summing up the administration's work is archived in the presidential library.

Lesson 2. Be Prepared to Consult on Policy Issues:
"One President at a Time" Is More a Truism Than a Reality

A president-elect and his team can expect to be involved in government policy before Inauguration Day. Constitutionally, a president exercises power until noon on January 20. In practical terms, however, presidents and their staffs, aware that power is about to change hands, acknowledge the coming change by not taking actions they might have taken earlier in their administration. They also involve the president-elect in what they are planning to do.

During the period between the election and the inauguration, presidents and their senior staff are reluctant to take actions the incoming administration is not going to buy into. That was the case in late 2008 when, for instance, NSC advisor Steve Hadley did not take any action that Jones didn't also favor. The incoming Obama administration, for example, decided not to accept as their own the Bush administration's Afghan report.

Waning Influence for an Incumbent Administration. The 2008 transition was unusual because a major financial crisis had occurred less than two months before the presidential election. The Bush White House team was only partially successful in getting their financial initiatives adopted in Congress. They were unable to get an auto bailout package and sought help from the Obama people to get an auto czar named well before the end of the Bush administration. Political muscle is useful right up to the end, but presidents rarely have it.

Another instance where the White House lacked the requisite muscle was on making cabinet members move on regulations in the eight-month schedule that Bolten established in his April 2008 memorandum to department and agency heads. They dragged their feet on doing it and came in late trying to get exceptions to Bolten's schedule. In the latter part of an administration those in leadership positions want to meet their own goals for a department and are less concerned with accomplishing what the chief of staff wants them to do. The result was that few of the department and agency heads met their deadlines for regulations. Focused on the financial crisis, Bolten had little time to follow up on the issue of department secretaries meeting their deadlines.

Vacancies in Government. There are many vacancies at the end of an administration, which makes it difficult for a president to carry through on things he might like to do. As we saw in chapter 7, there is a substantial leadership vacuum at the end of the administration at the implementation level in executive branch departments and agencies among the assistant secretaries, undersecretaries, and agency heads and their deputies. With few employees in the agencies where policy needs to be implemented, little work that the president is pushing for gets done.

Lesson 3. Move Up the Transition Calendar:
Planning Begins with Presumptive Candidates

Forget planning after the presidential election; the transition calendar starts months earlier. Although current legislation defines early transition planning as beginning after the major-party nominating conventions, the reality is that government agencies and candidates start their planning and informal contacts when there are presumptive nominees. Even though the Pre-Election Presidential Transition Act of 2010 provides for transition work after the party conventions, in reality those in and outside of government recognize that transition planning can begin in a practical way when there are presumptive candidates. The deciding date for the Democrats in 2008 was June 7, when Hillary Clinton announced her withdrawal from the presidential race, not September 4, when the second of the two major-party nominating conventions concluded. Government officials want transitions to work just as much as the candidates and their teams do.

Government Agencies Make Early Contacts with Presumptive Candidates. Once Hillary Clinton was out of the presidential race, Senator Obama was the presumptive nominee. Practically, at this point there was no other serious challenger for the Democratic presidential nomination. Then John Podesta, who had been a Clinton supporter, could sign up to work under Obama, and GSA could say we now have two clear candidates and we can begin informal discussions with them. Gail Lovelace saw it as the point where GSA could personally deal with the candidates' operations: "We knew McCain was going to be running. We had to wait . . . until we knew both, and then we contacted both. We actually started before both conventions, but it's not something we openly talk about," Lovelace said. "We just reach out and sit down and start quietly talking, and we're very careful to ensure that people don't really know what we're doing. . . . We respect their privacy. . . . We respect their needs in terms of not being out in public talking about what they're doing."[2]

Actions Taken before the Election. Because they began well before the election, the Obama operation had its transition organizational structure in place, its agency review and policy teams lined up, two hundred people cleared by the FBI for a national security background check, and detailed lists of positions they were looking to fill on a priority basis. On the latter point, for example, Phil Schiliro, who went on to become legislative director in the Obama administration, went to Senator Harry Reid's assistant, Jim Manley, on October 27, 2008, with a list of forty-five positions they wanted to fill quickly.[3] The list stated merely the positions, not the names of the people the Obama administration would want to have in them. All the same, they knew which positions they wanted to focus on. The Obama people were already moving on central transition tasks before the election.

The Right People at the Right Time. Getting information to the right people at the right time is crucial and currently seems to be a gap in the transition process. There are many instances of people saying that they didn't get information prepared for them until they had gotten into office. Lisa Brown found White House staff "verbally very forthcoming and helpful," but written material came after her in-person discussions.[4] That is a poor time to learn, as there is so much coming at a new employee at the White House that it is difficult to carve out time to learn from the past. All of the agency material that Clay Johnson provided to the Obama team did not get to the people coming into the White House until after they had taken office. Additionally, it is often routine to send materials to more than one place, especially when they are policy papers on issues cutting across government agencies and departments. Those papers need to get several places and not receiving them impacts more than just those working in the White House. There is no clearly established pattern that encourages the sitting administration to provide materials shortly after the election around the time that members of the new presidential White House and administration teams are being selected.

Lesson 4. Begin Information-Gathering Early in the Year: Mine Accessible Institutional Documents and Public Information

Changes in technology and in government practices about the availability of information on publicly accessible sites benefit candidates who want to begin an early transition planning operation. There is a great deal of available government information on programs, institutions, and personnel. Additionally, both political parties have documents from earlier transition planning efforts and have people knowledgeable about transition operations.

Government Information. The transition of 2008 was the first for which there was a great deal of information online about government agencies, including descriptions of programs and analyses of their effectiveness. Preparatory work in the personnel area was much easier in 2008 than in earlier years because of this available information. One benefit of online information is that participants can gather information in the early stages without talking to anyone, which has the disadvantage of giving away what they are doing. Russ Gerson and his group in the McCain personnel operation went through public searches without doing legal search services to look for arrests or payments due. When asked if they had consulted websites with information about criminal records, both sides emphatically said that they had not.

GSA has its own institutional memory and is the first agency to begin transition work. Gail Lovelace of GSA began work on the 2000 transition years earlier. In June 2009 she was beginning to gather her team to prepare for the 2012 transition. In June 2011 she had acquired space to accommodate the transition and the inaugural committee, which required finding a federal building location in the Washington area—preferably in Washington itself—that was also approved by GSA and the Secret Service. There are now stringent security requirements for transition office space since, the key members of the incoming administration will work there, including the president-elect and the cabinet secretaries. After each presidential election, the GSA planning group comes together to discuss their efforts and plan for the next transition.

Documents and People from Earlier Transition Planning Operations. By 2008, there was an institutional memory consisting of documents and people who could help guide candidates in the planning of a transition operation. The gradual creation of an institutional memory for offices as well as for particular transitions is important as well. In the past, people left information behind for others who were to follow in the next election on a somewhat random basis. On the Democratic side, Harrison Wellford, who worked on transition issues for candidate and President Carter and subsequent Democratic presidential transition efforts, represents an institutional memory, as does Jim Johnson, who worked on the John Kerry campaign and in earlier efforts as well, going back to Walter Mondale's unsuccessful race in 1984. Republicans, who have not had a comparable set of documents that can be used to form an institutional memory, do talk to people from prior Republican administrations, including William Timmons and Tom Korologos, who have served on all recent Republican transition teams and on several White House staffs in Republican administrations.

Lesson 5. Don't Be Afraid to Create a Large Transition Team: They Can Be Managed Successfully

This transition has taught us that it is possible to assemble and direct a large organization of transition team members without the group getting out of hand. With a transition structure of 617 people, the Obama operation could easily have gone in many different and conflicting directions without generating significant governing information. That has happened in many previous transition efforts, but good management kept the operation in this transition on track.

Management Is Important, not Size. The 2008–2009 transition showed that organizing a transition into office hinges on management, not the size of the organization. If effective ground rules are established by the incoming and outgoing administrations for the transition team to gather information from government agencies and departments, a large operation can stay within the rules and produce reports structured to meet presidential needs. But such organizational work takes time. In the 2000–2001 transition, the Memorandum of Understanding (MOU) was not signed by the outgoing and incoming administrations until December because of the complexity of the postelection judicial process between George W. Bush and Al Gore. The MOU is required in order to establish the rules for the transition people coming into departments and agencies to review their programs, positions, budgets, and policies. With just thirty-seven days left over for the transition, the Bush team did not want to have a large group going in for such a short period of time. Instead, the incoming political leaders in the departments and agencies undertook those reviews when they came into office. In earlier administrations, the review teams met with complaints from those in office who thought there was little overall coordination of what transition team members were looking for. There were no such complaints about the agency review process in 2008.

The Transition Chief as Manager. If an administration prepares early for the transition, there is more time to absorb what is taking place. Having John Podesta handle the transition worked well on the time front, as he was not involved in the campaign, and his ideas were in sync with those of Obama. He is located in Washington where the transition can best be headquartered for organizing the agency review and policy teams. Of particular importance was the reality that Podesta could fund the operation himself and not have to worry about being public about what he was doing. Additionally, he had the staff with the expertise to do some of the early work themselves before they brought in a large cadre of people. Many of those doing the transition work had worked for Podesta when he served in the White House during the Clinton years. After the transition and when Obama became president, he brought in many people who had worked at the Center for American Progress. He made use of the expertise Podesta had developed and the opportunity to emphasize some major CAP priorities, such as a focus on alternative energy.

Lesson 6. Welcome a New Transition Partner: White House Staff as Transition Facilitators

While President Truman imagined himself and his staff working with both major-party candidates at the White House, it took fifty-six years for such an arrangement to be worked out. Even then, the White House transition connections with both candidates did not unfold in just the way Truman had thought would be useful. What was unprecedented in 2008 about the White House role was asking the two presumptive candidates to assign representatives to come to the White House for meetings with the chief of staff and others on the president's staff and to do so well before the national party nominating conventions.

Candidate Representatives Come to the White House. When Bolten sent out the call to the two sides to appoint representatives to come to the White House, the Obama team sent Chris Lu, and the McCain operation sent Will Ball. There were several issues they worked on with White House staff, such as personnel, the software to handle incoming resumes, the memorandum of understanding that lays out the rules for the transition for agency review teams. On personnel issues, they met several times at the White House with people in that office, but not with both camps together except for the software.

White House Arranges Early Security Clearances for Transition Staff. The White House arranged for meetings at the Department of Justice for the candidate representatives to work through what the national security background check involves. Chief of Staff Joshua Bolten set up the clearance procedures such that no names of possible transition staff for either candidate went through the White House. That way, no one on the White House staff would know anything about that process and there could be no possibility of leaked information.

The Memorandum of Understanding. Working through the Memorandum of Understanding with both sides was unprecedented as well. By coming to agreement on what the MOU would provide—no matter who won—shortly after the election, the president-elect's team would be ready to have their agency review teams go into the departments and agencies.

The people who attended the sessions as well as those who set them up thought that these meetings and arrangements had gone well. In the future, when there is transition planning at the end of a two-term presidency, the president's White House staff have an important role to play in organizing the operation and bringing in people important in the first stages of a new administration.

Lesson 7. Employ Two Complementary Information Sources: People and Documents

The key arrangements for outgoing and incoming administration officials was, first, providing them with information in written form and, second, having them talk to each other about their work and what they were reading about the operations. The Bush people wanted to make sure that the people at the highest levels—

cabinet secretaries and senior White House staff—on the way out would talk to those coming in. The meetings were often preceded by the provision of information to the new team. In the press area, for example, Dana Perino gave Gibbs a briefing book on the Press Office, as did Kevin Sullivan with a similar book on the Office of Communications.

Two Information Sources. Steve Hadley was particularly concerned with providing both types of information and was in a position to do so. The advantage of the principal-to-principal exchanges is that people can ask questions and get answers that some participants might not want to write down and would prefer to give verbally. The forty memoranda on issues and countries was helpful to incoming National Security Council staff when they came into the White House. After observing the information in the memoranda, the incoming team members asked questions of those they sat next to for several weeks while they learned how the office operated.

While it was fairly easy to set up for the foreign policy and national security parts of change-of-party transitions, comparability across White House operations does not work quite as naturally in the domestic policy area, except for budgeting. Budgets have the same process from one administration to another. In the domestic policy area, however, there are differences in the shape of office operations and in their policy interests. The priorities and types of initiatives favored by Democratic and Republican administrations make it difficult to have people work together other than in the area of the processes that are required in handling their domestic issues. "The Obama health care proposal was so dramatic in what it was going to do that you couldn't have found anybody in . . . the DPC [Domestic Policy Council]," Jonathan Breul commented.[5] "There wouldn't have been a corresponding person to pair them up with."

Assembling Chiefs of Staff. While an outgoing White House staff can leave behind documents about their office operations, bringing together those who have previously held the position with newcomers provides a good opportunity to learn about continuity and change in White House office operations. Chief of Staff Joshua Bolten assembled a meeting of former chiefs of staff for incoming chief Rahm Emanuel. With thirteen of the sixteen chiefs of staff there, the session was particularly useful as it was done more than a month before he came into office in the White House. Bolten reflected on the session: "It was the first Friday in December and . . . before the election, I had invited all the chiefs of staff to breakfast in my office." Bolten saw it as a "chance for all of us to gather and to share stories and wisdom. . . . It was a really interesting session. I went around the table and asked all the chiefs to give Rahm a few sentences of advice. The vice president's

[Cheney's] advice was, 'Watch out for the vice president.' Then he went on to give some real advice."[6] Judging by the discussions with the president, on the Hill, in White House offices, the question of delineating the responsibilities of the vice president was an important one for many people and institutions.

Working with Counterparts. Another aspect of principals and the information they provided was the opportunity for incoming staff to sit beside their counterparts and work through issues. When it was principal to principal or a mid-level staff person to someone in the same position, people were more honest with one another about how things really worked. A senior administration official said that the memoranda were not particularly informative about how things worked on the subject under study, especially about cases where someone had screwed up. They were historical documents, from his viewpoint. At the same time, the documents led to good sessions about how government units were organized and what actions they took. Particularly in the NSC, these sessions were very useful.

Lesson 8. Systematize Information Collection: Use Templates

More than was true in most administration preparations, those inside and outside the government gathered information in a systematic way in multiple government units by asking the same questions of data. Starting early in their preparations for the transition, those inside the Bush administration determined in fairly expansive groups the key pieces of information and materials the newcomers would need. The same was true of those preparing to come into office. Comparable information is particularly useful for the president-elect, who has to quickly weigh volumes of information and programs from the departments and agencies. Having categories that reflect his interests and priorities makes his tasks and those of his advisors more meaningful.

Using Templates to Provide Comparable Information. Templates were used by both the outgoing and incoming administrations as a way of systematizing the gathering of information in order for the results to be useful for the incoming administration. They were used in a variety of unconnected areas with Clay Johnson, in his role of head of the President's Management Council, using them for departments and agencies preparing information; John Podesta used them for agency review teams and policy teams; Steve Hadley had them for contingency plans and memoranda; Joel Kaplan had them for his domestic memoranda; as Joie Gregor in the Office of Presidential Personnel used them to assemble information for President Bush on the nominees appointed by him.

Preparing templates provided an opportunity to gather information administration-wide and to decide, in advance of the information-gathering process, just what knowledge they thought was important for those coming into office. More and more, information crosses the boundaries of departments and agencies, and this was reflected in the transition by the efforts to collect information wherever in government a subject was covered.

Templates as Historical Records. Some of the templates preceded the transition, and many of them had more than one purpose. Steve Hadley, for example, developed the contingency plans for his own purposes and then provided them for the transition. At least one senior administration official in the Obama administration said that he would use them on the way out. In wrapping up what happened on his watch, he planned to start with the memoranda even though he saw them only as moderately helpful. He thought they were useful in historical terms. That was true as well with those in the Bush White House who prepared the memoranda. The documents will be a part of the record of the administration that the public can access when the documents are made available in the George W. Bush Library. These materials matter to the quality of the history that is left behind. Preparing to leave gives an administration an opportunity to sum up their time in office, which is useful to those working in it as well as to the public and those coming into an administration.

Lesson 9. Shift from Campaigning with a Staff Ready to Govern

There is always enormous pressure on a president to bring in with him those who got him to the White House. Campaign aides expect White House positions, and presidents often want to surround themselves with the people with whom they have worked for several years. That can cause an imbalance in the White House staff, because of the necessity of shifting to governing and lining up policy initiatives and working with Congress to get them passed. As it happens, campaign people are often not the best-qualified people to accomplish policy initiatives. Campaigning and governing require different kinds of people. During an election the campaign team is dealing with a world in which there are no shades of gray. There is one goal: to win the election. The focus is short-term, with the team's candidate representing the good and the opponent representing the malevolent.

Campaign v. Governing Staff. Once a successful presidential campaign comes into office, its campaign people often enters with a string of people they have offended, government officials of the opposing party. Governing requires dealing with people in a nuanced way, which is not necessarily a strength of campaign professionals. When working on individual policy initiatives, those in a White House often find their timetable to be controlled by others, particularly people in Congress. The president, forced to compromise, needs a team around him that has experience fashioning compromises and also knows the bureaucracy and the preexisting history on issues in previous administrations.

Balancing the number of campaign people who want jobs with the appropriateness of their backgrounds is a challenge that confronts every president. Most administrations try to farm out many of them to the departments and agencies, although some senior-level campaign strategists come into the White House as well. What some administrations do is make certain that they have people coming into the White House who have experience in an earlier administration of the same party. There were many people with experience in Clinton White House policy operations who came in with President Obama in 2008, particularly in the economic and environmental policy areas. That was particularly true in the policy area, but not where operations were concerned. In areas having to do with politics and process, the president brought in his associates from the campaign and from his Senate office. The Press Office, for example, only had people with campaign experience, with no one who had served in the Clinton press operation. The same was true as well for most of the people in the Office of Communications. It is difficult to get an effective press office in place without people who know the continuities of White House press operations.

Lesson 10. Create a Presidential Governing Narrative

Once the election has taken place and the country has a president-elect, the public wants to know who that person is and what he is going to do now that he has won. What will his policy initiatives and priorities be? When President-elect Obama and Mrs. Obama appeared on *60 Minutes,* the public was eager to get to know its new presidential family. The audience for that program was larger than for most of the speeches he gave once he came into office. He had an audience of 24.5 million people, which was the largest audience the program had had in nine years. People want to know the people who are moving into the White House and what they want to initiate during their years in office. These occasions and the speeches as well as the announcements a president makes all help build a narrative of who the president is and how he plans to govern now that he has won the election.

Transitions as a Series of Disaggregated Tasks. During the days following the election and before the inauguration, the president-elect works on several tasks, which are to shape a policy agenda with priorities lined up, to staff his White House operation, to establish how he wants to form the organization, to nominate cabinet secretaries, and to line up their deputies. He sends out his agency review teams into the departments and agencies to get a sense, before appointing and nominating people, of the functions the organizations perform and the programs they will be overseeing. When the president-elect holds a press conference during the postelection period, it is generally to nominate people for cabinet and agency positions, although occasionally a press session does deal with policy. President-elect Obama focused immediately on the financial collapse and returned to it during this period.

Presidential Appearances One by One. The appearances a president arranges during this period and the work that is done by those operating on his behalf make it difficult for a president to pull together everything he is doing into a single strong narrative for his administration. He has separate tasks to accomplish during this period, and that is reflected in the public appearances he makes. The transition parts do not naturally create a whole that speaks for the new president and how he will bring together government to answer the issues and problems that lie ahead.

With so much happening prior to coming into office and then a rush of policy demands in the early days, it is difficult for the new team to focus on how to bring together the politics of their policy issues together with the publicity to let the people know what is happening. Once a president comes into office, it takes several months before he can do that. In President Obama's case, it was a speech at Georgetown University in mid-April 2009 in which he discussed his priorities for his term in office.[7] Those priorities identified by Obama as pillars for a renewed economy and the growth of jobs—energy, regulation of Wall Street, health care, education, deficit—remained core issues for his administration throughout the first term.[8] By April, the public was paying little attention, though, and the Congress was focusing on its own issues. Few noticed the importance of that speech even though the central parts have come up in the 2010 State of the Union message and its parts in separate speeches throughout Obama's first term.

Lesson 11. Prepare for a Volatile and Contentious Presidential Appointments Process

The presidential appointments process has been marked by gains and setbacks with no clear road ahead. Since the 2008 election, there have been two pieces of legislation aimed at untangling the difficult confirmation process. First, the 2010 presidential transition legislation created an environment for early planning by requiring each major-party candidate to name a transition director after the party conventions. At that point, the government provides assistance to the candidates in terms of office space and technological assistance for their communications. Second, the Presidential Appointment Efficiency and Streamlining Act of 2011 sponsored by Senators Charles Schumer and Lamar Alexander, the chairman and ranking minority member of the Senate Rules and Administration Committee, respectively, grappled with the problem of the gradual increase in the number of departments and agencies created in the last decade that brought additional officials requiring Senate confirmation. The bill went into effect October 10, 2012.

The 2011 Legislation. The Presidential Appointment Efficiency and Streamlining Act of 2011 reduces by 166 the number of officials that are required to go through the confirmation process as well as looks forward to creating a working group to come up with additional ways to reduce the time and workload of the nomination process.[9] The reduction in appointees that must go through Senate confirmation has made the possibility for an incoming president getting up and running more quickly a better one. A resolution accompanying the act holds out the possibility of clearing out the executive calendar so that some nominations can get fast-walked through the confirmation process. So far that has not happened, but it could be a possibility at the beginning of a new administration when the appointment process gets clogged. A companion Senate resolution (S Res 116) created a new category of executive nominations, known as privileged nominations, with another 272 positions that if all senators agreed could go straight to the new category of the executive calendar for a vote.[10] Resolution sponsor Senator Schumer said of the new privileged nominations category and procedure: "The presumption for these part-time positions is, as I said, that they will be approved by unanimous consent and not be held up as a part of other battles or leverage or whatever else."[11] Any senator, however, could request more information from the committee of jurisdiction and send the nomination into the track used for most executive branch nominations. In the 112th Congress in mid-year 2013, the Privileged Calendar had twenty-five names on it, all of which have requests for information from the committee. Since this procedure is a relatively new one, it is difficult to tell how it is going to used.

A Compromise. While the confirmation process has been a thorn in the side of all recent presidents, with congressional intransigence increasing with each chief executive, there are signs that both party leaders in the Senate have recognized the issues and are moving to make some changes, though they have often done so in a contentious way. In July 2013, Senators Reid and McConnell agreed to a compromise to allow a vote on two of President Obama's nominees who had been denied a confirmation vote. Secretary of Labor nominee Tom Perez and administrator for the Environmental Protection Agency Gina McCarthy were allowed a vote after having been held up for several months in Perez's case and over a year for McCarthy. The compromise involved Democratic Majority Leader Reid agreeing to keep the filibuster rules as they were. "They [Republicans] are not sacrificing their right to filibuster, and we for damn sure aren't sacrificing our right to change the rules" to ban them, commented Reid. For his part, Senate Minority Leader Mitch McConnell said: "Put this down as progress in the right direction."[12] As contentious as the nomination process has been, there are clear gains for both party leaders to build on. The incentive is there to reduce the contentious nature of the process, because both sides realize that at some point there will be a president from the same side and there will be a need to shepherd his nominees through the Senate gauntlet.

Compromise Followed by the "Nuclear Option." On November 21, 2013, Majority Senate Leader Harry Reid brought to a vote a change in the rules governing presidential appointments coming to the Senate floor except for Supreme Court nominations, which would continue to be subject to filibusters requiring sixty votes to stop a nomination. For all other nominations, a simple majority would be needed. The full Senate vote was 52–48 in favor of the rules change. While Republicans decried the move, as we saw in the last chapter, President Obama's nominations for district and circuit courts of appeal nominees moved much more quickly after the rules change than had been earlier the case. By the numbers, the same has not been the case with executive branch nominees, but many of those are for ambassadorships. Federal Reserve nominees who languished for months in the Senate have gotten through. It is unclear how the situation is going to work out after the November 2014 elections when Republicans gained control of the Senate and are thus in a stronger position to oppose President Obama's initiatives, including his nominees requiring Senate confirmation.

Lesson 12. To Make a Transition Last: Make Management a Priority

Perhaps the greatest challenge that each president faces is how to make an effective transition last as long as possible. The initial problem in making a transition last is that the new team has the greatest opportunity for change in the early days before the key players know the ropes. That is why it is useful to bring in seasoned hands who can sense what kinds of change they can bring about and where concentrated action might be a waste of time.

There is a tendency to accept the organization of the previous administration and then gradually shift it to fit the purposes of the new administration. That was true in the communications/press area until 2011 when Media Affairs was shifted into the Press Office in order to have a consistent message, where those dealing with the out-of-town press—the Office of Media Affairs—are saying the same thing as those in the press office who are dealing with the national press corps.

Except for folding the homeland security advisor into the NSC and its advisor, the NSC followed the organization of the Bush White House NSC.

Organizing according to Past Practices. The pressures of getting a White House and an administration up and running means, in practical terms, that new administrations pretty much organize the way previous administrations did. Max Stier, who focuses his Partnership for Public Service organization on executive management, discussed the need to think differently about the appointments process as a part of general government organization: "But part of the problem is if you start from the proposition that you're going to staff the agencies as they've been done historically and the same kind of time table, then you're not going to have a team in place forever." If you do not reorganize early, with an eye to how you are going to use the departments and agencies effectively as resources in achieving your policy agenda, then you risk not having them work together to achieve what the president wants. If the president finds that the bureaucracy is not a helpmate in achieving his goals, then he will lean on the White House staff to serve as the spark plug for getting things done that he wants to accomplish. As Max Steir observed, "It places a natural gravitational pull to activity in the White House."[13]

Staff Secretary Lisa Brown, who entered the White House with President Obama, said that the result of dealing with the urgent rather than the long range is that "you plug into existing organizational structure." There is simply no time to work through organizational restructuring. "There is so much else to do that you end up getting taken over by events and lose the chance to make those broad changes."[14] The same problem existed for the Bush administration as well. Clay Johnson said that they kept the same number of people as the Clinton people had because they needed to create a budget very early in their first year. The easiest thing to do was take the budget the Clinton people had used. What they did not figure into their calculations was that the needs at the beginning of an administration are far greater than they are later on. What some administrations did, and the Clinton administration was one of them, was to staff up at the beginning of their administration with volunteers who later will leave once they have the initial rush of appointments out of the way. Restructuring the organization and the budget is an almost impossible task at the very outset even if that is when the most goodwill exists.

Getting the Right People in Place and Having a Management Agenda. For Stier, making a transition last means getting people in place early and then having an effective management operation that lasts throughout the entire administration: "I think they last throughout the whole term, because . . . a good transition is getting your people into jobs quickly and having them be educated about what the demands are and having a team created to achieve an agenda," Stier said. "The transition ought to encompass all of those things, not just seats and chairs, but rather seats and chairs that actually know something about what they're supposed to be doing, can avoid mistakes, and then work well together. And that should be the collective goal in my mind. And that should last . . . because you're building a team throughout for the whole administration." Above all, it is important to avoid getting it wrong because "it's a lot harder to fix something that you've messed up than it is to just get it right at the outset."[15]

Limits for Transition Benefits. There is every reason for an incoming administration to try to buy as much time as possible. Others, though, think there is a time limit for transition benefits and that a president can expect only a few months of goodwill. From a practical viewpoint, Chris Lu, executive director of the 2008 transition for Senator Obama, thinks that the benefits cannot last because the same people are not involved along the way with the memory of the earlier period. Consistency gets lost through the full period. "I think the area that we were most limited in [where] we didn't do enough planning before Election Day was on a communications plan," he says. This was because the communications plan for transition and governing was different than what was needed once the team entered into the White House. "The people who were doing the communications plan did a perfectly fine job Election Day, but they weren't the people who ended up on the transition, and then they weren't the people in the White House." So "having the people who are actually going to carry the thing all the way through makes all the difference in the world, because if I've developed a plan and I'm going to implement the plan, that has much more utility than if somebody else develops the plan for me, and I look at it, and I probably take some of it, and I reject some of it. So having those people all the way through helps."[16]

Transition Issues May Change. The nature of the issues can change, and that turned out to be an important factor in 2009. As Chris Lu said, "What we perceived to be the economic crisis on the day after Election Day was significantly different than what we thought it was two months before, and then when we came into office on January 20th, it was significantly different. [The financial situation] continued to deteriorate, and that causes you to rethink a lot of your plans along the way." If the issues change, and it is difficult to plan coming in, then where should the emphasis be in transition planning? For Lu, "transition planning helps people get up to speed for their jobs and is useful in the first . . . 100 days. . . . And it works out really well for the first month, and then after that events change along the way. It's always a useful exercise to do, and it's better than not doing anything, and even if you don't adopt everything in the plan, it's always better to have a plan than not to have a plan, and you end up using more of it than you think you are, and it certainly depends on how static the world you're operating in is."[17]

For the Obama team, the nature of the issues changed fairly quickly from the time of the election to the transition and then into the White House. Lu described the changes they faced in issues they needed to deal with: "Before I came into government, I never focused on the monthly jobs numbers, and we focus on them intensely here in the White House and obviously in light of where things have gone. But I remember very distinctly that first Friday of February of 2009, when we got the first jobs numbers under our watch, . . . we had lost eight hundred thousand jobs or whatever the number finally ended up being. That has a way of completely recalibrating everything you're trying to do."[18]

An administration may come into the White House thinking that it is going to be focusing on its campaign agenda, but fairly soon it finds that it needs to respond to an unfolding situation that requires it shift to addressing a financial crisis, for example. That means putting off the plans laid out in the *Blueprint for Change* until a later time. How far a president has to divert from the path he laid out depends on the conditions he has to deal with once he comes into office. All is not known beforehand.

But there is no other way for an administration to come into the White House other than to do all of the preparation it can. Some of the reports it develops and the process for appointments may change, but having a governing plan is far better than it is coming without one. For the Obama team, going through the preparations it did made a difference in what it was able to do getting an agenda settled even if that agenda was diverted for the financial crisis. At the same time, the work that President Bush ordered be done to provide for an effective transition, with the people entering the White House and administration informed on government programs and actions, allowed the Obama team to make informed choices about what it needed to do in the coming days and months.

The preparations for the transition followed a different model than any we have had in earlier administrations. The extensiveness of the effort as well as the early planning of what the new administration would need established a path that future incumbent presidents might—and should—follow as they leave office. With national security at risk, sitting presidents are likely to view that as part of their legacy, and in keeping with that, they should prepare their successors for office. An effective handoff of power from an incumbent to his successor is an aspect of leaving the institution of the presidency in good order.

People

Joshua Bolten: Director, President George W. Bush's transition out of office; chair, Transition Coordinating Council. Chief of staff, President George W. Bush, 2006–2009; director, Office of Management and Budget, 2003–2006; deputy chief of staff for policy, 2001–2003.

Lisa Brown: Co-chair (with Donald Gips and Melody Barnes), President-elect Barack Obama's Agency Review Teams, 2008. Staff secretary, President Obama.

Richard Cheney: Vice president, 2001–2009; director of the transition for President-elect George W. Bush; headed vice presidential search for Governor George W. Bush, 2000.

Gregory Craig: Advisor to Obama transition team on foreign policy and on executive action. White House Counsel to President Obama, 2009–2010.

Thomas Daschle: President Obama's nominee for Secretary of Health and Human Services who withdrew his name from consideration. Senate Democratic leadership, 1994–2005; Senator (D-S.D., 1987–2005), member, House of Representatives, 1979–1987.

Rick Davis: Member, six-person transition team for Senator McCain; National Campaign Chairman, McCain for President, 2007–2008.

Rahm Emanuel: During transition period named Chief of Staff, President Barack Obama, 2009–2010. Member of House of Representatives, 2003–2009; mayor of Chicago, 2011–.

Russell Gerson: John McCain transition team handling personnel preparations, 2008. Chief Executive Officer, Gerson Global Advisors.

Donald Gips: Co-chair (with Lisa Brown and Melody Barnes), President-elect Barack Obama's Agency Review Teams, 2008. Director, Office of Presidential Personnel, 2009; U.S. Ambassador to South Africa, 2009–2013.

Blake Gottesman: Handled many of the transition issues as deputy chief of staff to President G. W. Bush, 2008–2009. Special assistant to the president, 2001–2006.

Joie Gregor: Director, Office of Presidential Personnel, 2007–2008. Vice chair, Heidrick and Struggles, 1993–2007.

Valerie Jarrett: Co-director (with John Podesta and Pete Rouse), Obama-Biden Transition Project, 2008–2009. Senior Advisor to the President and Assistant to the President for Public Engagement and Intergovernmental Affairs, 2009–.

Clay Johnson III: Deputy director, Office of Management and Budget, 2003–2009; director of the President's Management Council, 2003–2009. Executive director, transition under President George W. Bush, 2000–2001; director, Office of Presidential Personnel, 2001–2003.

General James L. Jones Jr.: Campaign and transition advisor on national security issues. National Security Advisor to President Obama, 2009–2010. Commander United States European Command (COMUSEUCOM) and Supreme Allied Commander Europe (SACEUR), 2003–2006; Commandant of the Marine Corps, 1999–2003.

Senator Ted Kaufman (D-Del.) Co-chair, Senator Biden's transition team, 2008.

Nancy Killefer: Nominee, President Obama's first Chief Performance Officer, 2009. Senior partner, McKinsey and Company, 2006–.

Mike Leavitt: Director, Romney Readiness Project, 2012. Secretary, Department of Health and Human Services, President George W. Bush, 2005–2009; administrator, Environmental Protection Agency, 2003–2005; governor (R-Ut.), 1993–2003.

Joseph Lieberman: Chair, Senate Homeland Security and Government Affairs Committee, which handles transition legislation, 2007–2013. Senator (D-Conn.), 1989–2006; Senator (I-Conn.), 2006–2013.

Gail Lovelace: General Services Administration; senior career executive for presidential transition, 2008.

Christopher Lu: Executive director, President Obama's presidential transition team. Cabinet affairs secretary, President Obama, 2009–2013; legislative director, Senator Obama, 2005–2008; deputy secretary of labor, 2014–.

Anita McBride: Chief of staff for Laura Bush, 2005–2009. Special assistant for White House management for President George W. Bush; director of personnel for White House employees for Presidents Reagan and George H. W. Bush.

Jim Messina: Director of personnel in transition. Deputy chief of staff for operations under President Obama, 2009–2011; campaign manager for President Obama, 2012.

John Podesta: Co-director (with Valerie Jarrett and Pete Rouse), Obama-Biden Transition Project, 2008–2009. Director, Center for American Progress, 2001–2008; chief of staff, President Clinton, 2000–2001; counselor to President Barack Obama, 2013–.

Stephen W. Rochon: White House chief usher, 2007–2011. Rear Admiral, Coast Guard.

Pete Rouse: Co-director (with Valerie Jarrett and John Podesta), Obama-Biden Transition Project, 2008–2009. Acting White House chief of staff, 2010–2011; senior advisor to President Obama, 2009–2010; counselor to the president, 2011–2014; chief of staff, Senator Obama, 2004–2008.

Harrison Wellford: Gathered information on White House operations for Obama transition (2008), for Senator John Kerry (2004), for Vice President Mondale (1988); transition into office of President-elect Carter and transition out of President Carter.

Jeffrey Zients: U.S. chief performance officer, economic advisor to President Obama, acting director of the Office of Management and Budget, 2010, 2012–2013. Director, White House National Economic Council, 2014–.

Laws and Executive Orders

American Recovery and Reinvestment Act (ARRA): Public Law 111-5, signed by President Obama, February 19, 2009. The act provides for economic stimulus measures designed to help shore up the weak economy by providing jobs and building up the country's infrastructure.

Dodd-Frank Wall Street Reform and Consumer Protection Act: Public Law 11-203, signed by President Obama, July 21, 2010. This legislation is named for its Senate and House sponsors Senator Christopher Dodd (D-Conn.) and Representative Barney Frank (D-Mass.). The act aims at preventing the types of problems in the financial services sector that led to the deep 2008 recession.

Ethics Pledge and Waivers: Rules covering the conduct of executive appointees; every executive appointee signs an ethics agreement. The agreement may be waived when it is not in the public interest. The rules are laid out in Executive Order 13490, Ethics Commitments by Executive Branch Personnel, signed by President Obama, January 21, 2009.

Federal Vacancies Reform Act of 1998: Public Law 105-277, signed by President Clinton, October 21, 1998. Executive branch departments and agencies are required to report to Congress and to the Government Accountability Office vacant positions occupied by presidential appointees confirmed by the Senate (PAS). The act provides rules regarding how the positions can be filled.

Freedom of Information Act (FOIA): Public Law 104-231, signed by President Johnson, July 4, 1966. Provides for the disclosure to the public of government information held by administrative agencies, unless the documents requested fall into one of the specified exemptions described in the law.

Intelligence Reform and Terrorism Prevention Act of 2004: Public Law 108-458, signed by President G. W. Bush, December 17, 2004. Section 7601 on Presidential Transition provides for preelection security clearances for transition team members.

Lilly Ledbetter Fair Pay Act of 2009: Public Law 111-2, signed by President Obama, January 29, 2009. Corrective legislation to a 2007 Supreme Court case, *Ledbetter v. Goodyear Tire and Rubber Company*, where the Court held that Lilly Ledbetter's claim of unequal pay was barred by the statute of limitations, even though she had not been aware for some years of the company discriminatory pay actions that impacted her.

Lobbying Disclosure Act of 1995: Public Law 104-65, signed by President Clinton, December 19, 1995. A person must register as a lobbyist in the House and the Senate if 20 percent of their income in a three-month period derives from lobbying on issues before the Congress.

National Commission on Terrorist Attacks upon the United States (9–11 Commission): Public Law 107-306, signed by President G. W. Bush, November 27, 2002. The commission was established by Congress to report on the circumstances leading up to the September 11, 2001, attacks on the United States. The commission was called upon to report on measures that could be taken to prevent similar attacks in the future. The commission report on August 21, 2004 included recommendations relating to presidential appointments and transition actions.

Presidential Appointment Efficiency and Streamlining Act of 2011: Public Law 112-166, signed by President Obama, August 10, 2012. The act eliminates from Senate consideration certain executive branch positions that previously required Senate confirmation. It also established a working group to consider ways of reducing the paperwork for nominees to executive branch positions requiring Senate confirmation.

Presidential Records Act of 1978: 44 U.S.C. Section 2201-2207: Establishes rules governing the official records of the official records of presidents and vice presidents beginning with President Reagan in 1981. The PRA established that presidential records are public documents owned by the federal government rather than owned by the president himself and deeded to the government, as had earlier been the case.

Presidential Transition Act of 1963: Public Law 88-277, signed by President Johnson, March 7, 1964. This is the basic legislation on presidential transitions that provides funds for both incoming and outgoing presidents. The act has been amended several times to reflect greater government support for presidential transitions and additional monies for the presidents in transition.

Presidential Transitions Effectiveness Act of 1988: Public Law 100-398, signed by President Reagan, August 17, 1988. The act requires reporting for private contributions of monies and in kind contributions to presidential transitions, including staff. It established contribution limits for individuals and organizations.

Presidential Transition Act of 2000: Public Law 106-293, signed by President Clinton, October 13, 2000. Requires disclosure of in-kind contributions; the act provides one million dollars for the training of senior staff and administration members. The General Services Administration is required to provide certain information and services to major party presidential nominees.

Pre-Election Presidential Transition Act of 2010: Public Law 111-283, signed by President Obama, October 15, 2010. The act provides government assistance for presidential candidates after the major party nominating conventions. The act formalizes many of the practices adopted in the 2008 transition.

Troubled Asset Relief Program (TARP): Public Law 110-343, signed by President G. W. Bush, October 3, 2008. The Emergency Economic and Stabilization Act is the legislation that includes funds for the TARP program. TARP included several programs aimed at stabilizing financial institutions.

Government Agencies and Committees

Executive Office of the President: Signed into law in 1939 by President Franklin D. Roosevelt. The EOP now has several key units, including the White House Office, the Office of Management and Budget, the National Security Council, and the Council of Economic Advisors.

General Services Administration (GSA): Created by President Truman in a 1949 agency reorganization. GSA is an independent federal government agency that manages government facilities and supports department and agency operations. It supports presidential transitions through the development of office space, technology, and support for people and operations.

Office of Management and Budget: The Bureau of the Budget was created in 1921 to assemble the president's budget. When Congress created the Executive Office of the President (EOP), the budget office moved from the Treasury Department to the EOP. In 1970, the bureau was reorganized to include management functions as well as budgetary ones.

National Archives and Records Administration (NARA): As the institution tasked with preserving executive branch decision-making records, NARA carries out the provisions of the Presidential Records Act of 1978. The Office of Presidential Libraries is a unit within NARA.

National Security Council (NSC): The NSC was established in the National Security Act of 1947 to provide advice to the president on national security and foreign policy matters. The Council is chaired by the president. The act created the position of National Security Advisor.

Office of Government Ethics (OGE): Provides advice to departments and agencies on ethics laws and policies. It works with federal government employees on issues of conflict of interest and oversees the development and implementation of Standard Form 278 Financial Disclosure form that employees fill out.

Office of Personnel Management (OPM): Created in 1979 in a government reorganization that assigned the new agency the functions performed by the Civil Service Commission, which was founded in 1883. It is the human resources agency responsible for establishing employment practices for the federal workforce.

President's Management Council: Created by President Clinton in 1993. This body serves as an advisory council on management issues for the president. The deputy for management of the Office of Management and Budget serves as its director. The council is composed of chief operating officers, typically the deputy secretaries in the departments and large agencies.

Senate Committee on Homeland Security and Governmental Affairs: Chief oversight committee of the U.S. Senate for most presidential transition-related issues. Many presidential nominees come through this committee for their confirmation hearings. The House Committee on Oversight and Government Reform handles transition issues in the House of Representatives.

Terms

Acting official: An "acting" position is one filled on a temporary basis to replace a federal government official who has left the position vacant. The rules and practices relating to how long a Senate confirmed official can serve on an acting basis is governed by the Federal Vacancies Act of 1998.

Agency review teams: Presidential transition teams for the president-elect assigned to departments and agencies to gather information on the programs, people, and positions for the incoming team, including the officials who will serve in positions there.

Burrowing in: Converting political positions into federal career staff. At the end of an administration, particularly one of the opposing party, those preparing to come into the White House are often concerned that outgoing officials will seek to embed their officials in career jobs.

Center for American Progress: A think tank founded by John Podesta in 2003. It was the center for early transition policy planning for the Obama team and served as a talent bank for the incoming administration to fill White House and executive branch positions.

Contingency plan: A plan designed to take into account possible future events or circumstances. In 2008, the National Security Council created a series of plans designed to present alternative responses to possible crisis events.

Executive Order: An order signed by the president that implements statutes or is based on his role as chief executive. The orders have the force of law. Presidents Clinton and George W. Bush issued executive orders that resulted in the creation of the Transition Coordinating Council.

New America Foundation: Think tank focusing on issues ranging from national security studies to the economy. President Obama recruited from the organization a sizable number of appointees for executive branch foreign and national security positions.

PA: Presidential appointees for executive branch positions not requiring Senate confirmation.

PAS: Presidential appointees for executive branch positions requiring Senate confirmation.

Presidential Directive (PDD): Memoranda on national security issues signed by the president and sent to relevant department and agency heads.

Presidential Memorandum: A presidential instrument used to manage the practices and policies of executive branch departments and agencies.

Senate hold: A parliamentary procedure allowing one or more Senators to prevent a motion from reaching a Senate floor vote.

Situation Room: Series of secure rooms in the White House West Wing where the latest intelligence and military information is gathered and a place where the president and his national security team meet.

Standard Form (SF) 86 National Security form: A form presidential appointees must fill out posing questions concerning where people have worked, lived, traveled. Those required to fill out the form work on national security issues or are in a location where there is classified information.

Introduction

1. Bush, *Decision Points*, 473.
2. Bush, *Decision Points*, 473–74.
3. Anita McBride interview.
4. Gary Walters interview.
5. McBride interview.
6. "Inside the President's Armored Limo."
7. Stephen J. Hadley interview, June 10, 2009.
8. James L. Jones interview.
9. Hadley interview, June 10, 2009.
10. On February 26, 2008, the State Department designated the organization as a terrorist group, citing that it "poses a significant risk of committing, acts of terrorism that threaten the security of U.S. nationals or the national security, foreign policy, or economy of the United States." *Federal Register*, "Designation of al-Shabaab."
11. Baker, "Obama's War Over Terror."
12. Richard Cheney, interview for the White House Interview Program, Martha Joynt Kumar, Washington, D.C., July 27, 1999.
13. Joshua Bolten interview.

Chapter 1 • A Time of Opportunity and Hazard

1. See Burke, *Presidential Transitions*, ch. 9; Burke, "Lessons From the Bush Experience"; Pfiffner, "Conclusion: The Strategic Presidency"; Kumar et al., "Meeting the Freight Train Head On"; Burke, "Lessons from Past Transitions."
2. Baker, "Obama's War over Terror."
3. Hadley interview, June 10, 2009.
4. Hadley interview, June 10, 2009.
5. Hadley interview, June 10, 2009.
6. Hadley interview, June 10, 2009.
7. Hadley interview, August 16, 2011.
8. Bolten interview.
9. Bolten interview.
10. Bush, *Decision Points*, 474.

11. Raghavan, "Bomb in Yemen Kills 25."
12. Broder, "Bush, Gore Better Begin Planning."
13. See Hananoki, "Media Advance False Claim."
14. John Podesta interview, June 24, 2009.
15. Hechler, "Oral History Interview," 179.
16. Hechler, "Oral History Interview," 180.
17. Jones, "Oral History Interview," 29.
18. Jones, "Oral History Interview," 99.
19. Truman, "Message to Dwight D. Eisenhower."
20. Truman, "Message to Dwight D. Eisenhower."
21. Eisenhower, "Message to Dwight D. Eisenhower."
22. Brauer, *Presidential Transitions,* 15.
23. Joel Kaplan interview.
24. Joseph Hagin interview.
25. Bolten interview.
26. Patterson, *To Serve the President,* 94–95.
27. Patterson, *To Serve the President,* 94–95.
28. "Obama Seeks New Taxes on the Rich"; Office of Personnel Management, "Executive Branch Civilian Employment since 1940."
29. Reagan, "Remarks on Signing the Federal Employee Hiring Freeze Memorandum and the Cabinet Member Nominations."
30. Reagan, "Memorandum Directing Reductions in Federal Spending."
31. Hagin interview.
32. Max Stier interview.
33. McBride interview.
34. "Clinton's First Blunder."
35. Howard and Cerio, "Not All Smooth Sailing," 7.
36. Stier interview.
37. James Manley interview, December 6, 2011.
38. Clymer, "43rd President."
39. Manley interview, December 6, 2011.
40. Manley interview, December 6, 2011.
41. Daniel Chenok interview.
42. "Gallup Daily: Obama Job Approval."
43. Edwards, *On Deaf Ears,* 193.
44. Edwards, *On Deaf Ears,* 194.
45. "Where's Dubya?" 2–3.
46. "Where's Dubya?" 3.
47. "Enter Clinton . . . Exit Bush," 2–3.
48. Rosellini, "Reagan Asks for a First Waltz."
49. Thomas, "Reagan Keeps Attention on the Economy."
50. Weisman, "Reagan's First One Hundred Days."
51. "Marc Rich Dies at 78."
52. General Accounting Office, "Allegations of Damage During the 2001 Presidential Transition," 19.

53. General Accounting Office, "Allegations of Damage During the 2001 Presidential Transition," 15.

54. Edsall, "Clintons Take Away $190,000 in Gifts."

55. Harris and Milbank, "At the White House, 'Moving On' or Piling On?"

56. Burros and Leland, "Clintons Return Household Gifts of Uncertain Ownership."

57. Sperling, "Bush's Promising Start," 11.

58. Harris and Milbank, "At the White House, 'Moving On' or Piling On?"

59. Author's notes, Transition Coordinating Council meeting, January 9, 2009.

Chapter 2 · *Transition Foundations*

1. General Services Administration, "Presidential Transition 2008–2009."

2. Presidential Transition Act of 1963, Public Law 88-277, "Purpose of This Act," Section 2.

3. Section 3 (b).

4. Section 5.

5. Smith, "CRS Report for Congress."

6. Gail Lovelace interview, June 19, 2009.

7. Clay Johnson interview, January 13, 2009.

8. Johnson interview, January 13, 2009.

9. "Pre-Election Presidential Transition Planning Act of 2010."

10. "Pre-Election Presidential Transition Planning Act of 2010," 3.

11. "Pre-Election Presidential Transition Planning Act of 2010," 3.

12. Theodore Kaufman interview.

13. "Pre-Election Presidential Transition Planning Act of 2010," 6.

14. "Pre-Election Presidential Transition Planning Act of 2010," 7.

15. "Pre-Election Presidential Transition Planning Act of 2010," 8.

16. "Pre-Election Presidential Transition Planning Act of 2010," 8.

17. Blue, "Letter with Five-Page Enclosure to Senator Joseph Lieberman"; see also Blue, "Letter to Senator Joseph Lieberman," September 28.

18. Background comments made separately in June and October by two White House officials familiar with the requirements of the legislation and transition planning operations.

19. Martin and Burns, "Mike Leavitt, the Man Planning the Mitt Romney Presidency."

20. Eggen, "Romney Picks Mike Leavitt to Head Transition Team."

21. Stanley and Niemi, *Vital Statistics on American Politics, 2013–2014*, 259–60.

22. "Presidential Appointment Efficiency Streamlining Act of 2011," 2.

23. National Commission on Terrorist Attacks upon the United States, *9–11 Commission Report*, 422.

24. "Intelligence Reform and Terrorism Prevention Act of 2004," (f)(1).

25. "Intelligence Reform and Terrorism Prevention Act of 2004," (c)(2).

26. Bolten interview.

27. Christopher Lu interview, June 1, 2009.

28. Author's notes, Transition Coordinating Committee meeting, December 4, 2008. In Executive Order 13476, "Facilitation of a Presidential Transition" October 9, 2008, President Bush established the Transition Coordinating Council "to assist and support the tran-

sition efforts of the transition teams for the 'major party' candidates." The order provided that outside groups and individuals could be consulted on transition issues and brought into council meetings if the director of the group chose to do so. Chief of Staff Joshua Bolten, who chaired the group, invited a half-dozen transition experts to several of those meetings. I attended the fourth and fifth sessions as an observer. I was invited in my role as director of the White House Transition Project (www.whitehousetransitionproject.org).

29. William Ball interview.

30. Russell Gerson interview.

31. Gerson interview.

32. Lovelace interview, June 19, 2009.

33. Lovelace interview, June 19, 2009.

34. Lovelace interview, June 19, 2009.

35. Lovelace interview, June 29, 2011.

36. Lu interview, June 1, 2009.

37. Lovelace interview, June 19, 2009.

38. Lovelace interview, June 19, 2009.

39. Lovelace interview, June 29, 2011.

40. Gail Lovelace, testimony, "After the Dust Settles: Examining Challenges and Lessons Learned in Transitioning the Federal Government," Committee on Homeland Security and Government Affairs, Subcommittee on Oversight of Government Management, the Federal Workforce, and the District of Columbia, April 22, 2010.

41. Lovelace testimony.

42. Lovelace testimony.

43. Lovelace interview, June 29, 2011.

44. Lovelace interview, June 19, 2009.

45. Lovelace interview, June 19, 2009.

46. Robert I. Cusick, testimony, Subcommittee on Oversight of Government Management, the Federal Workforce, and the District of Columbia, Senate Committee on Homeland Security and Government Affairs, September 10, 2008.

47. Cusick testimony, 1.

48. Cusick testimony, 2–3.

49. Cusick testimony, 3.

50. Presidential Transition Act of 2000, Section 2 Amendments to presidential Transition Act of 1963, section 3 (B) (9) (A) subsection (b).

51. Section 2 Amendments to Presidential Transition Act of 1963 Section 3(a) (3) (iii).

52. Gene Dodaro, acting comptroller general, testimony, House Subcommittee on Government management, organization, and Procurement of the Committee on Oversight and Government Reform, September 24, 2008, 16.

53. Both are noncompetitive, noncareer categories, the former for posts GS-15 or below and the latter for those above GS-15.

54. Dodaro testimony, 16.

55. As the director of the White House Transition Project (www.whitehousetransition project.org), a group of two dozen political science presidency scholars preparing information about presidential transitions and White House operations, I gathered and gave to each of the transition teams thirty-two published books relating to transitions and White

House operations. In June, I delivered them to Harrison Wellford to use in his work on White House staff structure and to give to the Obama transition team; in August, I gave the materials to Will Ball, who served on the transition board of the John McCain operation and was preparing information for his team on past transitions.

56. Johnson interview, January 13, 2009.

57. Lu interview, June 1, 2009.

58. Lu interview, June 1, 2009.

59. Ball interview.

60. Hadley interview, June 10, 2009.

61. Hadley interview, June 10, 2009.

62. Dana Perino interview.

63. Lu interview, June 1, 2009.

64. Lu interview, June 1, 2009.

65. Lu interview, June 1, 2009.

66. Ball interview.

67. Ball interview.

68. Gerson interview.

69. Lovelace interview, June 29, 2011.

70. Stier interview.

71. Max Stier, "Presidential Management and Transition Conference," letter included in packets of materials provided for participants.

72. The Obama administration had senior administration officials as conference participants along with six people from the Romney transition planning operation who in early May had begun their work. The Obama officials included Lisa Brown, acting chief performance officer, Office of Management and Budget; John Acton, Department of Homeland Security; Dan Tangherlini, acting administrator of the General Services Administration; Darren Blue, who focused on transition preparations; and Scott Gould, deputy secretary, Department of Veterans Affairs. The Romney team included Mike Leavitt, who headed the operation; Bob White, senior advisor to Mitt Romney who did very early transition work; Jim Quigley, who in August was designated to head the agency review operation; Chris Liddell, later chosen to serve as executive director of the transition planning operation; and Joe Davis from Boston Consulting, who later oversaw the timeline on management issues for the Romney transition operation. Over the two-day conference, the Romney group spoke with sitting administration officials, including those currently holding government positions.

Those who were central to the George W. Bush transition out of office were conference participants as well, including former White House chief of Staff Joshua Bolten; deputy chief of staff Blake Gottesman; and Clay Johnson, who directed the department and agency transition operations in 2008. Also present were members of Congress involved in transition issues, including former senator Ted Kaufman, who had authored the Pre-Election Presidential Transition Act of 2010, and former representative Tom Davis, who had headed the House Committee on Government Reform. Together, the group discussed past operations, the meaning of the 2010 act as well as the presidential appointments legislation (S 679), at the time resting at the House desk; the bill would become law in August. Both conferences were successful because they brought together principals involved in transitions at a time with people who were beginning their planning work. The Romney people could take advantage of the knowledge of those sitting around the table who had planned the 2008 transition and could discuss what had worked and what had not.

Presidential Management and Transition Conference, "Presidential Transition and Management Conference Attendee List," Pocantico Center of the Rockefeller Brothers Fund, Tarrytown, New York, May 17–18, 2012. Included in materials given to conference participants. The following were also in attendance: Tom Bernstein; Chelsea Piers; Dan Blair, president, National Academy of Public Administration; Mike Brown, Sears Road Partners; Martha Kumar; Gail Lovelace, former transition planning official at the General Services Administration; Kristine Simmons, vice president, Partnership for Public Service; Tina Sung, vice president, Partnership for Public Service; and Mel Wolfgang, partner and managing director, Boston Consulting Group.

Chapter 3 · The Transition Out of Office

1. "Pre-Election Presidential Transition Planning Act of 2010," 3.
2. Bush, "Remarks to White House Staff."
3. Bush, "Remarks to White House Staff."
4. Podesta interview, June 24, 2009.
5. Bolten interview.
6. Bolten interview.
7. Bolten interview.
8. Bolten interview.
9. For an excellent discussion of the rule making process at the time of political transitions, see O'Connell, "Agency Rulemaking and Political Transitions."
10. Matthew Madia, "For Bush-Era Regulations, the Clock Is Ticking."
11. Bolten interview.
12. Bolten interview.
13. Allen, "For Bush, the Starting Point Could Be Abortion."
14. Eilperin, "GOP Targets 45 Rules."
15. Eilperin, "GOP Targets 45 Rules."
16. Pianin and Skrycki, "EPA to Kill New Arsenic Standards."
17. Walsh, "Arsenic Drinking Water Standard Issued."
18. Bolten interview.
19. Kaplan interview.
20. For an example of the suspicions of groups tracking government regulations, see Madia, "For Bush-Era Regulations, the Clock Is Ticking." For criticism of the impact of their labor regulations, see the congressional testimony of Lynn Rhinehart, associate general counsel of the AFL-CIO, http://judiciary.house.gov/hearings/pdf/Rhinehart090204.pdf, accessed August 16, 2014.
21. Madia, "For Bush-Era Regulations, the Clock Is Ticking."
22. Bolten interview.
23. Bolten interview.
24. Bolten interview.
25. Background interview.
26. From the Administrative Conference of the United States website: "The Administrative Conference of the United States is an independent federal agency dedicated to im-

proving the administrative process through consensus-driven applied research, providing nonpartisan expert advice and recommendations for improvement of federal agency procedures." Available at www.acus.gov/about/the-conference/, accessed August 24, 2012.

27. "Midnight Rules," Administrative Conference Recommendations 2012, adopted June 14, 2012, p. 4.

28. Beck, "OMB Missing in Action."

29. Johnson interview, January 13, 2009.

30. Gerson interview.

31. See Johnson, "2000–2001 Presidential Transition," 311.

32. Clinton, "Memorandum for the Heads of Executive Departments and Agencies."

33. Johnson, "2008–2009 Presidential Transition."

34. Johnson interview, January 13, 2009.

35. Johnson interview, January 13, 2009.

36. Johnson to Bolten, "Transition Direction," memorandum, July 18, 2008.

37. Johnson to Bolten, "Transition Direction," memorandum, July 18, 2008.

38. Johnson interview, January 13, 2009.

39. Johnson interview, January 13, 2009.

40. Bolten interview.

41. Bolten interview.

42. Bolten interview.

43. Kaplan interview.

44. Kaplan interview.

45. Ball interview.

46. Johnson interview, January 13, 2009.

47. Lu interview, June 1, 2009.

48. Ball interview.

49. Ward, "Obama-Bush Officials Conduct 'War' Games."

50. Lu interview, June 1, 2009.

51. Bush, *Decision Points*, 468.

52. Bush, *Decision Points*, 470.

53. Bolten interview.

54. Bolten interview.

55. Bolten interview.

56. For a discussion of the meeting, see Keith Hennessey (director of the National Economic Council in the Bush White House), "Dr. Goolsbee Gets It Wrong on the Auto Loans." The discussion was vetted by several Bush administration people who were present for the session and represents their collective thinking about the meeting.

57. Paulson, *On the Brink*, 420.

58. Bolten interview.

59. Bolten interview.

60. "Presidential Approval Ratings—George W. Bush."

61. Bolten interview.

62. Wallace, "Transcript: Economic Roundtable on 'FNS.'"

63. Bolten interview.

64. President Clinton signed Executive Order 13176 on November 27, 2000; President Bush signed Executive Order 13476 on October 9, 2008.

65. The Transition Coordinating Council members included in Executive Order 13476 are: Chief of Staff to the President who will serve as co-chair, Deputy Chief of Staff for Operations who will serve as co-chair of the TCC, Deputy Chief of Staff for Policy, Assistant to the President for Personnel, Assistant to the President for National Security Affairs, Assistant to the President for Homeland Security and Counterterrorism, Assistant to the President for Economic Policy and Director, National Economic Council, Attorney General, Director of National Intelligence, Director of the Office of Management and Budget, Director of the Office of Personnel Management, Administrator of General Service, Archivist of the United States, Director of the Office of Government Ethics, and "such others as the President or the Chair of the Council may select."

66. The author attended the December 4 and January 9 meetings. The descriptions of what people said come from my notes taken during the two sessions. Because the sessions were not public and no information was released afterward detailing what happened in the sessions, I am only identifying who spoke about what topics when those same people said similar things on the public record in other places.

67. White House Office of the Press Secretary, "Fact Sheet."

68. Author's notes, Transition Coordinating Council meeting, January 9, 2009.

69. Eilperin and Leonnig, "Administration Protects Bush Appointees."

70. Riechmann, "Bush, Obama Teams Hold Disaster Drill."

71. Ward, "Obama Team Joins Bush 'War Gaming.'"

72. Kaplan interview.

73. Hadley interview, June 10, 2009.

74. Hadley interview, June 10, 2009.

75. Johnson interview, January 13, 2009.

Chapter 4 · Coming into the Presidency

1. Lisa Brown interview.

2. Clinton, "Clinton Schedule, January 30 and 31."

3. Lu interview, June 1, 2009.

4. Lu interview, June 1, 2009.

5. Lu interview, June 20, 2012.

6. Lu interview, June 20, 2012.

7. Lu interview, June 20, 2012.

8. Lu interview, June 1, 2009.

9. Johnson interview, September 4, 2001.

10. Johnson interview, September 4, 2001.

11. Chenok interview.

12. Lu interview, November 7, 2011.

13. Ball interview.

14. Ball interview.

15. Ball interview.

16. Harrison Wellford interview.

17. Lu interview, June 1, 2009.

18. Wellford interview.

19. Lu interview, June 1, 2009.

20. Wellford interview.

21. Wellford interview.

22. Wellford interview.

23. For a detailed discussion of the George W. Bush transition, see Burke, *Becoming President.*

24. Bolten interview.

25. Eggen, "Groups on the Left Are Suddenly on Top."

26. Eggen, "Groups on the Left Are Suddenly on Top."

27. Hadley interview, June 10, 2009.

28. Lu interview, June 1, 2009.

29. Chenok interview.

30. Bolten interview.

31. Ball interview.

32. Lu interview, June 1, 2009.

33. Lu interview, June 1, 2009.

34. Lu interview, June 1, 2009.

35. Burke, *Presidential Transitions,* 99.

36. Johnson, "2000–2001 Presidential Transition."

37. Brown interview.

38. Brown interview.

39. Brown interview.

40. Brown interview.

41. "Augspies," "Barack's Transition to Ethical Government."

42. Brown interview.

43. Brown interview.

44. Wellford interview.

45. Gerson interview.

46. Ball interview.

47. Ball interview.

48. Ball interview.

49. Ball interview.

50. Ball interview.

51. Lu interview, June 1, 2009.

52. Lu interview, June 1, 2009.

53. Lu interview, June 1, 2009.

54. Lu interview, November 7, 2011.

55. Lu interview, November 7, 2011.

56. Dan Pfeiffer interview, May 27, 2009.

57. Edward Gillespie interview.

58. Hadley interview, August 16, 2011.

59. Hadley interview, August 16, 2011.

60. Pfeiffer interview, May 27, 2009.

61. Lu interview, June 1, 2009.

62. Paulson, *On the Brink,* 13.

63. Kaufman interview.

64. Kaufman interview.

65. Caro, *Passage to Power.*

66. Kaufman interview.

67. Allen, "Biden to Limit Role of Vice President."

68. Allen, "Biden to Limit Role of Vice President."

69. Johnson interview, September 4, 2001.

70. Kaufman interview.

71. Lu interview, June 1, 2009.

72. Lu email to author, July 13, 2014.

73. Lu interview, June 1, 2009.

74. Office of the President-Elect, "Policy Working Groups."

75. Office of the President-Elect, "Obama-Biden Transition: Agency Review Teams."

76. The basic link to transition groups is contained within the Obama transition website, change.gov at http://change.gov/learn/transition/. The Policy Working Groups are at http://change.gov/learn/policy_working_groups/, and the Agency Review Teams are at http://change.gov/learn/obama_biden_transition_agency_review_teams, while the listing of board members overseeing the transition is at: http://change.gov/learn/transition/.

77. Podesta interview, June 24, 2009.

78. Podesta interview, June 24, 2009.

79. Podesta interview, June 24, 2009.

80. Brown interview.

81. Brown interview.

Chapter 5 · *Transition Plans and Campaign Promises*

1. Reagan, *Personal Diary*, January 19 and 20, 1989.

2. Reagan, *Personal Diary*, January 19 and 20, 1989.

3. Leeder, "Staff Must Clear the White House Out."

4. Bush, "First Ladies."

5. McBride interview.

6. Leeder, "Staff Must Clear the White House Out."

7. Brown interview.

8. Kumar, "Recruiting and Organizing the White House Staff."

9. McBride interview.

10. Podesta interview, May 30, 2014.

11. Jones interview.

12. Allen and Parnes, *HRC*, 73.

13. Allen and Parnes, *HRC*, 73.

14. Jones interview.

15. "Remarks in Chicago Announcing the Nomination of Tom Daschle as Secretary of Health and Human Services."

16. Podesta interview, May 30, 2014.

17. Podesta interview, May 30, 2014.

18. Background interview.

19. Starobin, "Rise and Fall of Bill Daley."

20. Background interview.

21. Background interview.

22. Background interview.

23. Background interview.

24. Jones interview.

25. Reagan, "Remarks on Signing the Federal Employee Hiring Freeze Memorandum and the Cabinet Member Nominations."

26. Reagan, "Memorandum Directing a Federal Employee Hiring Freeze."

27. Reagan, "Remarks on Signing a Memorandum Directing Reductions in Federal Spending."

28. Clinton, "Remarks on Signing Memorandums on Medical Research and Reproductive Health."

29. Clinton, "Memorandum on the Title X 'Gag Rule.'"

30. Obama, "Memorandum on Mexico City Policy."

31. Obama, "Executive Order 13495—Nondisplacement of Qualified Workers Under Service Contracts."

32. Obama, "Executive Order 13497—Revocation of Certain Executive Orders Concerning Regulatory Planning and Review."

33. Obama, "Memorandum on Transparency and Open Government"; Obama, "Memorandum on the Freedom of Information Act."

34. Obama, "Executive Order 13489—Presidential Records."

35. Obama, "Executive Order 13491—Ensuring Lawful Interrogations"; Obama, "Executive Order 13492—Review and Disposition of Individuals Detained at the Guantánamo Bay Naval Base and Closure of Detention Facilities"; Obama, "Executive Order 13493—Review of Detention Policy Options"; Obama, "Memorandum on Review of the Detention of Ali Saleh Kahlah al-Marri."

36. Carter, "Executive Order 11967—Executive Order Relating to Proclamation of Pardon."

37. Obama, "Remarks at an Obama Victory Fund 2012 Fundraiser in New York City."

38. Obama, "Remarks on the National Economy."

39. Obama, "Remarks Announcing the Appointment of Nancy Killefer as Chief Performance Officer."

40. Podesta interview, May 30, 2014.

41. Podesta interview, May 30, 2014.

42. Podesta interview, May 30, 2014.

43. Department of Justice Archive, "The Vacancies Act."

44. Orszag, "Best Places to Work in the Federal Government."

45. Partnership for Public Service, "Best Places to Work Agency Index Scores" and "Best Places to Work: Agency Report Office of Management and Budget."

46. Jones, "Americans' Ratings of President Obama's Image at New Lows."

47. Jonathan Breul interview, January 13, 2014.

48. Johnson interview, August 9, 2002.

49. Obama, "Remarks of Senator Barack Obama."

50. Obama, "Executive Order 13490—Ethics Commitments by Executive Branch Personnel."

51. Sherman, "New Ethics Rules."

52. White House, "William Lynn Ethics Pledge Waiver."

53. Sherman, "New Ethics Rules."

54. Sherman, "New Ethics Rules."

55. "The President Orders Transparency."

56. Kahn, "Two Days After Instituting Ethics Rules."
57. Obama, "State of the Union Message," 2010.
58. Council for Lobbying in the Public Interest, "Collateral Damage," 21–22.
59. Council for Lobbying in the Public Interest, "Collateral Damage," 1.
60. Council for Lobbying in the Public Interest, "Collateral Damage," 8.
61. Council for Lobbying in the Public Interest, "Collateral Damage," 9, footnote 25.
62. Council for Lobbying in the Public Interest, "Collateral Damage," 9.
63. American Bar Association, "Resolution, Lobbying Disclosure Act," 4.
64. Eisen, "Waiver Pursuant to Section 3 of Executive Order 13490."
65. "Ethics Pledge Waivers Released by the White House."
66. Farnam, "Don't Cry for Biden Counselor Steve Ricchetti."
67. Office of Government Ethics, "Executive Branch Agency Ethics Pledge Waivers."
68. Burke, *Presidential Transitions*, 305, 309, 339–40.
69. Clinton, "1993 Executive Order 12834—Ethics Commitments by Executive Branch Appointees."
70. Minz, "Clinton Reverses 5-Year Ban on Lobbying by Appointees."
71. Babington, "White House May Rethink Lobbying Ban."
72. Clinton, "Executive Order 13184—Revocation of Executive Order 12834"; Clinton, "Statement on Efforts to Ensure Safe, Clean Drinking Water."
73. Background interview.
74. Background interview.
75. Database developed by the author.
76. Office of the Historian, Department of State, "Travels of the President," 2014.
77. Office of the Historian, Department of State, "Travels of the President," 2014.

Chapter 6 · *The National Security Council Transition*

1. This piece builds on an earlier article about the 2008 transition, particularly in the discussion of transition memoranda and contingency plans. Some of the quotations and observations found in the earlier piece appear here. The piece cited here is "The 2008–2009 Transition through the Voices of Its Participants," *Presidential Studies Quarterly* 39, no. 4 (December 2009).
2. For a discussion of the creation of the office and the roles played by NSC advisors, see Burke, *Honest Broker*.
3. Hadley interview, June 10, 2009.
4. Hagin interview.
5. Kumar, "Getting Ready for Day One," 614.
6. Keen, "For Some in Somalia."
7. Campbell and Steinberg, *Difficult Transitions*, 25.
8. Campbell and Steinberg, *Difficult Transitions*, 27.
9. Hadley interview, August 16, 2011.
10. Hadley interview, August 16, 2011.
11. Hadley interview, August 16, 2011.
12. Sanger, *Confront and Conceal*, x.
13. Background interview.
14. Worth, Mazzetti, and Shane, "Drone Strikes' Risks."
15. Hadley interview, August 16, 2011.

16. Hadley interview, August 16, 2011.

17. Hadley interview, August 16, 2011.

18. Hadley interview, June 10, 2009.

19. Hadley interview, June 10, 2009.

20. Hadley interview, June 10, 2009.

21. Jones interview.

22. Kumar, "2008–2009 Presidential Transition," 823–24.

23. Hadley interview, June 10, 2009.

24. Sanger, "Obama Order Sped Up Wave"; Sanger, *Confront and Conceal*, xii–xv and passim.

25. Hadley interview, June 10, 2009.

26. Background interview with two members of the Obama administration.

27. Background interview with two members of the Obama administration.

28. Background interview with two members of the Obama administration.

29. Background interview with two members of the Obama administration.

30. Hadley interview, June 10, 2009.

31. Hadley interview, June 10, 2009.

32. Hadley interview, June 10, 2009.

33. Hadley interview, June 10, 2009.

34. Hadley interview, June 10, 2009.

35. Hadley interview, June 10, 2009.

36. Hadley interview, June 10, 2009.

37. Hadley interview, June 10, 2009.

38. Hadley interview, June 10, 2009.

39. Jones interview.

40. Jones interview.

41. Jones interview.

42. Jones interview.

43. Warrick, "Lawmakers Urge Special Counsel Probe."

44. Background interview with two members of the Obama administration.

45. Background interview with two members of the Obama administration.

46. Background interview with two members of the Obama administration.

47. Hadley interview, June 10, 2009.

48. Hadley interview, June 10, 2009.

49. Hadley interview, June 10, 2009.

50. Hadley interview, June 10, 2009.

51. Hadley interview, June 10, 2009.

52. Hadley interview, June 10, 2009.

53. Hadley interview, June 10, 2009.

54. Hadley interview, June 10, 2009.

55. Hadley interview, June 10, 2009.

56. Hadley interview, August 16, 2011.

57. Hadley interview, August 16, 2011.

58. Hadley interview, June 10, 2009.

59. Bolten interview.

60. Hadley interview, June 10, 2009.

61. Hadley interview, June 10, 2009.

62. Hadley interview, June 10, 2009.

63. Hadley interview, June 10, 2009.

64. Hadley interview, June 10, 2009.

65. Hadley interview, June 10, 2009.

66. Hadley interview, June 10, 2009.

67. Hadley interview, June 10, 2009.

68. Hadley interview, June 10, 2009.

69. Background interview with two members of the Obama administration.

70. Background interview with two members of the Obama administration.

71. Background interview with two members of the Obama administration.

72. Hadley interview, August 16, 2011.

73. Background interview with two members of the Obama administration.

74. Background interview with two members of the Obama administration.

75. Background interview with two members of the Obama administration.

76. Background interview with two members of the Obama administration.

77. National Commission on Terrorist Attacks upon the United States, *9–11 Commission Report*, 422–23.

78. Kumar, "2008–2009 Presidential Transition," 830.

79. Author's notes, Transition Coordinating Council meeting, December 4, 2008.

80. Author's notes, Transition Coordinating Council meeting, December 4, 2008; Kumar, "2008–2009 Presidential Transition," 830.

81. Bolten interview.

82. Hadley interview, June 10, 2009.

83. Hadley interview, June 10, 2009.

84. Hadley interview, June 10, 2009.

85. Hadley interview, June 10, 2009.

86. Hadley interview, August 16, 2011.

87. Background interview with two members of the Obama administration.

88. Hadley interview, August 16, 2011.

89. Jones interview.

90. Jones interview.

91. Jones interview.

92. Jones interview.

93. Jones interview.

94. Jones interview.

95. Jones interview.

96. Cooper, "National Security Adviser Tries Quieter Approach."

97. Woodward. *Obama's Wars*, 197–98.

98. Jones interview.

99. Gerson interview.

100. Jones interview.

101. Jones interview.

102. Jones interview.

103. Jones interview.

104. Jones interview.

105. Kaufman interview.

106. Jones interview.

107. Obama, "Remarks on the Resignation of General James L. Jones, Jr."

108. Jones interview.

109. Jones interview.

110. Jones interview.

111. Jones interview.

112. Burke, *Honest Broker*, 169–77.

113. Jones interview.

114. Hadley interview, January 16, 2013.

115. Jones interview.

116. Jones interview.

117. Jones interview.

118. Jones interview.

119. Hadley interview, January 16, 2013.

120. Jones interview.

121. Jones interview.

Chapter 7 · Presidential Appointments

1. Obama, "Interview with Brian Williams of NBC News."

2. Gregg, "Statement From Gregg on Withdrawal of Commerce Nomination."

3. Baker, "Education of a President."

4. Hounshell, "Daschle Effect Strikes Gordon Brown."

5. Woodruff, *NewsHour*, March 9, 2009.

6. Bolten interview.

7. Stanley and Niemi, *Vital Statistics on American Politics, 2009–2010*, 202.

8. American Presidency Project, "Statements of Administration Policy."

9. *Federal Register*, "U.S. Government, National Archives and Records Administration."

10. American Presidency Project, "Search for 'Memorandum,'" 2009.

11. Stanley and Niemi, *Vital Statistics on American Politics, 2009–2010*, 328.

12. Office of the Historian, Department of State, "Travels of the President," 2013.

13. Carlstrom, "Broken Appointment Process."

14. The personal data statement can be found at http://graphics8.nytimes.com/packages/pdf/national/13apply_questionnaire.pdf; the Office of Government Ethics SF 278 Public Financial Disclosure Report form can be found at www.oge.gov/Forms-Library/OGE-Form-278—Public-Financial-Disclosure-Report/; and the SF 86 Questionnaire for National Security Positions form can be found at www.opm.gov/forms/pdf_fill/sf86.pdf, all accessed June 17, 2014.

15. Patterson, *To Serve the President*, 93–95.

16. O'Connell, "Let's Get It Started."

17. O'Connell, "Let's Get It Started," 8.

18. O'Connell, "Let's Get It Started," 8.

19. National Commission on Terrorist Attacks upon the United States, *9–11 Commission Report*, 422.

20. "Intelligence Reform and Terrorism Prevention Act of 2004." Public Law 108-458, (f)(1).

21. "Intelligence Reform and Terrorism Prevention Act of 2004." Public Law 108-458, (c)(2).

22. Bolten interview.

23. Ball interview.

24. Donald Gips interview.

25. Podesta interview, June 24, 2009.

26. Joie Gregor interview.

27. Chris Lu interview, June 1, 2009.

28. Gregor interview.

29. Lu interview, June 1, 2009.

30. Lovelace interview, June 19, 2009.

31. Lu interview, June 1, 2009.

32. Byrne, "Please Resign, Bush Tells Political Appointees."

33. Boyd, "Reagan Asks the Cabinet."

34. Schwartz, Devroy, and Rich, "HHS Pink Slips Sent."

35. Marquis, "Transition in Washington."

36. Johnson interview, January 13, 2009.

37. Johnson interview, January 13, 2009.

38. Johnson interview, January 13, 2009.

39. Johnson interview, January 13, 2009.

40. Kaplan interview.

41. Johnson interview, January 13, 2009.

42. Johnson interview, January 13, 2009.

43. Robert Shea interview.

44. Carey, "Presidential Appointments," 19–21.

45. Shiner and Raju, "Richard Shelby Places Hold on President Obama's Nominees."

46. Shiner, "Richard Shelby Lifts Hold on Obama Nominees."

47. Montopoli, "Richard Shelby Holds Up Senate for Home State Pork."

48. Kumar et al., "Meeting the Freight Train Head On."

49. Johnson interview, September 4, 2001.

50. Gerson interview.

51. Lu interview, June 1, 2009.

52. Lu interview, June 1, 2009.

53. Podesta interview, June 24, 2009.

54. Lu interview, June 1, 2009.

55. Gerson interview.

56. Gerson interview.

57. Gerson interview.

58. Lu interview, June 1, 2009.

59. Gips interview.

60. Gips interview.

61. Lu email to author, July 12, 2014.

62. Gips interview.

63. Podesta interview, May 30, 2014.

64. Bush, "President's News Conference."

65. Johnson interview, February 11, 2008.

66. G. Calvin Mackenzie, "Real Invisible Hand," 330.

67. Breul interview, February 29, 2008.

68. O'Connell, "Waiting for Leadership," 9.

69. Obama, "President's News Conference."

70. Lewis, "How Much Will Obama Nudge the Judiciary?"

71. Wheeler, "Judicial Nominations and Confirmations," 5.

72. McMillion, "President Obama's First-Term U. S. Circuit and District Court Nominations," 10.

73. McMillion, "President Obama's First-Term U. S. Circuit and District Court Nominations," 10.

74. Wheeler, "Judicial Nominations and Confirmations," 6.

75. Wheeler, "Judicial Nominations and Confirmations," 7.

76. Wheeler, "Judicial Nominations and Confirmations," 12.

77. Fram, "Filibuster Weakened, Senate OK'ing Judges Faster."

Chapter 8 · *The 2008 Transition*

1. Eisenhower, *Mandate for Change*, 85.

2. Lovelace interview, June 29, 2011.

3. Manley interview, November 4, 2011.

4. Brown interview.

5. Breul interview, January 13, 2014.

6. Bolten interview.

7. Obama, "Remarks on the National Economy."

8. Obama, "Remarks on the National Economy."

9. Lisa Brown (Chair), "Working Group Report Streamlining Paperwork for Executive Nominations."

10. Carey, "Presidential Appointments," 22–24.

11. Carey, "Presidential Appointments," 16.

12. Ferraro and Cowan, "Senate Reaches Deal on Obama Nominees, Filibusters."

13. Stier interview.

14. Brown interview.

15. Stier interview.

16. Lu interview, June 20, 2012.

17. Lu interview, June 20, 2012.

18. Lu interview, June 20, 2012.

Interviews by the Author

Ball, William. Washington, D.C. June 16, 2009.

Bolten, Joshua. Washington, D.C. June 25, 2009.

Breul, Jonathan. By telephone and in Washington, D.C. February 29, 2008; and January 13, 2014.

Brown, Lisa. Washington, D.C. June 7, 2012.

Chenok, Daniel. Washington, D.C. February 21, 2014.

Gerson, Russell. New York. September 16, 2011.

Gillespie, Edward. Washington, D.C. January 13, 2009.

Gips, Donald. Washington, D.C. June 9, 2009.

Gregor, Joie. New York. September 15, 2011.

Hadley, Stephen J. Washington, D.C. June 10, 2009; August 16, 2011; and January 16, 2013.

Hagin, Joseph. Washington, D.C. February 11, 2008.

Johnson, Clay III. By telephone, email, and in Washington, D.C. September 4, 2001; August 9, 2002; August 27, 2007; February 11, 2008; and January 13, 2009.

Jones, James L. Vienna, Virginia. November 29, 2011.

Kaplan, Joel. Washington, D.C. June 23, 2009.

Kaufman, Theodore. Wilmington, Delaware. November 1, 2011.

Lovelace, Gail. Washington, D.C. June 19, 2009; and June 29, 2011.

Lu, Christopher. Washington, D.C. June 1, 2009; November 7, 2011; and June 2012; and email July 13, 2014.

Manley, James. Washington, D.C. November 4 and December 6, 2011.

McBride, Anita. Washington, D.C. February 5, 2014.

Perino, Dana. Washington, D.C. January 12, 2009.

Pfeiffer, Dan. Washington, D.C. May 27 and November 18, 2009; and August 17, 2011.

Podesta, John. By telephone and Washington, D.C. June 24, 2009; and May 30, 2014.

Shea, Robert. Washington, D.C. June 11, 2009.

Stier, Max. Washington, D.C. April 30, 2012.

Walters, Gary. By telephone. July 29, 2014.

Wellford, Harrison. Washington, D.C. June 11, 2009.

Print and Digital Sources

Abramowitz, Michael. "In the Loop at the White House." *Washington Post*, February 25, 2008.

Administrative Conference Recommendations. "Midnight Rules." Adopted June 14, 2012.

Allen, Jonathan, and Amie Parnes. *HRC: State Secrets and the Rebirth of Hillary Clinton*. New York: Crown, 2014.

Allen, Michael. "For Bush, the Starting Point Could Be Abortion; President to Review Orders of Clinton Administration." *Washington Post*, January 22, 2001.

———. "Biden to Limit Role of Vice President." *Politico*, December 6, 2009. Available at www.politico.com/news/stories/1208/16261.html, accessed August 16, 2014.

American Bar Association. "Resolution, Lobbying Disclosure Act." August 8–9, 2011. Available at www.americanbar.org/content/dam/aba/directories/policy/2011_am_104b.authcheckdam.pdf, accessed August 18, 2014.

American Presidency Project. "Presidential Elections Data." Available at www.presidency.ucsb.edu/elections.php, accessed August 17, 2014.

———. "Presidential Job Approval Ratings Following the First 100 Days, Eisenhower–Obama." Available at www.presidency.ucsb.edu/data/100days_approval.php, accessed August 17, 2014.

———. "Search for 'Memorandum.'" 2009. Available at www.presidency.ucsb.edu/ws/index.php, accessed June 17, 2014.

———. "Statements of Administration Policy." 2009. Available at www.presidency.ucsb.edu/saps.php, accessed July 28, 2013.

"Augspies." "Barack's Transition to Ethical Government." *Daily Kos*, October 9. Available at www.dailykos.com/story/2008/10/09/624899/-Barack-s-Transition-to-Ethical-Government, accessed August 16, 2014.

Babington, Charles. "White House May Rethink Lobbying Ban." *Washington Post*, June 25, 2000.

Baker, Peter. "Education of a President." *New York Times*, October 12, 2010.

———. "Obama's War over Terror." *New York Times Magazine*, January 4, 2010.

Beck, Leland E. "OMB Missing in Action: Unified Agenda and Presidential Transition Planning." August 23, 2012. Available at www.fedregsadvisor.com/2012/08/23/omb-missing-in-action-unified-agenda-and-presidential-transition-planning/, accessed August 16, 2014.

Blue, Darren. "Letter to Senator Joseph Lieberman, Chairman of the Senate Committee on Homeland Security and Government Affairs." September 28, 2012.

———. "Letter with Five-Page Enclosure to Senator Joseph Lieberman, Chairman of the Senate Committee on Homeland Security and Government Affairs." June 2012.

Boyd, Gerald. "Reagan Asks the Cabinet to Resign to Give Bush Flexibility in Choice." *New York Times*, November 11, 1988.

Brauer, Carl M. *Presidential Transitions: Eisenhower through Reagan*. New York: Oxford University Press, 1986.

Broder, David. "Bush, Gore Better Begin Planning." *Contra Costa Times*, June 4, 2000.

Broder, John. "Raising Millions More for Separate Transitions." *New York Times*, November 11, 2000.

Brown, Lisa (Chair). "Working Group Report Streamlining Paperwork for Executive Nominations." Report to the President and the Chairs and Ranking Members of the Senate Committee on Homeland Security and Government Affairs and the Senate Committee on Rules and Administration, November 2012. Available at www.rules.senate.gov/ public/?a=Files.Serve&File_id=823659d3-b173-40b6-8afa-a261d561eba3, accessed June 11 2014.

Burke, John P. *Becoming President: The Bush Transition, 2000–2003.* Boulder, CO: Lynne Rienner Publishers, 2004.

———. *Honest Broker: The National Security Advisor and Presidential Decision Making.* College Station: Texas A&M University Press, 2009.

———. "Lessons from Past Transitions: Organization, Management, and Decision Making." *The White House World: Transitions, Organization, and Office Operations,* edited by Martha Joynt Kumar and Terry Sullivan, 25–44. College Station: Texas A&M University Press, 2003.

———. *Presidential Transitions: From Politics to Practice.* Boulder, CO: Lynne Rienner Publishers, 2000.

Burros, Marian, and John Leland. "Clintons Return Household Gifts of Uncertain Ownership." *New York Times,* February 8, 2001.

Bush, George W. *Decision Points.* New York: Crown Books, 2010.

———. "The President's News Conference." American Presidency Project, December 20, 2008. Available at www.presidency.ucsb.edu/ws/index.php?pid=76179, accessed June 17, 2014.

———. "Remarks to White House Staff." American Presidency Project, November 6, 2008. Available at www.presidency.ucsb.edu/ws/index.php?pid=84772, accessed August 11, 2012.

Bush, Laura. "First Ladies: Influence and Image." C-SPAN. Available at http://firstladies .c-span.org/FirstLady/45/Laura-Bush.aspx, accessedMay 31, 2014.

Byrne, John. "Please Resign, Bush Tells Political Appointees." Rawstory.com. December 9, 2008.

Campbell, Kurt M., and James B. Steinberg. *Difficult Transitions: Foreign Policy Troubles at the Outset of Presidential Power.* Washington, DC: Brookings Institution, 2008.

Cannon, Lou. *President Reagan: The Role of a Lifetime.* New York: Public Affairs Press, 1991.

Carey, Maeve P. "Presidential Appointments, the Senate's Confirmation Process, and Changes Made in the 112th Congress." Congressional Research Service, October 9, 2012. Available at www.fas.org/sgp/crs/misc/R41872.pdf, accessed July 27, 2013.

Carlstrom, Gregg. "The Broken Appointment Process." Fedline, FederalTimes Staff Blogs, August 24, 2009. Available at http://blogs.federaltimes.com/federal-times-blog/2009/ 08/24/the-broken-appointment-process/, accessed June 17, 2014.

Caro, Robert A. *The Passage to Power: The Years of Lyndon Johnson.* New York: Vintage, 2012.

Carter, James Earl. "Executive Order 11967—Executive Order Relating to Proclamation of Pardon." *American Presidency Project,* January 21, 1977. Available at www.presidency .ucsb.edu/ws/index.php?pid=7366, accessed June 12, 2014.

Clinton, William J. "Clinton Schedule, January 30 and 31." January 30, 1993, pp. 3–4, and January 31, 1993, pp. 1–2.

———. "Executive Order 12834—Ethics Commitments by Executive Branch Appointees." *American Presidency Project,* January 20, 1993. Available at www.presidency.ucsb.edu/ ws/?pid=61530, accessed March 10, 2008.

———. "Executive Order 13184—Revocation of Executive Order 12834." *American Presidency Project*, December 28, 2000. Available at www.presidency.ucsb.edu/ws/?pid=61672, accessed March 10, 2008.

———. "Memorandum for the Heads of Executive Departments and Agencies. Subject: Implementing Management Reform in the Executive Branch." October 1, 1993. Available at http://govinfo.library.unt.edu/npr/library/direct/memos/2552.html, accessed August 17, 2014.

———. "Memorandum on the Title X 'Gag Rule.'" January 22, 1993.

———. "Remarks on Signing Memorandums on Medical Research and Reproductive Health and an Exchange with Reporters." *American Presidency Project*, January 22, 1993. Available at www.presidency.ucsb.edu/ws/?pid=46219, accessed March 10, 2008.

———. "Statement on Efforts to Ensure Safe, Clean Drinking Water." American Presidency Project, January 17, 2001. Available at www.presidency.ucsb.edu/ws/?pid=73568, accessed March 10, 2008.

"Clinton's First Blunder: How a Popular Outcry Caught the Washington Elite by Surprise." *Time*, February 1, 1993.

Clymer, Adam. "The 43rd President: The President-Elect: A 'Humbled' Bush Visits His New Home." *New York Times*, December 19, 2000.

Cooper, Helene. "National Security Adviser Tries Quieter Approach." *New York Times*, May 7, 2009.

Cooper, Helene, and Jeff Zeleny. "Obama's Transition Team Restricts Lobbyists' Role." *New York Times*, November 11, 2008.

Council for Lobbying in the Public Interest. "Collateral Damage: How the Obama Administration's Ethics Restrictions on Public Service Have Harmed Nonprofit Advocacy and the Public Interest." September 2011. Available at http://opensocietypolicycenter.org/wp-content/uploads/CollateralDamageCLPI1020111.pdf, accessed June 11, 2014.

Curl, Joseph. "McCain Vows Tax, Spending Restraint; Calls Democratic Foes 'Liberal.'" *Washington Times*, February 18, 2008.

Department of Justice Archive. "The Vacancies Act." Available at www.justice.gov/archive/transition/vacancies-act.htm, accessed June 12, 2014.

Edsall, Thomas B. "Clintons Take Away $190,000 in Gifts; Hollywood Helped with Furnishings." *Washington Post*, January 21, 2001.

Edwards, George C. III. *On Deaf Ears: The Limits of the Bully Pulpit.* New Haven: Yale University, 2006.

Eggen, Dan. "Groups on the Left Are Suddenly on Top; Obama's Election Has Elevated the Influence Industry's Liberal Side." *Washington Post*, June 4, 2009.

———. "Romney Picks Mike Leavitt to Head Transition Team." *Washington Post*, June 3, 2012.

Eisen, Norman L. "Waiver Pursuant to Section 3 of Executive Order 13490." WhiteHouse.gov. April 28, 2010. Available at www.whitehouse.gov/sites/default/files/rss_viewer/jones_.pdf, accessed November 9, 2013.

Eisenhower, Dwight D. *Mandate for Change: 1953–1956.* Doubleday: New York, 1963.

———. "Message to Dwight D. Eisenhower Inviting Him to a Luncheon and Briefing at the White House." August 14, 1952. *Public Papers of the President, Harry S. Truman,* Item 227. Government Printing Office.

Eilperin, Juliet. "GOP Targets 45 Rules to Overturn Clinton Policies Include Abortion, Energy Issues." *Washington Post*, April 8, 2001.

Eilperin, Juliet, and Carol D. Leonnig. "Administration Protects Bush Appointees by Converting Positions to Career Civil Service Jobs." *Washington Post*, November 18, 2008.

"Enter Clinton . . . Exit Bush: TV News Coverage of the Presidential Transition." Center for Media and Public Affairs. *Media Monitor* 7, no. 2 (February 1993).

"Ethics Pledge Waivers Released by the White House." Whitehouse.gov. Available at www .whitehouse.gov/briefing-room/disclosures/ethics-pledge-waivers, accessed November 7, 2013.

Farnam, T. W. "Don't Cry for Biden Counselor Steve Ricchetti." *Washington Post*, April 25, 2012. Available at www.washingtonpost.com/blogs/in-the-loop/post/dont-cry-for-biden -counselor-steve-ricchetti/2012/04/25/gIQAvnlFfT_blog.html, accessed August 17, 2014.

Federal Register. "Designation of al-Shabaab as a Specially Designated Global Terrorist." Vol. 73, no. 53, February 26, 2008. Available at www.state.gov/j/ct/rls/other/des/102448 .htm, accessed October 15, 2014.

———. "U.S. Government, National Archives and Records Administration." 2013. Available at www.archives.gov/federal-register/executive-orders/2009-obama.html, accessed July 28, 2013.

Ferraro, Thomas, and Richard Cowan. "Senate Reaches Deal on Obama Nominees, Filibusters." Reuters, July 16, 2013.

Fram, Alan. "Filibuster Weakened, Senate OK'ing Judges Faster." Associated Press, June 16, 2014.

"Gallup Daily: Obama Job Approval." Gallup. Available at www.gallup.com/poll/113980/ Gallup-Daily-Obama-Job-Approval.aspx, accessed August 16, 2014.

General Accounting Office. "Allegations of Damage During the 2001 Presidential Transition." GAO-2-360. June 2002.

General Services Administration. "Presidential Transition 2008–2009." Video, 2009. Available at www.youtube.com/watch?v=kcT7myxNoWE, accessed August 16, 2014.

Gregg, Judd. "Statement From Gregg on Withdrawal of Commerce Nomination." *Wall Street Journal*, February 12, 2009.

Hananoki, Erik. "Media Advance False Claim that Obama's Reported Transition Plans Are Unusual or Unprecedented—but Presidents Bush, Clinton, Reagan, and Carter Also Planned Ahead." *Media Matters*, July 25, 2008.

Harris, John F., and Dana Milbank. "At the White House, 'Moving On' or Piling On? Bush and GOP Gain, Democrats Blush, and Ex-President's Allies Cry Foul Over Tales of Messy Exit." *Washington Post*, February 18, 2001.

Hechler, Kenneth. "Oral History Interview." Conducted by Niel M. Johnson. Harry S. Truman Presidential Library. November 29, 1985. Available at www.trumanlibrary.org/ oralhist/hechler.htm, accessed August 17, 2014.

Hennessey, Keith. "Dr. Goolsbee Gets It Wrong on the Auto Loans." June 7, 2009. Available at http://keithhennessey.com/2009/06/07/dr-goolsbee-gets-it-wrong-on-the-auto-loans/, accessed August 16, 2008.

Henry, Laurin L. *Presidential Transitions.* Washington, DC: Brookings Institution, 1960.

Hounshell, Blake. "The Daschle Effect Strikes Gordon Brown." *Foreign Policy*, March 10, 2009. Available at http://blog.foreignpolicy.com/posts/2009/03/10/the_daschle_effect _strikes_gordon_brown, accessed July 25, 2013.

Howard, Lucy, and Gregory Cerio. "Not All Smooth Sailing." *Newsweek*, February 1, 1993.

"Inside the President's Armored Limo." *Autoweek.* October 18, 2013.

"Intelligence Reform and Terrorism Prevention Act of 2004." Public Law 108-458. 2004. Subtitle F. Sec. 7601 Presidential Transition (f)(1). Office of the Director of National Intelligence. Available at www.dni.gov/index.php/about/organization/ic-legal-reference -book-2012/ref-book-irtpa, accessed June 17, 2014.

Johnson, Clay III. "The 2000–2001 Presidential Transition: Planning, Goals, and Reality." In *The White House World: Transitions, Organization, and Office Operations,* edited by Martha Joynt Kumar and Terry Sullivan. College Station: Texas A&M University Press, 2003.

———. "The 2008–2009 Presidential Transition Preparing Federal Agencies." *Presidential Studies Quarterly,* December 2009.

Jones, Jeffrey M. "Americans' Ratings of President Obama's Image at New Lows: More View Him Unfavorably Than Favorably." Gallup, June 12, 2014. Available at www.gallup .com/poll/171473/americans-ratings-president-obama-image-new-lows.aspx, accessed June 12, 2014.

Jones, Roger W. "Oral History Interview." Conducted by Jerry N. Hess. Harry S. Truman Presidential Library, August 14, 1969. Available at www.trumanlibrary.org/oralhist/ jonesrw.htm, accessed August 17, 2014.

Kaufman, Tim. 2010. Federal Times Blog. February 3. Available at http://blogs.federal times.com/federal-times-blog/tag/political-appointees/, accessed July 28, 2013.

Keen, Judy. "For Some in Somalia, U.S. Legacy Is Blood, Hate." *USA Today,* March 24, 1994.

Khan, Huma. 2009. "Two Days after Instituting Ethics Rules, President Obama Waives Them for Deputy Pentagon Secretary Nominee." ABC News, January 23.

Kumar, Martha Joynt. "The 2008–2009 Presidential Transition through the Voices of Its Participants." *Presidential Studies Quarterly* 39, no. 4 (December 2009).

———. "Getting Ready for Day One: Taking Advantage of Opportunities and Minimizing the Hazards." *Public Administration Review,* July/August 2008.

———. "Recruiting and Organizing the White House Staff." *PS: Political Science and Politics* 35, no. 1 (March, 2002): 35–40.

Kumar, Martha Joynt, George Edwards III, James P. Pfiffner, and Terry Sullivan. "Meeting the Freight Train Head On: Planning for the Transition to Power." In *The White House World: Transitions, Organization, and Office Operations,* edited by Martha Joynt Kumar and Terry Sullivan, 5–24. College Station: Texas A&M University Press, 2003.

Kumar, Martha Joynt, and Sullivan, Terry, eds. *The White House World: Transitions, Organization, and Office Operations.* College Station: Texas A&M University Press, 2003.

Leeder, Jessica. "Staff Must Clear the White House Out, Repaint, Redecorate, and Unpack before Parade Ends." *Globe and Mail,* January 17, 2008.

Leiby, Richard, and Valerie Strauss. "The Future First Lady, Finding Her Place in History." *Washington Post,* November 11, 2008.

Lewis, Matt K. "A Storm Is Brewing Inside the Romney Campaign." *Daily Caller,* August 27, 2012.

Lewis, Neil. "How Much Will Obama Nudge the Judiciary? Vacancies to Be Filled in 12 Appeals Courts." *International Herald Tribune,* March 12, 2009.

Mackenzie, G. Calvin. "The Real Invisible Hand: Presidential Appointees in the Administration of George W. Bush." In *The White House World: Transitions, Organization, and Office Operations.* College Station: Texas A&M University Press, 2003.

Madia, Matthew. "For Bush-Era Regulations, the Clock Is Ticking." Center for Effective

Government, May 28, 2008. Available at www.foreffectivegov.org/node/3703, accessed August 16, 2008.

"Marc Rich Dies at 78; His Pardon by Clinton Stirred Controversy." *Los Angeles Times,* June 27, 2013.

Marquis, Christopher. "Transition in Washington: The Confidante; Tripp Is Fired from Pentagon after Failing to Resign Post." *New York Times,* January 20, 2001.

Martin, Jonathan, and Alexander Burns. "Mike Leavitt, the Man Planning the Mitt Romney Presidency." *Politico,* June 3, 2012. Available at www.politico.com/news/stories/0612/76983.html, accessed August 16, 2014.

McMillion, Barry J. "President Obama's First-Term U.S. Circuit and District Court Nominations: An Analysis and Comparison with Presidents since Reagan." Washington, DC: Congressional Research Service, May 2, 2013.

Minz, John. "Clinton Reverses 5-Year Ban on Lobbying by Appointees." *Washington Post.* December 29, 2000.

Montopoli, Brian. "Richard Shelby Holds Up Senate for Home State Pork." CBS News, February 5, 2010.

National Commission on Terrorist Attacks upon the United States. *The 9–11 Commission Report: Final Report of the National Commission on Terrorist Attacks upon the United States.* New York: W.W. Norton, 2004.

Obama, Barack. "Blueprint for Change: Obama and Biden's Plan for America." 2008. Available at https://archive.org/details/346512-obamablueprintforchange, accessed August 17, 2014.

———. "Executive Order 13489—Presidential Records." January 21, 2009. Available at www.presidency.ucsb.edu/ws/index.php?pid=76782, accessed June 12, 2014.

———. "Executive Order 13490—Ethics Commitments by Executive Branch Personnel." *American Presidency Project,* January 21, 2009. Available at www.presidency.ucsb.edu/ws/index.php?pid=85673, accessed June 11, 2014.

———. "Executive Order 13491—Ensuring Lawful Interrogations." *American Presidency Project,* January 22, 2009. Available at www.presidency.ucsb.edu/ws/index.php?pid=85669, accessed June 12, 2014.

———. "Executive Order 13492—Review and Disposition of Individuals Detained at the Guantánamo Bay Naval Base and Closure of Detention Facilities." *American Presidency Project,* January 22, 2009. Available at www.presidency.ucsb.edu/ws/index.php?pid=85670, accessed June 12, 2014.

———. "Executive Order 13493—Review of Detention Policy Options." *American Presidency Project,* January 22, 2009. Available at www.presidency.ucsb.edu/ws/index.php?pid=85671, accessed June 12, 2014.

———. "Executive Order 13495—Nondisplacement of Qualified Workers Under Service Contracts." January 30, 2009. Available at www.presidency.ucsb.edu/ws/index.php?pid=85716, accessed June 12, 2014.

———. "Executive Order 13497—Revocation of Certain Executive Orders Concerning Regulatory Planning and Review." *American Presidency Project,* January 30, 2009. Available at www.presidency.ucsb.edu/ws/index.php?pid=85754, accessed June 12, 2014.

———. "Interview with Brian Williams of NBC News." *American Presidency Project,* February 3, 2009. Available at www.presidency.ucsb.edu/ws/index.php?pid=85748, accessed June 17, 2014.

————. "Memorandum on Mexico City Policy and Assistance for Voluntary Population Planning." American Presidency Project, January 23, 2009. Available at www.presidency .ucsb.edu/ws/index.php?pid=85685, accessed June 12, 2014.

————. "Memorandum on Review of the Detention of Ali Saleh Kahlah al-Marri." *American Presidency Project*, January 22, 2009. Available at www.presidency.ucsb.edu/ws/ index.php?pid=85672, accessed June 12, 2014.

————. "Memorandum on the Freedom of Information Act." *American Presidency Project,* January 21, 2009. Available at www.presidency.ucsb.edu/ws/index.php?pid=85678, accessed June 12, 2014.

————. "Memorandum on Transparency and Open Government." *American Presidency Project,* January 21, 2009. Available at www.presidency.ucsb.edu/ws/index.php?pid =85677, accessed June 12, 2014.

————. "The President's News Conference." American Presidency Project, August 9, 2013. Available at www.presidency.ucsb.edu/ws/index.php?pid=104008, accessed June 17, 2014.

————. "Remarks Announcing the Appointment of Nancy Killefer as Chief Performance Officer." *American Presidency Project*, January 7, 2009. Available at www.presidency.ucsb .edu/ws/index.php?pid=85356, accessed August 17, 2014.

————. "Remarks at an Obama Victory Fund 2012 Fundraiser in New York City." *American Presidency Project,* June 12, 2012. Available at www.presidency.ucsb.edu/ws/index.php ?pid=100986, accessed October 26, 2013.

————. "Remarks in Chicago Announcing the Nomination of Tom Daschle as Secretary of Health and Human Services." *American Presidency Project,* December 11, 2008. Available at www.presidency.ucsb.edu/ws/index.php?pid=85064, accessed September 26, 2013.

————. "Remarks of Senator Barack Obama," *New York Times,* June 22, 2007. Available at www.nytimes.com/2007/06/22/us/politics/22text-obama.html, accessed October 7, 2014.

————. "Remarks on the National Economy." *American Presidency Project*, April 14, 2009. Available at www.presidency.ucsb.edu/ws/index.php?pid=86000, accessed October 27.

————. "Remarks on the Resignation of General James L. Jones, Jr. as National Security Advisor and the Appointment of Thomas E. Donilon as National Security Advisor." *Public Papers of the President.* October 8, 2010.

————. "State of the Union Message." *American Presidency Project*, January 27, 2010. Available at www.presidency.ucsb.edu/ws/index.php?pid=87433, accessed November 6, 2013.

"Obama Seeks New Taxes on the Rich." *Wall Street Journal,* February 14, 2012.

O'Connell, Anne Joseph. "Agency Rulemaking and Political Transitions." *Northwestern University Law Review* 105, no. 2 (2001): 471–90.

————. "Let's Get It Started: What President-Elect Obama Can Learn From Previous Administrations in Making Political Appointments." Washington, DC: Center for American Progress. April 2009.

————. "Waiting for Leadership: President Obama's Record in Staffing Key Agency Positions and How to Improve the Appointments Process." Washington, DC: Center for American Progress, April 2010.

Office of Government Ethics. "Executive Branch Agency Ethics Pledge Waivers." Available at http://www.oge.gov/Open-Government/Executive-Branch-Agency-Ethics-Pledge -Waivers/, accessed August 17, 2014.

————. "SF 278 Public Financial Disclosure Report Form." Available at www.oge.gov/ Forms-Library/OGE-Form-278—Public-Financial-Disclosure-Report/, accessed June 17, 2014.

Office of Legal Counsel. Department of Justice. The Legal Significance of Presidential Signing Statements, memorandum for Bernard N. Nussbaum, Counsel to the President. November 3, 1993. Available at www.usdoj.gov/olc/signing.htm#N_6_, accessed March 10, 2008.

Office of Personnel Management. "Executive Branch Civilian Employment since 1940." 2012. Available at www.opm.gov/feddata/HistoricalTables/ExecutiveBranchSince1940 .asp, accessed August 17, 2014.

Office of the Historian, Department of State. "Travels of the President." 2014. Available at https://history.state.gov/departmenthistory/travels/president, accessed June 11, 2014.

————. "Travels of the President: Barack Obama." 2013. Available at http://history.state .gov/departmenthistory/travels/president/obama-barack, accessed July 28, 2013.

Office of the President-Elect. "Obama-Biden Transition: Agency Review Teams." Available at http://change.gov/learn/obama_biden_transition_agency_review_teams, accessed May 26, 2014.

————. "Policy Working Groups." Available at http://change.gov/learn/policy_working _groups/, accessed May 26, 2014.

Orszag, Peter, "Best Places to Work in the Federal Government: Double Bronze!" Office of Management and Budget website, May 20, 2009. Available at www.bestplacestowork .org/BPTW/rankings/detail/BO00#trends, accessed October 7, 2014.

Partnership for Public Service. "Best Places to Work Agency Index Scores." 2013. Available at www.bestplacestowork.org/BPTW/rankings/overall/small, accessed August 17, 2014.

————. "Best Places to Work: Agency Report Office of Management and Budget." 2013. Available at www.bestplacestowork.org/BPTW/rankings/detail/BO00#trends, accessed August 17, 2014.

Patterson, Bradley. *To Serve the President: Continuity and Innovation in the White House Staff*. Washington, DC: Brookings Institution Press, 2008.

Paulson, Henry M., Jr. *On the Brink: Inside the Race to Stop the Collapse of the Global Financial System*. New York: Hachette Book Group, 2010.

Pfiffner, James P. *The Strategic Presidency: Hitting the Ground Running*. Lawrence: University Press of Kansas, 1996.

Pianin, Eric, and Cindy Skrycki. "EPA to Kill Arsenic Standard; Whitman Cites Debate on Drinking Water Risk." *Washington Post*, March 21, 2001.

"The President Orders Transparency." Editorial. *New York Times,* January 23, 2009.

"Presidential Approval Ratings—George W. Bush." Gallup. Available at www.gallup.com/ poll/116500/presidential-approval-ratings-george-bush.aspx, accessed August 16, 2014.

Raghavan, Sudarsan. "Bomb in Yemen Kills 25 after Leader Is Sworn In." *Washington Post,* February 26, 2012.

Reagan, Ronald. "Memorandum Directing a Federal Employee Hiring Freeze." *American Presidency Project*, January 20, 1981. Available at www.presidency.ucsb.edu/ws/?pid =43601, accessed October 14, 2014.

————. "Memorandum Directing Reductions in Federal Spending." American Presidency Project, January 22, 1981. Available at www.presidency.ucsb.edu/ws/index.php?pid =43624, accessed August 16, 2014.

————. *The President's Daily Diary*. National Archives and Records Administration.

————. *Personal Diary*. Available at www.reaganfoundation.org/white-house-diary.asps, accessed September 18, 2013.

————. "Remarks on Signing a Memorandum Directing Reductions in Federal Spending." *American Presidency Project*, January 22, 1981. Available at www.presidency.ucsb .edu/ws/?pid=43613, accessed March 10, 2008.

————. "Remarks on Signing the Federal Employee Hiring Freeze Memorandum and the Cabinet Member Nominations." *American Presidency Project*, January 20, 1981. Available at www.presidency.ucsb.edu/ws/index.php?pid=43490, accessed August 16, 2018.

Riechmann, Deb. "Bush, Obama Teams Hold Disaster Drill." Associated Press, January 13, 2001.

Rosellini, Lynne. "Reagan Asks for a First Waltz and Wins Hearts in the Capital." *New York Times*, November 19, 1980.

Saad, Lydia. "Kennedy Still Highest-Rated Modern President, Nixon Lowest." *Gallup Politics*, December 6, 2010. Available at www.gallup.com/poll/145064/kennedy-highest -rated-modern-president-nixon-lowest.aspx, accessed August 17, 2014.

Sanger, David E. *Confront and Conceal: Obama's Secret Wars and Surprising Use of American Power*. New York: Random House, 2012.

————. "Obama Order Sped Up Wave of Cyberattacks against Iran." *New York Times*, June 1, 2012.

Schwartz, Maralee, Ann Devroy, and Spencer Rich. "HHS Pink Slips Sent." *Washington Post*, March 7, 1989.

Sherman, Jason. "New Ethics Rules Trip Up Lynn's Nomination to Key Pentagon Post." *Inside the Air Force*, January 23, 2009.

Shiner, Meredith. "Richard Shelby Lifts Hold on Obama Nominees." *Politico*, February 8, 2010.

Shiner, Meredith, and Manu Raju. "Richard Shelby Places Hold on President Obama's Nominees." *Politico*, February 5, 2010.

Smith, Stephanie. "CRS Report for Congress: Presidential Transition." Congressional Research Service, December 27, 2007.

Sperling, Godfrey. "Bush's Promising Start and Clinton's Sorry Exit." *Christian Science Monitor*, January 30, 2001.

Stanley, Harold W., and Richard G. Niemi. *Vital Statistics on American Politics, 2005–2006*. Washington, DC: Congressional Quarterly Inc., 2006.

————. *Vital Statistics on American Politics, 2009–2010*. Washington, DC: Congressional Quarterly Inc., 2011.

————. *Vital Statistics on American Politics, 2013–2014*. Washington, DC: Congressional Quarterly Inc., 2013.

Starobin, Paul. "The Rise and Fall of Bill Daley: An Inside Account." *New Republic*, January 12, 2012.

Thomas, Helen. "Reagan Keeps Attention on the Economy." United Press International, February 15, 1981.

Truman, Harry S. "Message to Dwight D. Eisenhower Inviting Him to a Luncheon and Briefing at the White House." August 13, 1952. *Public Papers of the President, Harry S. Truman*, Item 227. Government Printing Office.

"Two-Thirds Approve of Obama's Job." Associated Press, January 24, 2009.

Wallace, Chris. "Transcript: Economic Roundtable on 'FNS,'" Fox News Sunday, June 8, 2009. Available at www.foxnews.com/on-air/fox-news-sunday-chris-wallace/2009/06/08/transcript-economic-roundtable-fns, accessed August 16, 2014.

Walsh, Edward. "Arsenic Drinking Water Standard Issued; After Seven-Month Scientific Review, EPA Backs Clinton-Established Levels." *Washington Post,* November 1, 2001.

Ward, Jon. "Obama Team Joins Bush 'War Gaming.'" *Washington Times,* January 14, 2009.

———. "Obama-Bush Officials Conduct 'War' Games." *Washington Times,* January 13, 2009.

Warrick, Joby. "Lawmakers Urge Special Counsel Probe of Harsh Interrogation Tactics." *Washington Post,* June 8, 2008.

Weisman, Steven R. "Reagan's First One Hundred Days." *New York Times Magazine,* April 26, 1981.

Wheeler, Russell. "Judicial Nominations and Confirmations after Three Years—Where Do Things Stand." Washington, DC: Governance Studies at Brookings, January 13, 2012. Available at www.brookings.edu/~/media/Files/rc/papers/2012/0113_nominations _wheeler/0113_nominations_wheeler.pdf, accessed July 23, 2013.

"Where's Dubya? TV News Coverage of President Bush's First 50 Days in Office." Center for Media and Public Affairs. *Media Monitor* 15, no. 2 (March/April 2001).

White House. "William Lynn Ethics Pledge Waiver." January 22, 2009. Available at www .whitehouse.gov/assets/documents/lynn_waiver_final.PDF, accessed June 11, 2014. Ethics Pledge Waiver, "National Security Advisor, General James Jones," April 28, 2010, http://www.whitehouse.gov/sites/default/files/rss_viewer/jones_.pdf.

White House Briefing Room. "Presidential Memoranda." Available at www.whitehouse.gov/ briefing-room/presidential-actions/Presidential-Memoranda/2009, accessed July 28, 2013.

White House Office of the Press Secretary. "Fact Sheet: Ensuring a Smooth and Effective Presidential Transition." October 28, 2008. Available at http://georgewbush-whitehouse .archives.gov/news/releases/2008/10/20081028-1.html, accessed August 16, 2014.

———. "President Obama Announces Intent to Nominate Key Administration Posts." June 4, 2009. Available at www.whitehouse.gov/the_press_office/President-Obama -Announces-Intent-to-Nominate-Key-Administration-Posts-6-4-09/, accessed August 10, 2013.

Woodward, Bob. *Obama's Wars.* New York: Simon and Schuster, 2010.

Woodruff, Judy. *NewsHour.* Public Broadcasting System. March 9, 2009.

Worth, Robert F., Mark Mazzetti, and Scott Shane. "Drone Strikes' Risks to Get Rare Moment in the Public Eye." *New York Times,* February 5, 2013.